Archaeology of the Lower Muskogee Creek Indians, 1715–1836

A Dan Josselyn Memorial Publication

Archaeology of the Lower Muskogee Creek Indians, 1715–1836

H. THOMAS FOSTER II

With Contributions by Mary Theresa Bonhage-Freund
and Lisa O'Steen

THE UNIVERSITY OF ALABAMA PRESS
Tuscaloosa

Typeface: Minion

∞

The paper on which this book is printed meets the minimum requirements of American
National Standard for Information Sciences—Permanence of Paper for Printed Library
Materials, ANSI Z39.48-1984.

Library of Congress Cataloging-in-Publication Data

Foster, Thomas, 1970–
    Archaeology of the Lower Muskogee Creek Indians, 1715–1836 / H. Thomas Foster II ; with
contributions by Mary Theresa Bonhage-Freund and Lisa O'Steen.
        p.   cm.
    Includes bibliographical references and index.
    ISBN-13: 978-0-8173-1239-8 (cloth : alk. paper)
    ISBN-10: 0-8173-1239-0
    ISBN-13: 978-0-8173-5365-0 (pbk. : alk. paper)
    ISBN-10: 0-8173-5365-8
    1. Creek Indians—Chattahoochee River Valley—Antiquities. 2. Creek Indians—Material
culture—Chattahoochee River Valley. 3. Excavations (Archaeology)—Chattahoochee River
Valley. 4. Chattahoochee River Valley—Antiquities. I. Bonhage-Freund, Mary Theresa.
II. O'Steen, Lisa, 1956– III. Title.
    E99.C9F67 2007
    758.004′97385—dc22
                                                                        2006014322

To the Maskókalkî

Excavating or collecting artifacts from federal property without a permit is a criminal offense punishable by fines, imprisonment, and confiscation of property.

Contents

Figures

Tables

Preface

The purpose of this book is to investigate the diversity of the people referred to as the Muskogee (Maskókî) Creek Indians who lived along the Lower Chattahoochee and Flint River watersheds of southeastern North America during the eighteenth to early nineteenth centuries as revealed through archaeological remains. This investigation will synthesize all known archaeological research at Lower Muskogee Creek sites.

The Muskogee Indians were and continue to be a diverse people. During the Historic Period (circa 1540–1836), they and other Indians of the southeastern United States had a profound influence on the development of that region. Our knowledge of those cultures is limited to what we can learn from their descendants and from archaeological and historical sources. This book is about what we can learn from archaeological data.

This is the first published comprehensive archaeological summary of the Lower Creek Indians. While its intended audience is archaeologists, I expect that the readership will be more widespread than just professionals, and I hope that the synthesis described here is useful for a wider audience, including the modern descendants of the historic tribes that I discuss. Given the potential for a larger readership, I will briefly discuss the limitations of the methods and perspectives used in this book.

I have worked for many years to collaborate with the descendants of the people described here and know from their advice that I cannot hope to "summarize" their past or culture (Mihesuah 1998; Wickman 1999:5–6). Since this book focuses on the realm of information that can be identified from archaeological data, I want to point out that the view of the Muskogee Creek Indians as revealed from those data is limited. Studying archaeological remains provides a biased view of the lives and cultural heritage of a group of people, and the results in this book are no exception. This book leaves out significant portions of culture because it is limited to what we can learn from the preserved remains of behaviors. Archaeological data are limited to material remains. Consequently, archaeological knowledge is narrowly focused. For example, the review here does not cover the religious beliefs of the Indians or what kinds of traditional beliefs were held about life events. I don't want to claim that it is impossible for archaeologists to deal with these subjects, but nonemperical subjects have not been traditionally the subject of archaeological inquiry. Therefore, there is little for me to say in this book, which is a synthesis of existing work.

Archaeological data, however, have significant advantages over other types of data such as interviews, oral histories, and historic documents. Archaeological data are systematic and can be indiscriminately represented for large portions of the population. In other words, archaeological data can be relatively comprehensive and unbiased toward diverse sections of the society. For example, historic documents are biased, as they are written by individuals and represent the perspective, interpretation, and agenda of a single individual. Similarly, oral histories are told, remembered, and interpreted by individuals (Saunt 1999:31–34) and vary by clan and town (*talwa*) (Wickman 1999:61). The Muskogee Creek Indians have a rich tradition of oral histories, but I have not drawn significantly upon that source for this book because doing so would incorporate a new set of biases (Jackson 2003:30–32). Other researchers (Grantham 2002; Jackson 2003; Swanton 1928a, b; Wickman 1999) have addressed oral histories; therefore, my focus is on what can be learned from archaeological data. Archaeological artifacts such as food remains may be preserved for all members of a given household. In this way archaeological data complement oral histories and historic documents. Archaeological data are unique in that they provide information about daily life that was not preserved in oral histories. Other than oral histories, archaeological data are, possibly, the only source of information that is directly from the people themselves. Archaeological remains are not *necessarily* biased by an "other" perspective (Mihesuah 1998; Watkins 2000; Wickman 1999); however, their interpretation may be biased.

This book provides a synthesis of the archaeological perspective and is an attempt to describe the *variation* of that perspective over time and space. By quantifying the variation of the material culture over space and time, archaeologists will be able to better identify causes for change among the Indians. It is only after we understand the geographic and temporal variation that we can understand the causes of material change and adaptation through time and can distinguish the differences between individual Creek Indian towns (Piker 2003, 2004:6–8). Consequently, I spend a considerable amount of time describing the variation in the archaeological assemblages and feature types. I also identify the archaeological context where the artifacts were found so that the reader can evaluate the conclusions without referring to unpublished and unavailable reports. Sometimes, archaeological interpretations are based on the remains found in a single feature. Since the perspective of an entire culture or people cannot be determined with reasonable reliability or validity from a single feature, it is important to clarify how our conclusions were determined. I have attempted to list all known sources while drawing on the more systematically collected data. It is important that the reader know the entirety of the sites while understanding that not all collected data are equally useful. I discuss these limitations so that the reader can evaluate my conclusions.

Archaeologists are beginning to have a relatively comprehensive view of the variation among the material culture that represents the Lower Muskogee Creek Indians. Large sections of the habitat where they lived have been surveyed for archaeological remains. Some of the region has been completely surveyed. It is timely, therefore, to take account of that variation in order to better understand the diversity of the material culture of the Muskogee people and to better protect the remaining sites.

Much is known, but there is much more to learn about these people. For example, we certainly don't know much about the subsistence variation over large regions or changes in the economy in any detail. We have practically no idea about the meaning of most of the artifacts that are recovered. We don't know much about demography at a reasonable accuracy. We don't know about health or reproductive changes during the eighteenth century, although we think that they were dramatic. This book is a starting point rather than an end.

One of the goals of this book is to synthesize the vast amount of research on Lower Muskogee Creek Indian sites. There have been decades of cultural resource management research on those archaeological sites, but little of it has had peer review or been published. Most of the data sources are in museums, unpublished manuscripts and cultural resource management reports, and personal collections.

Archaeological investigations from cultural resource management projects are often designed with nonanthropological research goals that make the samples collected relevant to nonanthropological questions and more difficult to combine with anthropological studies. While most cultural resource management reports summarized here listed culture history research problems as a goal, the purposes of the studies were for evaluation in the National Register of Historic Places (NRHP). Consequently, samples collected and budgets and time allocated were solely for NRHP assessment. For example, we may have archaeological data on only a portion of a site that was within a construction area of a road. Consequently, our interpretation of that site is biased by the cultural resource management goals, which were to assess NRHP eligibility of or mitigate the cultural resources within a particular distance from the road. While we are blessed with a great deal of information from cultural resource management, the reporting of that data is, to say the least, frustrating. Site reports are difficult to obtain and are rarely in a peer-reviewed published format. If we do not adequately disseminate and review the results from cultural resource management projects, the information gained from them is lost. At the same time, we have to recognize that most of the research on Lower Muskogee Creek Indian sites has been on such funded projects. These applied archaeology research projects have their own biases and goals, but the mere volume of data makes them impossible, if not irresponsible, to ignore. A synthesis of the Lower Muskogee Creek Indian archaeology is a synthesis of cultural resource management-funded projects. This book establishes a baseline of knowledge about the material remains of the Muskogee people partly by publishing data that have been difficult to obtain because they were in unpublished and rare reports.

To characterize fully the material remains of the Muskogee, a book, ideally, should discuss their origins and all aspects of their society. I feel that we do not know enough about the origins or boundaries (social, economic, temporal, or geographic) of those people to accomplish that. So another goal of this book is to isolate and describe some of the boundaries and variation of what we do know. The temporal and geographic boundaries of this book are limited to the period after the Muskogee Creek Indians settled on the Chattahoochee River in the beginning of the eighteenth century until the state and federal governments in the beginning of the nineteenth century forcibly removed them (circa 1715–1836). That time period also corresponds to an archaeological phase, the Lawson Field phase (Knight 1994b). I intentionally limited the book to this phase so that we could characterize the variation within that archaeological and temporal unit. I am not convinced that we understand quantitatively the difference between Creek Indian artifacts of the eighteenth century and those of the seventeenth century, nor do we understand population migration during that period. I didn't want to introduce more confounding archaeological variables by including multiple phases in the synthesis. I also limited the book to the Lower Creek Indians instead of incorporating all of the Creek Indians because the survey region of the Lower Creek Indians is better defined than the Upper Creek region. Many of the Upper Creek archaeological excavations are either ongoing or not yet completely reported. Last, there is ethnic and political justification for the division between the Lower and Upper Creek towns (Jackson 2003). This book is about the people, but it is also about how archaeologists know what they know. It examines the evidence for the archaeological cultural unit that currently represents the Lower Creek Indians.

Chapters are organized by archaeological data type. Chapter 1 is a survey of ethnohistoric and ethnographic information about the Muskogee Creek Indians that is specifically relevant to the interpretation of archaeological investigations. There are many books on Creek Indian ethnohistory and ethnography, some of them recent (Braund 1993; Ethridge 2003; Hahn 2004; Jackson 2003; Piker 2004; Saunt 1999; Swanton 1922, 1928a, b; Waselkov and Braund 1995; Wickman 1999; Wright 1986). The ethnohistoric background in this chapter is based on some primary but mostly secondary sources and is an attempt to find generalizations that can be used as an interpretive framework for the archaeological data. The Muskogee Creek Indians during the eighteenth century were a dynamic people and generalization is not always warranted, but not all aspects of their lives changed dramatically, and, therefore, some generalization may be helpful. I review what we know from firsthand observations in historic documents pertaining to social organization, demography, subsistence, settlement, and political organization. There has been a wealth of recent historical studies on the Muskogee Creek Indians, and researchers are beginning to characterize how these people adapted to a changing social and physical environment.

Chapter 2 is a review of the landscape and biophysical environment of the Lower Chattahoochee and Flint Rivers during the eighteenth century. The environmental context is designed to give the reader a perspective of the physical conditions and constraints to which the Lower Muskogee Creek Indians were adapting. Chapter 3 is a review of the history of archaeological investigations in the Lower Chattahoochee River area. It also traces the archaeological evidence of specific towns and populations. This section is partly intended as a sort of "methods" section for a direct historic approach to studying the archaeological remains of the Lower Creek Indians because it associates particular artifact assemblages with known Creek towns and populations. The town description will serve as an ethnographic population to compare observed samples of archaeological remains. It also sets a baseline of archaeological data from which we can assess migratory patterns of the Lower Creek Indians. We have ethnohistoric evidence that they began dispersing during the late eighteenth to the early nineteenth century. In order to adequately and accurately assess the degree and cause of that dispersal, we need to understand where individual towns were located and the evidence to support those conclusions. For example, Marvin Smith (1987) has argued that the Southeastern Indians, including ethnic groups that contributed to the Muskogee Creek Indian populations, migrated during the Protohistoric Period. By defining the archaeological variation in a known town, of known population size, known duration of occupation, and known ethnic affiliation, we can better assess the archaeological evidence of migration. To reconstruct the location and archaeological evidence of the known Lower Creek Indian towns, the town section in Chapter 3 uses all major ethnohistoric sources, including the recently published Viatory journals by Benjamin Hawkins that list the geographic features and the distances between them (Foster 2003a), historic land survey maps, and reports and artifact assemblages for all known Lower Creek Indian archaeological sites.

Chapter 4 is a synthesis of the most frequently recovered artifact type from archaeological sites, pottery sherds. The analysis of pottery sherds is problematic, and I propose various methods to deal with the biases of this artifact type. Then I demonstrate geographic, ethnic, and temporal variation in the pottery that was manufactured by the Lower Creek Indians. This section builds upon and uses conclusions from a recently published article (Foster 2004d). Chapter 5 is a synthesis of the ethnohistoric and archaeological evidence for Creek Indian structures in the Lower Chattahoochee Valley. Structures reveal information about household use and demographic patterns through time. Chapter 6 by Mary Theresa Bonhage-Freund reviews archaeological plant remains, and Chapter 7 by Lisa O'Steen reviews archaeological animal remains from Lower Creek Indian sites. These two artifact classes are commonly used to represent subsistence foods and ecological context of archaeological sites. I don't describe trade goods in this book because of the sheer volume and the uncertainty of their function to the Indians. Trade goods were used for a variety of purposes (Piker 2004:146; Waselkov 1989, 1998), but no one has systematically identified the changing function of that diverse artifact class. Furthermore, one of the goals of the book is to advocate a more direct historic approach and continuity between the Historic, Protohistoric, and Prehistoric Southeastern Indians, so there is justification for focusing only on the Indian-manufactured material culture.

I have not attempted to spell all native proper names in an orthographically correct form. While this is not a linguistic study, various authors have consistently stated that the term *Creek Indians* is a foreign-imposed term that has a history that is offensive to their modern descendants. In addition, it could be argued that it is a less useful ethnographic unit of study because of the ambiguity of the ethnic constituents. Therefore, I have attempted to refer to the specific Indian people by their individual talwa name. I refer to the larger group of culturally related people who spoke a form of the Maskókî language as the Maskókalkî, which means "People who speak the Maskókî language," or by the more general English form Muskogee Creek Indians. The less precise term Creek Indians for the Maskókalkî is useful for comparative purposes for other researchers (Wickman 1999:185) and is commonly used among descendants today (Martin and Mauldin 2000:xiii). I use the names Muskogee, Maskókî, Muskogee Creek Indians, and Creek Indians interchangeably, but they are not equivalent. As I will explain later in the ethnohistory section, the term Creek Indians includes many people other than the Muskogee.

Acknowledgments

This book builds on and summarizes the contributions of decades of research, and the first acknowledgments should go to the individuals who have worked in the Lower Chattahoochee for decades and on whose work I have depended. A few of these individuals are Frank Schnell, Jr., Dan Elliot, Dean Wood, Chad Braley, Vernon J. Knight, Tim Mistovich, and Paul Jackson. Dean Wood, Southern Research, Frank Schnell, Jr., Jerald Ledbetter, and Chris Hamilton gave me copies of many reports. Thanks to my two book collaborators, Mary Theresa Bonhage-Freund and Lisa O'Steen, for putting up with my pestering. Chris Hamilton has always been hospitable and encouraged me over the years of my research at Fort Benning, and I could not have completed this project without his help. Thank you to Fort Benning, Chris Hamilton, Panamerican Consultants, Inc., and Paul Jackson for permission to reproduce images in Chapters 4 and 5 from cultural resource management reports commissioned by the United States Army, Department of Environmental Management. The Southeastern Archaeological Conference allowed me to reprint sections of a previously published article of mine in *Southeastern Archaeology*, volume 23, number 1, pages 65–84 (copyright 2004, Southeastern Archaeological Conference). Thank you to the Lilly Library for permission to reproduce the image by Basil Hall. Thank you to the Columbus Museum and Mike Bunn for permission to reproduce the "Chute de la Chattahoutchie." Thanks to Paul Jackson and Panamerican Consultants for the position at Fort Benning and the opportunity to work on the Cussetuh project. Marvin Smith and two reviewers read an earlier version of this manuscript, and their helpful comments are greatly appreciated. Adam King commented on parts of the ethnohistory section, particularly on my ideas about Southeastern chiefdoms and their political organization; I appreciate his input and advice. Ramie Gougeon and David Hally commented on the architecture chapter. Virgil Beasley and Jon Marcoux read and commented on sections of the ceramics chapter. Howard and Kara Foster read sections of an earlier draft and improved the writing considerably. Kara Foster carefully read and checked the manuscript for accuracy. Josh Piker and Steve Hahn advised me on sections of the ethnohistory chapter. Kathryn Braund has supported me in ways over the years that she doesn't even realize. Greg Waselkov, John Worth, and George Milner gave advice on the content of the book. Miriam Syler and the Cobb Memorial Archives graciously let me use their archives and lent materials. Thanks to Fort Benning Division of Environmental Management for support and access to maps and materials over the years. Thank you to Frank Schnell for advice and for lending me copies of Huscher's Walter F. George survey maps. Thanks to Steve Engerrand and the Georgia Archives for permission to photograph the Georgia plat maps and their hospitality while I was there. Miriam Syler and Cobb Memorial Archives graciously lent manuscripts and maps. Dean Wood and Southern Research gave me many manuscripts. Thank you to Kara and Waverly for the time I have spent on this over the years.

Notes on Orthography and Pronunciation

In this book, I have defaulted to spellings of native words, such as the proper names of talwas, to those used by Benjamin Hawkins in the late eighteenth century (Foster 2003a). I used his spellings because he lived among and studied the language of the Creek Indians during the time with which this book deals. He wrote native words in a syllabic form in an attempt to preserve the pronunciation. Elsewhere, I have spelled Muskogee (Maskókî) words according to their English spelling. Muskogee is the English term for the Maskókî (Martin and Mauldin 2000:xiii, 74). In Maskókî, the "k" is pronounced like a soft "g" in English. A "g" is pronounced with a hard "g" sound. All vowels are in their short form. The suffix -alkî is pronounced like "algee." Pronunciations are derived from Martin and Mauldin (2000).

Archaeology of the Lower Muskogee Creek Indians, 1715–1836

1
Ethnohistoric Context

The Creek Indians were an amalgam of diverse people who lived in southeastern North America during the historic period (circa 1540–1836). The core population of the Creek Indians were Maskôkî (Muscogee, Muskogee, Muskhogee, Creek) speakers, but it also included Hitchiti, Euchee, Natchez, and Alabama speakers (Braund 1993; Brown 1989; Hahn 2004:242–243; Hann 1988, 1996; Harper 1998:292–293; Martin and Mauldin 2000:xiii; Stiggins et al. 2003; Swanton 1922). Maskôkî is a language family that includes Alabama, Apalachee, Chickasaw, Choctaw, Muskogee Creek, Hitchiti-Mikasuki, and Koasati (Martin and Mauldin 2000: xiii). Maskôkalkî means Maskôkî people and is used here as a loose descriptive term for the Indians who spoke one of a collection of Maskôkî languages that were in use prehistorically and historically. The term Creek Indians is useful for comparative purposes and is used by modern Maskôkî (Creek) speakers.

These Indians settled into what is now central Georgia and Alabama in various waves of migration that occurred throughout the Historic and Prehistoric Periods (Ethridge 2003; Foster 2004d; Knight 1994a, b; Russell 1976; Smith 1987; Swanton 1922; Waselkov and Smith 2000; Worth 2000). The ethnic groups that made up the Creek Indians were always in flux at the individual level (Wickman 1999:157). However, the majority of the town populations that constituted the Creek Indians were relatively stable throughout that period. For example, the Cussetuh and Cowetuh towns were old towns and were in existence for hundreds of years (Hahn 2004:10–12, 26–29), but the demographic constituency of these towns varied over time.

The Maskôkî Creek Indians were divided by early European observers into two large groups based on geography, the Lower Creek and the Upper Creek (Figure 1.1). While some cartographers added a third division, the division into Upper and Lower is most common. These divisions were maintained in the postremoval settlement patterns in the Indian territories, although the geographic pattern was reversed. During most of the eighteenth century, the Upper Creek Indians consisted of the Abihka- and Coosa-allied people who lived on the Coosa River, the Alabama-speaking people who lived on the upper Alabama River near the confluence of the Coosa and Tallapoosa Rivers, the Tallapoosa-allied people who lived on the lower Tallapoosa River near the fall line, and the Okfuskee and allied people who lived on the upper Tallapoosa River in the Piedmont (Ethridge 2003; Hahn 2004; Swanton 1922; Waselkov and Smith 2000; Worth 2000). The Lower Creek Indians consisted of the Cowetuh- and Cussetuh-allied people who lived on the middle Chattahoochee and Flint Rivers and the Hitchiti and allied people who lived on the lower Chattahoochee and Flint Rivers. I retained the term Lower Creek here because it was used historically and has comparative purposes, and because the Maskókalkî descendants maintained the geographic division of the Upper and Lower towns in Oklahoma although the geographic placement was reversed (Jackson 2003:34). I also use the term to clarify that I am describing archaeological sites that are along the Chattahoochee and Flint Rivers and not along the rivers of central Alabama.

The exact origin of the term Creek Indians is not known. However, Verner Crane (Braund 1993:3–4; Crane 1918; Martin and Mauldin 2000:xiii) attributes it to the period when the British colonists in South Carolina referred to all the Indians who lived in what is now Georgia and Alabama by the name of their closest neighbors who lived on the Ochisee Creek. The South Carolina residents also referred to all the Indians as the Ochisee Creek Indians and later simply as the Creek Indians. Other etymologies of the Creek Indian name exist, however (Braund 1993; Gatschet 1884; Swanton 1922). Similarly, a few decades earlier, the Spanish colonists in Florida referred to the Indians who collectively made up the Creek Indians as "Apalachicola" Indians because the Apalachicola were the closest to the Spanish settlements (Hann 1988; Worth 2000).

While the term Creek Indians is an English-assigned name that detracts from the unique history and cultures of individual towns or talwas (Piker 2003, 2004:6–8), this book is a summary of archaeological data that also does not distinguish between the culture histories of individual talwas and uses the term as an analytic unit (Foster 2004d; Knight 1994b). Consequently, it is necessary to refer to the people living along the Chattahoochee and Flint watersheds as the Lower Creek Indians rather than by their more correct native individual town names. Following Wickman (1999:185), I will use *Creek Indians, Maskókî Creek Indians,* and *Maskókalkî* as equivalent terms.

It could be argued that using the term Creek Indians as an ethnographic group is so unsystematically defined and loosely applied over time that it isn't useful as an analytic unit. I hope that one result of this book will be a greater understanding of the variation in the material culture and archaeological sig-

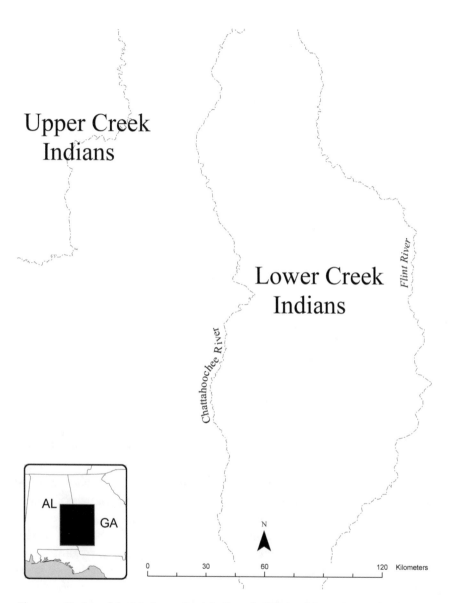

Figure 1.1. Region of the Muskogee Creek Indians during the eighteenth to early nineteenth centuries in the southeastern United States.

nature of individual talwas. I have retained the term Creek Indians so that we can understand its archaeological manifestation and perhaps not need it anymore. As a result we may finally take David Hally's advice and address the individual history of specific towns (Hally 1971).

There are numerous, detailed, and recent ethnohistorical studies that cover various aspects of the Maskókî and allied people (Braund 1993; Ethridge 2003; Foster 2001; Grantham 2002; Green 1990; Hahn 2000, 2004; Piker 2004; Saunt 1999; Swanton 1922, 1928a, b, 1946; Wickman 1999; Wright 1986). This chapter is intended to be a brief overview of the ethnohistoric evidence describing the cultural and economic history of the Creek Indians during the eighteenth to early nineteenth centuries. In this review, I am focusing on ethnohistoric sources that are directly relevant to the Lower Creek Indians and those that are directly relevant to behaviors that would have a greater effect on the archaeological record. In doing so, I have to make some generalizations about the Creek Indians during this time period. Generalizations are not always accurate, particularly for such a long time period and a wide range of ethnic groups that are interacting in a frontier exchange economy. Recent research by Robbie Ethridge (2003), Claudio Saunt (1999), Joshua Piker (2004), Barnet Pavao-Zuckerman (2005), Steven Hahn (2004), and Patricia Wickman (1999) has suggested that there were social, demographic, economic, geographic, and political changes for the Creek Indians during the time period that I cover in this chapter.

HISTORIC SETTLEMENT HISTORY

The earliest and best documentary record of the populations that would become the Creek Indians comes from 1540, when Hernando de Soto's exploratory expedition described the Southeastern Indians in what is now Georgia and Alabama. The Indians he encountered in those regions were the immediate ancestors of the Creek Indians described in this book (Clayton et al. 1993; Knight 1994b; Russell 1976). Those Indians were agriculturalists who had settled in relatively concentrated towns. De Soto also encountered individuals characterized by his chroniclers as "chiefs." These individuals seemingly had the power to muster armies; they were treated differently than other Indians and resided in special buildings (Clayton et al. 1993:75, 95, 230, 239, 278). Assuming that De Soto's chroniclers were unbiased, recorded the events correctly, and interpreted the native behaviors correctly, these observations seem to indicate a political structure not unlike chiefdoms elsewhere in the world (Service 1962). Marvin Smith and David Hally (1992) identify a number of behaviors that they attribute to chiefdoms of the Southeast and by extension to the ancestors of the Creek Indians. They use the chronicles of the De Soto expedition to identify patterns of behavior regarding gifts of tribute, women, housing, transportation, guides, burden bearers, and food to the Spanish explorers. Then they argue that these were typical of gifts given to chiefs and were therefore exemplary of chiefdom power in the Southeast during the sixteenth century and, by extension, the earlier Mississippian period. They do not question the validity of the De Soto accounts (Muller 1997:109). Rather they interpret the accounts literally and identify patterns of behavior among the different accounts. Smith and Hally argue (1992:105–106) that these gifts were given to the Spaniards because the Spaniards were viewed as chiefs. The evidence for the Indian interpretation of the Spaniards as chiefs is from two events when, according to the Spanish account, Indians asked if tribute should be paid to the Spaniards instead of the former native tribute recipient (Smith and Hally 1992:105).

The assumption of the unbiased nature of the De Soto chronicles, however, has not been adequately demonstrated (Clayton et al. 1993; Galloway 1997a, b; Muller 1997:72–78). Given what we know about the purpose of the Spanish explorations and De Soto's own political agenda, we should assume that the chronicles are *not* unbiased and prove them otherwise instead of the other way around (Wickman 1999:13–15). Jon Muller (1997) and Patricia Galloway (1995, 1997a, b) have analyzed this issue extensively, and I will not discuss the biases of the Spanish accounts any further.

Recently, Adam King (2002) has used theory developed by Richard Blanton and others (1996) to characterize the political organization of the Southeastern Indians from the Mississippian through the Historic Period, including the Creek Indians. He argues (222) that the chiefdom term also applies, at a fundamental level, to the Creek Indian political organization as well as the pre-Creek, Mississippian groups. He also argues that chiefdoms are not limited to using network strategies where power is focused on the individual. Instead chiefdoms also include political mechanisms that derive power from corporate groups. He argues further (222) that we know that Creek and Mississippian groups were characterized by the "fundamental organizational elements of chiefdoms: institutionalized social ranking, permanent political leadership, and a centralized decision making apparatus."

The Historic Period Creek Indians lived in a political organization where no single individual had power over another person (Hahn 2004:129, 146; Harper 1998:313–315; Waselkov and Braund 1995:146–148). Nevertheless, the members of towns worked on collective projects such as gardening, clearing agricultural fields, and building public structures (Harper 1998:326), participating in a collective pooling of economic resources in a redistribution system. Individuals voluntarily contributed portions of their harvest to a centralized storage system (Harper 1998:326). If this centralized food storage structure were found near a Mississippian period mound, Mississippian period researchers would attribute its function to a powerful chiefdom and centralized taxation (Muller

1997:40–41; Peebles and Kus 1977). Yet we know through Bartram's observation that contribution to this redistribution system was voluntary (Harper 1998:326). Either Creek social and political organization changed dramatically in a 200-year period, or there is more cultural consistency between the Creek Indians and the Mississippian period Indians. I prefer the simpler explanation that (1) the political organization of the Creek Indians did not change that drastically and (2) Creek political organization was corporate, therefore (3) Mississippian political organization was corporate.

The historic Creek Indians recognized certain individuals who were called Mico, who often came from high-ranking families, although the title holder seems to have been elected (Brown 1989:49; Waselkov and Braund 1995:117–118). While the ranking was inherited, the title was not (Hahn 2004:200). There is significant evidence that these Micos or chiefs gained power because of interaction with the bureaucratic political system of European settlers of South Carolina and Georgia. Steven Hahn documents the growth of power of Micos and the formation of the Creek Nation as a result of artificially attributed prestige in the form of European trade goods and titles (2004:70, 124, 170, 259, 262). European colonists wanted to deal with single representatives of the Creek people rather than groups of people because it was more efficient. For example, Thomas Nairne increased the power of the Lower Creek Indian Mico called "Emperor Brims" by bestowing titles upon him and other Micos during the early eighteenth century (Hahn 2004:70, 124). The English went so far as to name Brims's successor (Hahn 2004:124).

Even at the beginning of the eighteenth century, when intensive interaction with Europeans began, the Mico received special treatment in council and special foods and offerings. Other members of the society showed deference and respect to the Mico or high-status individuals with body positioning and submissive behaviors such as bowing (Hahn 2004:97; Harper 1998:285–286; Milfort 1959:99–100; Waselkov and Braund 1995:147). The Mico had the power to distribute the common foods in the public granary and often gave these "taxed" goods to visitors (Waselkov and Braund 1995: 147). These behaviors and characterizations are not unlike those described in formal encounters by De Soto. The societies he encountered have been classified as chiefdoms (Hudson et al. 1985). If chiefdoms can take the form argued by Blanton et al. (1996), then some Creek tribes were probably corporate chiefdoms. But that is a big "if." Power was probably inherited through clan affiliation but was not limited to or held by single individuals. The institution of the public corncrib seems to be consistently present and has a consistent function from the Mississippian period through the historic Creek Indians. I argue that this consistency is evidence of commonality between the Mississippian and Creek societies, and I suspect that the evolution of this collective behavior is related to the rise in the centralized organization of the Mississippian period, but that is beyond the scope of this book.

My interpretation of the ethnohistoric and archaeological data regarding the Creek Indians is that they are not what is commonly referred to as a chiefdom. There is centralized leadership in Creek society in the form of all adult males contributing to decisions at the council. Even the characterization of leadership is tenuous because council decisions were not binding. While part of this argument is semantics and classification, I do not find it useful to expand the definition of the chiefdom unit of classification to organizational structures that constitute almost half of the population (adult males). My argument here is that the Creek Indians were not chiefdoms, yet they participated in some behaviors such as collective pooling of resources and body posturing that are consistent with prehistoric Southeastern Indians. So we need to reassess our interpretation of the prehistoric populations instead of redefining the classification unit to fit the historic populations. We know more about the historic populations. It does not make sense to argue about the known from the unknown.

Vernon Knight argues that there is consistency from the prehistoric to the Historic Period in institutions that are larger than the talwa (Knight 1994a). He argues that the super-talwa organization of Red and White towns supports the argument for an organization above the talwa and that this institution is consistent with a chiefdom organization. I agree with his observation but not the conclusion. The presence of a confederation or cooperative organization in the form of a classification and organizational structure of towns is certainly true before the influence of the Europeans. However, the moity system of Red and White towns is a loose organization and its evidence for a chiefdom is weak.

After the initial sixteenth-century exploration by the Spanish, there was a relative dearth of exploration and therefore a lack of documentary sources of the Southeastern Indians for a few decades around the turn of the seventeenth century (Hudson and Tesser 1994; Worth 1994). Current interpretation of the sixteenth century is that the centralized populations encountered by De Soto broke up into smaller, more autonomous populations. There seems to be indirect evidence of that population dispersal in the form of archaeological sites showing frequency of population decrease (Knight 1994b; Knight and Mistovich 1984:231) and migration (Smith 1987). This political decentralization and migration may have been the result of mass population decrease from European-introduced diseases (Smith 1987). It is tempting to assume that Indians increased their dispersion from centralized chiefdom centers. However, archaeologists have not demonstrated that the migration that has been documented during the Historic Period wasn't a normal pattern of population dispersal during the Prehistoric Period. While there is evidence that migration occurred during the Protohistoric Period (Smith 1987), archaeologists haven't established that pattern for large regions or extended time periods in the Southeast. There is historic documentation and archaeological evidence for multiple regions and extended time periods during the Historic Period when Indians moved residences frequently and for a variety of social and ecological reasons (Muller 1997:61; Wickman 1999:157). Archaeologists should clearly characterize the causation for migration during the Historic Period because we have more information and can control for various confounding variables before making extrapolations about prehistoric causes for migration. I have begun to analyze historic migration for that very reason (Foster 2001, 2004d).

Vernon Knight used site frequency and distribution on the Chattahoochee River during the sixteenth century (Abercrombie phase, 1550–1650) as the clearest and most "dramatic" case of depopulation because of disease (Knight 1994a:383). Indeed there is a significant decrease in the number of sites dating to the period immediately after compared to the period before the Spanish exploration (Knight and Mistovich 1984:231–232). However, as will be discussed in more detail, we see a similar drop in site frequency during the late seventeenth century in the same region, but we know that that depopulation resulted from migration, not disease. Recently, Patricia Wickman has argued that the effect of European diseases was relatively short lived and that the Indians had recovered by 1565 (1999:158). So a more parsimonious explanation for the change in site frequency immediately after the Spanish exploration in the Chattahoochee River valley could be that it resulted from out-migration. I am certainly not arguing that the Spanish explorations had no effect or did not introduce diseases. Consistent with Jon Muller's approach, I am examining the empirical evidence for these "dramatic" changes that may have occurred and comparing it to what we know from the Historic Period (1997:56, 61).

It is not until the late seventeenth century that we begin to have significant descriptions of the Creek Indians. In the mid-seventeenth century, the Spanish missions of La Florida describe Apalachicola Indians living near what is now the lower Chattahoochee River. These Indians are not well known through documentary sources but are mentioned in some "town lists" of the period (Hann 1988:357–364). These lists were censuses of Indian towns made by the Spanish associated with the missions in Florida and give geographical information because they are usually itemized in an order that reflects the position of the town relative to the missions (Hann 1988:362, 1996; Worth 2000:273). The lists indicate that the geographical position of the Lower Creek Indian towns in the late seventeenth century is not inconsistent with their location during the eighteenth century. In other words, many of the Lower Creek Indian towns had settled onto the Chattahoochee River *at least* by the mid-seventeenth century. Steven Hahn has documented the Muskogee town of Cussetuh on the

Chattahoochee River by 1662 (2004:28). Where the town was located before that time is debatable, although initial regional analysis of ceramic artifacts indicates that occupants may have migrated from what is now central Alabama (Knight 1994b).

This argument about migration and the location of towns is based on the identification of towns with the same name. Unfortunately, this method of tracing population migration through town names is probably biased in unknown degrees, irrespective of the popularity of the method (Muller 1997:95–96). We do not know how many different towns of the seventeenth century had the same name. We only have a sample of some population of towns in the Southeast during the seventeenth century. We need to know the sample population before we can make unbiased statements about the migratory history of a single town. Furthermore, we do not understand the naming conventions of place-names for the Southeastern Indians. In other words, how valid is our method of tracing names (Knight 1994a:378)? The late-eighteenth-century town of Nuyaka was founded by a population of people from a town called Tote-pauf-cau (Foster 2003a:45s). The name of the Upper Creek town of Tal-lo-wau mu-chos-see means "new town" but was formerly called Took-au-bat-chee tal-lau-has-see (Tukabatchee Old Town) and implies that this "new town" was the former location of Tukabatchee. Recent studies by Douglas Hurt (2000), Karen Booker et al. (1992), and Patricia Wickman (1999:57, 74–78, 158) may begin to address these issues of naming conventions. Last, most researchers are not really interested in the location of places with the same name. They are interested in the people who lived at that location. Nevertheless, we do not yet understand the demographic relationship between the individuals who lived in a town and the town's naming history, particularly over numerous generations. For example, it is unlikely that all individuals from the same families lived in the same geographic location for multiple generations and that they all migrated together—in fact we have evidence to the contrary. During the eighteenth century, there are numerous observations of individuals and groups of individuals from specific towns joining residents of other towns (Foster 2003a: 42s, 45s, 46s, 47s, 48s, 62s; Wickman 1999:157).

We know that during the seventeenth century the Spanish traded with Indians living in the Apalachicoli province (Hann 1996:68). That province has the name that the Spanish attributed to the Indian towns distributed along what is now called the Chattahoochee River. The earliest town list for the Chattahoochee River region was made in 1675 by Bishop Gabriel Díaz Vara Calderón. It lists, in order from south to north, Chicahuti, Sabacola, Oconi, Apalachicoli, Ilapi, Tacusa, Usachi, Ocmulgui, Ahachito, Cazithto, Colomme, Cabita, and Cuchiguali (Hann 1988:362). Cazithto may be the same town as Casiste, which is a Muskogee town and was mentioned by the missionaries as early as the

1660s. Cazithto may be the same Casiste that was mentioned by the De Soto chroniclers in 1540. The 1540 Casiste has been estimated to have been located to the west in what is now central Alabama, however (Hudson 1994: 87). The discrepancy between the location of the 1540 location of Cussetuh (Casiste) and the seventeenth-century location of Cussetuh (Cazithto) is part of the justification for a west-to-east migration into the Chattahoochee River valley. Cazithto (later Cussetuh), Cabita (later Cowetuh), and Colomme (later Kolomi) spoke Muskogee languages, whereas the majority of the remaining towns probably spoke Hitchiti languages (Hann 1996:66–67). These town lists probably demonstrate that Muskogee-speaking people had settled on the Chattahoochee River by the mid-seventeenth century and perhaps earlier. Spanish missionaries described a group of nine towns settled by Indians who had migrated from the "far west" to the Chattahoochee River region during the seventeenth century (Hann 1988:33). This migration may be the origin of the Muskogee immigration to the Chattahoochee River area. The Muskogee migrated in and settled among the native Apalachicola, Hitchiti-speaking Indians. These Spanish references are generally consistent with the migration legend told to General Oglethorpe in 1735 by Chekilli (Swanton 1928b:38) but they are inconsistent with the cause for the migration. That migration account recorded that the Cussetuh people came from the west and eventually settled along the Chattahoochee River among the Apalachicola people who were already there.

The Spanish and English documents and maps from the late seventeenth century indicate that a number of towns remained on the lower Chattahoochee River until around 1685 when some, if not all, of the people settled there migrated farther east and settled along the Ochisee River (now the Ocmulgee River) watershed in central Georgia (Hann 1988:231–232; Worth 2000:278–279). This eastern migration was partly in response to the Indians' desire to be closer to English traders who, in the late seventeenth century, were settled in and trading out of Charles Town in what is now South Carolina. The Chattahoochee River settlements were likely almost completely abandoned between 1685 and 1715 (however, see Worth 2000:279). A letter by Nathanial Johnson and others in 1708 lists Apalachicola Indians living on the Savannah River in east Georgia, eleven towns settled on the "Ochasee River," and one town settled on the "ChochtarRuchy River" (Chattahoochee River), which was situated about 150 miles west of the "Ochasee" Indians (Johnson 1708). It was during this time that the English began to refer to these Indians as the Ochisee Creek Indians and eventually as the Creek Indians.

In 1715, Indians on the Savannah and Ochissee Rivers migrated back to the Chattahoochee River watershed because of trader abuses and in response to the Yamasee War (circa 1715). While it is tempting to believe that the 1715 resettlement locations were the same as pre-1685 locations, we do not have sufficient evidence yet to make that claim (Worth 2000). The well-documented repopulation of the Chattahoochee River valley after the Yamasee War, therefore, serves as a good temporal division for the history of Indian settlement along the Chattahoochee River. This repopulation is also the beginning of the Lawson Field archaeological phase, which currently defines the archaeological representation of the Lower Creek Indians of the eighteenth and early nineteenth centuries (Knight 1994b:189). This temporal boundary also serves to define the limits of this book.

Beginning in 1715, the Indians from the Ochisee Creek in central Georgia began migrating at an unknown rate back to the Chattahoochee River in western Georgia. We do not know if they all moved back at once or in what order. We do know, from various maps, that shortly after 1715, many of the same towns had relocated to the Chattahoochee River (Worth 2000). The Indians who settled along the Chattahoochee River in 1715 remained in relatively stable settlement locations until they were removed by the Georgia, Alabama, and U.S. governments between 1825 and 1836. A few towns resettled short distances away during the eighteenth to early nineteenth century, but they remained on the Chattahoochee River. For example, Cussetuh occupied at least two locations on the Chattahoochee River between 1715 and 1825 (Foster 2003a:58s).

DEMOGRAPHY

Population statistics on the Creek Indians of the eighteenth century are abundant, although the validity of those statistics is unknown. Since the populations that made up the Creek Indians were so variable, estimation of the numbers of the entire Creek people is not meaningful over time. However, a series of censuses taken of individual towns throughout the eighteenth and early nineteenth centuries are useful in estimating population size (Swanton 1922). Amos Wright (1999) recently summarized much of that census data so I will not reproduce it here. These censuses were taken for a variety of purposes; consequently, there are biases of each that must be addressed in order to compare them over time. Paredes and Plante (1983) have performed the most detailed analysis of the data for bias and temporal trends to date. They found that the Creek population generally increased during the eighteenth century. Between 1738 and 1750, the population decreased from about 8,000 to about 4,500. Then the population began increasing until it reached around 22,000 when the Indians were enumerated in preparation for removal to the Oklahoma territories in 1836 (Paredes and Plante 1983:19, fig. 1; Swanton 1922:434–437). This increase in population is consistent with archaeological investigations (Knight and Mistovich 1984:231) and paleodemographic data (Foster 2000b).

The 1832 censuses were the most accurate and actually counted all individuals instead of only adult males as did most of the earlier censuses. Since most censuses did not enumerate all individuals, it is not possible to specify statistics on sex ratio over time. However, the 1832 Creek Indian census enumerated the number of males, females, and slaves in each household for every town and village in the Upper and Lower Creek region. While the Creek Indian economy and household structure may have changed over the eighteenth century (Ethridge 2003; Saunt 1999), the census is useful for its quantitative detail.

While not as detailed as the 1832 censuses, a census in 1725 by Captain Glover also enumerated males, females, and children and is useful for comparison (Feest 1974). This census listed the number of people by town. There were 1,452 men, 1,560 women, and 990 children in the Upper and Lower Maskókî towns, resulting in a male-female ratio of 0.93:1 and less than one child per two parents (Feest 1974:163).

The 1832 census listed a total population in the 66 Creek Indian towns of 21,487, including 745 slaves. Of those people, there were 10,037 Creek Indian males and 10,711 Creek Indian females, a male-to-female ratio of 0.94:1. Slaves consisted of about 3 percent of the total population. There were 6,254 households in all of the towns, and each consisted of 3.44 individuals, on average (Douthat 1995). This is a slight increase in the number of children per parents over the 1725 census.

SOCIAL AND POLITICAL ORGANIZATION

Since the Creek Indians were an amalgam of different cultural groups, generalization about their social and political organization is tenuous. Nevertheless, the majority spoke a similar language and all were Southeastern Indians who shared common cultural characteristics (Hudson 1976; Urban 1994). While the ultimate decision-making unit of Southeastern Indians was the individual, the economic unit was the *hûti*, or household (Ethridge 2003:142; Hudson 1976; Saunt 1999:40; Waselkov and Braund 1995:127). The household consisted of a wife and husband, their daughters and sons-in-law, and unmarried grandchildren (Swanton 1928b:79, 170). The house and its associated property belonged to the eldest female in the household (Foster 2003a:73s; Saunt 1999:39). Family descent in the household also belonged to and was traced through the female line (Urban 1994; Wickman 1999:85–86). When a man married, he moved in with his wife's family (Foster 2003a:73s). The husband helped build a new house for his wife and their children. John Swanton described the development of a household:

> A man, assisted by other members of his family or clan, might build a house in a new situation and clear the usual yard by hoeing up the surface weeds and grass for a considerable space about it. Now, when one of his

daughters married her husband, drawn from some other, perhaps distant, locality, [he] would build another house on part of the same cleared space or in the immediate neighborhood where the pair would set up housekeeping. As his other girls would continue to occupy the ancestral dwellings, or others erected for them in the neighborhood, the boys would marry elsewhere. A man might erect and pay for a house and call it "my house" but it was to all intents and purposes the property of his wife. (Swanton 1928b:170–171)

Since property and ancestry were traced from the female line, children were reared and educated accordingly. Young girls learned female behaviors from their mother and her relatives, and a young boy learned male behaviors from his mother's male relatives such as her brothers. A man did not raise or significantly influence his own sons (Swanton 1928b:363). He raised his sister's sons. When a husband and wife divorced, the children and household property belonged to the woman.

A woman and her children belonged to a clan (Wickman 1999:63, 82). Membership in the clan defined an individual's mythological family and gave them relations to people in other towns (Urban 1994: 176). In this way, clanship extended relationship and social ties all over the Southeast (Brown 1989:64–65). The number of clans varied among the various linguistic groups that constituted the Creek Indians, but there were common clan families such as Wind, Bear, and Panther (Brown 1989:65; Swanton 1928b:115–117). Clans were ranked in social value so that membership and ancestry with a particular clan provided inherited status (Urban 1994:178). Marriage was exogamous with the clan because marriage within one's clan was like marrying a sibling (Swanton 1928b:166). A man married a member of another clan and his children became the clan of his wife (Brown 1989:65). Greg Urban has pointed out that this view of the Creek Indians is rigid and simplistic. I have described the basic variation of the Lower Maskókî Creek Indians, whereas other Maskókalkî such as the endogamous Chickasaw practiced different marriage patterns (Urban 1994:175).

Women owned the household economic products for good reason. They provided the bulk of the subsistence goods in the economy. Men and women worked together to clear the agricultural fields, but women planted the crops and harvested them. They also collected firewood and foraged for nonagricultural plant foods. Men hunted for animal products and foods, but animal foods did not contribute a significant fraction of the diet. A more detailed review of the subsistence economy follows and in Chapters 6 and 7.

Recent research by historians and archaeologists have cast doubt on the stability of this labor allocation system. Joshua Piker, Claudio Saunt, and Kathryn

Braund have argued that interaction with European traders altered the economy to a degree that had effects on the gender roles of the household economy and, by extension, the archaeological representation of it. The European colonies of South Carolina and Georgia stimulated trade in deerskins and slaves, among other items. The increased demand for deerskins created a dependence of the Indians on trade goods (Braund 1993:67, 121–138; Piker 2004:82, 138, 142, 145; Saunt 1999), which in turn increased the trade between the Indians and the colonists. It could be noted that modern Maskókalkî respect this pattern of matrilineality (Wickman 1999:86), so if there was any effect it was not to a degree that would completely eliminate the lineage system.

Kathryn Braund and Claudio Saunt have argued that this increased trade with Europeans altered the Creek Indians' values of property ownership (Braund 1993:129–138; Saunt 1999:63, 71–73, 164–185). If such a change did occur, it should be visible in the archaeological record in the form of the distribution and "hoarding" of prestige items. Cameron Wesson uses this argument but applies it to food storage and chiefly power among the Southeastern Indians (Ethridge 2003:306, 29n, 32n; Wesson 1997, 1999). Storage of food is unlikely to be the result of chiefly or elite control of resources among the Creek Indians but rather is more likely the result of risk management strategies (Foster 2003b; Winterhalder et al. 1999).

The deerskin trade was a sexually dimorphic economic activity that had specific male and female roles. Traditionally, males hunted for deer during the late fall and early winter, and women processed the deer (Braund 1993:67–68; Saunt 1999). Sometimes males would take their wives and children with them on the hunts (Braund 1993:figs. 6, 7). Consequently, the demography of the villages changed for a portion of the annual economic and religious cycle. The male-to-female ratio in towns decreased during at least part of the year. William Bartram visited and described an Indian town in the late 1770s and said "we saw their women and children; the men being out hunting" (Harper 1998:133).

Claudio Saunt and others have argued that this demographic shift intensified during the eighteenth century, particularly after about 1760 (Piker 2004:79, 97; Saunt 1999:42, 143–144). Archaeologists have argued that this trade-induced demographic shift resulted in a change in the type of houses that were built by the Creek Indians during the eighteenth century (Waselkov and Smith 2000; Waselkov et al. 1990). Because of the depopulation in the villages during the winter, the older-style winter houses were built less frequently during the seventeenth and eighteenth centuries. Whether this pattern is valid beyond the Upper Creek sites where it was observed has not been verified. Chapter 5 addresses this issue.

Cameron Wesson has argued that the social and political organization of the historic Maskókalkî was "dramatically" altered (Wesson 2002). He analyzed the number and type of burial accompaniment in prehistoric through the Historic Period burials among the Maskókî archaeological sites of the Tallapoosa River in what is now central Alabama. He used burial artifacts as a measure of "prestige goods" and defined prestige goods as items that are nonlocal and that are used by "elites" to control power (Wesson 2002:114–115). He equates elites and power with prehistoric chiefs and historic Micos, presumably, though he does not define either elite or power.

During the Protohistoric Period, the number of European trade goods in burials is less than during the Historic Period. Wesson says that it is "possible" that the use of European trade goods during the Atasi (protohistoric) phase indicates their function as prestige burial goods, although he doesn't justify why (Wesson 2002:119). During the Tallapoosa phase (Historic Period and the period discussed in this book), almost all burials contained European trade goods (Wesson 2002:fig. 7.3). He interprets this as evidence that power has been dispersed away from a central, elite power figure such as a chief and distributed among the people. An alternative interpretation is that European trade goods had become common and "cheap" by the Historic Period. Wesson's data do not demonstrate declination of chiefly power but do support a change in the function and value of European trade goods over time. During the Historic Period, some European trade goods lost their "prestige" if they ever had it. Hahn (2004) has argued, as discussed in detail below, that Europeans used power roles and prestige goods in a manipulative way that was variable over time and in relatively isolated cases.

As mentioned, the Maskókî political organization was corporate. Political decisions such as the declaration of war or cooperation with another group of people were made at the level of the town or talwa (Piker 2004:3, 6–8, 29). Each talwa maintained a council of respected adult males. These men collectively made decisions only about the individuals who lived in the town, but their decisions were nonbinding. Power and status in Maskókî culture were obtained through inheritance, age, religious role, oratory, and warfare (Wickman 1999:101).

The council was presided over by the Mico (Harper 1998:313–314, 316). The holder of the title was elected, but the process of election is not clear (Brown 1989:49; Harper 1998:313–314), and there is some evidence that it may have been inherited (Braund 1993: 20; Wickman 1999: 93). The Mico was more of a council manager than an executive (Braund 1993:74; Hahn 2004:146, 200). The Mico called the council to order, but, according to William Bartram in the 1770s, "[the Mico] has not the least shadow of exclusive executive power" (Waselkov and Braund 1995:118). The European settlers and representatives viewed these Micos as having executive power not unlike kings in Europe. The bureaucratic structure of European government and the military dictated that the Europeans discuss treaties with representatives of the Indians. They used the Mico as representative of the Indians and thereby gave extraordinary power to him, particularly through access to trade goods and, in the late eighteenth and early nineteenth centuries, direct payment (Foster 2003a:221–222; Hahn 2004:70, 124, 200, 259, 262, 270; Swanton 1928b:317). The power of the Micos, which was bestowed by the European prestige goods and titles, was not inherited and did not confer power other than that from persuasion (Hahn 2004:146, 200; Harper 1998:314–315).

Cameron Wesson has recently argued that chiefly or elite power decreased from the prehistoric through the Historic Period (Wesson 1997, 1999, 2002). By extension, the "elites" of the Historic Period Maskókalkî were the least influential. The ethnohistoric evidence described here is consistent with an interpretation of the Historic Period elites, however defined, as a dispersed power. Wesson (2002) doesn't clarify whom he means as elites. He argues that elite power was diminishing to a point at which it was almost nonexistent during the Historic Period being discussed here (Wesson 2002:123). He argues for a "dramatic decline" and cultural "erosion" during the Historic Period. Although his support for these dramatic changes is not empirically demonstrated, I don't disagree that power was dispersed and relatively weak during the Historic Period.

The town councils held influence over the town's inhabitants only (Piker 2004:3, 6–8). The National Council, in contrast, made decisions for the entire body of Creek towns. Like the town councils, its power was minimal. Nevertheless, the European governments used it to represent the decisions of all the Creek people. Clearly, in many cases, it did not represent the desires of the common Creek people (Ethridge 2003:107–108; Hahn 2004:262–270; Piker 2004:6–8). Benjamin Hawkins, the Indian agent who lived among the Creek Indians between 1796 and 1816, worked to establish and fund a National Council because it was more efficient than to solicit decisions from each town (Foster 2003a:57). Steven Hahn has argued that the National Council and the Creek Nation were bureaucratic units artificially created in order to interact with the European legislative and political systems. He documents that the Creek Nation was not united in 1735 but was created as a legal entity in the early eighteenth century to justify a land claim and in response to British territorialism (Hahn 2004:173, 204, 229–270). Research by Patricia Wickman supports the interpretation that the confederacy was a European creation (1999:183–187) and did not exist prehistorically.

Archaeologists Vernon J. Knight and Marvin Smith also have argued that the confederacy of the Creek Indian towns was in response to outside influences (Knight 1994a; Smith 1987:129–142). Smith pointed to migration and warfare of the late seventeenth century. Knight argued that the confederacy of Creek Indian towns was a historically recent development but that the social mechanisms that allowed its development were remnants of chiefdom organization (1994a:386). He does not define what he means by chiefdom organization but points to cultural commonalities that allowed for interaction between independent towns. He argues that these Creek Indian towns formed larger political organizions "conditionally" (1994a:386).

Individuals of mixed European and Indian ancestry used the National Council to collaborate with the European governments to further their own wealth and influence (Hahn 2004:170; Saunt 1999:67–89). These few individuals such as Alexander McGillivray used their unique power and position to dominate the relationship that the Creek Indians had with foreign European governments. Since historic documents come from the Europeans, these few powerful individuals bias our view of Creek social and political organization. While they appear, in the documents written by Europeans, to have significantly influenced the Creek people, it is unlikely that these intergovernmental relationships significantly affected the day-to-day activities of the Muskogee people.

SUBSISTENCE ECONOMY

The Muskogee and Southeastern Indians generally engaged in a mixed subsistence economy that varied over space and time. During most of the eighteenth century, they were primarily horticulturalists and collectors. There are a number of ethnohistoric sources that reveal information about Creek Indian subsistence, and, in addition, there has been a resurgence of research by archaeologists and historians on the subsistence economy of those Indians (Braund 1993; Ethridge 1996, 2003; Foster 2000a, 2001, 2003b; Foster et al. 2004; Harper 1998; Piker 2004; Waselkov 1997; Waselkov and Braund 1995).

The renowned botanist William Bartram, who traveled among and wrote about Creek Indians during the 1770s, was astute in his observations of plants used and grown by the Indians. He observed that the Creek people grew corn, rice, sweet potatoes, beans, squash, and watermelons (Waselkov and Braund 1995:165). Benjamin Hawkins noted a dependence on similar produce 20 years later, in 1796 (Foster 2003a:21). Some Indians had begun growing European-introduced foods like rice, but the main diet for the majority of people came from native products such as corn and beans. A synthesis of plant and animal archaeological remains found at Creek Indian sites is presented in Chapters 6 and 7.

Corn was the staple subsistence item of the Creek Indians (Foster 2003a:21, 41–42, 2003b; Harper 1998:325). It was prepared in a number of ways. It was shucked in the fields and carried home usually in skin bags carried on the back but sometimes by canoe (Swanton 1928b:444). Still on the cob, it was laid out to dry and placed in corncribs (Harper 1998; Waselkov and Braund 1995:54, 56).

The better quality corn was placed in the back of the corncrib and the poorer quality corn was consumed first because it would rot faster. Dried corn was ground into flour and made into cakes, which were baked on open fires (Harper 1998; Waselkov and Braund 1995: 37, 39, 63, 106). Kernels were mixed with lye from ashes to make hominy, a staple item that was cooked in large clay pots over an open fire (Waselkov and Braund 1995:39, 44, 77).

Agricultural products such as corn and beans were planted in two garden areas, one communal and the other private (Foster 2003b; Harper 1998:325–326). The communal garden or horticultural fields, outside the habitation area, were larger and provided most of the food (Ethridge 2003:147; Foster 2003b). A single town had use rights to the land that was communally farmed by the town members (Waselkov and Braund 1995:158). These plots were located in the river floodplains immediately adjacent to the town during the Historic Period. However, there is some evidence that some Southeastern Indians in the very late Historic Period (1800–1836) were abandoning river bottom settlements and "settling out" into the uplands for a variety of reasons (Waselkov 1997), but the degree of this change in settlement has not been quantified over space or time. For example, we do not know if this change was stimulated by individuals who began ranching in the late nineteenth century, by population growth, or by environmental variables, or if it was a normal shifting of population. Recent research, which uses ecological modeling and ethnohistoric data, has indicated that the primary variable contributing to garden placement and duration was soil productivity (Foster 2003b).

The produce from a town's communal agricultural fields was distributed among the families of the town. Since Creek Indians were matrilineal, adult females owned and worked the farmland (Foster 2003a:21). Individual plots were identified in the large communal fields by borders between the plots, but everyone worked together on all plots during the planting.

> Every town, or Community, assigns a piece, or parcels, of Land, as near as may be to the Town, for the sake of conveniency—This is called the *Town Plantation,* where every Family or Citizen has his parcel or share, according to desire or conveniency, or largeness of his Family—The shares are divided or bounded by a strip of grass ground, poles set up, or any other natural or artificial boundary,—thus the whole plantation is a collection of lots joining each other, comprised in one inclosure, or general boundary. In the Spring when the Season arrives, all the Citizens as one Family, prepare the ground & begin to plant, beginning at one end or the other, as conveniency may direct for the general good; & so continue on until finished; & when the young plants arise & require culture, they dress and husband them until their crops are ripe. The work is directed by an

overseer, elected or appointed annually, I suppose, in rotation throughout the Families of the Town. He rises by day break, makes his progress through the Town, and, with a singular loud cry, awakens the people to their daily labour, who, by sunrise, assemble at the public square, each one with his hoe & axe, where they form themselves into one body or band, headed by their superintendent, who leads them to the field in the same order as if they were going to battle, where they begin their work & return at evening. The females do not march out with the men, but follow after, in detached parties, bearing the provisions for the day. When the Fruits of their labours are ripe, and in fit order to gather in, they all on same day repair to the plantation, each gathering the produce of his own proper lot, brings it to town & deposits it in *his own crib*, allotting a certain proportion for the *Public Granary* which is called the *King's Crib* because its contents is at his disposal, tho' not his private property, but is to be considered the Tribute, or Free Contribution of the Citizens for the State, at the disposal of the King. (Waselkov and Braund 1995:158–159; original italics)

Techniques for field preparation were relatively consistent between Indian groups. The Indians used fire to clear the understory (Ethridge 1996:229; Foster 2004d) and reused old fields before new ones were cleared because of the labor involved in clearing virgin forest. Virgin forests were rarely cleared for agricultural land. Large trees were girdled and left to fall in the winter storms (Silver 1990; Williams 1930:435). On average, the communal agricultural fields for a single Southeastern Indian town were several hundred acres (approximately 100 ha) in size and were immediately adjacent to the towns (Ethridge 2003:140–157, figs. 12, 13, 16, 17; Foster 2003b; Waselkov 1997). James Adair was a trader who lived among the Southeastern Indians and wrote about them in the eighteenth century. He noted, "Now, in the first Clearing of their plantations, they only bark the large timber, cut down the saplings and underwood, and burn them in heaps; as the suckers shoot up, they chop them off close by the stump, of which they make fires to deaden the roots, till in time they decay" (Williams 1930:435).

After the field was clear, the women created "hillocks" (Lafitau 1974:54), small hills of dirt about two to three feet apart, in which to plant seeds. Three to ten seeds were planted in each hillock (Baden 1987:22; Lafitau 1974:54; Lescarbot 1968:248–249; Will and Hyde 1964:81). The hillocks gave support to the growing plants. James Adair, again, described these rows of hills as compact: "[The Indians] plant the corn-hills so close, as to thereby choak up the field. They plant their corn in straight rows, putting five or six grains into one hole, about two inches distant. They cover them with clay in the form of a small hill.

Each row is a yard asunder, and in the vacant ground they plant pumpkins, water-melons, marsh-mallows, sunflowers, and sundry sorts of beans and peas, at least two of which yield a large increase" (Williams 1930:439).

These hills were formed and worked with digging sticks and hoes made of stone, shell, or the shoulder blade of a large animal. Later, metal hoes were used. William Baden, using mostly northeastern ethnohistoric sources, noted that Indians worked only about six weeks in the fields (1987:24). This work included only occasional weeding. He also points out that the techniques and labor involved in this type of agriculture have important effects on the yield of corn in a single plot of land. Since the Indians were not tilling the ground, the ash from burned and harvested plant matter on the ground was not being reincorporated into the soil. Under this system, nitrogen and other important nutrients were rapidly lost to erosion (Baden 1987).

Two crops of corn were planted by the Creek Indians, an "early corn" or "little corn" and a "great corn" (Hudson 1976:295). The early corn was planted in the individual family plots near the houses around March and harvested around May. A Natchez Indian from Louisiana described the season for harvesting the "little corn." "The third moon is that of the Little Corn. This month is often awaited with impatience, their harvest of the great corn never sufficing to nourish them from one harvest to another" (Swanton quoted in Hudson 1976:366). The early corn contributed to an important annual festival, the boosketau or Busk ceremony (Foster 2003a:75s–78s; Harper 1998:326; Hawkins 1807). The "great corn" was harvested around September and was planted in the larger, communal fields on the edge of town; it provided most of the corn for the annual diet.

Every household had an individual garden for private use adjacent to the house compound inside the town. The size of these gardens is unknown; they are only described as "small" (Waselkov and Braund 1995:54). Again, Bartram observed, "Besides this general plantation, each Habitation in the Town incloses a garden spot adjoining his House, where he plants, *Corn, Rice, Squashes,* &c, which, by early planting & closer attention, affords an earlier supply than their distant plantations" (Waselkov and Braund 1995:160, original italics).

Toward the beginning of the nineteenth century, some Creek Indians began to own and sell cattle and pigs (Ethridge 2003:158–174). While the cattle and pig industry may have become important for individuals in particular towns, it was not a primary source of economic dependence. Josh Piker argues that the cattle were reluctantly raised by a few Creek individuals and represented unwanted change in the traditional economy (2004:99–100). Because data were unsystematically collected from historical sources and archaeological collections, archaeologists still do not understand the degree of influence that cattle and pig products had on the economy and subsistence of the Indians. A significant contribution to the argument that the Creek Indians raised cattle and pigs is from the writings of Benjamin Hawkins (Ethridge 2003:158–174; Foster 2003a:4j, 30, 31s, 35s–36s, 38s, 40s, 42s–43s, 50s–51s, 60s, 62s, 103, 393). However, his documents were biased because one of his major goals was to convert the Indians to cattle and pig raising. While there is no question that some Creek Indians in parts of the Southeast began to use domesticated animals for their economic value, we still don't know how widespread the practice was among individual households. Archaeological investigations provide an alternative data source that may inform us about the relative contribution of domesticated animals to the Indian economy; it will be discussed in Chapter 7.

The Creek Indians hunted and greatly depended on deer for meat and products. Indian use of deerskins and its relationship to European trade has been a source of significant research in the last decade (Braund 1993; Foster and Cohen 2005; Pavao-Zuckerman 2000, 2005; Piker 2004; Saunt 1999). European demand for the skins of deer created a market in the southeastern United States during the eighteenth century. That market, it is argued, drastically altered the society, economy, and environment of the Creek Indians (Braund 1993; Foster and Cohen 2005). Along with those changes, the use of deer and deer products probably changed, and these changes are visible in the archaeological record as will be seen in Chapter 7.

There is evidence that deer hunting changed throughout the eighteenth century. Joshua Piker has documented a change in the hunting territories of the Creek Indians throughout the eighteenth and early nineteenth centuries (Piker 2004:84, 154). These changes may have been related to and influenced diplomatic involvement between the Creek Indians and the colonists of South Carolina, Georgia, and Florida. Although the justification for his conclusion is not clear, Piker argues that diplomacy was affected by hunting because the Indians visited the colonists and traded while on hunting trips (Piker 2004:76).

Deer hunting and the deerskin trade may have also affected town demography because Indians may have begun hunting for longer periods of time. A number of researchers have argued that Indians became dependent on the trade goods that were obtained in return for deerskins (Braund 1993; Ethridge 2003:9–10; Piker 2004:79, 82, 84, 138, 148–151; Saunt 1999:139–163; Waselkov et al. 1990). Consequently, the Indians may have increased their hunting frequency and duration during the middle of the eighteenth century. If the deerskin trade market increased dramatically during the early to middle part of the eighteenth century, then we should expect to find a temporal change in the frequency of trade goods in archaeological deposits from that period. Documented changes in the faunal assemblage of archaeological deposits have been documented at Upper Creek sites (Pavao-Zuckerman 2000) and will be discussed in detail in Chapter 7.

SETTLEMENT

A Creek town, or talwa, was the normal political unit for the majority of Creek Indians during the eighteenth to early nineteenth centuries (Harper 1998:313–314; Piker 2003, 2004:6–8, 29). Therefore, the town and its identification are significant to the political history of the Maskókî people. Most towns had a similar physical layout, and ethnohistoric descriptions help identify their location among archaeological sites. However, the talwa was more than a physical location. It was a social entity in that it constituted the tribal affiliation of its members (Jackson 2003:42; Opler 1952). Consequently, a talwa's members did not *necessarily* have to be physically located in one place.

A Creek Indian town had geographic and social space. Patricia Wickman describes a talwa as a place where people cooperate and come together to "make medicine" and sing and dance together around one fire (1999:94–95), which is the sacred fire in the square ground that will be discussed more fully. Wickman's interpretation of a talwa is consistent with the formation of new talwas. A new talwa was not officially formed until a square ground and sacred fire was built.

At the center of the town's geographic space was a square ground, chunky yard, and council house. The square ground was an area with four rectangular structures, one on each side, and a ceremonial fire in the middle. It was used in warmer weather for council meetings and ceremonies. In 1772, David Taitt, a British officer, gave the best firsthand description of a square ground during the eighteenth century: "The Square is formed by four houses about forty feet in Length and ten wide. Open in front and divided into three different Cabins each. The seats are made of Canes Split and worked together raised about three feet off the Ground; and half the width of the House, the back half being raised above the other about one foot; these Cabins serve for beds as well as seats in Summer" (Mereness 1961:503).

The chunky yard was adjacent to the square ground and was a large, flat, cleared field. It was often swept clean so that a slight mound of earth encircled it from the sweeping. It was the location of a ball game played by the Creek Indians. Also located adjacent to the square ground was the council house, or "hothouse" or "winter council rotunda," a large circular structure that could house hundreds of individuals. David Taitt again described the Tukabatchee council house in the Upper Creek towns: "The hot house is generally built at the north west Corner of the Square having the door fronting the South East. The one in this Town is a square building about 30 feet diameter rounded a little at the Corners; the walls are about four feet high; from these walls the roof rises about twelve feet, terminating in a point at top. . . . In this house the Indians Consult about the affairs of their Nation in the Winter Season and in

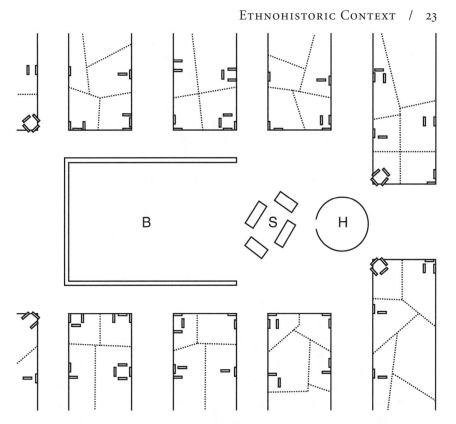

Figure 1.2. Creek town layout, adapted from Ephraim G. Squier's engraving of "Creek Towns and Dwellings" (redrawn and adapted from Bartram in Waselkov and Braund 1995:figure 33). B is the ball field, S is the square ground, and H is the hot house or council house.

their Square in the Summer" (Mereness 1961:503). William Bartram provided an idealized town layout in 1789 (Figure 1.2; Waselkov and Braund 1995:fig. 33).

Surrounding the square ground, chunky yard, and council house were the individual residences (see Figure 1.2). The small rectangles represent individual house structures within a house lot indicated by dotted lines. Each family ideally had four house structures organized around a courtyard forming a square about the size of a half-acre (Waselkov and Braund 1995:93). This courtyard was like a miniature "square ground" as described above, but not all families were large enough or wealthy enough to subscribe to this idealized house compound layout as seen in Bartram's sketch of individual house lots in figure 1.2. Individual families had small gardens immediately adjacent to their house.

Towns were located along the major rivers in the area, the Tallapoosa, Coosa, Alabama, Flint, and Chattahoochee, usually for access to natural resources

(Waselkov and Smith 2000; Worth 2000). William Bartram described the variables contributing to Creek Indian town location:

> An Indian town is generally so situated, as to be convenient for procuring game, secure from sudden invasion, a large district of excellent arable land adjoining, or in its vicinity, if possible on an isthmus betwixt two waters, or where the doubling of a river forms a peninsula; such a situation generally comprises a sufficient body of excellent land for planting Corn, Potatoes, Beans, Squash, Pumpkins, Citruls, Melons, &c. and is taken in with a small expence and trouble of fencing, to secure their crops from the invasion of predatory animals. At other times however they choose such a convenient fertile spot at some distance from their town, when circumstances will not admit of having both together. (Waselkov and Braund 1995:126–127)

Recent research into the environmental variables that contributed to the location and duration of the physical location of towns (Foster 2000a, 2001, 2003b; Foster et al. 2004) has shown that the most limiting and significant variable contributing to town abandonment was soil fertility. While lack of fuel wood was mentioned by eighteenth-century Creek Indians as a reason for moving town locations, it probably was not a widespread cause for town abandonment (Foster 2001:174–177). In some cases, social factors such as access to trade goods or communication networks may have been more important than biophysical factors.

In the 1770s, towns were described as compact (Harper 1998:133, 245). Few households were "out of sight of the town" (Waselkov and Braund 1995:156), although this pattern varied throughout the region because of localized warfare (Harper 1998:133). In addition, this pattern of a population tightly focused on a central town location may have been changing in the very late Historic Period (1800–1836) when ranching became more popular (Ethridge 2003:158–174). When this "settling out" occurred, the physical location of the talwa changed, but the social context probably remained the same since individual members of a town maintained allegiance to their town.

We do not know the degree to which this demographic dispersal was widespread throughout the Creek Indian towns. Since our sample of documents that are numerous enough and detailed enough are limited to about a 100-year period (circa 1715–1836), we can't rule out the possibility that the "settling out" wasn't a normal shifting and fissioning of towns over time. Indeed there may be crosscultural evidence across the southeastern United States that it was a normal process of long-term population demography (Blitz 1999). For example, well before the acceptance of cattle ranching, Thomas Nairne, in 1708, described the process of town division in a letter regarding the customs of southern Indians:

> Sir that at once you may have a notion of the Indian Government and the progression of on Village out of another, I'le Illustrate by an Example:
>
> C

>   1   2

> A B D E
>
> Suppose 1:2 to be a river, A: a populous flourishing Town on the river side, straightned for planting ground. Upon some disgust, or other reason 2 Leading men lead out Colonies of 30 or 40 famelies Each and sattle 2 New Villages B: C: Bechancing to florish and increase much, out of it by the same means arise D and E. (Moore 1988:62–63)

Town fissioning and cycling (Anderson 1994; Blitz 1999) seems to have been a normal process of demographic growth, environmental degradation, and political formation for Southeastern Indians and other horticulturalists around the world.

CONCLUSIONS

In this chapter I have presented a review of the ethnohistoric literature that is based on firsthand accounts and observations of the Creek and allied Indians. Ethnohistoric sources such as documents, journals, and maps are immensely useful for details, which are not preserved in oral history or in the archaeological record. Since there are numerous and recent reviews of various aspects of Creek Indian society using ethnohistoric sources, this review deals with those cultural aspects that are more likely to affect archaeological deposits such as subsistence and architecture remains. The ethnohistoric sources present a relatively static perspective of an ethnographic present and do not quantitatively or even qualitatively demonstrate the variation between individual towns or households. Historic documents are also limited in temporal scope because most of our reliable documents are from the late eighteenth century. The rest of this book supplements with archaeological remains what we know about Creek Indian cultural heritage from the oral histories and ethnohistoric accounts.

Environmental Context

Thomas Foster and Mary Theresa Bonhage-Freund

The environmental context of the Maskókalkî is relevant to understanding the people and their heritage. Creek Country, as Robbie Ethridge (2003) has called it, was a dynamic environment that responded to the native and foreign settlers. The environment shaped the decisions of the people and the people shaped the environment. Recent archaeological, geological, and ethnohistoric research has begun to allow us to characterize that environment and how it changed over time in response to the Southeastern Indians. In her book on Creek Country, Ethridge (2003:32–53) reviewed the landscape of all of the Maskókalkî as described by Benjamin Hawkins in the late eighteenth century.

The Maskókalkî lived along the Lower Chattahoochee and central Flint River watersheds (Figure 1.1). The Chattahoochee was named after a town of the same name. According to Benjamin Hawkins, it means marked or flowered stones (Foster 2003a:52s). Rivers were frequently named for a prominent physiographic feature or town. The Chattahoochee River was called the "Rio del Spiritu Santo" and the "Apalachicola River" by the Spanish, who viewed it from the south and were more familiar with the Apalachicola people who were settled to the south (Cumming and De Vorsey 1998:plate 24; Hann and McEwan 1998:33). In the early eighteenth century, it was also referred to as the "River Cusitie" on an English map. In this case the river is named after the Maskóki town of Cussetuh (Utley and Hemperly 1975:336). John Goff's article on the town of Chattahoochee contains other names (Utley and Hemperly 1975:338).

Those watersheds formed the settlement patterns and biophysical environment of the people who lived there. The headwaters of the Chattahoochee River start in the mountains of what is now Georgia. They flow almost due southward and join with the Flint River to make the Apalachicola River and empty into the Gulf of Mexico. The Chattahoochee and Flint Rivers form a north-to-south orientation of the towns. The headwaters of the Flint River start in the Piedmont of Georgia and flow south and southwest. These watersheds formed the habitat of the Lower Creek Indians as usually defined. The habitat forms the subject of this book, but the Maskókalkî lived far beyond these watersheds.

The central Chattahoochee River was 120 yards wide in 1796 (Foster 2003a:53s). It flowed out of the mountains, over the Piedmont, over the fall line, and down through the Coastal Plain. The Piedmont is a gently rolling hillside with hardwoods and pines. It ends at the fall line hills, which begin the Coastal Plain (Figure 1.1). These hills are a transition zone in several ways: between the hilly topography of the Piedmont and the relatively flat Coastal Plain region; between elevations; and between plant and animal communities. It is not a coincidence that the majority of the Maskókalkî towns along the Chattahoochee River were situated along this ecotone. In 1796, Benjamin Hawkins described the falls, called the Cowetuh Falls because the town of Cowetuh was nearby:

[T]hese are over a rough, coarse rock, forming some islands of rock, which force the water into two narrow channels, in time of low water. . . . fish may ascend in this channel, but it is too swift and strong for boats; here are two fisheries; one on the right belongs to this town [Cowetuh]; that on the left, to the Cussetuhs; they are at the termination of the falls; and the fish are taken with scoop nets; the fish taken here are the hickory shad, rock, trout, perch, cat fish, and suckers. . . . The land on the right [western] bank of the river at the falls, is a poor pine barren, to the water's edge the pines are small; the falls continue three or four miles nearly of the same width, about one hundred and twenty yards; the river then expands to thrice that width, the bottom being gravelly, shoal and rocky. (Foster 2003a:53s)

In this quote, Hawkins relates many features of the fall line ecotone that are important to the people who lived there and still live there. Plant and animal resources abound at this confluence. Travel up the river was limited by the falls. In the early 1800s, the U.S. government studied and surveyed these falls as a place to put an armory, but they decided that travel up the Chattahoochee was too prohibitive (Willoughby 1999:67).

The land about the Cowetuh Falls was described by Hawkins as a poor pine barren. The region of the Lower Creek Indians was and could still be considered a poor pine barren. It is characterized by sandy soils that are conducive to pine trees and plants that live in nutrient-poor soils. In 1828, Basil Hall traveled through the southeastern United States and recorded images of his travels. He described the pine barrens:

A considerable portion of the Southern States of America, and even as far as North Carolina, is covered with boundless forests of pine-trees. These districts are called Pine Barrens, and the soil being generally sandy, with a scanty supply of water, they are probably destined to remain for ever in the state of a useless wilderness. Upwards of five hundred miles of our journey lay through these desolate forests, and I have therefore thought it worth while to give a Sketch, which is sufficiently character-istic of these singular regions. Occasionally villages gave some relief to the tedium of this part of the journey; and whenever a stream occurred, the fertility of the adjacent lands was more grateful to the eye than I can find words to describe. Once or twice, in traveling through the States of Georgia, we came to high knolls from which we could look over the vast ocean of trees, stretching without a break, in every direction, as far as the eye could reach, and I remember, upon one of these occasions, thinking that I never before had a just conception of what the word forest meant. (Hall 1829: entry for XXIII)

Hall's image of the towering forest was impressive, and despite his impression of the land as useless, the Indians had used those forests for generations.

Analysis of witness trees on land survey maps from the early eighteenth cen-tury gives a relatively unbiased and quantitative characterization of the forests that surrounded the Maskókalkî (Black et al. 2002; Foster et al. 2004). These trees were boundary markers for land surveys and were recorded on maps and field notes at the time of the surveys (1827 through the 1830s). They have been used by a wide number of ecologists as a reliable and valid characterization of the forest composition at the time of the surveys.

Witness trees in the area of the Maskókalkî on the Lower Chattahoochee River watershed indicate that most of the region can be characterized as a pine-blackjack forest type (Black et al. 2002:fig. 3) and is characteristic of the area as a xeric region (Braun 1950). Several species of pine such as shortleaf (*Pinus echinata*), longleaf (*Pinus palustris*), loblolly (*Pinus taeda*), slash pine (*Pinus eliottii*), and Virginia pine (*Pinus virginiana*) probably lived in the area, but the witness tree data do not distinguish pine by species (Black et al. 2002:2068; Harper 1998:21, 32, 239). Of all these, longleaf pine is the most common in nu-trient-poor, upland, dry soils prone to a high number of fire frequencies (Black et al. 2002:2068–2069).

Paleoethnobotanical analyses reveal different types of information about the environment than do witness tree data. Paleoethnobotany is the scientific investigation of the relationships between plants and people as manifested in the archaeological record (Ford 1979). Archaeobotanical data, including both macroplant and microplant remains, are the raw material of paleoethnobotanical research. Macroplant remains are those archaeologically excavated seeds, tubers, roots, wood charcoal, and other floral remnants that can be clearly examined either by the naked eye or with the assistance of a low-powered light microscope. Microplant remains include pollen, phytoliths, starch grains, and other floral remains that require high-powered microscopes, sometimes involving scanning electron microscopy. In addition, trace element analysis of cooking residues, wood ash, and similar preserved substances may be considered to be a category of archaeobotanical analysis. In this chapter we consider both kinds of remains, but no trace element analysis has been reported to date. Archaeobotanical remains have been systematically recovered and adequately analyzed at only a few Creek Indian archaeological sites. We will discuss what can be learned from the archaeobotanical assemblages from a series of well-studied sites: Cussetuh, Buzzard Roost, Ochillee Creek, and Yuchi Town.

Many of the plants represented in archaeobotanical assemblages from Creek Indian sites favor or require specific environments, and frequently entire ecosystems are directly or indirectly related to human activity. The opening or disturbance of fields for agriculture or settlement allows noncultivated open field taxa to gain a foothold, and successional processes are set in motion. One of the authors (Foster) has measured the compositional changes that occurred in forests that were used by Upper Creek Indians using witness trees. I found that early succession species were more frequent in specific regions of the river valleys, which were probably correlated with horticultural fields (Foster et al. 2004:43). Early succession species were not significantly higher within 2,000 meters of villages, however (Foster et al. 2004:39). In addition, some species, like maypops or purslane, were cultivated or encouraged in agricultural plots during historic times (Bonhage-Freund 1997; Gremillion 1989). Open-field taxa are those plants that occur naturally, invading those local fields that lack substantial brush or tree cover. Some of these plants are commensal with agriculture, and some, like maypops, may even be encouraged or otherwise tended in agricultural fields. They are native or naturalized to local conditions and show no signs of genetic modification.

Over time, forest encroaches on the edges of agricultural fields, and as soil fertility declines, people begin to manage succession rather than fight it (e.g., Alcorn 1984; Chagnon 1996). Edge zone/old field/understory taxa are those most likely to be found in the area of ecotone linking field and forest. Most of these plants are successional species that invade abandoned ("old") fields but also thrive in the more open areas of the forest edge created by land clearing. Hereafter these are referred to as "edge zone" taxa. Elsewhere in Georgia, Native Americans are thought to have managed successional plants to maximize the availability of such plants (Bonhage-Freund 1997). When agricultural productivity approaches the point of diminishing returns, entire towns or villages may be relocated and the cycle begins anew (Foster 2003b, 2006b).

Historic documents and macroplant remains suggest that Cussetuh Town followed the trajectory just described. This town relocated several times during its history (see Chapters 1 and 3). In the late eighteenth to early nineteenth centuries, agricultural soils proximate to Cussetuh town were in decline, and the town itself showed signs of preparing for relocation. Macroplant remains from this town give direct evidence of agricultural, open field, and edge zone taxa. In addition, wetland and forest ecosystems can be identified from the paleobotanical assemblage (Bonhage-Freund 2003).

Maize, barley and European cereal grains represent agricultural fields. All of the starchy seeded taxa favor or tolerate bottomland conditions. There were no identified plants that required dry open fields. All of the species producing fruits and edible pods recovered at Cussetuh Town favor abandoned agricultural fields and were probably regarded as "wild crops" (Bonhage-Freund 1997). These include blackberry/raspberry, elderberry, and honey locust. Pokeweed thrives in the area of ecotone between old fields and forest.

Sedge, flatsedge, bulrush, maygrass, and sumpweed all favor wetland environments. Today there is a swampy area near the site, and these paleobotanical data suggest that wetlands also existed during the historic Creek occupation. Gordon Willey (1938) described the same wetlands during his fieldwork at Cussetuh in the mid-1930s, which was before the topography was altered by grading, and his descriptions indicate the antiquity of the wetlands near the site. Wetlands support many economically useful plants beyond those recovered in these samples. They also provide critical habitat for waterfowl, fish, amphibians, and reptiles. Wood charcoal likewise supports proximity to wetlands (cane, sycamore, basswood, blackgum) but also to drier, better-drained soils (oak, hickory, poplar); black walnut, chestnut, and elm/hackberry all prefer well-drained mesic soils, while most oak, hickory, and poplar favor more xeric landscapes.

In summary, a variety of habitats are documented within the catchment zone of Cussetuh village. These provide diverse resources for both humans and wildlife. Cussetuh Town was positioned in what could be described as a broad area of ecotone. Old and agricultural fields, wetlands, mature forests, and edge zones provided a natural pantry as well as a source of a variety of raw materials.

Located along the Flint River in Taylor County, Georgia, Buzzard Roost (Salenojuh) was a daughter village of Cussetuh, occupied in the late eighteenth century. This town is represented by two archaeological sites, 9TR54 and 9TR41 (Ledbetter et al. 2002). Taylor County is contained within the Fall Line Sandhills physiographic province but is in close proximity to the Midland region of the lower Piedmont (Wharton 1978). A variety of habitats are inferred from the plant remains at the Buzzard Roost sites. Agricultural species present at this town include indistinguishable European cereal grains, maize, squash, common bean, marshelder, maygrass, peach, and perhaps cotton.

Open field taxa are represented at both sites. Copperleaf, doveweed, wild type goosefoot, grass seed, grass stem, and pigweed were present at both sites. In addition, wild lettuce was recovered at 9TR41, while clover, knotweed, maypops, and spurge appeared at 9TR54.

The ubiquity of open field taxa, or percentage of proveniences in which these taxa appear, was 22 percent at 9TR41 and 55 percent at 9TR54 (see paleoethnobotany chapter for discussion of ubiquity). At 9TR41, open field taxa were found in postmolds, small and large pits, and smudge pits. A total of eight different open field taxa were identified. At 9TR54. open field taxa had 55 percent ubiquity, including postmolds, small and large pits, fireplaces, trash pits, and root cellars. A total of 11 different open field taxa were identified.

Edge zone taxa that are present in both sites include blackberry/raspberry and pokeweed. Arrow wood and dogwood are unique to 9TR41, while bedstraw, elderberry, grape, greenbriar and serviceberry are found only at 9TR54. Edge zone plant remains have only 15 percent ubiquity at 9TR41 compared to 55 percent at 9TR54. Sedge, a wetlands species, was recovered from a single trash pit at 9TR54. It amounts to approximately 1 percent of the seeds and similar-sized macroplant remains from the site and is the only confirmed wetland taxon from either site.

Wood charcoal analysis is an additional tool for environmental reconstruction. Ten unique genera were identified at 9TR41 and 13–14 at 9TR54. At 9TR41, these include ash, black walnut, cherry/plum, elm/hackberry, hickory, oak (including red and white), sycamore, pine (including southern yellow), cane, and probably rattan. The 9TR54 samples included blackgum, black walnut/butternut, chestnut, elm, hickory, oak, sumac, sweetgum, tulip tree, eastern red cedar, pine (including eastern white and southern yellow), and cane. A possible additional genus is hackberry. All of these taxa, with the exceptions of chestnut and rattan, would be expected in a mature oak-hickory forest zone. Chestnut is found elsewhere in Georgia but would be unusual so far west and south. Rattan is not native to North America. Euro-American farmers have long used chestnut for fencing, and modern outdoor furniture is frequently fabricated of rattan. It is likely that these two taxa are intrusions from a more modern time period. They are, perhaps, contemporary with the cottonseeds discussed in Chapter 6.

Of the specifically identified wood species, ash, chestnut, elm/hackberry, sycamore, black walnut sweetgum, and sweetgum prefer mesic to hydric soils. Cane favors hydric soils, and canebrakes were often noted historically. Both pine and eastern redcedar prefer dry conditions and are also pioneer species of abandoned fields. While pine is found scattered throughout eastern deciduous forests, there have been vast tracts of pines in the Southeast since late prehistoric times (Bonhage-Freund 1997; Wagner 2003). This may be related to regional climatic conditions, may be a by-product of the clearing of land for agriculture, or both (Bonhage-Freund 1997). Cedar was found to be significantly more frequent near Indian villages in the analysis of witness trees mentioned (Foster et al. 2004).

The environment of Ochillee Creek (9CE379) in the early nineteenth century consisted of a mixed forest dominated by pine (Bailey 2002). The principal overstory trees in the immediate site vicinity would likely have consisted of a mixture of oaks, pines, and hickories (O'Steen and Raymer 1999). This is probably a successional forest, produced by land clearing, burning, and deliberate maintenance of open space by prehistoric and historic Indians. Open spaces created by such activity would have attracted a spectrum of wild plants for human and animal consumption. Likewise, the floodplain supported a high density and wide variety ranging from herbaceous plants to mast-producing trees (O'Steen and Raymer 1999).

Pine comprised 86 percent of the identified archaeobotanical charcoal found at the Ochillee Creek site and had 100 percent ubiquity (O'Steen and Raymer 1999). Approximately half of the pine was identified as southern yellow pine, confirming that pine was a major component of the local forest in the site vicinity. The pine barrens were impressive forests because they had an open understory. These forests are usually open with a two-story community with a subcanopy of blackjack-oak, bluejack oak (*Quercus cinerea*), and turkey oak (*Quercus laevis*) (Black et al. 2002:2068; Braun 1950). Early historic travelers described these forests as "gothic cathedrals" (Ethridge 2003:43). The river bottoms had a more varied forest composition (Black et al. 2002:2069–2070; Ethridge 2003:42–45). Stream valleys were a white oak–mixed mesophytic community consisting of sweet gum, water oak, and red maple.

Vegetation in the region has been significantly altered owing to human impacts. The Indians altered the forests near their habitation areas. A quantitative study of forest composition changes in association with the Maskókalkî economic behaviors identified alterations in the forest composition (Foster et al. 2004). Foster found through an analysis of the witness tree data that the Indians were increasing the frequency of hickory trees within 2,000 meters of their villages, reducing the number of pines within 2,000 meters of their villages, and increasing early succession species such as cherry trees within 6,000 meters of their villages. Pines became less frequent because the Indians were using pine for building materials (Foster et al. 2004:38). Hickory increased because the Indians gathered the nuts in great quantity and brought them to the vil-

Table 2.1: Percentage of land cover at Fort Benning, Georgia, over time (Olsen, et.al. 2001: table 1)

Date	Forest %	Pine %	Mixed %	Deciduous %	Barren %	Non-Forest %	Non-forest on steep slopes %
1999	76.231	34.06	21.537	20.629	4.6059	19.1631	13.9975
1991	77.987	29.06	22.913	25.9187	3.8312	18.2716	13.344
1983/86	80.479	27.46	29.862	23.1516	4.1953	15.3252	11.1388
1974	82.900	23.98	23.385	35.529	3.2056	13.8939	9.3257
1827	97.447	78.18	11.735	11.7355	NA	2.5525	0.5983

lages. Early succession species increased because of agricultural clearing and burning (Foster et al. 2004:38–40, 44). Recent analyses of palynological data indicate that hunting activities may have also affected the forests because the Indians burned the forests in order to drive out the deer (Foster and Cohen 2005). Fire decreases hardwoods and increases pine (Abrams 1992).

After the Indians were forcibly removed, settlers from the newly formed United States began intensive agriculture and cut down almost all of the trees. Old growth forests exist in only a few locations now. A recent study of historic aerial photos from a U.S. army base (Fort Benning) and the witness trees described above indicated that the percentage of nonforest vegetation found on steep slopes (greater than 3 percent) is increasing. Areas of pine forest are probably increasing. Areas of deciduous forest are decreasing (Table 2.1). The modern forest at Fort Benning is highly managed, however (Dale et al. in press; Olsen et al. 2001).

Another feature of the living environment of the Creek Indians of the Chattahoochee and Flint Rivers was their transportation network. Trade routes were ancient paths that were probably originally deer paths (Myer 1928:735). They were dynamic, and locations shifted according to the needs of the travelers. However, many were in use for a long time and became arteries of communication, cooperation, and trade among a wide range of populations. Recent research by Foster (2001) indicates that the location of trade routes was valuable for the placement of towns and affected their economic decisions about agriculture.

These routes were also the paths taken by European explorers. Consequently, the perspectives recorded in their writings are often tempered by the location of roads and paths. For example, distances and cultural landmarks in the Viatory by Benjamin Hawkins (Foster 2003a) are made along transportation routes

(Foster 2004b). Reconstructions of town locations and cultural and geographic features using these historic sources need to consider the transportation routes (Foster 2004b).

The analysis of historic roads and paths is best made through the inspection of historic maps. Occasionally these transportation networks are visible in historic aerial photos, but those paths are usually limited to the larger roads and the coverage is not as complete. John Goff researched a variety of sources and has provided the most thorough investigation of early transportation routes in Georgia (Utley and Hemperly 1975). He documented a series of roads that were used to enter the territory of the Maskókalkî from the east. These paths passed through Upper Creek towns of Okfuskee and Okfuskeneena and Lower Creek towns such as Salenojuh and Cussetuh (Utley and Hemperly 1975:194). One of the southern paths that traversed from Augusta to Mobile and passed through Cussetuh was eventually used by the U.S. government for a postal route and the Federal Road (Foster 2005a; Southerland and Brown 1989).

There were countless other smaller paths that connected households and families. These paths later became roads used by U.S. settlers. Many of them are recorded on historic land survey maps that were drawn in 1827 (Foster 2004b). I have reconstructed the location of paths and roads that were in use in the years immediately following the forced removal of the Maskókî from their homeland along the Chattahoochee River. These transportation routes are recorded, although not always systematically, in great detail. Figure 2.1 shows the myriad paths and roads that were in use around 1827 in Creek Country. Some of the paths appear to stop and start. This may be an artificial function of the fact that they were digitized from land survey maps that were drawn by different land surveyors. Different surveyors did not always record the same cultural features such as paths and roads. The figure, nevertheless, shows paths generally traveling in a northeast to southwest direction and in a north to south direction. However, there are a number of smaller paths in the uplands that probably went to dispersed homesteads.

The climate where the Maskókalkî lived is currently warm and humid. According to Stahle and Cleaveland (1992), the paleoclimate was one of transition with much of the eastern United States experiencing a period of environmental fluctuations. By the sixteenth century, the climate achieved the essential form that it possesses today with minor fluctuations. The overall climate when the Creek Indians were living along the Chattahoochee River was very similar to the present. Caleb Swan described the climate during the late eighteenth century as "remarkably healthy; the wet and dry seasons are regular and periodical. The rainy season is from Christmas to the beginning of March, and from the middle of July to the latter end of September. Between these two periods there is seldom much rain or cloudy weather" (Swan 1855:258).

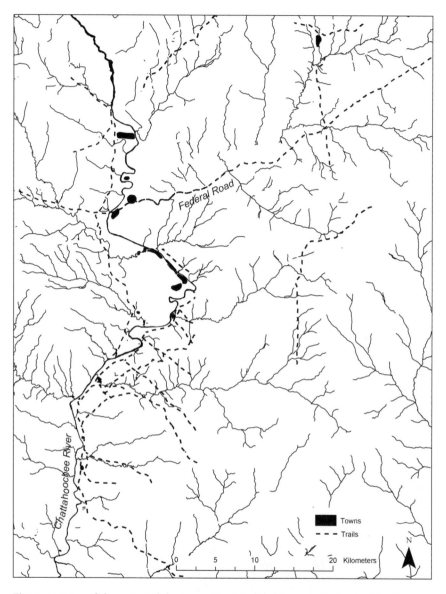

Figure 2.1. Map of the region of the Lower Creek Indians (1715–1836) showing the Chattahoochee River watershed and travel routes as digitized from historic land surveys (1827 to
1830s).

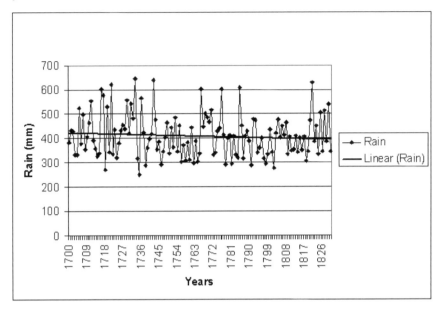

Figure 2.2. Georgia rainfall between 1700 and 1836 as estimated from dendrochronology. Graph was created from raw data (Stahle and Cleaveland 1992).

Stahle and Cleaveland (1992) have reconstructed paleoclimates for the southeastern United States from tree ring analyses. These data show that the eighteenth century witnessed a gradual reduction in rainfall between 1700 and 1836 (Figure 2.2). This figure is an adaptation from the raw data available from Stahle and Cleaveland (1992). The Creek Indians described the years between 1804 and 1812 as the "hungry years" because of a long drought (Ethridge 2003:154). These years correspond to a sequence of below-average rainfall according to the reconstructions by Stahle and Cleaveland, although there are others of equal and greater magnitude.

3
History of Archaeological Investigations

There has not been a major summary of the archaeology of post–Yamassee War (circa 1715) Lower Creek Indians since Huscher's unpublished Lower Creek summary (1959). The archaeological classification of post–Yamassee War Indian sites is called the Lawson Field phase (Foster 2004d; Knight 1994b:189; Knight and Mistovich 1984; Schnell 1990, 1998; Willey and Sears 1952), which spans 1715–1836. The history of the definition of that phase will be described in detail below. Recently John Worth provided the most thorough synthesis since Huscher, but his chapter was focused on early Creek settlements (pre-1715) and particularly on ethnohistoric sources (Worth 2000:266). Marvin Smith (1992) and Chad Braley (1995) summarized the number of sites and history of excavation on Historic Indian sites of the Piedmont and Coastal Plain regions of Georgia for a cultural resources management synthesis for the Georgia Historic Preservation Office. The majority of recent archaeological work has been on post–Yamassee War sites as a result of cultural resource management in and around Columbus, Georgia, and Fort Benning, Georgia, and Alabama. Figure 3.1 shows the relative position of the Lower Creek region and the surveys that are discussed here. Since most Creek Indian settlement was along the major rivers, almost all of the Lower Creek Indian residential habitat has been surveyed. This summary will be a comprehensive description of the archaeological surveys of Lower Creek settlements occupied after the Yamassee War as currently described in published and unpublished reports.

This chapter serves multiple purposes. A survey of the archaeological investigations places the investigations in context and helps to explain the historical development of the Lawson Field phase, which is the archaeological manifestation of the Lower Creek Indians as it is currently defined. This phase has become known as the archaeological signature of a group of people (Knight 1994b). As the phase is currently defined, it represents multiple linguistic groups and vast economic and social changes as described in Chapter 1. I feel that it is timely to reassess the archaeological manifestation of the Lower Creek Indians

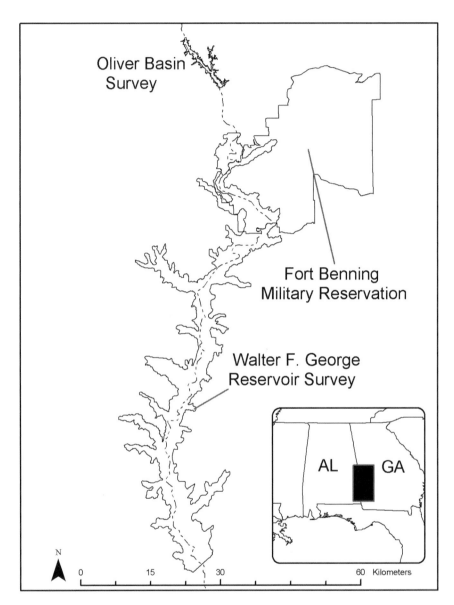

Figure 3.1. Region of the Chattahoochee River showing the Walter F. George Reservoir, the Fort Benning Military Reservation, and the Oliver Basin archaeological surveys.

from a direct historic approach since we know so much about the composition of the people and archaeological sites. In addition, there are a number of advances in our knowledge of the Maskókalkî owing to historic and archaeological research in the last few decades. We can begin to systematically address these hypotheses and ideas about culture change (Braund 1993; Ethridge 2003; Foster 2000b, 2003b, 2004d; Foster and Cohen 2005; Hahn 2004; Hudson and Tesser 1994; Knight 1994a, b; Piker 2004; Wickman 1999).

Our current definition of the Lawson Field phase is limited in its ability to distinguish linguistic variation, temporal changes, spatial variation, and known economic and social changes (Foster 2004d). We need to understand why we define the Lower Creek assemblages the way we do and to understand the utility of that archaeological phase. In other words, we need to measure the reliability and validity of the metric in order to use it effectively, where the metric is an archaeological assemblage identified as the Lawson Field phase.

Another function of this chapter is to provide a synthesis of all known documentary and archaeological evidence for the location of the Lower Creek towns. This approach will serve to define the archaeological signature of the different towns since each town was politically and economically unique and should be studied as an independent entity (Hally 1971; Piker 2003, 2004). It will also help to identify patterns of migration and temporal changes within talwa populations. Ethnohistoric documents reference various towns by name, but we need to understand the relationship between the events in the ethnohistoric documents at a given time and the archaeological manifestation of the people at the town. The archaeological manifestation can sometimes represent single sites continuously occupied or multiple sites occupied in various degrees if the people migrated or the population changed. Understanding the causes of migration and population dispersal among the Southeastern Indians is important to a number of researchers (Anderson 1994; Blitz 1999; Foster 2001, 2003b, 2004d; Hally 1971; Williams and Shapiro 1990) because human population movement contributes to such a wide range of anthropological and ecological processes. In the second part of this chapter, I spend a significant amount of time reconstructing the archaeological evidence for the known Lower Creek Indian towns so that we can understand the fission process of these Southeastern Indians, use a direct historic approach in their analysis, and control for the validity of the archaeological remains that are documented.

ARCHAEOLOGICAL RESEARCH ON THE LOWER CREEK INDIANS

This section will review the history of our knowledge of archaeological resources in the Lower Chattahoochee River watershed in relation to Creek Indian sites. We need to understand the different methods that contributed to our collective archaeological knowledge of the Maskókalkî. Our current knowledge is a cumulative process and not all of it has been collected with the same level of confidence. In order to use that knowledge effectively, we need to understand its epistemology.

Unsystematic investigations by avocational collectors have impacted sites since the sites were first abandoned and are still to this day greatly affecting the preservation of these cultural resources (Hargrave et al. 1998; Scott 2004). This unsystematically collected information is of little use because the contexts of excavation are rarely recorded or published. This summary therefore will be primarily limited to systematic investigations. I describe each survey and the methods used so that readers can evaluate and compare the various methods. Since the methods used varied, the validity and reliability of the data produced also varied. This is why I have taken so much time in this volume to explain clearly the methodology and contexts of the data summarized here.

Benjamin Hawkins probably was the first to somewhat systematically record the location of Creek Indian archaeological sites. He was the Indian Agent to the southern Indians from 1796 to 1816 (Foster 2003a) and lived among and wrote extensively about the Creek Indians. He regularly traveled among the Lower Creek Indian towns and recorded abandoned towns, ball grounds, and other archaeological sites, although he did not necessarily classify them as such (Foster 2003a:46j, 16–17). I am classifying Hawkins as a systematic researcher because he regularly recorded abandoned cultural resources on his travels and Viatory. His Viatory serves as a sample of cultural resources distributed along trails and roads. William Bartram, 20 years earlier, recorded multiple archaeological sites such as abandoned towns and mound sites, but his recordings were less systematic than convenience samples (Waselkov and Braund 1995:35, 38–39, 42–43, 76).

In the late nineteenth century, Clarence B. Moore surveyed prehistoric Indian mounds for evidence of manufacture. In the process, he performed the most systematic and formal recording of archaeological sites that had yet been conducted in the Lower Creek region. Although he was interested in sites with mounds and the Creek Indians did not build mounds, he recorded the location of a number of Creek archaeological sites (Brose and White 1999). Moore visited the Creek Indian town of Cussetuh, which he called the "Dwelling site near Hall's Upper Landing, Chattahoochee County, Ga." (Brose and White 1999:437). He visited the Abercrombie Mound and Woolfolk's Mound, which are very near the towns of Cowetuh Talluahassee and Cussetuh Old Town, respectively.

Soon after Moore's survey and publication, Peter Brannon published a series of articles on the location of Lower Creek towns in relation to archaeological sites (Brannon 1909, 1920, 1922a, b, 1925, 1926, 1930). His data on the location of the towns were partly derived from a local informant using retrospective interviews. In the 1920s, at the time of the interviews, the informant claimed to be present at many of the sites approximately 100 years earlier, and Brannon usually believed him. Given the methods of the time, Brannon is to be commended for publishing much of his work and for his early research in the Lower Chattahoochee Valley.

The largest survey conducted in the homeland of the Lower Creek Indians was performed in preparation for the inundation of a section of the Chattahoochee River between Fort Gaines and Columbus, Georgia. The damming of the river created what is now called the Walter F. George Reservoir or Lake Eufaula. Two archaeological surveys were conducted in preparation for the dam. The University of Alabama, Museum of Natural History, conducted a survey of the Alabama (western) side of the Chattahoochee River from the Florida boundary north to Phenix City, Alabama, in 1947 (Hurt 1947, 1975). This survey was directed by Walter B. Jones and David DeJarnette of that museum and was authored by Wesley R. Hurt. Its goal was to identify sites that would be inundated by the proposed damming of the river (Hurt 1947:x, 1975). From June 10 to September 1, 1947, a team surveyed approximately 180 kilometers (112 miles) along the river. They did not collect artifacts at, test, or even visit all of the sites. Some of the sites were identified based on local informants. Wesley Hurt's report remains a major source for the reconstruction of the location of individual towns in the region.

The Walter F. George archaeological survey was also conducted in preparation for the damming of the Chattahoochee River. This second survey is often called the Walter F. George survey; it was conducted by the Smithsonian Institution and was led by Harold Huscher of that institution. He used methods similar to Hurt's. He visited some sites, made mostly surface collections, and tested a few sites. His results were summarized in a brief report (Huscher 1959). The report was issued after work elsewhere in the state had begun to define the variation of material culture and archaeological remains from Creek Indian sites (Kelly 1938; Wauchope 1966).

Another reservoir was surveyed farther north, nearer to Columbus, Georgia. This survey of the Oliver Basin was conducted by Edward McMichael and James Kellar (1960) as a joint project between the University of Georgia and the Georgia Power Company. It was a high quality report, particularly for the times, but covers an area mostly not settled by the Lower Creek Indians. They did record a few small settlements and individual homesteads in the survey, but the majority of the settlements were south, below the fall line. Another survey, farther north, was conducted by Harold Huscher of the University of Georgia (Huscher et al. 1972). It was of the West Point region, settled by Upper Creek Indians, and is not considered for this book.

The Walter F. George was surveyed again by the University of Alabama. That survey was funded by the U.S. Army Corps of Engineers and was directed by Vernon J. Knight, Jr. (Knight and Mistovich 1984). It was conducted mostly by boat and was limited to the water's edge. The reservoir was not drained at the time of the survey. The investigators revisited sites found by Huscher and Hurt in the earlier reservoir surveys. While the methods varied slightly depending on the land conditions and ownership by the U.S. Army Corps of Engineers, sites were generally identified with modern techniques. They shovel-tested sites with 30-meter interval transects and collected surface samples (Knight and Mistovich 1984:46–47).

Last, our knowledge of the prehistory of the Chattahoochee River region has been greatly affected by the fact that a military reservation is located there. Cultural resources management at Fort Benning Military Reservation has improved our understanding of Creek Indian sites quantitatively and qualitatively. All areas within the boundary of the base that are available for survey have been surveyed using modern methods. Sites were identified with 30-meter transects of shovel tests that were 30 meters apart. In general shovel tests were dug until sterile soil was encountered. When sites were encountered, transects were increased in order to delineate the site boundaries. Fort Benning Military Reservation is approximately 72,800 hectares (180,000 acres).

THE LAWSON FIELD PHASE

The Lawson Field phase has been defined as the artifact assemblage that represents the Lower Creek Indians (Knight 1994b:189; Knight and Mistovich 1984:225; Schnell 1990:69). It was first defined based on an excavation at the Creek Indian town of Cussetuh (Willey and Sears 1952). Gordon Willey defined an archaeological phase (Lawson Field) after excavating test units across Lawson Army Airfield at Fort Benning, Georgia, during the 1930s (Foster 2005a; Willey n.d.a, b; Willey and Sears 1952). He identified structures and burials containing European trade goods that dated to the eighteenth century. Based on detailed descriptions of the town's geographical location during the eighteenth century by the U.S. Indian Agent Benjamin Hawkins (Foster 2003a), Willey and Sears identified the site that they excavated as the historic town of Cussetuh. At the time, Cussetuh was the most thoroughly excavated eighteenth-century Creek town. They defined the ceramic assemblage based on the contents of five burials and mostly plow zone artifacts (Willey n.d.a, b; Willey and Sears 1952:4–5). The burials contained mostly European trade goods. Unfortunately, until recently, the location of Willey's excavations was ambiguous (Foster 2005a). Consequently, the Lawson Field ceramic assemblage was originally defined predominantly from ceramics from the plow zone at some unknown location of a site that probably represented some undefined section of Cussetuh town. In my recent excavation at Cussetuh, I reviewed historic aerial photographs and geo-referenced them to the survey notes left by Gordon Willey and to modern aerial photographs. I was able to locate Willey's units to within a few meters using a geographic information system (Foster 2005a).

The Willey and Sears publication identified a ceramic assemblage that consisted of a roughened ceramic type, Chattahoochee Brushed (Chattahoochee Roughened var. *Chattahoochee*), an incised ceramic type, Ocmulgee Fields Incised (Lamar Incised var. *Ocmulgee Fields*), undecorated types, and a red painted type, Kasita Red Filmed (Mission Red Filmed). All types were tempered with sand or grit. In contrast to seventeenth-century assemblages, no ceramics reported from this section of Cussetuh were shell tempered. The authors stated that the types found at Cussetuh were "closely related" to the ceramics found at Ocmulgee Fields near Macon, Georgia, although they did not specify how. Ocmulgee Fields was a seventeenth-century (circa 1685–1715) Creek Indian town (Kelly 1938; Mason 1963; Willey 1938; Willey and Sears 1952). Many of these same pottery types continued to be manufactured after the Creek Indians were forcibly removed to the Indian territories (circa 1836) and up until around the turn of the twentieth century (Gettys 1995; Quimby and Spoehr 1950; Swanton 1928b; Wenner 1948). Lawson Field pottery types will be described in detail in Chapter 4.

Since the Willey and Sears article defining the Lawson Field phase (1952), the number of types associated with this section of Lower Creek ceramic cultural evolution has increased, but the major types have not changed significantly. Table 3.1 shows a list of ceramic types found at Lower Creek Indian sites as defined by Knight (1994b). The most thorough synthesis of this assemblage was by Knight and Mistovich (1984) and Mistovich and Knight (1986) and summarized recently by Knight (1994b) and Foster (Foster 2004d). Knight (1994b:189) identified Lawson Field sites primarily from "abundant, datable English, French, and Spanish trade goods." He identified 1BR35, 9SW50, 1RU63, 1RU20/21, 1BR25, and other sites as Lawson Field. Tom Lewis (2004) recently analyzed a large sample of vessels from the Lawson Field type-site and performed the most detailed manufacturing analysis of these ceramics to date.

Since the synthesis of Knight and Mistovich (1984) and Mistovich and Knight (1986), two decades and millions of research dollars have been spent on intensive cultural resource management in the heart of the Lower Creek habitat. This recent research permits a reanalysis of the definition of Lower Creek material culture and the ability to distinguish population variation. This book proposes and uses a "direct historic" approach to the identification and definition of material culture (Brown 1993; Foster 2004d; Rubertone 2000; Steward 1942). Archaeological classification has historically used a deductive

Table 3.1: Ceramic types in the Lawson Field phase according to current definitions (Knight 1994)

Lawson Field Ceramic Types (Knight 1994)
Shell-tempered Plain
Shell-tempered Burnished Plain
Walnut Roughened, var. *McKee Island*
Shell-tempered Incised
Nonshell-tempered Plain
Nonshell-tempered Plain
Chattahoochee Roughened, var. *Chattahoochee*
Chattahoochee Roughened, var. *Wedowee*
Lamar Incised, var. *Ocmulgee Fields*
Mission (Kasita) Red Filmed
Lamar Complicated Stamped
Toulouse Plain
Toulouse Incised

technique to organize sites in space and time, but the models from which cultures were classified were induced from poorly understood sites. For example, the Lawson Field phase was originally defined based on plow zone artifacts and five burials of a convenience sample of the archaeological remains from the town of Cussetuh. Therefore, archaeologists often seriate, or temporally order, site occupations using phases that were defined decades earlier and were poorly understood. Sometimes, that is all that is available. However, we have a significant sample of data from sites that can be dated independently from ceramic seriation, so we should step back and reevaluate our definition of the archaeological manifestation of the Maskókalkî in the Lower Chattahoochee River valley watershed.

LOWER CREEK INDIAN TOWNS

A major purpose of this section is to provide a form of a population census with which archaeological and ethnohistoric study samples can be compared. Since these data are necessarily biased by preservation, excavation methods, collector bias, and research goals, we need to know the population from which those archaeological data are sampled. Adequately assessing the sample population for *each* archaeological data set is far beyond the scope of this work. However, assessing the number of towns and their location relative to archaeological sites is an important first step in that direction. The town location reconstructions in this chapter are used as a basis for the direct historic methodology (Steward 1942) in remaining sections of the book.

Robbie Ethridge (2003) and Amos Wright, Jr. (1999, 2003) recently synthesized significant ethnohistoric documents relating to the location of Creek Indian towns. For example, Ethridge (1996, 2003:29) constructed the first map of Creek Indian towns according to the journals of Benjamin Hawkins. Their sources were used extensively for this summary along with those of Margaret Ashley and Frank Schnell, Sr. (1928), Peter Brannon (1920), Franklin Fenenga and Barbara Fenenga (1945), Mark Fretwell (1954, 1962, 1980), Albert Gatschet (1884), Wesley Hurt (1947, 1975), Harold Huscher (1959), Vernon Knight and Tim Mistovich (1984), Edward McMichael and Edward Kellar (1960), Frank Mulvihill (1925), Thomas Owen (1950), Frank Schnell, Jr. (1970), John Swanton (1922), and John Worth (2000). Worth recently reassessed Huscher's correlation of archaeological sites with Creek towns. His reanalysis was the most significant study of its kind using modern data, but he concentrated mostly on pre–Yamassee War sites whereas this study is defined for post–Yamassee War sites. Also, Amos Wright, Jr. (1999, 2003) recently compiled an extensive body of historical references to Creek Indian towns. The only more extensive similar source is John Swanton's *Early History of the Creek Indians & Their Neighbors* (1922). I will not reproduce Wright's extensive lists in this book.

The rest of this chapter provides a list of Creek Indian populations who were living along the Chattahoochee and Flint Rivers between 1715 and 1836. It is organized by talwa. I list talwas as known through ethnohistoric documents, maps, and archaeological sites. As generations of ethnohistorians and archaeologists before me have noted, the synthesis of an entire group of people is difficult and highly inaccurate. In other words, the validity of a census that claims to list the names of towns over a 125-year period is questionable (Foster 2004c). With the following list, I am documenting some of the towns that existed between 1715 and 1836 on the lower Chattahoochee and Flint Rivers. These towns may have changed locations during that time period. Using minimally the criteria set forth by Trigger (1969) and Lolly (1996), I am synthesizing that knowledge and identifying archaeological sites which, to the best of our current knowledge, may represent the town's residents' material remains.

Apalachicola and Apalachicola Old Town

Apalachicola and Apalachicola Old Town are related because they represent the same Hitchiti-speaking people who moved the location of their town during the late eighteenth century. Apalachicola (Palachacola, Apalachucla, Palachocola) is a relatively old town that emigrated with the rest of the Creek Indians from central and eastern Georgia to the Chattahoochee River around 1715. A town named Apalachicola was settled on the Savannah River in the late seventeenth century (Caldwell 1948; Swanton 1922:131). Soon after that migration, some Apalachicola Indians settled at the confluence of the Flint and the Chatta-hoochee Rivers with a headman called Cherokee Leechee. That town was called by the name of the headman and later Apalachicola Fort (Swanton 1922:131).

Possibly not all of the Apalachicola Indians settled with Cherokee Leechee because Spanish and English documents of the early eighteenth century de-scribe a separate town called Apalachicolo. In 1716, Diego Peña listed Apalachi-colo as being six leagues from Caveta, which was the Spanish spelling of Cowe-tuh (Boyd 1949:25; Hann and McEwan 1998:363). From these Spanish accounts we have a general idea of the location of Apalachicola but not an exact one. Diego Peña's diary recorded that he visited a chief of Apalachicola who lived about two leagues (about five miles) from the town of Apalachicolo (Boyd 1949:22). Later, presumably on his way to Cowetuh, he said that he found a "small farm where once there was a fort" that was two leagues distant (Boyd 1949:26). That fort may have been the Spanish Fort of 1689–1691 (site 1RU101), but it isn't clear. Weisman and Ambrosino (1997:121) interpret this to indicate that Apalachicola was located near Cowetuh, far to the north of the Spanish Fort (see Cowetuh section). If the 1716 location of Apalachicola was at site 1RU65, as I argue below, then Peña could have encountered the fort on his trav-els north toward Cowetuh. It is not until the late eighteenth century that there are descriptions detailed enough to identify the town's location precisely.

In 1796, Benjamin Hawkins described Palachoocle as situated on the western bank of the Chattahoochee, one and one-half miles below Auhegee Creek (Swanton 1922:134). Note that one published version of Benjamin Hawkins's *Sketch of the Creek Country* (Foster 2003a:65s) says that Palachoocle is one and one-half miles below "Cheahau," not Auhegee Creek. The original manuscript at the Library of Congress in Washington, D.C., says "Auhegee" Creek, not Cheahau (Peter Force Collection, Series 8D, Items 62.2–70, 72/1, Mss. 17, 137, Reel 42 of 112). At another location in his journals, Hawkins says that "Pa,la,choo,cl,e is on the left ab.t 15 minutes [one mile] beyond Hitchiti on a poor pine flat" (Foster 2003a:42j). Auhegee Creek was called "Hitchiti" at its confluence with the Chattahoochee (Foster 2003a:41j, 64s), so this entry is consistent with the previous one. In addition, the William Bonar map of 1757 places "Palachocola" immediately south of "Aheigy Creek" (Cumming and DeVorsey 1998:plate 59E).

These observations place Apalachicola in the late eighteenth century at site 1RU18 (Figure 3.2) if distance is measured along the transportation route from the north. These transportation routes were recorded and georeferenced into a GIS from the 1830s-era land survey maps. Prior estimates of distance by Hurt (1947) and Huscher (1959) were made without this "travel distance" data. Hurt and Huscher measured distances in direct, linear space, so the use of the trade

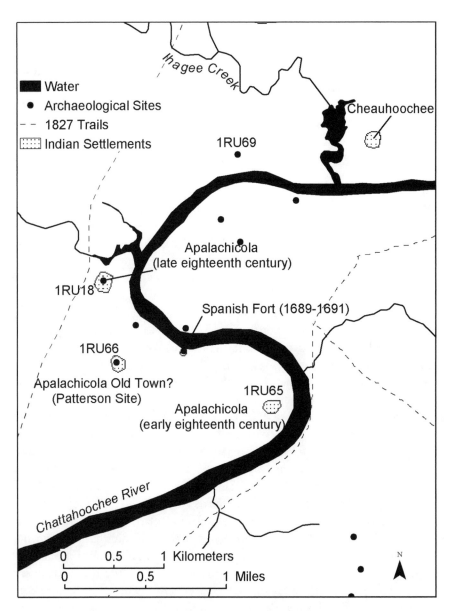

Figure 3.2. Location of Cheauhoochee, Apalachicola, and the Spanish Fort (1689–1691) on the Chattahoochee River during the eighteenth to early nineteenth centuries.

routes is a dramatic improvement that aids our use of the historic accounts from Hawkins and Taitt (Foster 2004b).

The late-eighteenth-century location may also be at 1RU66, which is consistent with reconstructions by Huscher (1959:33), Hurt (1975:21), and, more recently, Worth (2000:288–289); however, that distance from Ihagee Creek is much greater than one mile. Another option is that the late-eighteenth-century town of Apalachicola was located at 1RU69, the Cottonton Site (Figure 3.2). This site was excavated by Lewis Larson and reported by Edward Kurjack (1975:185–195) as a relatively small site with a late-eighteenth-century Creek component. Various trade goods were found at the site. Given that this site is off the main transportation route and Kurjack interpreted it as related to but not Apalachicola, I am arguing that the next most likely site to represent late-eighteenth-century Apalachicola is 1RU18, a short distance away.

Site 1RU18 was investigated by Wesley Hurt (1947, 1975:21). Based on 153 surface-collected artifacts, Hurt classified the site as a Creek Indian village about 100 by 150 yards in diameter (1947:86). He recorded his sites on Alabama Highway Department maps, the location of which are unknown as of this writing (personal communication, Eugene Futato, Alabama Site Files, University of Alabama, 2004). Consequently, the only source for the location of 1RU18 is Harold Huscher's map (1959), which places it south of an unnamed creek at the confluence of the Chattahoochee River (Figure 3.2). However, the 1975 edition of Wesley Hurt's survey places it slightly north of that location and closer to the Cottonton site (1RU69) (1975:30).

Site 1RU66 has been identified as the seventeenth- to early-eighteenth-century (pre-1715, Blackmon phase) village (Knight 1994b:189), but Kurjack (1975:180, 185) clearly states that the European ceramics found at the site in association with Indian-made artifacts date to the late eighteenth century, which is the Lawson Field phase. Sites 1RU18 and 1RU66 are separated by a mile and, based my field investigations, could not be confused as the same habitation area, in contrast to Huscher's statement otherwise (Huscher 1959:90). Site 1RU18 is on a higher elevated terrace relative to the Patterson site, 1RU66.

In 1772, David Taitt spent a number of days in Pallachocola while surveying the Creek Indian Territory (Mereness 1961:554–560). He said that Pallachocola was about six miles south-southwest from Geehaw (Cheahau). If Cheahau was at site 1RU54 as described in the Cheahau section, then site 1RU18 is almost exactly six miles south-southwest and represents Apalachicola of the 1770s, as it did during the 1790s when Benjamin Hawkins described it (Foster 2003a:42j, 65s). Mark Fretwell independently identified the same area for the location of Apalachicola of Taitt and Hawkins's time (1962:37). Therefore, Apalachicola did not relocate between 1772 and 1796. However, it had apparently moved around 1755, according to accounts in 1772 by David Taitt (Mereness 1961:557), and in the late 1770s, according to William Bartram (Harper 1998:246).

David Taitt visited the former location of Apalachicola on a "point" about a mile and a half "below" Apalachicola (Mereness 1961:557, 558). William Bartram also made a similar visit in the late 1770s. Bartram reported that he walked about a

> mile and a half down the river, to view the ruins and site of the ancient Apalachucla: it had been situated on a peninsula formed by a doubling of the river. . . . We viewed the mounds or terraces, on which formerly stood their town house or rotunda and square or areopagus, and a little back of this, on a level height or natural step, above the low grounds is a vast artificial terrace or four square mound, now seven or eight feet higher than the common surface of the ground; in front of one square or side of this mound adjoins a very extensive oblong square yard or artificial level plain, sunk a little below the common surface, and surrounded with a bank or narrow terrace, formed with the earth thrown out of this yard at the time of its formation: the Creeks or present inhabitants have a tradition that this was the work of the ancients, many ages prior to their arrival and possessing this country. (Harper 1998:246)

If the former location of Apalachicola was about one and one-half miles below the location of Apalachicola in the late eighteenth century (at 1RU18), then the former location was approximately at 1RU65 or, less likely, the Patterson site (1RU66) or 1RU27 which underlies the Spanish Fort (1689–1691). These sites were recorded by Harold Huscher and investigated in various degrees. Site 1RU65 was recorded as a Creek Indian "village" (Huscher 1959:59, 95) with Ocmulgee Fields and Chattahoochee Brushed ceramics. He called site 1RU27 the Indian village surrounding the Spanish Fort (Huscher 1959:90) and described it as containing Ocmulgee Fields, burnished-plain, and Chattahoochee Brushed ceramics. It was located within about 100 meters of the Spanish Fort site. While site 1RU65 is more consistent with the distance of one and one-half miles that Bartram and Taitt described for the distance between Apalachicola and Apalachicola Old Town, 1RU65 has no evidence that it ever had a mound or a large population (Brose and White 1999:414; Huscher 1959:95). However, there is evidence of a low mound approximately 30 feet in diameter somewhere on that peninsula, according to Brother Finbarr, a local resident and amateur archaeologist who surveyed the region. Site 1RU65 hasn't been investigated beyond simply recording its location (Huscher 1959). Frank Schnell, Jr. worked with Huscher and visited the mound site with Finbar. As of this writing, he remembers the mound as an erosion remnant (personal communication 2005). Further evidence of a mound near Apalachicola is a map produced by the Alabama Anthropological Society in 1925 indicating that there is a mound at "Opalachukla" (Edwards 1921).

Although the 1689 Spanish Fort trace ruins are not significantly elevated beyond the surrounding topography, it is possible that Bartram and the host Indians mistook the fort trace and ruins as a "square" mound or terrace (Harper 1998:246; Frank Schnell, Jr. personal communication 2005). By Bartram's visit, the fort constructed by Apalachee Indians would have been abandoned for approximately 85 years; it does have a trench or moat surrounding it, which makes the fort ruins appear higher. The site at the village, 1RU27, has been identified as having a late-seventeenth-century occupation. Huscher reported that Smith tested this site (Huscher 1959:91), but that reference is not in his list of references so further information about site 1RU27 is not available.

Auputtaue

Auputtaue (Upatoi) is a small village formed by a "splinter" population from Cussetuh. It is estimated to have been settled around 1790, based on ethnohistoric reference (Elliott et al. 1996). Dan Elliot and other researchers (Ethridge 2003; Foster 2001) use a quote in the documents of Benjamin Hawkins to argue that the town was settled in 1790. The quote was from a resident of the town who said that he moved with his family to the town six years earlier (Foster 2003a:59s). Unfortunately, this is not conclusive evidence that the entire town was formed at the same time that this particular individual migrated there, although it is not inconsistent with that interpretation. Nevertheless, artifacts found at the site are consistent with that occupation date and the town was not mentioned by earlier ethnohistoric sources (Elliott et al. 1996:262–276, 1999).

Benjamin Hawkins stated in 1799 that the town was situated about twenty miles upstream from Cussetuh on the Hatche-thlucco. The Hatche-thlucco is currently called the Upatoi Creek. A significant number of sites such as 9ME395 and 9ME42 in that location have been investigated and are highly likely to be associated with individual houses and public structures of the town of Auputaue (Figure 3.3) (Elliott et al. 1996:259). Furthermore, structures associated with the town are mapped on the 1827 Muskogee County District 10 land survey map in section 252 (Elliott et al. 1996; Foster 2001).

Broken Arrow

Broken Arrow seems to be synonymous with the towns of Likatcka (Swanton 1922:229), Clay Catskee (Mereness 1961:548, 549), and Tlocorcau (Foster 2003a: 63), and it may be an English translation of the Indian word. If this is so, then Amos Wright notes the earliest mention of the town as "Thloyeatka" in 1786

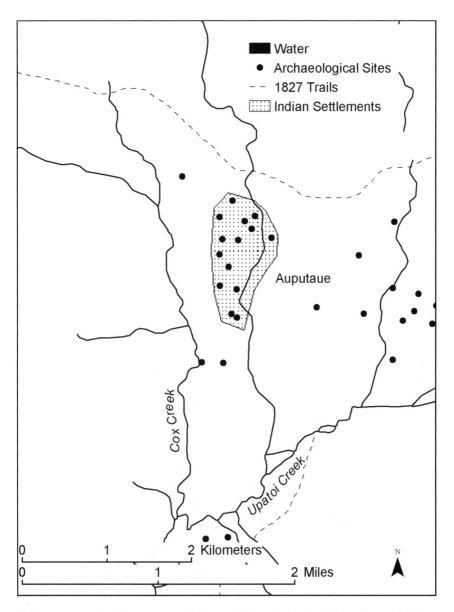

Figure 3.3. Location of Auputaue on the Upatoi Creek during the eighteenth to early nineteenth centuries.

(2003:21). However, David Taitt traveled through Clay Catskee on April 28, 1772, and he said that the village was about six miles upriver from Eutchie (Yuchi) town and on the west side of the Chattahoochee River (Mereness 1961:548). The town consisted of 60 gunmen in 1772 (Mereness 1961:549). Caleb Swan in 1790 crossed the Chattahoochee at Broken Arrow, "twelve miles below the Cassita and Coweta towns" (Swan 1855:229; Swanton 1922:254). The 1795 Barker map lists "Clay Cotska or Broken Arrow" on the west side of the Chattahoochee River south of Cussetuh and Cowetuh and north of Cheahau (Barker 1795). In 1796, Benjamin Hawkins recorded that residents of "Tlocorcau (broken arrow)" moved to Coweta Talluahassee. This reference seems to be John Swanton's justification for placing Likatcka (2) at the location that is later called Cowetuh Talluahassee (1922:229, plate 2). Albert Gatschet (1884:137–138) and Thomas Owen (1950:188–189) attribute Broken Arrow to a river crossing on the Chattahoochee and the name of a small village also known as Broken Arrow. Gatschet says that William Bartram refers to it by Tukauska (1884:138; however, see Harper 1998:653–654).

Even given all of these references to the location, the placement of Broken Arrow is still problematic. The earliest reference to the location of the town is by David Taitt in 1772. He says that Clay Catskee is six miles north of Euchie (Yuchi) town. If Yuchi town was in the same location that it was when Benjamin Hawkins described it in 1796, then Yuchi town was south of the current Yuchi Creek and adjoining the Chattahoochee River on the west bank (Figure 3.4). Yuchi town has been identified as partly represented by archaeological site 1RU63 (Braley 1991, 1998; Foster 2004a; Hargrave et al. 1998; Huscher 1959; Schnell 1982). Given that location of Yuchi town, then during David Taitt's visit, Clay Catskee was near the location of Cussetuh but on the western bank of the Chattahoochee.

In 1790, Caleb Swan says that Broken Arrow was located approximately 12 miles below Cussetuh and Cowetuh. Since Cowetuh and Cussetuh are a few miles apart, that description covers a wide area and doesn't place this town very well. Swanton locates it on the eastern bank of the Chattahoochee approximately across from Yuchi town (1922:plate 2). This and subsequent investigations have led some to believe that Broken Arrow is represented by site 9CE68, 9CE66, 9CE171, 9CE172, or 9CE709 (Buchner 1996; Huscher 1959; Schnell 1982). These sites produced artifacts that are consistent with a Creek Indian town. Using Swanton (1922) extensively, Harold Huscher originally identified 9CE66 as Likatcka. Frank Schnell, Jr. (1982) investigated 9CE66 and concluded that it was not occupied during the period that Broken Arrow or Captain Ellick's town was occupied. Instead, those two towns were probably downstream. Frank Schnell (1982) and Buchner (1996) identify Broken Arrow a little downstream, starting at 9CE68 but not inconsistent with Swanton's Likatcka (2). This is the

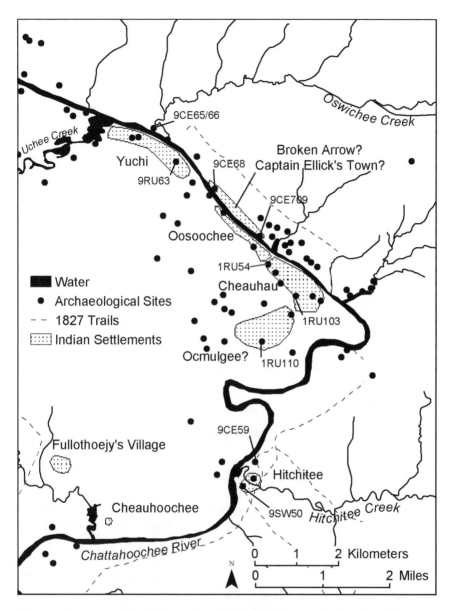

Figure 3.4. Location of Yuchi, Oosoochee, Captain Ellick's town, Cheahau, Ocmulgee, and Hitchitee on the Chattahoochee River during the eighteenth to early nineteenth centuries.

same location of "Euchee Town" on the 1827 Georgia Land Survey map. While this location is not inconsistent with the descriptions by Swan and Taitt, it isn't very accurate and there are a number of towns in the area that could also be represented by any particular archaeological site. Swanton (1922:229), citing Hawkins, says that Broken Arrow was burned in 1814, but it is listed in the 1832 census so it had reformulated as a town in some unknown location by that date.

There are a number of possible interpretations of the existing data. Clay Catskee may not be synonymous with Likatcka or Tlocorcau. Hawkins states that Tlocorcau is Broken Arrow (Foster 2003a:63). Since Hawkins is considered by many to be a reliable and valid source of information about these Indians, Tlocorcau probably meant Broken Arrow. However, that doesn't mean that there wasn't another town called Likatcka or Clay Catskee 20 years earlier. The correlation between sites 9CE68, 9CE66, 9CD171, 9CD172, or 9CE709 (Figure 3.4) seems to be founded in Swanton's placement of Likatcka (2) on plate 2 (1922). Schnell (1982:4–8) agrees with this interpretation. There doesn't seem to be any good reason to believe that the area surrounding 9CE68 is Broken Arrow. Those sites were probably settled by Captain Ellick's town "opposite" Uchee town, but there isn't any reason to believe that Captain Ellick's town is the same as Clay Catskee, Likatcka, or Broken Arrow. John Worth's recent study came to a similar conclusion (2000:table 10.3). The most consistent placement of Broken Arrow is at or near 1RU11, although that is still ambiguous (Figure 3.5).

Cheauhau

Many towns by the name of Cheauhau or some variation of that name are identified throughout the Historic Period beginning with the De Soto travels in 1540. While it is unlikely that these were all one population, they may have been related. This section is about the town that was settled along the Chattahoochee River between 1715 and 1836. Cheauhau was often grouped with Osochi and Ocmulgee, and they were collectively called the "point towns" because they were located at a large bend of the Chattahoochee River. At times, they were labeled simply as the "point towns" on maps and censuses (Harper 1998:289; Swanton 1922). The anonymous "Indian Villages" map of 1715 (Cumming and De Vorsey 1998:map 157; Swanton 1922:plate 3) places the town of Chehaw on the upper Altamaha River in central Georgia. Soon after 1715, the Cheauhau people and the rest of the Creek Indians living in central Georgia migrated back to the Chattahoochee River.

After the 1715 migration to the Chattahoochee River, the Cheauhau apparently settled among the "point towns" in the big bend of the Chattahoochee River where they were visited by David Taitt in 1772 (Mereness 1961:545–546), William Bartram in 1776 (Harper 1998:289, 413), and Benjamin Hawkins in 1796 (Foster 2003a:63s). In 1772, David Taitt said that Geehaw (Cheauhau) was

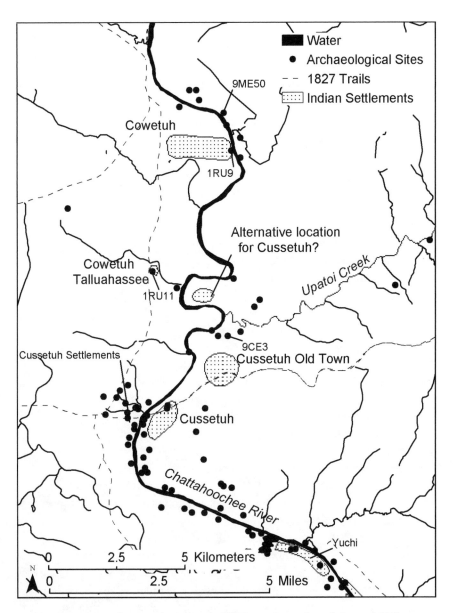

Figure 3.5. Location of Cussetuh, Cussetuh Old Town, Cowetuh, and Cowetuh Talluahassee on the Chattahoochee River during the eighteenth to early nineteenth centuries.

about three miles south of Yuchi town. At that time, Yuchi town was probably at site 1RU63 (Figure 3.4), which places Cheauhau of 1772 around site 1RU12, 1RU54, and south to 1RU103, all of which have Indian components dating to the mid-eighteenth century.

It should be noted that the modern boundary of sites in this "point" region is affected by water level, which is higher from the damming of the Walter F. George reservoir. Since these site boundaries were defined for cultural resource management at Fort Benning, the survey results are controlled by the research designs at Fort Benning. Fort Benning cultural resource surveys do not require surveys where there is standing water. Consequently, we are not confident about the actual pre-reservoir boundary of these sites.

When Wesley Hurt first surveyed the "point" region, he identified two sites that he labeled 1RU12 and 1RU24 that contained artifacts consistent with an eighteenth-century Indian occupation (Hurt 1947:196, fig. 24j; Hurt 1975:fig. 7). Hurt reported that 1RU12 was a medium-sized village with artifacts that would date to the late seventeenth to early eighteenth centuries and that 1RU24 dated to the late eighteenth century; however, he did not visit it, and his information was apparently based on interviews (1947:195–196). When Harold Huscher surveyed that region, he identified a site that he named 1RU54. This site, he claimed, was Hurt's 1RU12, and he identified it as Cheauhau. Site 1RU54 contained mostly artifacts predating the Creek occupation (Huscher 1959:91).

Water and Air Research (Dickenson and Wayne 1985) and Panamerican Consultants, Inc. (Jackson, Crutchfield, et al. 1998) revisited site 1RU54. Dickenson and Wayne (1985:C-67) reported ceramics and daub that are consistent with a Creek Indian occupation. Jackson, Crutchfield, et al. reported 56 out of 1,341 diagnostic Creek ceramics (1998:77–78). This small Creek component is consistent with Huscher, who reported a Lake Jackson component and a few Ocmulgee sherds (1959:91). Although Huscher suggested that 1RU54 was Cheauhau and other investigators have accepted that assessment (Dickenson and Wayne 1985; Jackson, Crutchfield, et al. 1998:88; Worth 2000:table 10.3), neither Huscher's nor recent investigations are consistent with a site that was occupied by Creek Indians for 125 years.

The location of sites 1RU103 and 1RU104 is more consistent with David Taitt's description of Cheauhau relative to Yuchi town. These two sites were identified by Dickenson and Wayne (1985) and redefined by Southern Research (Elliott, Keith, Weisman, et al. 2001). Site 1RU103 contained artifacts that were consistent with a Creek occupation. These sites are also not consistent with sites that were occupied for over 100 years, but the distance from Yuchi town is more consistent with David Taitt's description. Sites 1RU103 and 1RU104 are 2.8 miles from the center of 1RU63, whereas 1RU54 is about 2.4 miles from its center.

Sites 1RU110, 1RU111, and 1RU56 have been lumped together as related sites (Jackson, Crutchfeld, et al. 1998). This site complex is also in a location that is consistent with historic descriptions of the location of Cheauhau between 1715 and 1836. These sites were investigated by shovel testing by Dan Elliott (1992) and Weisman and Ambrosino (1997) and with six test units by Paul Jackson (Jackson, Crutchfield, et al. 1998:106). Their investigation revealed that the site had little stratigraphic integrity (Jackson, Crutchfield, et al. 1998:117). They found ceramics possibly consistent with an earlier seventeenth-century Creek Indian component according to phase definitions at the time (Jackson, Crutchfield, et al. 1998:118; Knight 1994b). Dickenson and Wayne (1985:c95) reported a very small number of nondiagnostic artifacts at 1RU110.

In summary, the only significant evidence that Cheauhau was settled in the area of 1RU54/1RU103/1RU104/1RU110 (Figure 3.4) is the description given by David Taitt (Mereness 1961) and the consistency that the Bartram and Hawkins accounts give. Cheauhau seems to have stayed in the same general position from about 1715 until removal, circa 1836. The archaeological investigations in that region are not inconsistent with the ethnohistoric documents, but they do not significantly support the ethnohistoric accounts either.

Cheauhoochee

Cheauhoochee was a small town associated with Cheauhau. In 1796, Benjamin Hawkins said that it was approximately one and one-half miles west of the town of Hitchiti on a creek called Au-he-gee, although the creek was called the Hitchiti Creek at its confluence with the Chattahoochee River (Foster 2003a:64s). Auhegee Creek is currently called Ihagee Creek (Figure 3.2). This is consistent with Hawkins's Viatory entry which calls the creek "Hitchitee hatche au,hiqu" (Foster 2003a:41j). Although Hurt (1947, 1975) and Huscher (1959) surveyed this area, no sites of the Creek period were identified by them. One site, the Cottonton site (1RU69), was identified approximately 0.9 miles to the west of this location. It may be associated with Cheauhoochee. Lewis Larson investigated the Cottonton site and concluded that it was a small mid- to late-eighteenth century Creek Indian village that may be associated with Apalachicola (Kurjack 1975).

Cherokeeleeche. *See* Apalachicola

Cussetuh and Cussetuh Old Town

Cussetuh was a politically and religiously important town to the Lower Creek Indians. Consequently, it was mentioned often in historic documents and its location is relatively well documented and investigated. However, there are two well-documented locations of this town between 1715 and 1825, one better known than the other.

Cussetuh migrated with the Ochesee Creek towns in central Georgia back to the Chattahoochee River after the Yamassee War (Brannon 1925:44–45; Foster 2003a, 2004d, 2005a; Swanton 1922:220; Willey and Sears 1952). Benjamin Hawkins, in the late eighteenth century, wrote that they first settled in on a "high flat" near the late-eighteenth-century location. That "high flat" is a well-defined landform (Figure 3.5) and has been identified by many researchers as the location of the first Cussetuh settlement after the 1715 emigration to the Chattahoochee River (Brannon 1925; Ethridge 2003; Foster 2003a, 2004d, 2005a; O'Steen et al. 1997:22–23; Swanton 1922; Willey and Sears 1952:3–4).

Although the bluff immediately north of 9CE1 is likely the location of Cussetuh Old Town, there are no sites there that match an early-eighteenth-century Indian settlement. The most likely site on that landform that could represent the Old Cussetuh town location is 9CE3. It is also known as the Wool-folk site and was investigated by Clarence B. Moore (Brose and White 1999), Margaret Ashley and Frank Schnell, Sr. (1928), Peter Brannon (1909), Harold Huscher (1959), Southern Research (Elliott, Keith, Price et al. 2001), and prob-ably Robert Wauchope. The Georgia Archaeological Site Files form for site 9CE1 confuses 9CE3 with 9CE1 and indicates that Wauchope visited 9CE3 (O'Steen et al. 1997:22). I investigated Wauchope's collection at the Middle American Research Institute and the Center for Archaeology at Tulane University in 2005 but did not find any evidence of a site from Chattahoochee County with a late-eighteenth-century Indian artifact assemblage. Another site in the vicinity, the Quartermaster site (9CE42), contains a historic Indian component but has been investigated only at a very cursory level by David Chase (Fort Benning), Southern Research, Inc. in 1999, and Panamerican Consultants, Inc. in 2001 (Beasley 2003:4; Elliott, Keith, Price, et al. 2001). The residents of Cusse-tuh probably occupied this bluff location until around the middle of the eigh-teenth century and then moved down to the floodplain location at 9CE1, where Hawkins and others described them in the late eighteenth century (O'Steen et al. 1997; Foster 2001).

Although the reference is a little ambiguous and the town may be Cowetuh, Benjamin Hawkins indicated that a town, perhaps Cussetuh, was previously on the Georgia side of the river immediately north of Upatoi Creek in the bend of the river where the Cussetuh agricultural fields were in the late eighteenth century (Foster 2003a:64). Hawkins said, "Some years ago, the town was built here, and during the winter when the Indians were out hunting, a flood carried off the houses and all their corn. They then sat down at a rise a little back, and in a few years after removed to its present site" (Foster 2003a:64). The "rise" may have been the location of Cussetuh Old Town. This reference may indicate a third location of Cussetuh on the Chattahoochee River. It is possible that he is referring to the pre–Yamassee War location of Cussetuh or perhaps a very short lived town location. It is labeled "Alternative location for Cussetuh?" in Figure 3.5.

The location of Cussetuh in the late eighteenth century is better known and investigated. It was investigated by Clarence Moore (Brose and White 1999), Margaret Ashley and Frank Schnell, Sr. (1928), Willey and Sears (1952), John Cottier (1977), O'Steen et al. (1997), Panamerican Consultants, and myself (Foster 2001, 2003a, 2005a). All of these investigations and many historic references (Brannon 1925; Foster 2003a; O'Steen et al. 1997; Swanton 1922) are consistent with 9CE1 representing the core of the late-eighteenth- and early-nineteenth-century town of Cussetuh. There may have been other parts of the Cussetuh town near 9CE1, but that site seems to be the center of the town and was occupied until at least 1820 (Swanton 1922:224); however, on the 1827 Land Survey maps, there is no indication of a town.

Cowetuh and Cowetuh Talluahassee

Talluahassee means "old town" in Maskókî. Hence, in theory, Cowetuh Talluahassee is the name given to the older location of Cowetuh after Cowetuh moved. However, we don't understand Creek Indian town-naming conventions very well. While Talluahassee does mean "old town" in the Maskókî language, we don't *necessarily* know that Cowetuh Talluahassee was the previous location of Cowetuh or that the population from Cowetuh moved from Cowetuh Talluahassee to Cowetuh. Also, we don't know exactly when this occurred.

During the late eighteenth to early nineteenth centuries, the time when we have the most accurate descriptions, we know of the existence of two towns named Cowetuh and Cowetuh Talluahassee. Benjamin Hawkins clearly described the location of these two towns, and research in those regions has identified a series of archaeological sites with the towns (Foster 2003a). Sites 1RU11 and the 1RU60 area are associated with Cowetuh Talluahassee, and 1RU8 and 1RU9 are associated with Cowetuh of Hawkins's time (Figure 3.5). The sites associated with Cowetuh Talluahassee have been investigated more intensively yet sporadically because there is an Indian mound nearby. Clarence B. Moore and Peter Brannon investigated the mound at 1RU60, Abercrombie mound, and the associated cemetery. Numerous others have investigated it since (Chase, DeJarnette, Cottier, and Huscher). The mound is mostly a platform mound with intrusive burials that was used before the Creek Indian town of Cowetuh was settled, but there are Creek-period burials nearby. A short distance away is 1RU11, most recently investigated by Rick Richardson and Eric Duff (1998) as a contract from the landowner. Their shovel-testing investigations served, mostly, to define the boundaries of site 1RU11 so that the owners could mine the region for gravel.

During the mid-eighteenth century, there were two towns in existence called, by David Taitt, "Coweta" and "Little Coweta." Taitt visited both towns and definitely distinguishes between them. He said that Cowetuh was about five miles north of Cussetuh (Mereness 1961:549). If Cussetuh during Taitt's time (1772) was in the same location as it was during Hawkins's time (1796), then the town referred to as Cowetuh by David Taitt is the town referred to as Cowetuh by Benjamin Hawkins in 1796 and is associated with 1RU8 and 1RU9. The town called "Little Coweta" by David Taitt in 1772 was probably the Cowetuh Talluahassee of the late eighteenth century. Just because Cowetuh Talluahassee was called "Old Town" in the late eighteenth century doesn't mean that the residents of Cowetuh in the Hawkins period lived at the location of Cowetuh Talluahassee immediately preceding their occupation at Cowetuh. For example, Cowetuh Talluahassee could have been named such because it was the seventeenth-century (pre–Yamassee War) location of Cowetuh.

We know that at least some of the residents from Cowetuh Talluahassee were from a town called Tlocorcau (see also Broken Arrow) (Foster 2003a:63). The evidence from the David Taitt manuscript shows that Cowetuh Talluahassee was at one time referred to simply as "Little Coweta." Although his reference to the town is a little ambiguous and may be Cussetuh, Benjamin Hawkins indicates that a town, perhaps Cowetuh, was previously on the Georgia side of the river in the bend of the river where the Cussetuh agricultural fields were in the late eighteenth century (Foster 2003a:64) (Figure 3.5; however, see entry for Cussetuh).

Eufaula

There were multiple towns called Eufaula (Yufaula), but there was probably just one town by that name settled among the Lower Creek Indians on the Lower Chattahoochee between 1715 and 1836. Benjamin Hawkins described the Lower Creek Eufaula in 1799 as being situated "fifteen miles below Sau-woog-e-lo, on the left [eastern] bank of the river, on a pine flat . . . they have spread out their settlements down the river" (Foster 2003a:66s). Harold Huscher identified sites 9QU22, 9QU23, and 9QU25 with Eufaula (Huscher 1959:101; Worth 2000:288). All three of these sites were described as "extensive" and yielded Creek Indian ceramics, although no other diagnostic materials (Huscher 1959:101). While this location is approximately 15 miles south of the location that Huscher (1959) identified for Sauwoogelo, I have argued that Sauwoogelo (see Sauwoogelo section) was farther downstream (Figure 3.6). Consequently, Eufaula was also probably farther downstream near sites 9CY4, 9CY7, and 9CY15 and between Drag Nasty Creek and Pataula Creek (Figure 3.7). Sites 9CY7 and 9CY15 were investigated by Huscher; he described 9CY7 as an extensive and "important multicomponent site . . . the surface has considerable amounts of historic material" (1959:97). Site 9CY15 was described by Huscher as similar to 9CY7.

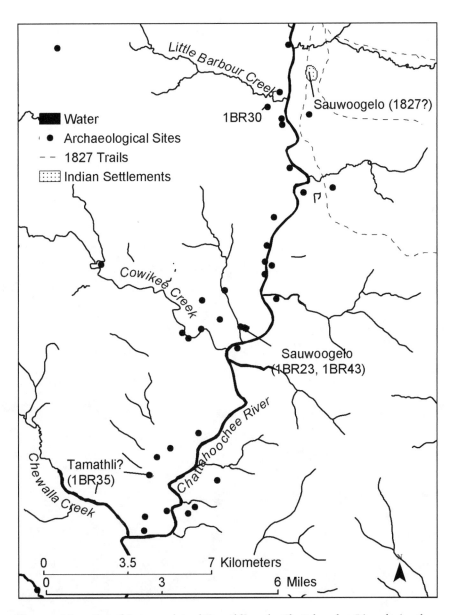

Figure 3.6. Location of Sauwoogelo and Tamathli on the Chattahoochee River during the eighteenth to early nineteenth centuries.

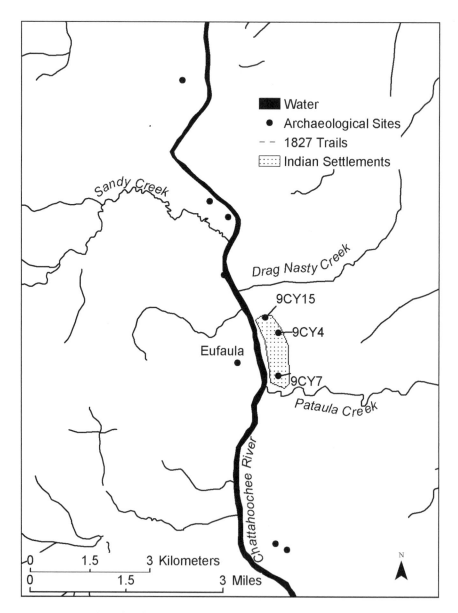

Figure 3.7. Location of Eufaula on the Chattahoochee River during the eighteenth to early nineteenth centuries.

Hitchiti

During the late eighteenth and early nineteenth centuries, a town called Hitchiti was located on the eastern bank of the Chattahoochee near the confluence of present-day Hichitee Creek at the Chattahoochee River (Ethridge 2003:63–64; Wright 2003:88–89). In 1796, Benjamin Hawkins located the town four miles below Cheauhau and on the east bank of the Chattahoochee River (Foster 2003a:64s). If Cheauhau was at 1RU54 area (see Cheauhau entry), then four miles along the eastern bank of the Chattahoochee places the town at the confluence of present-day Hichitee Creek (Figure 3.4). David Taitt mapped Hitchiti relative to Cheauhau also, but he said that Hitchiti was about three miles SSW from Chehaw (Mereness 1961:548). Although there is a slight discrepancy between these two accounts, they are not incompatible with each other if there was variation in how Taitt and Hawkins measured the distance between the towns or if the towns moved up or down river slightly. For example, if Taitt measured the distance between the towns along the western bank, then the distance is approximately three miles (Figure 3.4).

Arthur Kelly (Kelly et al. 1961:36) unquestionably correlates site 9SW50 as a significant portion of the town. The site revealed Creek Indian artifacts as well as trade goods. The A. R. Kelly report (Kelly et al. 1961) classified the site as "Ocmulgee Fields." The Ocmulgee Fields phase at the time of that report constituted Creek Indian sites. It did not distinguish between settlements that were pre- and post–Yamassee War (1715) as is done here and in studies since then (Knight 1994b). Given the presence of Abercrombie and Complicated Stamping at the site, I believe that *either* 9SW50 probably has a pre–Yamassee War date *or* the current definition of Creek Indian sites in relation to shell tempering is incorrect (Knight 1994b). Recent research by Foster (2004d) shows that shell tempering correlates with Hitchiti-speaking Lower Creek towns.

Part of the justification that Kelly et al. (1961:36) used for the identification of 9SW50 with Hitchiti is a map source in a history of Stewart County (Terrill and Dixon 1958). These authors claim that an 1828 map shows "Hitchile" town in lot 344 of Lee County District 34 (Kelly et al. 1961:35). The map in the Terrill and Dixon (1958:52–53) book is labeled "Map of Stewart County drawn from early Surveys of Georgia by Mrs. Wm A. Fitzgerald, 1927." That map was redrawn from the Georgia Lee County Land survey map of 1827, which does *not* label a town called "Hitchile" in that land lot (see Oosoochee section). Instead, it lists a town called "Osucha" in the adjacent land lot (350; Figure 3.8) of District 22. District 34 doesn't exist. Kelly et al. (1961:35) misinterpreted the redrawn map in the Terrill and Dixon book.

Other sites in that general area that may also correlate with the town of Hitchiti are 1RU70, 1RU141, and 9CE59 (Figure 3.8). Artifacts were collected at

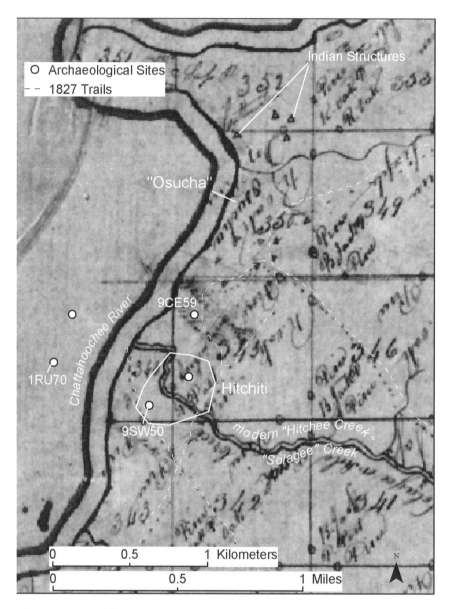

Figure 3.8. Portion of 1827 Lee County (currently Stewart County), Georgia, District 22, plat map showing the location of Hitchiti and Osucha (courtesy of Georgia Division of Archives and History).

1RU70 from the surface by a diligent and dedicated amateur archaeologist over approximately 14 years and summarized in an unpublished manuscript (McPike 1992; Schnell 1984:8). An excess of 3,000 European trade goods, including 1,414 kaolin pipestems, were dated to the 1740s (McPike 1992:9). The artifacts were donated to the Columbus Museum in Columbus, Georgia. While the occupants of this site may have been residents of Hitchiti, the site is on the western side of the Chattahoochee River, which contradicts the late-eighteenth-century descriptions of the town above.

Oconee

William Bartram said that Oconee was one of the towns situated in central Georgia that relocated to the Chattahoochee soon after the Yamassee War (circa 1715; Harper 1998:240). We don't know exactly where the residents of Oconee settled immediately after the migration to the Chattahoochee River in 1715. In the late eighteenth century, Benjamin Hawkins placed the town of Oconee approximately six miles below Palachoocle (see Apalachicola) and on the east bank of the Chattahoochee (Foster 2003a:65s). The creek on the western (Alabama) bank, which is opposite this proposed location of Oconee town, was called "Oconee" creek by Benjamin Hawkins in 1799 (Foster 2003a:41j) and is presently called Hatchechubbee Creek (Figure 3.9).

Sites 9SW52 and 9SW3 have been identified as representing Oconee (Worth 2000:288; Huscher 1959:33). These sites are approximately five and one-half miles south of the Apalachicola area, so there is a slight inconsistency with Hawkins's description. Worth (2000:Table 10.3) identified Oconee with a series of sites that span almost four miles. The Lee County Land Survey map of District 22, section 195, shows four structures that are almost exactly six miles south of Apalachicola and about one-half mile south of site 9SW3, which has been identified as Oconee (Huscher 1959:33). This is opposite the confluence of Hatchechubbee Creek and the Chattahoochee River at Cottonton, Alabama. I would argue from the Hawkins reference and the 1827 map that Oconee in the the late eighteenth century was approximately at section 195 of Lee County District 22 Land Survey Map. Site 9SW3 is nearby and is probably associated with the late-eighteenth-century town of Oconee. Mark Fretwell's analysis agrees with my interpretation (Fretwell 1962:40), and Huscher considered that site an alternative location for Oconee. The site was described as a ceramic "village" (Huscher 1959:73).

Ocmulgee

Ocmulgee settled on the Chattahochee with the 1715 migration from central Georgia. They are listed in censuses from 1716 through 1764 and seem to be located in approximately the same location throughout that period. They were

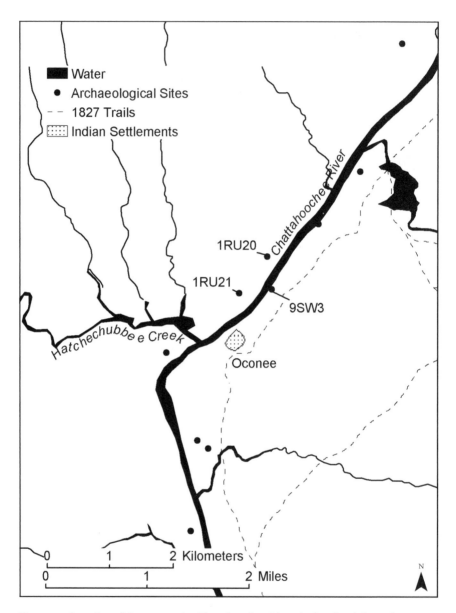

Figure 3.9. Location of Oconee on the Chattahoochee River during the eighteenth to early nineteenth centuries.

linked with the "Point towns" (see Oosoochee). Huscher (1959:32, 92) identified 1RU55 and 1RU56 as representing Ocmulgee. Worth (2000:288) agrees with that assessment. Those sites were reported as "poor" sites (Huscher 1959:92). Presumably Huscher's measurement of "poor" was the number of artifacts found. Since Huscher's investigations, other investigators have redefined those sites in relation to each other and to 1RU110 (Weisman and Ambrosino 1997:286–297; Dickenson and Wayne 1985:C-92; Elliot 1992:201) (Figure 3.4). These three sites are probably one site and are related to one another (Weisman and Ambrosino 1997:290). The Ocmulgee settlers apparently abandoned that location around 1764. They aren't mentioned as a large town on the Chattahoochee again. Benjamin Hawkins mentioned that a few Ocmulgee families were living on the Flint River in 1797 (Foster 2003a:173).

Oosoochee. *See* Worsita

Sauwoogelo

Sauwoogelo was an old town also known as Sawokli and Swalaw (Harper 1998:293). References to its existence go back to the early seventeenth century when the Spanish called it Sabacola (Worth 2000; Hann 1988, 1996:Table 1). Towns of these name variants apparently existed in multiple locations throughout the seventeenth to nineteenth centuries, which makes conclusions about individual town locations ambiguous.

In the late eighteenth century, Benjamin Hawkins recorded the location of Sau-woo-ge-lo as "six miles below Oconee, on the right [west] bank of the river [Chattahoochee], a new settlement in the open pine forest . . . here We-lau-ne, (yellow water,) a fine flowing creek, joins the river; and still lower, Co-wag-gee, (partridge,) a creek sixty yards wide at its mouth" (Foster 2003a:65s). Practically all researchers have placed this town near site 1RU30 and Little Barbour Creek in Alabama because that site and creek are approximately six miles below the reconstructed location of Oconee near the mouth of Hatchechubbee Creek (Figure 3.6) (Harper 1998:639; Huscher 1959:34, 86; Worth 2000:288; Wright 2003:136). Worth (2000:289) suggests that the nearby site of 1BR25 may represent the pre–Yamassee War town (circa 1715). These sites are consistent with one line of evidence, the description of Sau-woo-ge-lo in the *Sketch of the Creek Country* by Benjamin Hawkins (Foster 2003a:65s). They are inconsistent with another line of evidence, the name of creeks.

According to the land survey maps for Townships 11, 12, and 13, Range 29, of the St. Stephens district in Alabama, the Hatchechubbee Creek, Little Barbour Creek, and Cowagee Creek had the same names in 1834 as they have today. That fact doesn't demonstrate that they were not named differently in Hawkins's time, 30 years earlier, but it is not consistent with it. If those creeks were named the same during the time of Hawkins's observations as they were in 1834, then the location of Sauwoogelo is probably much farther downriver, between Wy-launee (Welaune) Creek and Cowikee (Cowegee) Creek. If the more northerly Little Barbour Creek location is incorrect, then two creeks of approximately the same size and distance from each other would both have had to change names between 1796 and 1834. Since this is less likely than the single distance error in Hawkins's Sketch (Foster 2003a:65s), I am interpreting the Cowikee Creek and Wylaunee Creek to be the Hawkins period location (Figure 3.6). Note that in the Oconee section I argue that present-day Hatchechubee Creek was called Oconee Creek and that the Little Barbour Creek was called Coshis-see Creek by Hawkins in 1799 (Foster 2003a:41j; Fretwell 1962:20).

Brannon and Battle considered this location but dismissed it because of in-formation from a retrospective interview from a local informant (Battle 1921: 81–82). The informant claimed to remember (almost 100 years earlier) when the town was occupied and identified sites 1RU20 and 1RU21 as representing the town (Figure 3.9). Filling in for Harold Huscher and the Smithsonian In-stitution, C. S. Holland investigated those sites and found the major occupa-tion to be from the first half of the eighteenth century (Holland 1974:43–44; Huscher 1959:34, 52–53). Sites 1RU20 and 1RU21 are therefore probably not the Sauwoogelo of Hawkins's time.

Huscher (1959:86) followed Hurt's (1947, 1975) assessment of 1BR30 as a likely representative of Sawokli town, but Hurt (1975) was the only one to in-vestigate the site. Given the reconstruction of the location above, 1BR21 or 1BR43 is more consistent with the geographical description of the location of Sauwoogelo when Benjamin Hawkins described it (Figure 3.6). However, on the 1827 Georgia Land Survey maps for Lee County, District 22, section 17, 20, 53, and 54 maps have a number of structures that are labeled "Sciokalah town." This location is approximately opposite 1BR30, which is consistent with Huscher (1959:86) and Hurt (1975) but on the eastern bank of the Chattahoochee (Fig-ure 3.6).

Tamathli

Tamathli was also called Tama in the seventeenth century (Swanton 1922:181), Tamaxli in 1738 (Hann 1988:364; Swanton 1922:183), Tamatley in 1772 (Mereness 1961:551), and Tum-ault-la in 1796 (Foster 2003a:26s). It was an old town and seemed to have moved around a number of times during the seventeenth and eighteenth centuries, eventually merging with the Seminole groups in Florida (Foster 2003a:25s–26s; Swanton 1922:181–184). Unfortunately, during the period for which we have more and reliable historic documentation (the late eigh-teenth century), these people were probably not settled on the Chattahoochee among the Lower Creek Indians and were therefore not described in any detail.

The latest reference by anyone whose accounts are considered reasonably reliable is by David Taitt in 1772. He simply mentions Indian resistance to his visiting the town of Tamatley because of the danger in traveling by canoe to the town (Mereness 1961:551). Taitt was at Cheauhau, so Tamatley was south of Cheauhau. This is consistent with the interpretation that Tamathli had migrated far to the south where the Seminole were living by the late eighteenth century and also with Benjamin Hawkins's description of the town of Tumaultlau and the origin of the Seminole (Foster 2003a:26s).

David DeJarnette and Edward Kurjack identified Tamathli with site 1BR35 (Figure 3.6) (Kurjack 1975:109). David DeJarnette led an excavation at that site and revealed a circular structure, three burials, and trash pits, as well as many European trade goods that date to the mid-to-late eighteenth century (Kurjack 1975:109–130). Harold Huscher (1959:86–87) and John Worth, in his recent reassessment (2000:288–290), agree with their interpretation of 1BR35 as representing Tamathli. DeJarnette and Kurjack's justification for the identification of the site as Tamathli is based on the 1733 De Crenay map (Kurjack 1975:109). It shows a town called "Tamatle" between "Chya," which is presumably Cheauhau, and the confluence of the Flint and Chattahoochee Rivers (Swanton 1922:Plate 5). If Cheauhau was where I argue that it was in 1733, then Tamathli was somewhere within a 100-mile area along the lower Chattahoochee. In other words, the De Crenay map of 1733 is not accurate enough to make the conclusion that these researchers have made. Unfortunately, we do not have enough information at this time to locate Tamathli within a reasonable range of error.

Taskegee

Taskegee was settled on the Chattahoochee River for only a few years, probably fewer than 20. According to the diary of the expedition of Diego Peña in 1716, the town of "Tasquique" was located along the Chattahoochee River between Yuchi town and Cussetuh (Boyd 1949:25). Taskegee (Tuskeegee, Tasquique) is listed in the 1725 census as well but not in any later censuses of Chattahoochee River towns (Swanton 1922; Wright 1999). Instead, a town by that name is identified elsewhere in what is now Alabama. Perhaps the Taskegee town from the Chattahoochee River moved to the central Alabama location after 1725 and before 1738 (Waselkov and Smith 2000).

Unfortunately, the descriptions of Taskegee on the Chattahoochee are not detailed enough to identify its location unambiguously. Assuming that Yuchi town was approximately at 1RU63 (see Yuchi section) in the early eighteenth century (Braley 1998) and that Cussetuh was in the Cussetuh Old Town location as described (see Cussetuh section), then Taskegee could have been anywhere within a three-to-four-mile range, including sites 1RU44, 1RU45, or even the Lawson Field sites such as 9CE125, 9CE126, or 9CE1. Huscher (1959:33) and Worth (2000:288) place the town significantly farther south near sites 1RU34, 1RU35, 1RU36, and 1RU37.

Usseta. *See* Worsita

Worsita, Usseta, and Oosoochee

I will argue below that these three names represent the same town. The location of Worsita is tied to the location of Cheauhau (see section on Cheauhau). David Taitt says that Cheauhau adjoins the Worsita square (Mereness 1961:550). The Worsita town that Taitt mentioned in 1772 is probably the Usseta that William Bartram says borders Cheauhau in 1776 (Harper 1998:289). Since Hawkins says that Oosochee borders Cheahau 20 years later, Usseta and Worsita may be Oosochee. If that is true, then, Bartram lists the presence of a second town—Hooseche—that sounds like Oosochee (Harper 1998:293). Consistent with this interpretation, Robbie Ethridge's recent analysis of the Benjamin Hawkins journals concluded that the town mentioned by Hawkins in 1796 as Oosochee was the same Usseta mentioned by Bartram and, by my extension, the same as Taitt's Worsita (Ethridge 2003:62). However, some have argued that Usseta is Cussetuh (Harper 1998:413; Swanton 1922:169, 308) or a Westo village (Wright 2003:186). Oosooche is listed in the censuses of 1738, 1750, and 1760 as being associated with Cheauhau, Ocmulgee, and Yuchi town, all of which were called "point towns" and were therefore settled near Cheauhau, as argued above, during that time (Swanton 1922:166).

If Worsita is the same as Usseta and Oosochee, then these names refer to a town that remained in the same relative location, probably from 1715 until 1836. However, the 1827 Lee County Land Lot map (Georgia Archives), in lot 350, which is near the Hitchiti Creek, shows a town called "Osucha." This may indicate that as late as 1827, Osoochee moved south along the Chattahoochee (see Hitchiti section). It was immediately upstream and adjacent to Cheauhau. According to the reconstruction of Cheauhau above, the sites upstream and adjoining the 1RU54 region represent Oosochee (Figure 3.4). Sites 1RU52 and 1RU53 may represent that adjoining town. Harold Huscher investigated these two sites and concluded that 1RU52, because of the greater frequency of trade goods, was occupied slightly more recently (1959:91). Both sites are consistent with an occupation by an eighteenth-century Oosochee (Worsita, Usseta) population. Dickenson and Wayne (1985:c56–c63) also investigated these sites and found similar results.

Yuchi

The residents of Yuchi town aligned with and settled among the Lower Creek towns on the Chattahoochee during the migration associated with the Yamassee War (circa 1715). They were mapped and listed in various censuses during the eighteenth century and seem to have remained in the same location from about 1715 until removal (circa 1836). In the late eighteenth century, when we have the best quality descriptions of the town's location, it is immediately south of Uchee Creek at the confluence of that creek and the Chattahoochee River on the western bank. David Taitt visited the town and described it as "about three miles up the Chatahutchie River" from Cheauhau (Mereness 1961:545). Benjamin Hawkins said in 1796 that Yuchi town was "on the right bank of Chat-to-ho-che, ten and a half miles below Cowe-e-tu-tal-lau-has-see. . . . Above the town and bordering on it, Uchee creek, eighty-five feet wide, joins the river" (Foster 2003a:61s). Cowetuh Talluahassee was located at 1RU11 (see Cowetuh section) and Cheauhau at 1RU54, so Yuchi of the late eighteenth century was located approximately where 1RU63 and 1RU57 were (figure 3.4).

The site 1RU63 has been identified as representing Yuchi town for a long time and has attracted extensive investigation by authorized and unauthorized excavators (Braley 1991, 1998; Hargrave et al. 1998; Huscher 1959; Scott 2004). The most extensive investigations were by Harold Huscher and David Chase (Braley 1991, 1998). Most of the results from those investigations, those from Harold Huscher, still have not been properly analyzed. Chad Braley (1998) summarized the investigations by David Chase. Braley (1998) reports that there are two archaeological components and that the site was occupied almost continuously from the mid-seventeenth through the early nineteenth century. Since Yuchi town was not settled on the Chattahoochee until around 1715, then the pre-1715 occupants at site 1RU63 were not Yuchi Indians.

CONCLUSIONS

In this chapter I have reviewed the major archaeological projects that have revealed evidence of Creek Indian sites along the Chattahoochee and Flint Rivers. The chapter serves as a sort of methods section for a direct historic approach to the study of Maskôkî sites. Over 350 archaeological reports revealing 491 archaeological sites were included in the synthesis. The investigation of Creek Indian sites has been of interest to professionally trained archaeologists and to unsystematic collectors for over 100 years. I have attempted here to pull together into a single place the history of those investigations and to use them to inform us better about the cultural variability of the Indian inhabitants of the Chattahoochee River region. I provided a new analysis of the archaeological and historic evidence to identify the location of particular towns that serves to help understand the archaeological manifestation of population migration and dispersal among Southeastern Indians. The following chapters describe the material culture as revealed through these archaeological investigations.

4
Pottery

For a number of reasons, pottery has become the most studied Indian artifact type, and the pottery of the Lower Creek Indians is no exception. Pottery is related to and reflects the subsistence economy, which is an important cultural analytical unit. In addition, it is usually well preserved and is assumed to be time sensitive, two practical characteristics that are significant reasons it is one of the most studied of all the artifact classes found at archaeological sites. Eighteenth-century historic visitors of Southeastern Indian towns often talked about seeing pottery sherds and pieces in old mounds, middens, and accumulations around houses (Waselkov and Braund 1995:34, 45, 46, 96, 153, 211), and that artifact class is still used to identify sites. Pottery variation has been used and abused more than any other artifact class because it is assumed to be reflective of ethnicity, demography, migration, trade, and interaction and to be a tool for temporally dating artifact assemblages (Orton et al. 1993; Rice 1984; Sinopoli 1991).

Creek Indian pottery has been studied for over 100 years (Brose and White 1999; Speck 2004:25–28). The Creek Indians used pottery primarily for cooking subsistence foods but also for heating and roasting plant materials (Speck 2004:25–28; Swanton 1979:550–552). Stews and meats were boiled in large pots (Swanton 1979:551). Pottery served special functions and was renewed in religious ceremonies such as the Boosketuh (Foster 2003a:24, 77s), a ceremony of renewal and thanksgiving. In preparation, new pots were made to replace the old ones (Waselkov and Braund 1995:125).

Creek Indian women and girls made the pottery (Foster 2003a:22; Waselkov and Braund 1995:127, 152–153). They collected clay from pits near their houses inside the villages. Over time, the clay extraction pits became large and filled with rainwater, forming small ponds (Swanton 1912:fig. 43; Waselkov and Braund 1995:106). Specific clay sources were also known by the Indians and were perhaps used for specialized pottery such as the painted wares, which are often characterized as temperless and of finer clay. Benjamin Hawkins observed one such clay extraction area in the late eighteenth century on the Uchee Creek near the town of Yuchi (Foster 2003a:42j).

Caleb Swan was a U.S. official who observed and wrote about the Creek Indians of the late eighteenth century. He recorded "earthen pots and pans of various sizes, from one pint up to six gallons. But in these, they betray a great want of taste and invention, they have no variety of fashion; these vessels are all without handles, and are drawn so nearly to a point at the bottom, that they will not stand alone. Therefore, whenever they are set for use, they have to be propped upon three sides with sticks or stones" (Swan quoted in Swanton 1979:551).

Swan's description tells us about the form of the vessels. The form of southeastern Indian vessels has been demonstrated to be related to the function of those vessels (Hally 1986). Frank Speck recorded the function of Yuchi pottery vessels around the turn of the twentieth century. He recorded seven forms that were in use or at least constructed by the Yuchi at that time. Owing to a variety of context, dating, and sampling problems, I don't include Yuchi vessels in my analysis of Lower Creek pottery below. I want to identify ceramic variation between the ethnic and linguistic towns that constituted the Lower Creek Indians, and I don't feel confident in doing that yet. For example, Chad Braley identified an unusually low frequency of Chattahoochee Brushed pottery, which is the normal indicator of Lawson Field phase components (1998:102). So I don't feel that we can adequately distinguish between seventeenth- and eighteenth-century phases at Yuchi town. However, this discussion of Yuchi pottery vessels is informative about functions. In addition, there are some interesting differences between the Yuchi forms and the forms defined in my analysis, which is probably mostly from Maskôkî towns.

These vessel forms were used for a variety of functions. A "low flat form," identified below as a constricted rim bowl, was used for food dishes or "receptacles for boiled beans and corn"; it was about eight inches in diameter and about three inches in height and was decorated with incised lines (Speck 2004:26). According to Speck, the incising had no meaning or name (2004:27).

A large jar with a flat bottom was used for everyday cooking of boiled corn. The size of the jar depended on the size of the family using it, but Speck said that they would hold at least two quarts (2004:26). These jars were always in use because they held hot or cold food for consumption all day long. The Yuchi version of the jar had more vertical sides than the forms defined below. Note that Swan's description of Upper Creek vessels says that their pots were "pointed" at the bottom, not flat.

Small vessels are found in both Yuchi and Maskôkî pottery assemblages. Speck says that small vessels made by Yuchi were for holding seeds and were put in graves as burial accompaniments. A large flat-bottom jar with a decorative pinched rim was used to boil and make the "sacred concoction" at ceremonial events. These vessels were usually more than 12 inches in height. The pinched rim was formed with a "bent-up" twig and represented the sun and moon (Speck 2004:26–27). Women used another small vessel during menstruation. Ths vessel was a small platter or plate about three inches in diameter. Since the plates have such a specific function and were destroyed after use, they were not fired (Speck 2004:27). Consequently, they and other special function, short-lived vessels are probably not represented in archaeological assemblages.

In general, the pottery construction techniques were similar among various Creek Indian tribes. Based on Maskókî informants, John Swanton described pottery construction (1979:551–553). A woman used clay sources from particular outcroppings. She chose clay with a particular texture that would not crack upon firing. If the right clay could not be found, she mixed clay that she had with fine sand. Sometimes other tempers, or inclusions, were mixed with the clay, such as bone, crushed pottery pieces, or shell. To shape the pot, she first laid down a flat piece of clay to form the base; thus, the base was a separate and solid piece of clay. As will be seen, these bases are found archaeologically and attest to the continuity of the technique that Swanton recorded and to eighteenth-century manufacturing techniques. The woman rolled small sections of the clay onto a hard surface such as flat stone. The rolled clay formed coils, which were placed around the base in successive layers to form the wall of the vessel (Swanton 1979:551–552).

While the forming of pots seems to be relatively consistent between talwas, there are a variety of postformation, decorative techniques that were recorded by Swanton's informants. The outside of the pot was smoothed by scraping it with a mussel shell. The inside was smoothed with a small stone. These stones are found in protohistoric Maskókî burials (Foster 1993). Sometimes a corncob was rolled over the outside of the vessel to produce texture (Swanton 1979: 552); this treatment may be regionally variable. Swanton's informants were Alabama and Upper Creek while the pottery that is included in the study below are from Lower Creek towns. Corncob treatment is rare in Lower Creek pottery (Knight 1994b). Some pots were painted with a red pigment, then placed upside down on a fire to harden.

Understanding the archaeological manifestation of the diverse uses and contexts of pottery is complex enough that Swanton avoided the subject (Swanton 1979:555). Pottery is an unusual collection of material remains to study because it is breakable. Consequently, our analysis of pottery is almost always an analysis of fractions of samples of a population of pottery. The analysis of samples requires an understanding of the population from which the sample was derived and of the sample's characteristics as well as those of the fraction of the sample. It can be viewed as a sample of a sample that was chosen from a population. Sampling pottery is an extraordinarily complex sampling problem, and I have used specific analytical methods in order to deal with that problem and to characterize in a valid manner the variation within that population of pottery that the Creek Indians actually used. I have used regional analyses, a direct historic approach, and vessel analyses.

In order to measure the variation in ceramic ware assemblages found at Creek Indian archaeological sites over time and space, I used a direct historic approach to classification and regional analysis. I used town and ethnic identities as classified in Chapter 3 as a starting point for the identification of pottery assemblages. Since we know which sites were associated with specific towns and we know the location of the majority of the towns occupied along the Chattahoochee and Flint Rivers during the eighteenth to early nineteenth centuries, we can begin to define *empirically* the population of pottery used by the Creek Indians and by specific towns. The empirical, inductive approach used here is in contrast to a deductive, seriation approach used traditionally (Braley 1995, 1998; Fairbanks 1952, 2003; Kelly et al. 1961; Knight 1994b; Knight and Mistovich 1984; Mistovich and Knight 1986; Schnell 1982, 1990, 1998; Smith 1992; Willey and Sears 1952). The seriation models currently used to define Creek Indian material culture were formulated over decades of research and assume constant rates of change over time and space. Unfortunately, however, those phases were defined largely from samples of artifacts with uncontrolled provenience, such as surface collections. Furthermore, many of the collections were incompletely analyzed or even reported (for example, Huscher 1959).

A goal of this chapter is to describe and identify variation in the eighteenth- to early-nineteenth-centuries (Lawson Field phase) Lower Creek Indian pottery assemblage that has resulted from changes over time, changes over space, and variation between individual populations. In other words, I intend to segregate the variation within the archaeological unit called the Lawson Field phase, which currently represents the average material culture of all of the Indians who inhabited the Lower Chattahoochee and Flint Rivers during the eighteenth and early nineteenth centuries.

Since pottery is often the defining characteristic of Creek Indian archaeological sites (Foster 2004d; Gettys 1995; Knight 1994b; Quimby and Spoehr 1950; Schmitt 1950; Wenner 1948), I will spend a significant amount of space in this chapter to quantify clearly what we know about the variation of pottery found at *known* Creek Indian towns. Since pottery is the most used metric for the identification of Creek Indian sites in the Southeast and in postremoval Oklahoma sites, I want to define clearly the "population" of ceramics as best as possible so that we can understand the utility of that metric (Orton 2000: 44–57; Orton et al. 1993).

Pottery is used to identify ethnic boundaries, but we don't clearly under-stand the reliability and validity of pottery styles as a measure of ethnicity for the Creek Indians although some progress has been made (Foster 2004d; Knight 1994b; Worth 2000). In this chapter, I intend to characterize the pottery styles and forms of the Lower Chattahoochee and Flint River valleys as best as pos-sible over space and time within the eighteenth century. In other words, I am using the known towns as defined in Chapter 3 to identify talwa affiliations of ceramic assemblages and using that population of pottery to define my sample. We need to understand the differences between material culture at individual talwas and over time in order to understand larger changes of the Creek Indi-ans using archaeological data.

It is the opinion of myself and others (Foster 2004d; Opler 1952; Piker 2003; Schnell 1970, 1998) that Southeastern Indian populations including the Creek Indians were unique, at least at the level of the town, not the river valley or archaeological phase. Consequently, the talwa or town should be the unit of archaeological assemblage investigation *at a maximum*; ideally it would be the individual household or decision-making unit. There is little ethnographic, political, or historical justification for using large regions as the unit of assem-blage comparison.

POTTERY SAMPLE

I identified *all known* archaeological sites that contained components from the Lower Creek Indians: the sites dated between A.D. 1715 and 1836. I summarized the pottery assemblage for each site and then analyzed the total population of ceramics by town affiliation, occupation period, and geographic location. Some of the results described in this chapter were summarized elsewhere (Foster 2004d). Sites were identified from the Georgia and Alabama State Historic Preservation Office Site Files, the Fort Benning Military Reservation cultural resources data layer, Fenenga and Fenenga (1945), Huscher (1959), Hurt (1947, 1975), Knight (1994b), Knight and Mistovich (1984), McMichael and Kellar (1960), Mistovich and Knight (1986), and numerous cultural resource manage-ment reports. See Table 4.1 for a full list of references. While over 350 reports, publications, and manuscripts were reviewed for this synthesis, only those con-taining components relevant to this book are included in the table.

The sample in Table 4.1 represents the entire population of Lawson Field sites that have been investigated beyond simple shovel testing. There are hun-dreds of sites that have been investigated by shovel testing alone and have been identified with a Lawson Field component (Figure 4.1). However, sites with only shovel testing do not provide enough site contextual control for an adequate, unbiased assessment of ceramics (Foster 2004d; Orton and Tyers 1990, 1992;

Table 4.1: Lower Creek Indian archaeological sites included in the ceramics synthesis

Site Number	Feature	Reference	Average Occupation Date
1BR1	total	DeJarnette 1975	
1BR10	total	DeJarnette 1975	
1BR21	total	DeJarnette 1975	
1BR23	total	DeJarnette 1975	
1BR24	total	DeJarnette 1975	
1BR25	total	Mistovich and Knight 1986	
1BR3	total	DeJarnette 1975	
1BR30	total	DeJarnette 1975	
1BR31	total	DeJarnette 1975	
1BR35	total	DeJarnette 1975	1740
1BR37	total	DeJarnette 1975	
1BR4	total	DeJarnette 1975	
1BR5	total	DeJarnette 1975	
1BR6	total	DeJarnette 1975	
1BR7	total	DeJarnette 1975	
1HE15	total	DeJarnette 1975	
1HE16	total	DeJarnette 1975	
1HE25	total	DeJarnette 1975	
1HE26	total	DeJarnette 1975	
1HE31	total	DeJarnette 1975	
1HE32	total	DeJarnette 1975	
1HE38	total	DeJarnette 1975	
1HO12	total	DeJarnette 1975	
1HO17	total	DeJarnette 1975	
1HO5	total	DeJarnette 1975	
1LE21	total	McMichael and Kellar 1960	1796
1LE8	total	McMichael and Kellar 1960	
1RU20	square 5	Holland 1974	1735–1750
1RU20	total	Holland 1974	1735–1750
1RU21	total	DeJarnette 1975	
1RU22	total	DeJarnette 1975	
1RU227	total	Jackson et al. 1998a	
1RU28	total	DeJarnette 1975	
1RU35	total	Espenshade and Roberts 1992	1810–1825
1RU39	total	Jackson et al. 1998	none
1RU5	total	DeJarnette 1975	
1RU54	total	Jackson et al. 1998	1715–1825

Continued on the next page

Table 4.1: *Continued*

Site Number	Feature	Reference	Average Occupation Date
1RU63	total	Braley, 1998	1600–1750
1RU66	1	DeJarnette 1975	1700–1800
1RU66	2	DeJarnette 1975	1700–1800
1RU66	total	DeJarnette 1975	1700–1800
1RU69	total	DeJarnette 1975	1800s, perhaps early
1RU9	total	DeJarnette 1975	
9CE1	total	Willey and Sears 1952	
9CE1	various	Lewis 2004	~1750–1775
9CE1	total	Foster 2005a	~1750–1775
9CE1207	stp total		
9CE1207	total		
9CE1207	tu1		
9CE1207	tu2		
9CE379	5	Cowie 2001	variety, ~1807
9CE379	6	Cowie 2001	variety, ~1807
9CE379	8	Cowie 2001	variety, ~1807
9CE379	57	Cowie 2001	variety, ~1807
9CE379	61	Cowie 2001	variety, ~1807
9CE379	66	Cowie 2001	variety, ~1807
9CE379	70	Cowie 2001	variety, ~1807
9CE379	total	Cowie 2001	variety, ~1807
9ME394	tu1	Elliot et al. 1996	1790–1825
9ME395	3	Elliot et al. 1996	1790–1825
9ME395	total	Elliot et al. 1996	1790–1825
9ME42	f2	Elliot et al. 1996	1790–1825
9ME42	f3	Elliot et al. 1996	1790–1825
9ME42	f4	Elliot et al. 1996	1790–1825
9ME42	f6	Elliot et al. 1996	1790–1825
9ME42	f7	Elliot et al. 1996	1790–1825
9ME42	f8	Elliot et al. 1996	1790–1825
9ME42	tu1	Elliot et al. 1996	1790–1825
9ME42	tu2	Elliot et al. 1996	1790–1825
9ME42	tu3	Elliot et al. 1996	1790–1825
9ME42	tu4	Elliot et al. 1996	1790–1825
9ME42	tu5	Elliot et al. 1996	1790–1825
9ME42	tu6	Elliot et al. 1996	1790–1825
9ME42	tu7	Elliot et al. 1996	1790–1825
9ME42	tu8	Elliot et al. 1996	1790–1825

Continued on the next page

Table 4.1: *Continued*

Site Number	Feature	Reference	Average Occupation Date
9ME43	tu1	Elliot et al. 1996	1790–1825
9ME469	tu1	Elliot et al. 1996	
9ME469	tu2	Elliot et al. 1996	
9ME472	total	Elliot et al. 1996	
9ME479	total	Elliot et al. 1996	
9ME50	9ME52	Ledbetter et al. 1996	1760–1820
9SW50	1	Kelly et al. 1961	
9SW50	3	Kelly et al. 1961	
9SW50	4	Kelly et al. 1961	
9SW50	5	Kelly et al. 1961	
9SW50	test pits	Kelly et al. 1961	
9SW50	total	Kelly et al. 1961	
9TR18		Worth 1997	
9TR23		Worth 1997	
9TR41	Creek features	Ledbetter et al. 2001	1760–1790
9TR54	Creek features	Ledbetter et al. 2001	1760–1790

Orton et al. 1993). Consequently, only sites with at least test unit excavation were included in the artifact syntheses and comparisons in this chapter (Figure 4.1 and Table 4.1).

Sites were identified as Creek Indian or eighteenth- to early-nineteenth-century Indian according to the original investigator as specified in the respective original report. However, Creek components were usually assigned if the ceramic type Chattahoochee Roughened var. *Chattahoochee* was present at the site. This remains the standard method of identification even for Creek Indian sites in Oklahoma (Gettys 1995). The full range of ceramic types found at Lower Creek Indian sites and the history of that archaeological phase were reviewed in Chapter 3.

Occupation dates for the sites were identified from excavation reports, historic references, and trade good assemblages. The respective average occupation date for each feature at each site is summarized in Table 4.1. While these averages may not represent the most accurate summation of the occupation of the respective site, they do represent a best estimate based on all available documentary and artifact data. Table 4.1 reports on all Lower Creek sites that received at least test-unit excavation. Column 1 is the official site number. Column 2 is the archaeological context of the artifacts reported in this study. For

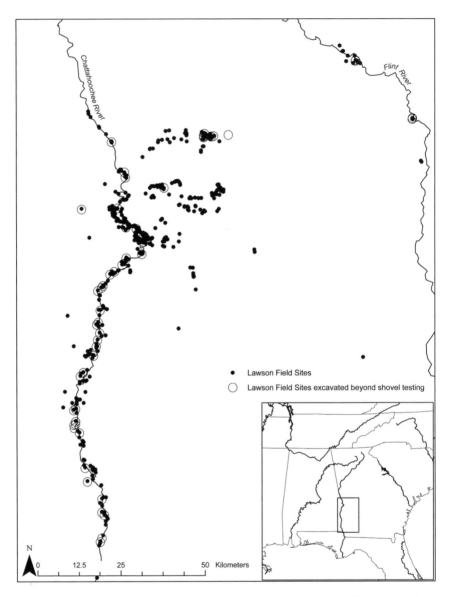

Figure 4.1. All archaeological sites situated along the Chattahoochee and Flint River valleys that contain Lawson Field (circa 1715–1836) components. Sites that were excavated beyond simple shovel testing are shown as open circles.

example, artifacts may have been found in a feature or may have been reported as the "total" or summary of all artifacts combined. Since the summary or total of all artifacts combined is biased relative to artifacts from controlled feature contexts, they were separated out in this analysis. Column 2 reflects that fact. Column 3 lists the most representative references used for the data in this study. Column 4 represents the average occupation date for each feature or site as determined from documentary or artifact data. While a single average date is not likely to be a valid measure of the duration of a town's occupation, a single value was necessary for the quantitative comparisons based on average occupation date.

CORRELATING ARCHAEOLOGICAL SITES
WITH TOWN LOCATIONS

This study is a summary of the archaeological signature of Lower Creek Indian towns. The archaeological signature of an entire town is almost impossible to identify and probably not that useful. It is, after all, the *summation* of all preserved trash accumulated over a period of time. Instead, archaeologists take samples of the town and then use them as a representative sample of artifacts that would be found in a town at a given time. Since we do not know the full population of artifacts in a given town, archaeologists often assume that the sample excavated is representative of the material remains of a town's inhabitants. That assumption is rarely likely or even confirmable. For this study, I used known archaeological sites and descriptions of the talwa's location from primary historic sources as identified in Chapter 3. Archaeological data were used to compare a hypothesized location of a town with the excavated remains at the site.

Even with the differences in the spatial definition of a town or talwa, an archaeological site can usually be associated with a particular named town of a particular time period. When I could not associate a site with a particular town of known occupation duration, I used European trade goods as described in excavation reports in order to identify the occupation duration of the region where the site was located.

Fifty-four sites with single components dating to the eighteenth and early nineteenth centuries were identified for inclusion in the synthesis and comparison in this book (Table 4.1). This is a study that compares the relative frequency of artifacts between different archaeological contexts. Comparing artifact frequencies between archaeological contexts is very problematic because of bias resulting from differential preservation and function of the artifact classes (Foster 2004d; Orton and Tyers 1990, 1992; Orton et al. 1993:169). For example, the frequency of a given ceramic type may be higher in one site or one feature simply because the vessel that it represents was more broken or differentially preserved. This is the bias of differential "brokenness" (Orton 1985; Orton and Tyers 1990, 1992). See Lewis (2004) and Foster (2004d) for attempts to deal with this problem among Creek Indian ceramics. Unless we know the degree of this bias or can control for it, comparing artifact frequencies from different archaeological contexts is of little use because we don't know the *significance* of the difference in the observed frequencies. Comparing artifact weights, percentage of vessel preserved such as rim percentages, and a variety of other methods allow us to control for this bias to some degree (Orton et al. 1993:169, 172–174).

Since the data that I am summarizing in this study were previously collected, I had to work with the measurements that were recorded. In almost all cases, artifact counts and not artifact weights were recorded in reports. Since artifact counts are biased, I limited my summary to features of known context (Table 4.1). In other words, I compiled artifact frequencies from features that are known to be from Native American settlements of the eighteenth to early nineteenth centuries. Since all artifacts originated from features, the degree of pottery brokenness should be similar (although not necessarily exact) for all artifacts in the sample.

I interpolated the relative frequency of each ceramic type over space using Kriging and ArcGIS 8.3 (ESRI 2003). Kriging is a geostatistical technique that takes surrounding measured data values into consideration when interpolating unknown values (McCoy and Johnston 2002:221). This technique is useful when data are probably spatially autocorrelated as ceramic assemblages are likely to be. The technique produced maps of ceramic type frequencies for the entire lower Chattahoochee River valley.

By default, the interpolation of a set of spatial quantities such as ceramic frequencies is defined over the space of all the items in the set. For example, the interpolated space is a large rectangular area (a matrix or raster) that encompasses the most northeasterly site and the most southwesterly site. Because of the arrangement of Lower Creek Indian towns along the north-south-flowing Chattahoochee River, the interpolated space includes a large area with no data, which skews the validity of the predicted values. Consequently, I defined an analytical space (analysis mask) for the Kriging interpolation that was no larger than 25 kilometers from all sites. This area represents the analytical space of the interpretation.

While I am using a biased measure of pottery assemblages (sherd counts), I am limiting the spatial characterization to sherds from a common depositional environment. I argue that the value of this GIS interpolation technique is in its spatial comprehensiveness. The results of the Kriging interpolation represent a spatial map of a given trait (ceramic surface treatment) over the entire Lower Creek habitat.

As an alternative method for characterizing the total population of pottery types used by the Lower Creek Indians, I synthesized the results from three major studies of minimum vessel counts (MNV) at three Muskogee towns that dated from the late eighteenth century. Vessel analysis can be a relatively unbiased method of comparing assemblages if the percentage of the vessel preserved is estimated in some way (for example, rim sherd percentage) (Orton et al. 1993:172). Unfortunately, not a single analysis of Creek Indian pottery has used these less biased methods of assemblage quantification. Vessel counts without estimates of the total vessel represented is a very biased measure of total vessel number because we do not know the relative probability of breakage of each pot type (Orton et al. 1993:169–171) or the amount preserved. For example, is the difference in relative proportion of bowls between two sites or features because the bowls were treated differently in the two features/sites, broke differently, functioned differently, or were manufactured differently, or because the frequency observed represents the frequency used in the population? The latter option assumes that the sample of vessels recovered within the feature or site is a random sample from a normally distributed sample of pots in the entire population of pots being used by the inhabitants and that both features/sites were used by the same number of individuals for the same amount of time. That scenario is highly unlikely. Given all these measurement problems, my approach to reducing these biases in the archaeological record is to be comprehensive and to limit my study to a minimum number of vessels analyses and to a direct historic and regional approach. I have attempted to include very large samples in my syntheses. Since a goal of this study is to characterize the population of vessels that were in use by the Indians, we will be able to compare sherd assemblages to the vessel population in order to estimate the represented vessels and more accurately compare assemblages.

There have been three major studies of Lower Creek Indian vessels. Other studies have identified vessels but did not specifically perform a vessel assemblage analysis. Usually that was because the sample of identifiable vessels was not sufficient for comparison or because vessel analysis was not a recognized analytical technique. The three major vessel studies were conducted by Jerald Ledbetter and Southeastern Archaeological Services, Inc. (SAS) at the Victory Drive Site (Ledbetter 1997) and Buzzard Roost town (Ledbetter et al. 2002) and by Thomas Lewis and Panamerican Consultants, Inc. at the Cussetuh site (Lewis 2004). All three sites are likely associated with Muskogee-speaking towns that were occupied during the latter half of the eighteenth century. Consequently, the vessel analysis is biased against non-Muskogee-speaking populations such as the Hitchiti or Yuchi as well as early-eighteenth-century artifact variation.

The Victory Drive site is located immediately across the river from the eighteenth-century town of Cowetuh (see Chapter 3). The site likely represents a sample of the pottery used by residents of the Cowetuh town, which was occupied during the second half of the eighteenth to the early nineteenth centuries. The vessels in the assemblage were from three different excavations at the site: the Dolly Madison site, the Go-Kart site, and excavations by SAS in 1993 (Ledbetter 1997:44). The first two sites were combined into the single site named the Victory Drive Site (9ME50) by Frank Schnell, Jr. All excavations were summarized in a recent report by Jerald Ledbetter and SAS (Ledbetter 1997). The majority of the 1993 excavation by SAS revealed Bull Creek and Averett phase occupation and are not relevant to this summary (Ledbetter 1997:107–119, 145). The Victory Drive site vessel assemblage as summarized in the report is therefore a multicomponent assemblage. For the summary in this chapter, I included only vessels from the Lawson Field phase features as described in the report (Ledbetter 1997). The Lawson Field vessels were from three households and one feature and constituted 98 minimum numbers of vessels based on "distinctly different rims" (Ledbetter 1997:213). They do not state a minimum rim size used or the percentage of the rim preserved or how they defined "distinctly different."

A total of 59 vessels analyzed were from a single feature from the Dolly Madison site (Ledbetter 1997:213, fig. 28), 17 vessels were from a single feature at the Go-Kart section of the site, and 22 vessels were excavated from one feature from the SAS excavation of the site (Ledbetter 1997:213). Vessels from the Go-Kart section of the site were from two features that contained eighteenth-century trade goods (Ledbetter 1997:46–47) and were in association with a possible structure, which probably "predates" the Creek occupation (Ledbetter 1997:48). Vessels from the Dolly Madison section of the site were from a single feature that contained a large number of Creek and Euro-American artifacts that dated to the early part of the nineteenth century (Ledbetter 1997:49–53). The one feature from the 1993 SAS excavation was situated within the remains of a Bull Creek phase (circa A.D. 1250–1400) structure (Ledbetter 1997:123). The SAS feature contained European ceramics that dated to the last half of the eighteenth to the early nineteenth centuries (Ledbetter 1997:233). The vessels from the Victory Drive site are, therefore, from a relatively unknown cultural context in relation to the Cowetuh people. The unknown context may bias the sample as a representative sample of the Cowetuh vessel assemblage. All features containing vessels used in this analysis contained artifacts that primarily dated to the last half of the eighteenth to the early nineteenth centuries (Ledbetter 1997:231–236) and are consistent with an interpretation that they are associated with the late-eighteenth-century occupation of Cowetuh as described in Chapter 3. Unfortunately, the association of these features with a household or structure is ambiguous.

Excavations at the town of Buzzard Roost (Salenojuh) were conducted by SAS as a part of a Georgia Department of Transportation project at two separate sites, 9TR41 and 9TR54. The two sites probably represent different sections of the Muskogee town of Buzzard Roost, a splinter town of Cussetuh occupied approximately between A.D. 1775 and 1805 (Ledbetter et al. 2002:47–64, 253). The sample from these sites consisted of a minimum number of 73 vessels; however, four of those vessels were recovered from unprovenienced surface collections and were discarded from the analysis in this chapter (Ledbetter et al. 2002:178–196). Unique vessels were identified from rim sherds larger than two centimeters. Vessel diameters were determined with the use of a concentric circle chart. Percentage of rim preserved was not reported (Ledbetter et al. 2002:176). Vessels from Buzzard Roost were recovered in feature contexts that were spatially associated with structures. The structures are described in more detail in Chapter 5. Finally, Thomas Lewis performed the last major vessel analysis on ceramics from the 2001 excavation at Cussetuh town (Lewis 2004). The vessels he identified probably represent the latter half of the eighteenth-century pottery assemblage of the residents of Cussetuh (see Chapter 3). The analysis by Lewis included over 81,000 sherds and sherdlets, and a minimum of 465 vessels were identified. His study was the largest of any to date and included an analysis of manufacturing techniques, which is unprecedented among Creek Indian studies. Manufacturing analyses are important for identifying mechanical properties of the vessels that may contribute to preservation biases in sherd counts and weights (Orton and Tyers 1990, 1992).

Lewis identified a minimum number of vessels from rim sherds greater than four centimeters (Redwine et al. 2004:53). He recorded MNV from rim diameter but not the percentage of rim that was preserved or included in the analysis. He recorded type, surface decoration, size, and manufacturing techniques (Lewis 2004:105). Unfortunately, he did not account for the feature or artifact context in which any of the vessels were found. Since vessel use, function, and preservation and our interpretation of these variables are dependent on the context, his analysis is difficult to interpret.

There are some other samples of Creek Indian vessels, which have been described in reports but cannot be included in this study for a variety of reasons. Chad Braley and SAS analyzed vessels from the Yuchi town site (Braley 1998). The Yuchi town site (1RU63) was excavated by numerous individuals over many decades (Braley 1991, 1998; Hargrave et al. 1998; Huscher 1959; Schnell 1982). Unfortunately, the results of some of those excavations were rarely reported and are ambiguous. Chad Braley (1998) argued that the Yuchi town site probably contained a Lawson Field phase (circa A.D. 1715–1836) and a Blackmon phase (circa A.D. 1650–1715) component. The majority of the excavations were conducted by Harold Huscher as a part of the Smithsonian's River Basin Survey. Those Smithsonian collections have not been completely analyzed. Since the site was heavily occupied, contained multiple components, and particularly because the analysis in this chapter is an attempt to isolate variation over time and space, results from the Yuchi town site will not be included in the synthesis in this book. This is a deficiency in our understanding of the Lower Creek Indians because the Yuchi were a significant component to the social environment of the Lower Chattahoochee region during the eighteenth century. The vessel assemblage from the Bull Creek site (Ledbetter 1996) should be mentioned because of the extensive number of preserved vessels but will not be included in the analyses in this chapter. This site was occupied primarily during the Bull Creek phase (circa A.D. 1250–1400) and is outside the scope of this book. Last, another large sample of single component Lawson Field ceramics was reported by Southern Research (Elliott et al. 1999:XIV-38–XIV-64) but did not identify individual vessels other than those selected for illustration. I will first describe the results from a spatial analysis of surface decoration; then I will describe the results from a vessel summary (n=635).

SURFACE TREATMENT FROM SHERD COUNTS

Although I argued above that artifact counts of broken artifacts are a highly biased measure and relatively useless (Orton et al. 1993:169–171) comparative measure of pottery assemblages, almost all reports summarize total artifact frequency. Consequently, I will show the total average relative frequency of each ceramic type for comparative purposes. Figure 4.2 shows the typical pattern of Lawson Field ceramic types. Chattahoochee Roughened, Mission Red Filmed, and Lamar Incised dominate the assemblage with a scattering of other types. Since this graph represents counts of ceramic types in mixed and, therefore, unknown archaeological contexts, these frequencies are biased to an unknown degree (Orton 2000; Orton and Tyers 1992).

Creek Indian sites are primarily defined by the presence of Chattahoochee Roughened types (Figure 4.3), a red painted type called Mission Red Filmed (Figure 4.4), and an incised type called Lamar Incised (Figure 4.5) (Knight 1994b; Knight and Mistovich 1984; Mistovich and Knight 1986). Figure 4.3 shows reconstructions of two Chattahoochee Roughened vessels that were found at the mid-to-late eighteenth-century town of Cussetuh. Figure 4.4 shows two Mission Red filmed vessels, and Figure 4.5 shows five Lamar Incised vessels. Each type will be discussed in detail below.

The rest of the results in this study are composed only of artifacts from fea-

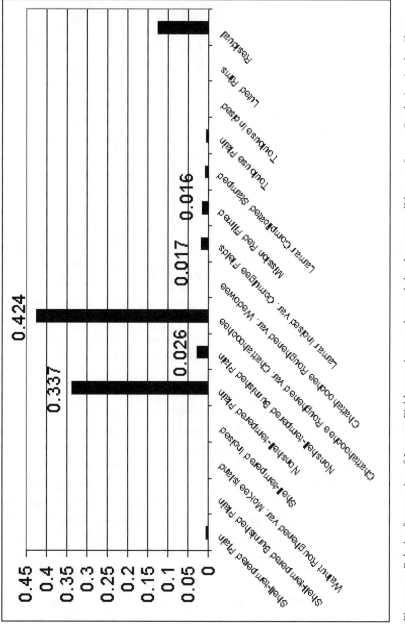

Figure 4.2. Relative frequencies of Lawson Field ceramic types by total sherd count at all known Lower Creek sites in the Chatta-hoochee and Flint River valleys.

Figure 4.3. Two Chattahoochee Roughened var. *Chattahoochee* vessels from Cussetuh (photo courtesy of Panamerican Consultants, Inc. and Fort Benning Military Reservation).

tures. This discrimination method reduces the bias due to differential preservation in the archaeological record. When only feature artifacts are included, the relative frequencies change slightly, but the qualitative visual pattern is the same (Figure 4.6). Unfortunately, since we do not know the cultural or depositional contexts of the surface artifacts, we don't know whether the similarity between these assemblages results from random chance or not. Nonshell Plain and Chattahoochee Roughened dominate the assemblage. Lamar Incised var. *Ocmulgee Fields* increases in frequency as do the Nonshell burnished types and Lamar Complicated stamped. This graph represents a summary of all reported Lower Creek ceramic sherd count assemblages that date between 1715 to 1836. Furthermore, it represents a summary of all Lower Creek ceramics in the total population of sites that were excavated beyond simple shovel testing and dated between 1715 and 1836 according to European trade good association and historic documents.

I analyzed these artifact assemblages relative to geographic variation by interpolating the existing assemblages with Kriging (Foster 2004d). The Kriging technique produced maps of the lower Chattahoochee River valley according to ceramic type. Since these Kriging maps have recently been published (Foster 2004d:figs. 7–11), I will not reproduce them here. The Kriging analysis

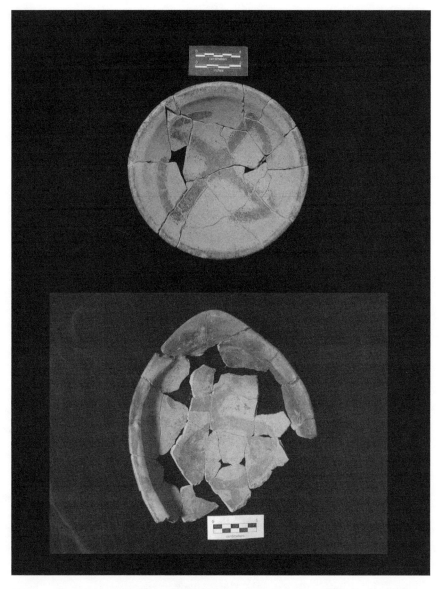

Figure 4.4. Two Mission Red Filmed vessels from Cussetuh (photo courtesy of Panameri-can Consultants, Inc. and Fort Benning Military Reservation).

of the geographic range of these types shows that the predominant type, Chat-tahoochee Roughened, increases in frequency from north to south, and Non-shell Plain increases from south to north (Foster 2004d:figs. 7, 8). Mission Red Filmed, thought to originate from the far south, is relatively consistent over the study region (Foster 2004d:fig. 9); however, it may increase slightly in the far

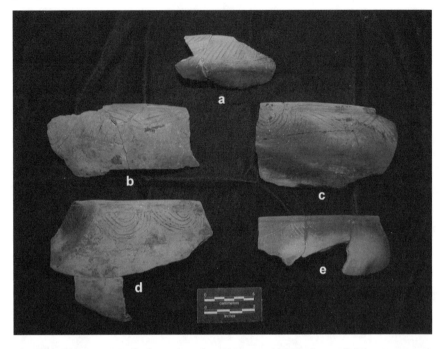

Figure 4.5. Five Lamar Incised var. *Ocmulgee Fields* vessels from Cussetuh (photo courtesy of Panamerican Consultants, Inc. and Fort Benning Military Reservation).

south and around the town of Hitchiti. Lewis (2004:123–124) argued recently that Mission Red Filmed could be subdivided into a series of types. While I wouldn't be surprised if there is geographic variation in that pottery type, Lewis didn't specify his methods or sampling strategy. Consequently, his conclusions are difficult to evaluate empirically or to replicate and, for the purposes of this analysis, are assumed not to be valid. Lamar Incised var. *Ocmulgee Fields* peaks around the "core" towns in the central Chattahoochee River valley and decreases north and south (Foster 2004d:10).

Shell tempering is traditionally considered to be a defining trait of the eighteenth century and is thought to decrease in use throughout the century. My analyses show that Shell-tempered Plain ceramic types peak among the southerly Lower Creek towns, the Hitchiti-speaking towns (Foster 2004d:fig. 11), for example, around Sawokli, Oconi, and Apalachicola. Shell-tempered Incised shows a similar pattern. These interpolations show that Chattahoochee Roughened increases from north to south. Since the southern towns were mostly Hitchiti-speaking, this may be a linguistically correlated trait (Foster 2004d). This conclusion is in contrast to the current model of the nonshell-tempered, roughened type evolving out of roughened types from central Alabama (Knight

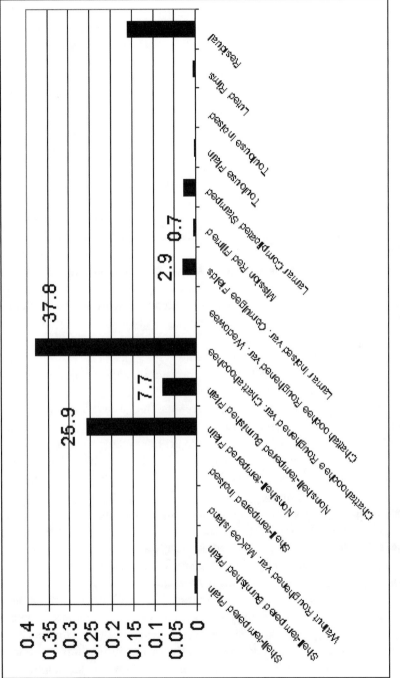

Figure 4.6. Relative frequencies of ceramic types by total sherd count in single Lawson Field component features at all known Lower Creek sites in the Chattahoochee and Flint River valleys.

1994b). Kelly (1938) and Fairbanks (Fairbanks 1952, 1955, 2003) argued the opposite, however.

These spatial analyses show that there is a significant amount of spatial variation in the Lower Creek ceramic assemblages. Consequently, I would argue that the definition of the Lower Creek ceramic assemblage is relative to geographic location and perhaps talwa. This fact plus the fact that there is a north-to-south ethnolinguistic segregation to Lower Creek towns led me to analyze the ceramic assemblages according to linguistic association. I assigned a given site to either Muskogee or Hitchiti according to Swanton (1922) and Hann (1996). Because of a small sample size (n=1) and mixed context of the artifacts, I did not analyze the Yuchi assemblages in this study.

Figure 4.7 shows the average relative frequency of each type summarized for all sites according to its linguistic association. There is a significant similarity between them, but the differences are interesting also. Hitchiti sites have a higher frequency of Nonshell Plain relative to Chattahoochee Roughened. They have higher frequencies of Ocmulgee Incised. And, perhaps most interesting, they have a much higher relative frequency of shell-tempered pottery in their assemblages. No Muskogee sites have shell tempering present. All the shell tempering in this sample came from sites that were attributed to Hitchiti-speaking populations. A principal components analysis of all ceramic types versus all sites reveals a strong division between shell-tempered ceramics and nonshell-tempered ceramics (Figure 4.8). The first two axes explain 57 percent of the variation. The horizontal axis in Figure 4.8 shows a strong correlation with temper variation.

Interesting, and consistent with the interpretation that the temper variation is owing to ethnic variation, is the town of Eufaula, a Muskogee-speaking town situated far to the south among mostly Hitchiti towns. Eufaula sites show no shell tempering. In other words, Eufaula is consistent with the interpretation that the variation in tempering that is observed is owing to ethnic variation and not geographic variation.

Shell tempering is usually attributed to a temporal change in the variation of the pottery assemblage of Creek Indian pottery (Knight 1994b). Shell tempering is defined as much more frequent in the Blackmon phase, the phase before the Lawson Field phase (Knight and Mistovich 1984; Mistovich and Knight 1986; Schnell 1990). This trait is usually defined as decreasing in frequency during the Lawson Field phase (the eighteenth century). To test whether shell tempering decreases over time, I performed a simple correlation analysis for each type with the average date of the site or the artifact assemblage with which it was associated. For example, I dated a given site by the European trade goods that were found there and then derived an average occupation date. Only two types were strongly correlated with time *and* statistically significant (Shell-

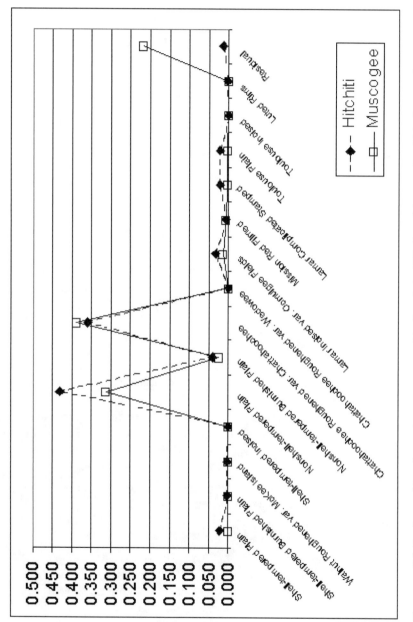

Figure 4.7. Relative frequencies of ceramic types segregated by linguistic affiliation of the town in which the ceramics were found. The graph illustrates total sherd count in single Lawson Field component features at all known Lower Creek sites in the Chattahoochee and Flint River valleys.

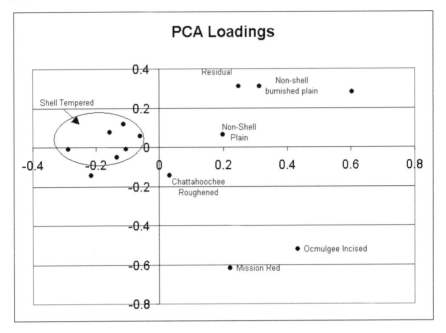

Figure 4.8. Principal components analysis (PCA) of relative frequencies of total sherd counts in single Lawson Field component features at all known Lower Creek sites in the Chattahoochee and Flint River valleys.

tempered Plain: −0.567, p=0.002, n=25; Walnut Roughened: −0.534, p=0.003, n=25). They were both shell-tempered types and negatively correlated with time. This is consistent with current definitions of the Lawson Field phase. However, given the strong spatial association and the Hitchiti language association, it is possible that the shell tempering is a Hitchiti trait and that it decreases in frequency during the Lawson Field phase because of the documented southerly migration of Hitchiti towns into Florida (Hann 1988; Worth 2000). While these data are comprehensive, the amount of shell temper is still relatively low. So these conclusions should be tempered by that fact.

VESSEL FORM

A synthesis of individual vessels (n=635) from three towns revealed patterns of the typical pottery vessel assemblage in use by the Lower Creek Indians during the late eighteenth century. While vessel numbers without estimates of total vessels represented can be a biased measure of vessel assemblage because of reasons discussed above, my approach is to be inclusive and to use a very large sample. While I cannot quantify or even qualify the relative bias of this sample (n=635), I am assuming that the sample size is large enough to capture all the variation within the original population of vessels. All of the vessels were from towns with Muskogee-speaking people so the study is biased against Hitchiti-speaking cultures.

This minimum number of vessels synthesis from Cussetuh, Buzzard Roost, and the Victory Drive site included 635 vessels identifiable to shape category and described six vessel forms (Figure 4.9): bottles (n=15; 2.4%), carinated constricted rim bowls (n=48; 7.6%), open bowls (n=203; 31.9%), flaring rim bowls (n=30; 4.7%), flaring rim jars (n=204; 32.1%), goblet/cups (n=6; 0.9%), and undefined (n=129; 20.3%). The studies summarized here used relatively consistent vessel form categories. Common characteristics collected by all studies were vessel form, rim diameter, and surface treatment. Each vessel form and function will be described below.

Vessel function of Creek Indian pottery has not been studied systematically for Muskogee pottery. Consequently, I have used David Hally's (1986) study of Indian vessels of the northwest Georgia–late Mississippian period as a model for vessel function, in addition to the ethnohistoric and ethnographic data reviewed in the beginning of this chapter. The Mississippian period Indians (sixteenth century) from northwest Georgia were probably ancestral to and culturally similar to the eighteenth-century Indians who made the vessels described here.

Bottles are represented by nine vessels totaling almost 2.36 percent of the total population. They are characterized by "a globular body, flat base, small orifice and short neck with vertical or insloping rim" (Hally 1986:278, table 4). Bottles were probably used to serve and store liquids. The orifice diameter has a mean of 10.3 cm with a standard deviation (s.d.) of 9.5 cm. However, there is a single outlier, a bottle with an orifice of 42 cm. When the outlier is removed, the mean orifice of bottles is 7.5 cm and the s.d. is 3.2 cm. Bottles tend to be undecorated (n=11; 73%), although a fraction is decorated with red filming (n=2; 13.3%) or incising (n=1; 6.7%). Some bottles exhibited evidence of handles (Lewis 2004:181, 184).

Carinated constricted rim bowls or "casuela bowls" are defined as "constricted rim vessels with a distinct shoulder break, which sometimes forms a well defined projecting keel or carination" (Hally 1986; Ledbetter 1997:221). Forty-eight carinated bowls were identified; they constitute 7.5 percent of the total vessel population. These bowls have an average rim diameter of 27.6 cm with an s.d. of 8.7 cm. David Hally (1986:288–289) and (Ledbetter 1997:222) identified two sizes of this form. The data presented here are not consistent with a bimodal distribution. Hally (1986:288) argues that these bowls were used for reheating foods and for foods that require mixing and stirring. These bowls tend to be incised (n=28; 58.3%) with a smaller fraction being Red Filmed (8%;

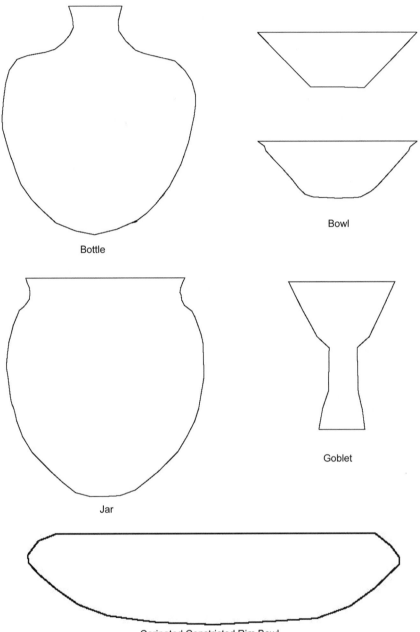

Figure 4.9. Vessel forms from a sample of Lower Creek Indian vessels (n=635) from excavations at Cussetuh, Buzzard Roost, and the Victory Drive sites.

16.7%) or undecorated (n=10; 20.8%). Lewis's analysis of carinated bowls at Cussetuh (Lewis 2004:176) noted that red filming on these bowls is sometimes present. That same manufacturing study at Cussetuh gave some indication that rims from carinated bowls may be overrepresented because rims and shoulders seem to be constructed from a single piece of clay whereas the base is formed from another (Lewis 2004:125–128). This manufacturing bias may affect the relative proportion of surface decorations present on bowls such as red filming and incising. Swanton and Speck observed that these bowls were used for presentation or "receptacles" for beans and corn (Speck 2004:26; Swanton 1979:553).

Flaring rim bowls were probably for conspicuous displays of food for presentation as they are often well decorated (Hally 1986:290; Ledbetter 1997). While the majority are undecorated (n=15; 53.6%), surface decorations can be red filmed (n=7; 25%), roughened (n=2; 7%), or incised (n=4; 14.3%) (Lewis 2004:179). In the Lower Creek sample described here, 30 vessels or approximately 4.7 percent of the total population of vessels were flaring rim bowls. The average diameter of these bowls is 27.2 cm with an s.d of 8.0 cm.

Open bowls were used for a variety of purposes (Hally 1986); consequently, they exhibit a variety of morphologies. Approximately 32% of all vessels are bowls (n=203). Surface decoration is well distributed between roughened (n=8; 3.9%), red painted (n=54; 26.6%), and incised (n=54; 26.6%). The majority were undecorated (n=87; 42.9%) A manufacturing study at Cussetuh gave some indication that rims from uncarinated bowls may be overrepresented because rims and shoulders seem to be constructed from a single piece of clay whereas the base is formed from another (Lewis 2004:125–128). This manufacturing technique may affect the relative proportion of surface decorations that are on bowls such as red filming and incising. Rim diameters of bowls range between 4 cm and 56 cm with a mean of 27.4 cm and an s.d. of 13.8 cm. There is evidence that some bowls are not circular or symmetric (Lewis 2004:128–130). The bases of these bowls are rounded or pedestaled.

Bowls and occasionally bottles are painted with a red pigment. The pigment from four vessels was analyzed for chemical content, and preliminary results indicate that the pigments are made of inorganic materials consisting of oxygen, silicon, and iron (Lewis 2004:130). John Swanton's early-twentieth-century Upper Creek informants said that the red pigment was from "red stones" found in the hills that were pounded into a powder and applied with a stick (Swanton 1979:552).

Painted figures are not fully understood, but the Cussetuh study produced the largest sample to date and may be a representative sample of painted vessels (Lewis 2004). Shapes include birds, "t," circles, "rays," "sunbursts," and a variety of four-sided shapes (Ledbetter et al. 2002:195; Lewis 2004:136–147). Painted zones are often inscribed by an incised line and may indicate a variety of the

Mission Red Filmed (Kasita Red Film) types (Lewis 2004). Pigments were possibly painted on the vessel surface with the manufacturer's finger instead of with a paintbrush or stick as Swanton recorded (1979:552). The symbolic significance of the figures painted on the vessels is not known. While some individuals have speculated about such meanings, no ceramics researchers have consulted with the descendant Muskogee communities. Given the relatively short period of time between the use of these eighteenth-century pots and the fact that the descendant communities were still constructing similar pottery until very recently, this seems to be a highly productive or at least justified source of information about meaning.

Flaring rim jars are the most frequent of all vessel types. The orifice diameter is as wide as the maximum diameter of the vessel body, although a proportion of openings is constricted (Ledbetter 1997:214). Rims are usually modified with an applied strip of clay that is pinched (Ledbetter 1997:218; Lewis 2004:181). Surface decoration is almost exclusively brushed-roughening (n=100; 49%) or cob-roughening (n=13; 6.4), although a large proportion is undecorated (n=84; 41.2%). Lewis attributes this to the fact that many flaring rim jars are roughened to the shoulder of the jar, and areas of the jar above the shoulder are often plain (Lewis 2004:111). Therefore, a single flaring rim jar can produce both brushed and plain sherds. Rim diameters of these jars are evenly and normally distributed with a mean of 30.7 cm and an s.d. of 19.4 cm. There is a wide variation of jar sizes with a minimum jar diameter of 7 cm and a maximum of 243 cm. David Hally and Jerald Ledbetter (Hally 1986; Ledbetter 1997) attribute the function of these vessels as general cooking pots. They were probably used for stews and foods that cooked for an extended period of time (Hally 1986:285). Ethnographic and ethnohistoric research indicates that boiled corn was cooked and stored in these pots.

Tempering agents used in flaring rim jars vary (Lewis 2004:114–115), but in all cases the temper is a form of sand of varying sizes. No shell temper was observed in this vessel analysis. Thomas Lewis (2004) noted that the tempering agent varied within a single vessel. The bottom half of the vessel was constructed from a single piece of clay and was tempered with coarser sand than the upper portion that was constructed with a coiling technique. Lewis's conclusions are not quantified so it is difficult to determine how much of this pattern is real or results from random variation, however. He lists a "[w]idely varying basal thickness, lack of coil seams, and complete absence of coil fractures" as support for his conclusion (Lewis 2004:115). It is consistent with Swanton's observations, however (1979:552).

The last identifiable vessel form, cups and goblets, is new to the Historic Period and probably contains forms made to resemble European ceramics called "Colono-ware." These vessels exhibit a wide range of morphological vari-

Table 4.2: Relative frequency of surface decoration type found in a sample (n=340) of vessels from excavations at Cussetuh, Buzzard Roost, and the Victory Drive sites in Georgia (totals are rounded).

Type-Variety	Count	Percent
Chattahoochee Roughened	72	21.18
Mission Red Filmed	77	22.65
Lamar Incised, *var. Ocmulgee Fields*	46	13.53
Lamar Incised	11	3.24
Undecorated	132	38.82
Total	340	100.00

ation and are relatively small. This vessel class constitutes only six vessels in the sample, less than 1 percent. All are either roughened or plainly decorated.

Surface decoration, when viewed from the minimum vessel counts, as opposed to the sherd counts used in the spatial analysis above, reveal a different pattern of assemblage composition (Table 4.2). The roughened types, Chattahoochee Roughened var. *Chattahoochee,* constitute about 20 percent of the total decoration. Mission Red Filmed types constituted *a higher frequency* of the total assemblage than the roughened types. This is in direct contradiction to the current model of the relative frequency of roughened types relative to red-filmed types (Knight 1994b). Lamar Incised types constitute approximately 17 percent of the total assemblage, and undecorated types constitute about 39 percent of the assemblage (Table 4.2). Since vessel counts are less biased than sherd counts in relation to the representation of surface decoration to the actual proportion of surface decoration on whole vessels (Orton 1982, 1985; Orton and Tyers 1990, 1992; Orton et al. 1993:168–171), we should reassess the model of relative frequencies of surface treatment of Creek ceramic types.

The traditional characterization of Creek Indian ceramic assemblages is that almost 50 percent of the assemblage is Chattahoochee Brushed (Knight 1994b). That characterization is based on ceramic counts, which are biased because the "relative breakage rates" of each pottery type are likely to vary and therefore affect the relative proportion of sherds representing each type. In other words, a composition of ceramic types by type frequency is more of an assessment of the relative degree to which each vessel type breaks (Orton et al. 1993:52). This is why manufacturing and vessel analyses are so important.

Thomas Lewis (2004) speculated that the proportion of sherds with red filming and incising would be abnormally high because of manufacturing techniques for the vessels decorated with those designs. Type frequencies based on minimum number of vessels are less biased if the assemblage is large, such as the one analyzed here, because there is a higher chance that the assemblage contains all types of vessels and is therefore complete (Orton et al. 1993:169–170, fig. 13.1). Consequently, the proportions observed here in Table 4.2 are probably the most valid representation of the relative proportion of these surface decorations in the population of Lower Creek Indian vessels used by the Muskogee Indians during the last half of the eighteenth century.

This is a new finding and improves our ability to assess changes in Creek Indian material culture. Because of the completeness of this analysis, we are more accurately characterizing the actual relative frequency of pottery types that were in use by the Creek Indians as opposed to characterizing the number of pottery pieces that were collected. The relative frequencies of each type in Table 4.2 represent the average of the pottery types used by Muskogee-speaking Indians during the eighteenth century. While this is the most complete and least biased characterization of the average Lower Creek Indian pottery assemblage, it represents the average of ceramic assemblages that were in use at Muskogee-speaking towns only. Now that we have an unbiased representation of the population of vessels and vessel treatments used by Muskogee-speaking people during the eighteenth century, we can begin to compare that population to samples of sherds that are found in archaeological sites over space and time.

CONCLUSIONS

In this chapter I have reviewed the ethnographic and ethnohistoric evidence for pottery use by Creek Indians and the empirical variation within a sample of archaeological ceramics as revealed in all known reports and publications. The sample was derived by reviewing all known archaeological sites that were occupied by Lower Creek Indians. In order to control for differential bias owing to preservation and function, only those artifacts from features were included. A geostatistical interpolation technique, Kriging, was used to analyze how ceramic traits varied over the area inhabited by the Lower Creek Indians. The same data were used to identify ethnolinguistic correlations within the ceramic assemblage and variation resulting from temporal changes. Last, I reviewed 635 vessels from three Muskogee town excavations. The analysis revealed six vessel forms, which probably constitute the entire population of vessels used by the majority of the Muskogee-speaking Lower Creek Indians during the last half of the eighteenth century. The analysis identified a less biased approximation of the relative frequency of pottery types and forms that were used by these Indians during the eighteenth century. The vessel form analysis here has used assemblage analytical units and spatial analysis in order to evaluate pottery assemblages with the least amount of bias in the assemblages.

I have taken advantage of the comprehensiveness of this pottery sample and the large collection of vessels that we have to define the sample populaion from which archaeological samples are selected. I hope that we can begin to use this sample population to understand better the preservation biases and functional variation in other pottery assemblages. For example, if we accept this pottery assemblage as the population sample, we can compare pottery assemblages from features or sites to determine differential function.

The assemblage defined here represents a total assemblage or a total population of pottery types and forms that were in use during the eighteenth century by the Lower Creek Indians. While we know that each talwa and its people were unique, as well as the pottery that they made, we can use this average assemblage to derive some general conclusions about the average Muskogee pottery functions. The vast majority of the vessels that the Muskogee people were using were flaring rim jars and open bowls. These two forms were probably used for everyday cooking and serving of soups and stews. The next most frequent identifiable form is the carinated bowl, which Hally (1986) interprets as a serving form. These bowls were probably for more formal occasions. These forms exhibited a significant amount of continuity and form through the years within the Muskogee culture. The Muskogee people in Oklahoma continued to use the same forms and reproduce the same decorations for decades. Pottery and the subsistence and social interaction that food sharing exhibits were resilient traits among these people.

5
Architecture

Architecture reflects social space. It reflects public and private areas and household organization. It can reflect gender roles and changes in society. Historians and archaeologists have argued that changes in Maskókalkî society and culture are reflected in architectural forms and household organization (Braund 1993; Waselkov and Smith 2000; Waselkov et al. 1990; Wesson 2002). However, just like their pottery, Maskókalkî architecture varied over time and space. In this chapter I will characterize the architectural variation that was in use by the Maskókalkî during the eighteenth to early nineteenth centuries. I will describe the ethnohistoric accounts of architectural forms and construction techniques. Then I will describe all known architectural structures that have been investigated while using the historic accounts to interpret the archaeological evidence. Last, I will evaluate the ethnohistoric and archaeological evidence for structures in the context of economic and social change during the eighteenth to early nineteenth centuries.

For a variety of reasons, Maskókalkî household architecture is more historically documented than other architectural forms. Much of that variation was recently reviewed by David Hally (2002). Most of the useful historic descriptions of Creek Indian houses and structures are from the late eighteenth century. However, between 1739 and 1740, an assistant to General Oglethorpe, the governor of Georgia, traveled to the Lower Creek towns on the Chattahoochee and described "[t]heir Houses or Hutts are built with Stakes and plaistered with Clay Mixed with Moss which makes them very warm and Tite" (Mereness 1961:221). This pattern of structures made of a wooden frame covered in hardened mud lasted for the next few decades.

In the last quarter of the eighteenth century, a number of travelers through the Creek territories gave descriptions of their buildings. David Taitt, a British agent hired to map the Creek Indian towns, gave one of the best descriptions of public architecture:

The Square is formed by four houses about forty feet in Length and ten wide. Open in front and divvied into three different Cabins each. The seats are made of Canes Split and woven together raised about three feet off the Ground; and half the width of the House, the back half being raised above the other about one foot; these Cabins serve for beds as well as seats in Summer. The hot house is generally built at the north west Corner of the Square having the door fronting the South East. The one in this Town [Upper Creek town of Tukabatchee] is a Square building about 30 feet diameter rounded a little at the Corners; the walls are about four feet high; from these walls the roof rises about twelve feet, terminating in a point at top. The door is the only Opening in this house for they have no window nor funnel for the smoke to go out at, there is a small entry about ten feet long built at the out side of the door and turned a little round the side of the house to keep out the cold and prevent the wind blowing the fire about the House. . . . In this house the Indians Consult about the affairs of their Nation in the Winter Season and their Square in the Summer. (Mereness 1961:503)

This pattern of two major public structures in Lower Creek towns is repeated by numerous authors (Foster 2003a:71; Milfort 1959:93–95; Swanton 1928b, 1946; Waselkov and Braund 1995:168–186). William Bartram, the renowned botanist, drew an idealized Creek Indian town in 1789 (Figure 1.2). He shows the enclosed round council house that was used in the winter and the open square ground that was used in the summer as described by Taitt. The U.S. Indian Agent Benjamin Hawkins described a round council house:

the rotunda or assembly room, called by the traders, "hot house" . . . is near the square, and is constructed after the following manner: Eight posts are fixed in the ground, forming an octagon of thirty feet diameter. They are twelve feet high, and large enough to support the roof. On these, five or six logs are placed, of a side, drawn in as they rise. On these, long poles or rafters, to suit the height of the building, are laid, the upper ends forming a point, and the lower ends projecting out six feet from the octagon, and resting on posts five feet high, placed in a circle round the octagon, with plates on them, to which the rafters are tied with splits. The rafters are near together, and fastened with splits. These are covered with clay, and that with pine bark; the wall, six feet from the octagon, is clayed up; they have a small door into a small portico, curved round for five or six feet, then into the house. (Foster 2003a:71s)

Both David Taitt (1772) and Benjamin Hawkins (1796) described a council house that was between 30 and 42 feet in diameter (9.2–12.8 meters). It was rounded, octagonal, or circular in shape. According to Hawkins, the exterior wall used 8 posts approximately 5 feet high (1.52 meters) placed in the ground. In 1813, a soldier in General Floyd's Army passed through the Lower Creek territories and described a circular council house similar to the earlier Taitt and Hawkins versions: "The town house is a large building built round at the bottom for three or four feet high out of sticks & mud with large post(s) of the same hight which supports a plate. Inside of this wall is other large post(s) set round which support other plates on which two rest the rafters. On the last plates rest a large beam which supports another large post in the center against which rest the remainder of the rafters so as to bring the roof to a point in a conical form. On these rafters are tied small lathes which support the bark of which the roof is made. There is only one door which makes it as dark as midnight" (Swanton 1946:391–392).

Basil Hall, a Scottish traveler, described a Lower Creek council house near Columbus, Georgia, on the Chattahoochee River in 1828. While not as detailed as those above, his description is of a conical roofed structure rising to at least 30 feet (9.2 meters). The roof descended to the ground and was thatched (Benton 1998:39). This council house was in the vicinity, if not at, the Muskogee town of Coweta.

These descriptions of council houses show relative consistency from the 1770s through 1828. Indians were removed from the Georgia side of the Chattahoochee River in 1825, and their lives were significantly disrupted (Ethridge 2003; Wright 1986). Nevertheless, historic descriptions during that time period indicate that the traditional public architecture was maintained.

The other major public structure found at Creek Indian towns is the square ground as described in 1772 by David Taitt (above). It was another public meeting place but was used primarily in warm or pleasant weather. Figure 1.2 (S) shows William Bartram's drawing of a square ground. It was situated adjacent to the circular council house but was constructed differently. There are fewer descriptions of the square grounds, possibly because they were not significantly different from other domestic structures. William Bartram recorded a drawing of a square ground (Figure 5.1) in the late 1770s (Waselkov and Braund 1995:172, fig. 21).

In 1772, Taitt described the square ground as consisting of four buildings. Milfort (1959) and Benjamin Hawkins (Foster 2003a:71) indicated that the four buildings were used as seating for individuals according to their ranking and clan affiliation. Figure 5.2 illustrates John Swanton's reconstruction of the Cussetuh square ground according to Benjamin Hawkins (Swanton 1928b:68). It shows that the various buildings were reserved for different classes of people. Basil Hall, in 1828, described the "square court" as "about twenty yards across, formed by four covered sheds, in which were seated several of the chiefs, and more than a hundred of the other natives. In each of these sheds there was

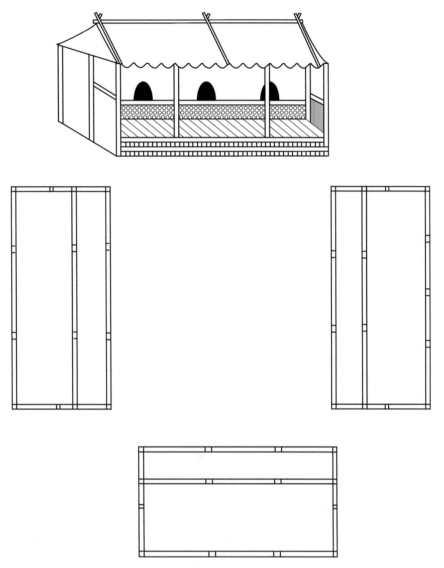

Figure 5.1. The Creek Indian Square Ground buildings, from William Bartram's drawing of "The Principal, or *Council House*" by Edwin Davis, redrawn and adapted from Waselkov and Braund (1995:figure 34).

erected a raised shelf or floor, about a foot and a half from the ground, dipping towards the court, and covered by a smooth, hard mat, made of split canes, sewed together. On this the principal Indians were seated in state, cross legged, or stretched, with equal dignity, at their full length" (Benton 1998:37).

The square ground layout was also the ideal form for individual household

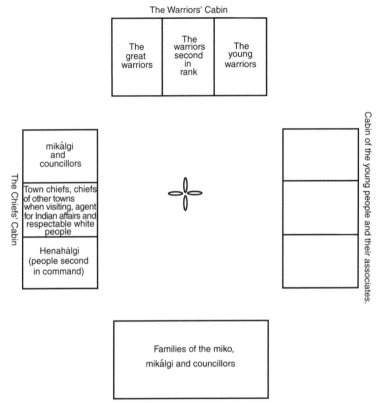

Figure 5.2. Plan of the Cussetuh Square Ground according to Benjamin Hawkins. Redrawn and adapted from Swanton (1928:figure 68).

buildings (Waselkov and Braund 1995:180). The rectangular building was the basis of the square, just as in the public square ground. Each family added buildings as their wealth and need determined; some had only one rectangular building. Bartram was illustrating individual households and the variation in the number of buildings of each household in his drawing of a typical Creek Indian town (Figure 5.1). The "footprint" or area of the household square, which ideally consisted of four rectangular buildings, was approximately ¼ acre (0.1 hectare), according to Bartram (Waselkov and Braund 1995:93). Bartram elaborated on this household pattern and the function of each building:

The habitations of the Muscogulges or Upper Crick Towns, consist of Little Squares, or four oblong square houses, encompassing a square area, exactly on the plan of the *Publick Square*,- every Family however have

not four of the Houses- some 3, - some 2, - and some but one, according
to their circumstances, of largeness of their family, &c. - but they are situated so as to admit of four building when conveniency or necessity require it - Wealthy citizens, having large Families, generally have Four
Houses; and they have particular use for each of these buildings - One
serves for a *Cook Room & Winter Lodging House* -another for Summer
Lodging House & Hall for Receiving Visitors - and a 3d for a Granary, or
Provision House, &c: - This is commonly two Stories high and divided
into two apartments transversely - the lower story of one end being a
potatoe house & for keeping such other roots & fruits as require to be
kept close or defended from cold in Winter - The chamber over it is
the Corn Crib - The lower story severs for a shed for their saddles, pack-
saddles, & geers & other Lumber; the loft over it is a very spacious airy
pleasant Pavilion - where the Chief of the Family reposes in the hot seasons & receives his Guests, &ca. - And the Fourth House (which com-
pleats the Square) is a Skin House or *Ware-house,* if the proprieter is a
wealthy man, and engaged in Trade or Traffick - where he keeps his Deer
Skins, Furs & merchandize & treats with his Customers - Smaller or less
Wealthy Families, make one, two or 3 houses serve all these purposes as
well as they can. (Waselkov and Braund 1995:180)

Bartram's terminology of Creek Indians is confusing and deserves elabora-
tion. He was describing a pattern of the "Upper Crick" towns which included
the towns on the Lower Chattahoochee River and are referred to as Lower
Creek Indian towns in this book. Bartram distinguished the Muskogee-speaking
towns, which he called the Upper Creeks, from the Hitchiti-speaking towns
settled along the far south Chattahoochee and in Florida. He called these latter
Creeks the "Lower Creeks." This naming convention is in contrast to that used
in this book and by most other writers. According to conventional terminology,
the Creek Indians settled in central and northern Alabama were called Upper
Creeks, and those Indians settled along the Lower Chattahoochee were called
the Lower Creeks (see Chapter 1).

Bartram's distinction between the Upper Creeks (Muskogee speakers) and
the Lower Creeks is informative about ethnic variations in structures among
the Lower Creek Indians (as defined in this book, not Bartram's terminology)
along the Lower Chattahoochee. The Lower Creek Indian settlements as defined in this chapter included both Muskogee- and Hitchiti-speaking Creek
Indians (see Chapter 3). The Hitchiti speakers were probably settled in the
Chattahoochee valley before the Muskogee (Foster 2004d; Hann 1988, 1996;
Knight 1994b; Worth 2000). The Muskogee populations settled mostly along
the central Chattahoochee River valley during the eighteenth to early nine-

teenth centuries, as described. Consequently, the distinction that Bartram makes about the "Lower Cricks or Seminoles" is probably referring to the Hitchiti-speaking populations. He said that the Hitchiti-speaking groups were

> not so regular & ingenious in their building either publick or private. They have neither the *Chunky-Yard* or *Rotunda* & the Publick-Square is imperfect—One, Two or Three Houses at farthest serve their purpose. And indeed they don't require it, for their Towns are but small, and consequently their Councils just sufficient for the government or regulation of the Town or Little Tribe, for in all great or publick matters they are influenced by the Nation (Upper Creeks).
>
> Their Private Habitations generally consist of two buildings—One a large oblong house, which serves for Cook-Room, eating house & lodging rooms, in 3 apartments under one roof—the other's not quite so long, which is situated 8 or 10 yards distance, one end opposite the front door of the principal house, thus. This is two stories high, and just like & serves the same purpose of the Granary or Provision House and Loft of the *Upper Creeks.* (Waselkov and Braund 1995:183)

Bartram goes on to describe how the Cherokee residential houses are similar except that each family has a round winter house and a rectangular summer house (Waselkov and Braund 1995:183–186). The pattern of each household using a round structure for winter and a rectangular structure for summer time apparently was also common among seventeenth-century Upper Creek towns (Waselkov et al. 1990). By the time of the eighteenth-century houses covered in the current summary, the round winter houses were not used any more among the Creeks (Hally 2002; Waselkov et al. 1990). The roundhouse architectural style was retained only for the public council house among Lower Creek Indians after the Yamassee War (circa 1715). The variation in numbers of square buildings and round buildings is probably a function of the cold temperatures. The Seminoles of warm-weather south Florida carried the pattern to an extreme; their residential structures were open canopies (Swanton 1946:plate 60).

Caleb Swan, who traveled among and wrote about the Creek Indians around 1790, described construction methods and structural details of houses. His description is probably of an Upper Creek household, but the pattern is similar for the Muskogee-speaking Lower Creek households also:

> The houses they occupy are but pitiful small huts, commonly from twelve to eighteen or twenty feet long, and from ten to fifteen feet wide; the floors are of earth; the walls, six, seven, and eight feet high, supported by

poles driven into the ground, and lathed across with canes tied slightly on, and filled in with clay, which they always dig for, and find near the spot wheron they build. The roofs are pitched from a ridge pole near the center, which is covered with large tufts of the bark of trees. The roofs are covered with flour or five layers of rough shingles, laid upon rafters of round poles, the whole secured on the outside from being blown away, by long heavy poles laid across them, and tied with bark or withes at each end of the house. In putting on these curious roofs, they seem to observe an uniformity in all their different towns; which, upon the approach of a stranger, exhibit a grotesque appearance of rudeness, not so easily to be described with the pen, as it might be with the pencil. The chimneys are made of poles and clay, and are built up at one end, and on the outside of the houses. On each side of the fire-place, they have small cane-racks or platforms, with skins whereon they sleep; but many of them, too lazy to make these platforms, sleep on the floor, in the midst of much dirt.

They have but one door at the side and near the center of the house; this, although nothing remains inside to be stolen, is barricaded by large heavy pieces of wood, whenever they quit the house to go out a hunting.

Their houses being but slightly made, seldom resist the weather more than one or two years, before they fall to pieces. They then erect new ones, on new plots of ground; thus, but continually shifting from one place to another, bulk of some of their largest towns are removed three or four miles from where they stood three or four years before, an no vestiges remain of their former habitations. (Swan 1855:692–693)

Swan's description is useful for the interpretation of features and archaeological remains of Creek Indian houses. Individual house buildings were rectangular structures approximately 6 meters long, 3.5 meters wide, and 2.4 meters high. They were made of a wooden frame with cane or wood splits woven between the frames to form a wattle or with lathes. The cane walls were then covered over with mud daub to form a wattle and daub wall. The mud for the daub was obtained near the structure so we would expect to find clay extraction pits near houses. The domiciliary structure described in Swan's account was relatively empty so few artifacts would be found in association with this structure. Bartram's description of the function of each residential building as given above indicates that other buildings in the residential square might be distinguished by artifact remains in and around the structure. For example, the Granary or Provision house in Bartram's account may show evidence of corn storage or horse tack.

The structures, according to Caleb Swan, would not have lasted more than a few years as the construction materials, wood and mud, would have deteriorated beyond use. Swan noted that rebuilding house structures resulted in the shifting of houses and eventually of the town over a period of time. The archaeological result of this rebuilding would be multiple postholes, daub collection pits, and the appearance of multiple structures for a single household.

Historical accounts also indicate that the construction of household structures may have changed over time. Two drawings of Creek Indian houses give evidence that some Indians in the late eighteenth and early nineteenth centuries may have adopted the more European-style log cabin construction. Given the current paucity of evidence it is impossible to quantify the degree of that change. Caleb Swan drew a Creek household in 1790 titled "The Creek house in its best state of native improvement in 1790" (Swanton 1946:plate 58). That Swan drew this household and titled it as he did indicates that this house was an outlier. The log cabin construction was rare at the time of his drawing in 1790. Another, much later drawing may have been equally unique, but the artist did not indicate such in the title. Basil Hall drew with his Camera Lucida a single household near the Chattahoochee River in 1828 (Figure 5.3). This sketch is of a log cabin structure. Note in the foreground, however, that one of the outbuildings, presumably the corncrib, was still an aboveground structure. Also, the presumed domiciliary structure in the background has a canopy. The overall layout of the log cabin residential structures is the same as the earlier types. The only difference is that the construction is of an aboveground alternating, horizontal and corner-notched log construction. The walls may or may not have clapboards in the drawing. This type of house may not utilize construction techniques that would have an archaeological signature. Contrary to the earlier Creek Indian rectangular structures, the aboveground log cabin probably did not utilize vertical posts that would leave postholes in the ground. Consequently, the only evidence of the type of construction illustrated in the Hall drawing would be artifactual. The four vertical posts, however, would reveal the "corn crib." While we do not know how widespread this construction technique was utilitized, an English missionary, Adam Hodgeson, traveled through the Lower Creek town of Cussetuh on the Chattahoochee in 1820 and described the town to "consist of about 100 houses, many of them elevated on poles from two to six feet high, and built of unhewn logs, with roofs of bark" (Swanton 1922:224). This pattern of houses is consistent with the older style, vertical post construction. Although the date was late (1820), houses at Cussetuh were still very traditional.

ARCHAEOLOGICAL EVIDENCE OF ARCHITECTURE

Recent archaeological investigations in the Lower Chattahoochee and Flint River valleys have revealed information about the structures described by early

Figure 5.3. "Indian huts west of the Chattahoochee river, 7, April 1828," by Basil Hall, MS no. 93. Courtesy, Lilly Library, Indiana University, Bloomington.

travelers and historic accounts. Most of the structural evidence from recent research has been of the smaller, individual household structures. This chapter is intended to be a comprehensive survey of the investigations that have revealed evidence for Lower Creek Indian structures that date to the post–Yamassee War era (1715). A list of references used in the study is included in Table 5.1. Reviews of Upper Creek architecture can be found in Hally (2002), Sheldon (1997), Waselkov and Smith (2000), and Waselkov et al. (1990).

One of only three possible circular structures that have been excavated and date to the eighteenth century was investigated by David DeJarnette at the "Jackson" site (1BR35). This site is probably the town of Tamathli or is directly associated with it (Kurjack 1975:115–130). The structure (Figure 5.4) measured 25 to 30 feet in diameter (7.6–9.2 meters). Daub or hardened clay was found in association with the structure as was a pit filled with stones. Burials were found at the site but not within the boundary of this structure. Based on historic reference and the European trade goods found, the site dates to the early to mid-eighteenth century.

C. G. Holland, filling in for Harold Huscher of the Smithsonian Museum, River Basin Surveys, excavated 1RU20 and 1RU21 during 1965. This site is probably the eighteenth-century historic Creek town of Oconee (see Chapter 3). Based on artifact remains found, it was occupied during the first half of the eighteenth century. The evidence for structures at this site is very scant. Holland's

Table 5.1: Creek Indian structures that have been excavated along the Chattahoochee and Flint Rivers dating between 1715 and 1836

Site Number	Structure	Type	Town Affiliation	Date of Occupation	Reference
1RU20/21	Structure	Vertical Post	Oconee	1715-175-	Holland 1974
1BR35	Feature 47	Circular	Tamathli	1700–1750	Kurjack 1975
1RU63	A	Vertical Post	Yuchi	1715–1830	Braley 1998
1RU63	Unit X4	Vertical Post	Yuchi	1715–1830	Braley 1998
9ME348	Structure	Vertical Post	Cussetuh	1775–1825	Keith 2003
9CE1	Structure	Vertical Post	Cussetuh	1750–1775	Willey n.d.a; Foster 2005a
9CE1	A	Vertical Post	Cussetuh	1750–1776	Foster 2004e
9CE1	B	Vertical Post	Cussetuh	1750–1777	Foster 2004e
9CE1	C	Vertical Post	Cussetuh	1750–1778	Foster 2004e
9CE1	D	Vertical Post	Cussetuh	1750–1779	Foster 2004e
9CE1	E	Vertical Post	Cussetuh	1750–1780	Foster 2004e
9CE1	F	Circular	Cussetuh	1750–1781	Foster 2004e
9CE1	G	Circular	Cussetuh	1750–1782	Foster 2004e
9CE1	H	Vertical Post	Cussetuh	1750–1775	Foster 2005a
9CE1	I	Vertical Post	Cussetuh	1750–1775	Foster 2005a
9CE1	J	Vertical Post	Cussetuh	1750–1775	Foster 2005a
9TR41	1	Vertical Post	Buzzard Roost	1770–1788	Ledbetter et.al. 2002
9TR41	2	Vertical Post	Buzzard Roost	1770–1788	Ledbetter et.al. 2002
9TR54	Northern	Log Cabin?	Buzzard Roost	1770–1788	Ledbetter et.al. 2002
9TR54	Southern	Log Cabin?	Buzzard Roost	1770–1788	Ledbetter et.al. 2002
9CE379	Southern	Log Cabin?	Unknown	1800–1820	Cowie et.al. 2001
9CE379	Eastern	Vertical Post	Unknown	1800–1820	Cowie et.al. 2001

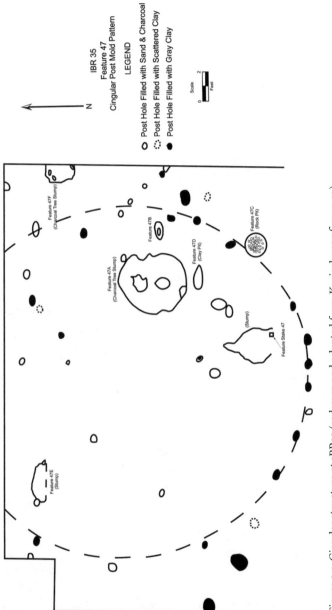

Figure 5.4. Circular structure at 1BR35 (redrawn and adapted from Kurjack 1975:figure 40).

published article and laboratory notes (River Basin Survey site reports, microfilm, Smithsonian Institution) indicate that he revealed a "fireplace" or hearth in close proximity to a line of small posts. He characterized the line of posts as "fence-like" and similar to a palisade (Holland 1974:34). While many Indian and European artifacts were found and evidence of a structure was suggested, no clear evidence of a structure was identified.

During a resurvey of the Walter F. George reservoir in the early to mid-1980s, Tim Mistovich and Vernon J. Knight investigated two feature patterns that were identified as structures at the Blackmon Site. This site is mostly associated with a mid-seventeenth-century Blackmon phase component (Mistovich and Knight 1986). The authors identified four amorphous structures, but all were dated to the seventeenth-century Blackmon phase component at the site and will not be discussed further here.

During the late 1990s, mitigation was undertaken on the site of the late-eighteenth-century town of Buzzard Roost (Salenojuh) for a Georgia Department of Transportation project (Ledbetter et al. 2002). This town was a daughter village of Cussetuh, which means that it was a population of the larger Muskogee town of Cussetuh that formed its own town (see Chapter 3). Based on ethnohistoric documentation and artifact analysis at the site, it was occupied mostly between 1770 and 1788 (Ledbetter et al. 2002:47–64, 210). Approximately four structures were identified, two of the typical eighteenth-century vertical post type and two potentially of a different type of manufacture.

Structures 1 and 2 at 9TR41 were of the rectangular vertical post design described above (Figure 5.5 shows structure 1). This site contained large oval pits. The rectangular outline defined by postholes was approximately 3 by 5 meters. The length of the structure was oriented east-west while the "front-back" orientation was north-south. Food remains and domiciliary remains were found in associated features (Ledbetter et al. 2002). The structure's frame consisted of approximately seven posts along the long "front" and "back" walls (east-west) and approximately five posts along the short "side" walls (Figure 5.5). Postmolds ranged from 6 to 20 cm in diameter (Ledbetter et al. 2002:79). The second structure was similar in shape but slightly larger in overall size.

At the second section of the Buzzard Roost town (9TR54), more structures were identified by the authors. They were of a different type and less well defined. Approximately two structures were identified based on the association of large pits, particularly rectangular pits (Figure 5.6). These pits were interpreted as "cellars" or depressed floors in a rectangular structure, with no or few vertical postholes preserved. The lack of vertical postholes may be from poor preservation or the lack of vertical posts in the structure surrounding the "cellar." The structures that enclosed these subterranean cellars may have been aboveground, log cabins such as were drawn by Caleb Swan and Basil Hall and

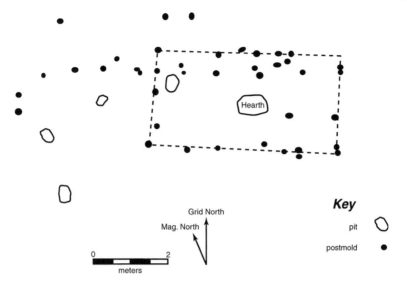

Figure 5.5. Vertical post design architecture excavated at 9TR41 (Buzzard Roost, circa 1770–1788; redrawn and adapted from Ledbetter et. al. 2002:figure 44).

described above. Aboveground corner-notched log cabins would leave little or no evidence in the subsurface ground. The rectangular pit was in association with large round pits and postholes (Figure 5.7).

Similar Creek Indian structures with "rectangular cellars" were found by Dan Elliot and Southern Research at Upatoi, another daughter village of Cussetuh (Elliott et al. 1996, 1999). Burials and many European trade goods were found in association with Creek Indian manufactured artifacts. These sites are well documented and are mapped on the 1827 Georgia land survey maps (see Chapter 3). The location and occupation of Upatoi relative to the sites investigated is unambiguous. The information about structures at this town is a good index of construction techniques during the very late eighteenth and early nineteenth centuries.

The "rectangular" features found at Upatoi sites 9ME394 and 9ME395 are defined less well than the ones found at Buzzard Roost. It is unclear if they are indeed subterranean cellars in a Creek Indian house. Given their amorphous shape, they may be clay extraction pits like those found on other Creek sites. The cellars at the Upatoi sites are approximately the same dimensions as the Buzzard Roost cellars (Elliott et al. 1999; Ledbetter et al. 2002).

While postholes are present at two of the Upatoi sites, they are not in a rectangular outline typical of wattle and daub vertical post construction (Elliott et al. 1996, 1999). The lack of posts in a recognizable rectangular pattern,

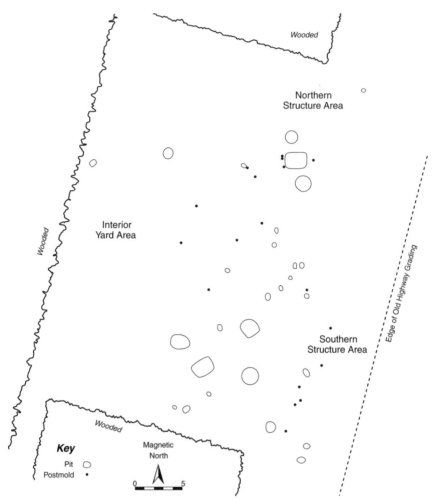

Figure 5.6. Block excavation of 9TR54, "Buzzard Roost," showing rectangular features. Redrawn and adapted from Ledbetter et. al. (2002).

large amounts of daub, and the presence of wrought and machine-cut nails indicates that nontraditional Creek Indian houses were constructed at the late historic (circa 1790–1825) town of Upatoi. A third site investigated at the town of Upatoi, 9ME42, does show evidence of traditional vertical post and wattle and daub construction. It was probably another household at the town. A burial was uncovered in immediate proximity to a number of posts (Elliott et al. 1996:33, fig. 7). The practice of burying individuals inside houses is well known among the historic Creeks from archaeological investigation (Hally 2002; Shel-

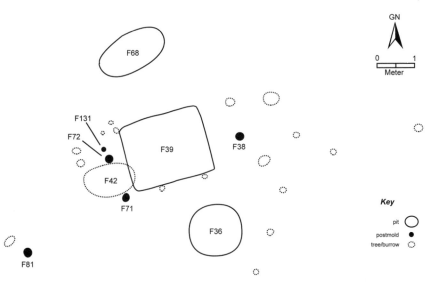

Figure 5.7. Feature concentration of 9TR54, "Buzzard Roost," showing rectangular feature and possible aboveground house. Redrawn and adapted from Ledbetter et. al. (2002).

don 1997) and ethnohistoric accounts (Swanton 1946; Waselkov and Braund 1995).

Another site that was extensively excavated recently revealed that individual households might have utilized mixed architecture construction types. Site 9CE379 was excavated by Southern Research (Cowie 2001) on Fort Benning Military Reservation. While the site's affiliation with a historic town is unknown, the site is relatively well dated from European trade goods to circa 1800–1820 (Cowie 2001:81). Given its proximity and relationship to other Muskogee-speaking towns such as Cussetuh, the individuals settled at 9CE379 were probably Muskogee-speaking Creek Indians.

When the site was first shovel-tested, it revealed an artifact scatter that closely approximated the spatial distribution of individual household square grounds (Cowie 2001:fig. 1.2 and discussion above). Four concentrations of artifacts were encountered; they were oriented roughly with the cardinal directions. Furthermore, the area of low artifact density between the four high-density areas was approximately 1/4 acre (0.1 hectare). One-fourth of an acre is the same size that Bartram mentioned when describing the size of an individual's household compound (Waselkov and Braund 1995:93). The archaeological signature of a single component Creek household is apparent in the interpolation of artifacts from shovel testing (Figure 5.8).

Test unit excavation was conducted in selected areas of the "square ground."

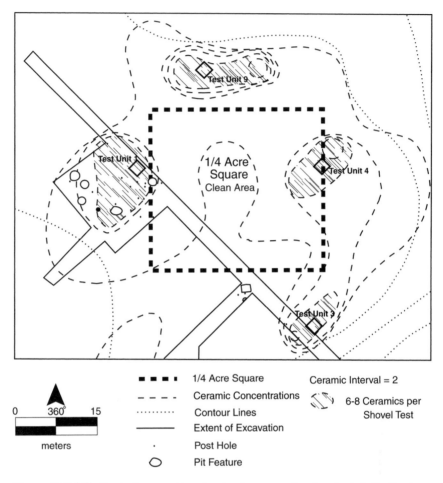

Figure 5.8. Ochille Creek site excavation showing features and archaeological distribution of a single rectangular household compound. Redrawn and adapted from Cowie (2001).

Figure 5.8 shows the artifact distribution from shovel testing and the test units that were placed on the site. Test unit excavation was undertaken to investigate the hypothesis that the artifact concentrations and spatial pattern represented individual buildings of a household square ground (Cowie 2001). Excavation units on the far east of the site revealed typical vertical post and wattle and daub construction architecture. Figure 5.9 shows posthole patterns and associated clay extraction pits on the eastern side of the household compound. According to archaeological investigation at other Creek Indian sites (Waselkov and Smith 2000) and that by Caleb Swan in 1790, these clay extraction pits were placed adjacent to wattle and daub construction houses (Swan 1855:692–693).

The western artifact and feature cluster had the highest concentration of

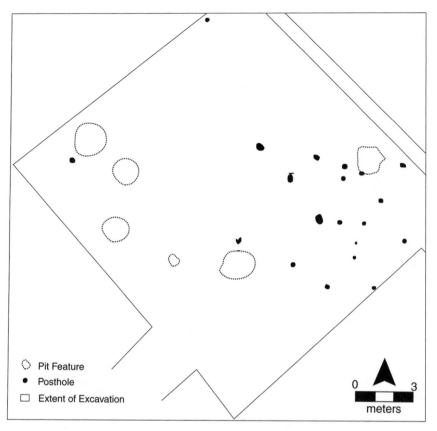

Figure 5.9. Ochille Creek site excavation showing posthole features from a structure and clay extraction pits in close vicinity of a single rectangular household compound. Redrawn and adapted from Cowie (2001).

"kitchen-related" artifacts: faunal remains, a peach pit, and mulberry seeds (Cowie 2001:118). The author associated this area with the "kitchen" and summerhouse. The western section revealed the largest amount of daub. A wattle and daub structure may have been on both the western and eastern side of the household square ground. As noted by the investigators (Cowie 2001), this pattern matches Bartram's account (quoted above) of variations in function between the different buildings that make up the square household pattern (Waselkov and Braund 1995:180). Thus the historic accounts of Upper Creek and Muskogee houses match the general pattern of outlying houses. There is some evidence of mixed architecture in the north of the site or in the south of the site in association with the cellar or subterranean floor of an aboveground structure.

Investigations at Yuchi town (1RU63) have been extensive. However, because of poor publication and reporting of the results, intermittent investigation, the length of occupation, presence of multiple components at the site, and destruction resulting from looting, the results are difficult to interpret (see Chapter 3). Nevertheless, there is evidence of Lower Creek Indian architecture at the site. Yuchi town was occupied approximately between 1715 and 1836 by Yuchi Indians and prior to about 1700 by another group of Indians, probably Hitchiti speakers. Since we do not yet have a good understanding of the material differences among Hitchiti, Yuchi, and Muskogee material culture, results from this site are tentative (Foster 2004d).

While many investigators have worked at the site (Braley 1991, 1998; Hargrave et al. 1998; Schnell 1982), David Chase of Fort Benning and Harold Huscher of the Smithsonian performed the most extensive excavations at 1RU63 and revealed the most information about structure types (Braley 1998). Their excavations are still not fully reported, but Chad Braley summarized part of the excavation. That report described the excavation of multiple posts, burials, and pits. Chase identified a house (A) in association with posts and daub. While the entire outline was not excavated, the structure was the rectangular vertical post, wattle and daub manufacture type. No round structures were found; however, only a small section of the town was excavated and the excavation sample was biased toward the hypothesized center of the site. Excavation unit X-4 also revealed a rectilinear vertical post structure. There is too little information to determine if these are public or private structures. Furthermore, the structures may date to the previous time period (Blackmon, circa 1650–1715) (Braley 1998; Worth 2000).

The most thoroughly investigated Lower Creek town is the historic town of Cussetuh. The majority of this eighteenth-century town is probably within site 9CE1. That site has been investigated through shovel testing, test unit excavation, and phase III mitigation. Gordon Willey (1938) first excavated at the site in the late 1930s for a short period. The results of that investigation were briefly summarized in 1952 in *Southern Indian Studies* (Willey and Sears 1952). This publication mentioned a "rectilinear building" (Willey and Sears 1952:5) but did not describe or illustrate it. Willey's unpublished report and maps did illustrate the structural evidence, however (Figure 5.10), and I have recently reconstructed his excavations (Foster 2005a).

Recently, approximately five hectares of 9CE1 were excavated as result of construction and Department of Defense research at Fort Benning, Georgia. These investigations have revealed the largest area ever investigated of a Lower Creek Indian town. Nevertheless, relatively little evidence of structures was found, and the results are unfortunately still preliminary (Foster 2004e, 2005a).

The evidence for structures at 9CE1 was defined from comparative ethnohistoric descriptions and archaeological investigations at other Maskókî sites (reviewed above). The identification of structures at Cussetuh is dependent on

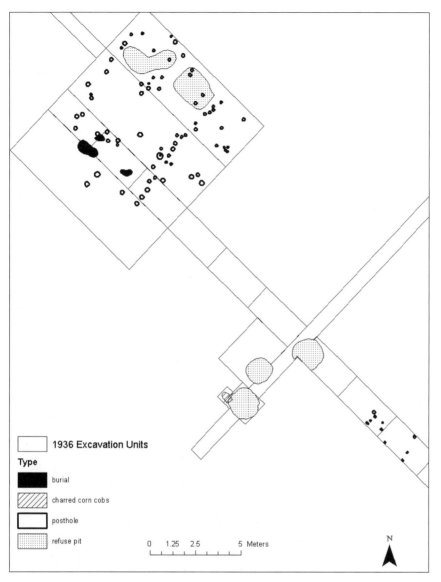

Figure 5.10. Rectangular "house" structure identified by Gordon Willey (1938) (Foster 2005a).

the association of postmolds with clay extraction pits and rectangular features. The rectangular features may have the same function as features identified within Creek households elsewhere and called "cellars" in the floors of houses (Elliot et al. 1996, 1999; Ledbetter et al. 2002). In no area of the recent excavations at 9CE1 was there unambiguous evidence of structures (Foster 2004e,

2005a). Variables used to indicate structures were (1) the presences of rectangular pits, (2) three or more postholes in a relatively straight line, (3) the presence of rounded pits outside the area of the probable structure, (4) consistency (low standard deviation) in the depth of postholes when measured from the local area, or (5) three or more postholes forming an arc. Given the ambiguity in identifying structures at Cussetuh, I defined probable structure areas. These areas are regions with a number of the archaeological elements that have been identified with Maskókî structures elsewhere and as defined above.

Probable Structure Area A was defined by a linear alignment of five postholes and a sixth that may or may not be related (Figure 5.11). The structure is 5.5 meters long. All of the postholes in structure area A were dug at approximately the same depth (s.d. = 2.5 cmbd). A similar linear alignment of posts with similar depths may have resulted from a "veranda" in front of a horizontal post, corner-notched structure similar to the one in Figure 5.3, however. Since rectangular pits ("cellars") have been found in association with the horizontal log-cabin-style structures and there is no such rectangular pit in association with these posts, they are presumed to be portions of a vertical log rectangular structure. Postholes in association with this structure contained Indian manufactured ceramics that are consistent with eighteenth-century Maskókî towns (Foster 2004e).

Structure Area B was defined by six linearly aligned posts with an average maximum depth of 33 cmbd (s.d. = 8.9 cmbd). No associated features were within the "structure area" other than two possible posts, and no artifacts were found within the posts. This posthole alignment may represent an arbor or a structure similar to Structure A (Foster 2004e).

Structure Area C is very tenuous (Figure 5.12) and is defined based on nonstructural elements. Evidence for the structure consists of a rectangular pit and a burial. Both feature types are found, though not exclusively, in nonvertical post domestic structures. For example, structures at Buzzard Roost described above were defined based on the presence of features outside the boundary of the structure. No postholes were associated with Structure Area C (Foster 2004e).

Structure Area D was loosely defined based on a concentration of postholes, three burials, and rectangular pits (Figure 5.12). The postholes may or may not be related to the structure. There is not a significant pattern of postholes to indicate a vertical post design.

Structure Area E is relatively well defined by linear posthole alignments (Figure 5.13). There were no internal pit or burial features. However, consistent with other Creek households, there were large round clay extraction pits in the immediate vicinity of the structure (Foster 2004e). Compare the clay extraction pit proximity at Structure Area E in Figure 5.13 to the clay extraction pits

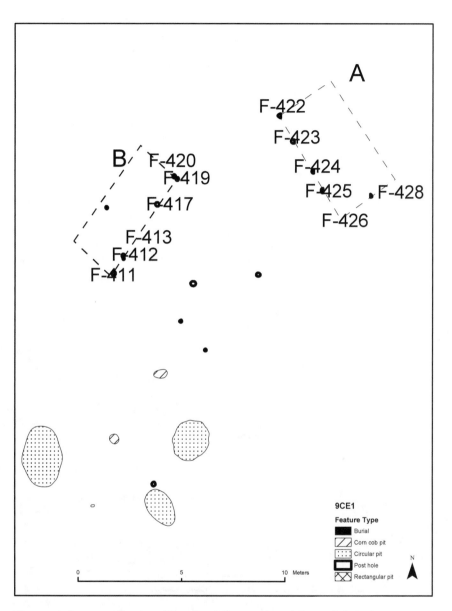

Figure 5.11. Structure areas A and B at the 2001 excavation of Cussetuh (9CE1) at Fort Benning Military Reservation, Georgia (Foster 2004e).

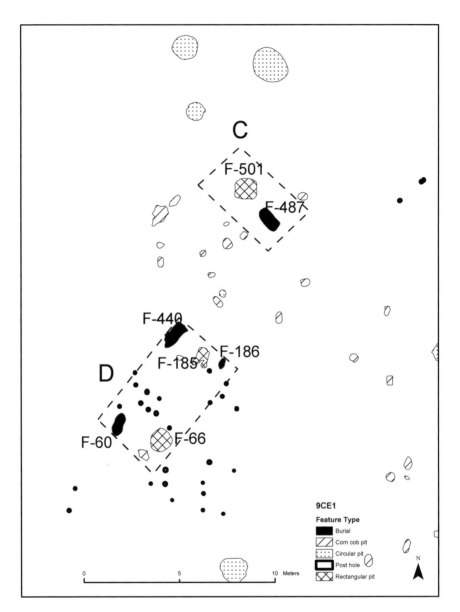

Figure 5.12. Structure areas C and D at the 2001 excavation of Cussetuh (9CE1) at Fort Benning Military Reservation, Georgia (Foster 2004e).

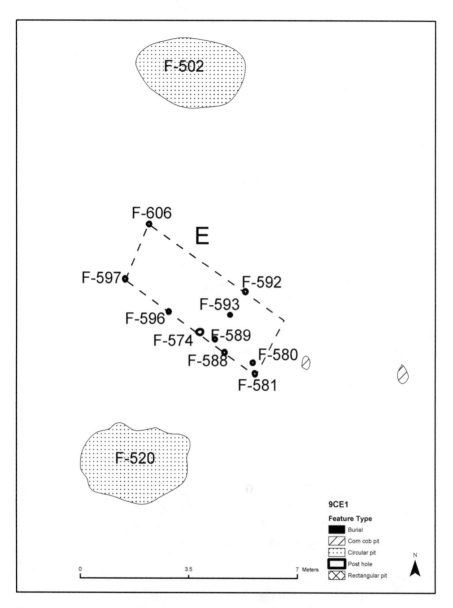

Figure 5.13. Structure area E at the 2001 excavation of Cussetuh (9CE1) at Fort Benning Military Reservation, Georgia. Note clay extraction pits, features F-502 and F-520 (Foster 2004e).

at the structure found at Buzzard Roost in Figure 5.7. Structure E defines a posthole pattern that outlines a structure approximately 5.4 by 1.97 meters. These dimensions are within the range of a small rectangular domestic structure or an arbor (Sheldon 1997). However, given the close proximity of a clay extraction pit, this structure was interpreted as a small domestic structure.

Depth of the postholes associated with Structure E (Figure 5.13) produced a bimodal distribution (Foster 2004e:table 14.2). All posts "inside" the dotted line defining a hypothetical area of the structure—features 589, 580, and 593— are significantly shallower than the post "on" the "wall." The three "internal" posts had an average depth of 15.3 cmbd (s.d. = 3.7 cmbd). The "wall posts" had an average depth of 44.5 cmbd (s.d. = 4 cmbd). While surface elevation varies at 9CE1 (Foster 2005a), these posthole depths are measured relative to each other. The depth of internal versus external posts has been shown to be significantly different in other Southeastern Indian structures (Hally 2002).

Probable Structure Areas F and G were identified as circular. The only other circular structure known among the Lower Creek sites is at the Jackson site, which may be the town of Tamathli (Figure 5.4; Kurjack 1975). Some fences or palisades may produce a circular posthole pattern, but the areas produced by Structures F and G are relatively small (52.8 m^2 and 329.9 m^2, respectively). Consequently these areas are not interpreted as corrals or palisades. Probable Structure F is defined by a sequence of five postholes that form an arc of a circle that is 8.2 meters in diameter (Figure 5.14). This diameter is within the range of the diameter of a council house as described by Hawkins and others above (Foster 2004e).

Probable Structure F is likely a round public structure. While most of the postholes for this structure were probably eroded or destroyed, there was an alternating pattern of large postholes with an average diameter of 20.6 cm with small postholes with an average diameter of 11.0 cm. The postholes were spaced approximately 1.5 meters apart. In the analysis of the features, I determined that if that pattern of postholes, 1.5 meters apart, is interpolated along the circumference of the outline of the structure identified in Figure 5.14, then the structure would consist of 16 posts of alternating size, 8 large and 8 small. In Figure 5.14, the solid black dots represent interpolated postholes in the structure. This reconstruction is almost identical to the description given by Benjamin Hawkins of a council house (Foster 2003a). He stated that the council house was octagonal in shape with eight posts. The alternating smaller posts identified in structure area F may have been for support of the wattle and daub wall and not visible from the exterior.

Probable Structure Area G (Figure 5.15) was defined by a circular pattern of four postholes. They may form a circle 20.5 meters in diameter (Foster 2004e). This diameter is twice the size of the typical council house of the late eigh-

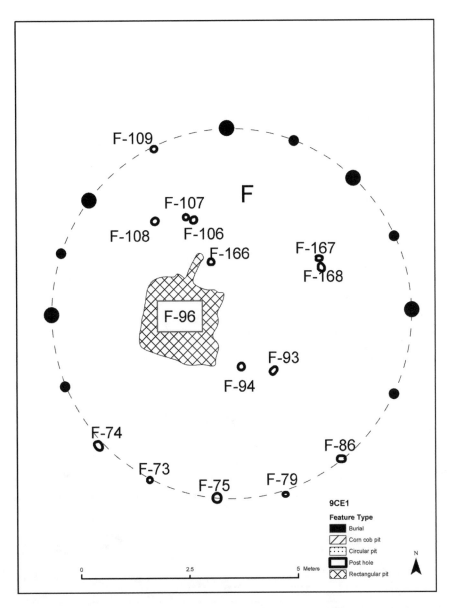

Figure 5.14. Structure area F at the 2001 excavation of Cussetuh (9CE1) at Fort Benning Military Reservation, Georgia. Solid circles represent interpreted locations of posts in circular structure (Foster 2004e).

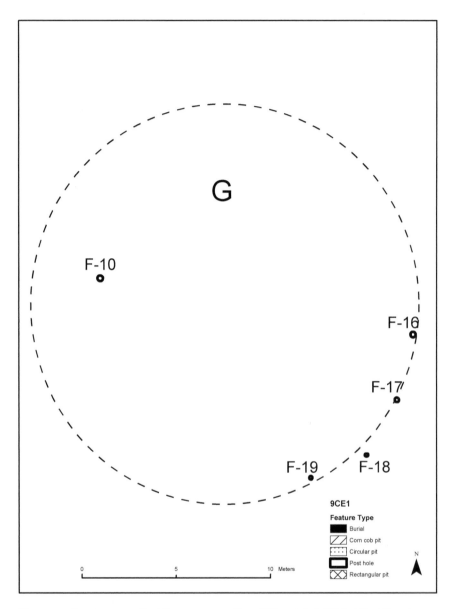

Figure 5.15. Structure area G at the 2001 excavation of Cussetuh (9CE1) at Fort Benning Military Reservation, Georgia (Foster 2004e).

teenth century as described above. The four posts have an average depth of 29 cmbd (s.d.= 8.3). The larger standard deviation of the depth of these posts may indicate that they are not related to a single building event. In other words, they may not represent the wall of a circular structure.

Probable Structure Areas H, I, and J were defined by recent excavations in what is presumed to be the center of Cussetuh (Foster 2005a). The research design of these excavations in 2005 did not allow for the expansion of excavation units beyond a width of about one meter, so identification of structures in this area is tenuous. While the density of architectural features was high, I was still only able to identify probable structure areas. In fact, the density of features was 151 times the number of features identified in the 2001 excavations (Foster 2004e, 2005a).

Structure areas in the 2005 excavations were defined based on the same criteria as in the 2001 excavations (Foster 2005a). All structure areas showed evidence of vertical post design. The size of the excavation units did not allow for the definition of the entire structure boundary. Structure Area H was defined from the alignment of postholes and a nearby oval pit (Figure 5.16). Structure Area I was defined by the alignment of postholes and a burial pit (Figure 5.17). Structure Area J (Figure 5.18) was a loosely defined region that contained a large number of postholes, daub concentrations, and burial pits. This area may represent an entire household compound (Foster 2005a).

EFFECTS OF ECONOMIC AND SOCIAL CHANGES ON ARCHITECTURE

Multiple researchers have argued that the Southeastern Indians underwent a significant number of changes during the Historic Period as a result of contact with Europeans (Braund 1986, 1993; Ethridge 1996; Hahn 2000; Hally 2002; Piker 2003; Saunt 1999; Sheldon 1997; Smith 1987; Waselkov 1989, 1997, 1998; Waselkov and Smith 2000; Waselkov and Wood 1986; Waselkov et al. 1990; Wesson 1999, 2002). One of the significant drivers of change for the Southeastern Indians and European setters was the deerskin trade (discussed in detail in Chapter 1). Market demand for deer leather products in Europe and elsewhere stimulated deerskin production in the Americas during the eighteenth century. Recently Kathryn Braund and Claudio Saunt have argued that the deerskin trade altered the gender relations, economy, and property rules of the Southeastern Indians (Braund 1993; Saunt 1999). Another change resulting from the deerskin trade may have occurred in architecture (Hally 2002; Schroedl 1986, 2000; Waselkov and Smith 2000; Waselkov et al. 1990). Architectural changes are the manifestation of cultural changes in the population density, economic production unit, and reproductive patterns within a society (Durrenberger

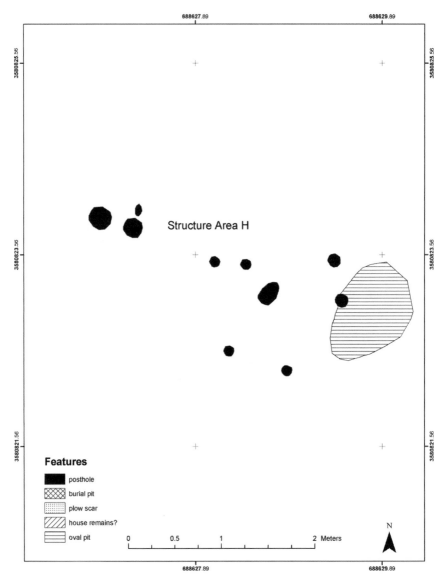

Figure 5.16. Structure area H at the 2005 excavation of Cussetuh (9CE1) at Fort Benning Military Reservation, Georgia (Foster 2005a).

and Tannenbaum 1992; Rogers and Smith 1995). While the evidence for architectural changes over time among Southeastern Indians seems valid, we still do not understand the degree of those changes. Since household architecture is a correlate of demography and society, change in architecture is a direct measure of change in demography, gender relations, and property rules.

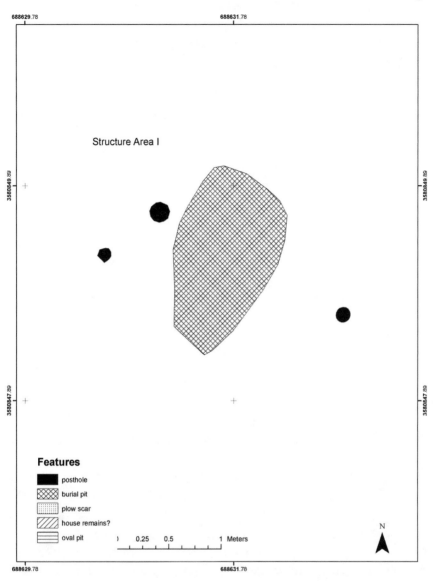

Figure 5.17. Structure area I at the 2005 excavation of Cussetuh (9CE1) at Fort Benning Military Reservation, Georgia (Foster 2005a).

During the eighteenth and nineteenth centuries, there was a significant amount of variation in architectural styles among the Lower Creek Indians. That variation is documented in ethnohistoric description and archaeological investigation of 25 structures, which date to the Lawson Field phase (circa 1715–1836). Archaeologists identified three basic architecture styles: vertical post rec-

Figure 5.18. Structure area J at the 2005 excavation of Cussetuh (9CE1) at Fort Benning Military Reservation, Georgia (Foster 2005a).

tangular residential structures, horizontal log "cabin" rectangular structures, and round public structures or "council houses."

Consistent with the findings of Waselkov et al. (1990) at the Upper Creek site of Fusihatchi in central Alabama, no subterranean rounded "winter houses" were found in use by the Lower Creek Indians during the eighteenth century.

Only one structure, the round public structure at the Jackson site, was occupied during the first half of the eighteenth century, so there may be a bias toward the latter half of the Lawson Field phase. The Chattahoochee River Valley was sparsely occupied during the late seventeenth and early eighteenth centuries because of emigration to the Ocmulgee River watershed in central Georgia (Worth 2000). So evidence of round subterranean structures may be lacking simply because of a lack of settlement on the Chattahoochee River during the seventeenth century to the beginning of the eighteenth century. There may be evidence of subterranean rounded structures at Muskogee Creek towns on the Ocmulgee River in central Georgia (Pluckhahn 1997) because the Creek Indians moved from the Ocmulgee River to the Chattahoochee River around 1715. Consequently, if subterranean round structures were being used by the Lower Creek Indians during the late seventeenth to early eighteenth centuries, they may be found only on the Ocmulgee River watershed.

Nevertheless, the effect of the deerskin trade on household composition and architectural style is probably evident in this structure assemblage. It is important to note that *no* subterranean rounded winter house structures are known from the Lawson Field phase in the Lower Creek region. According to Crane and Saunt, changes in the deerskin trade didn't affect gender roles and property until around 1760 (Crane 2004; Foster and Cohen 2005; Saunt 1999:42). Similarly, there is little evidence of rounded subterranean winter houses among the Lower Creek during the first half of the eighteenth century. If the deerskin trade was the driving force altering the household structure and the architecture used by those households, and if the effects of the deerskin trade weren't pronounced until around 1760, then we would expect to see at least some evidence of subterranean rounded structures among the Lower Creek Indian sites from the first half of the eighteenth century along the Chattahoochee River (Hally 2002; Sheldon 1997; Waselkov 1997; Waselkov et al. 1990; Wesson 1999). The effects of the deerskin trade do not seem to have caused the transition to aboveground rectangular structures among the Lower Creek. That architectural style was well established by the mid-eighteenth century. However, it must be noted that the number of well-preserved houses from the Lower Creek region is very small now, so these results are tentative.

There seems to be clear evidence of a change in architectural styles from rounded subterranean winter house to only rectangular vertical post design during the seventeenth and eighteenth centuries in central Alabama (Sheldon 1997; Waselkov et al. 1990) and Tennessee (Hally 2002; Schroedl 1986, 2000). However, given the regional perspective of the architectural variation of the Lower Creek Indian sites and the good temporal control of those sites, it seems unlikely that the general trend by Southeastern Indians away from subterranean winter houses was caused by changes in the deerskin trade. Cameron Wesson has argued that changes in the size of these houses reflect a decrease in chiefly power during the Historic Period. His evidence, however, is a graph that isn't explained and is difficult to evaluate (Wesson 2002:fig. 7.4). The graph is of floor size, but the units and sample size are not specified.

Regional climate variation seems to be a simpler explanation. During the period of the deerskin trade, the Cherokee still lived in the round houses, which may indicate that roundhouse construction is a northerly, cold-climate trait (Hally 2002:105). The use of round houses by central Alabama Indians could be related to a southern migration by Maskókî people who formerly lived in what are now the southern Appalachian Mountains (Smith 1987, 2000).

The ethnohistoric descriptions of structures demonstrate significant variation, particularly between the Muskogee and Hitchiti peoples along the Chattahoochee River. In the late eighteenth century, William Bartram described Seminole structures that were aligned differently than those of the Muskogee houses (Waselkov and Braund 1995:cf. figs. 21 and 34). The house compound in Bartram's drawing consisted of two buildings aligned perpendicular to one another. Bartram's description of the houses built by Hitchiti-speaking Seminoles who lived south of the Muskogee on the Chattahoochee River described variation that is probably evident in the archaeological record.

The deerskin trade may have drastically affected the economy, gender relations, and property rules (Braund 1993; Saunt 1999), but its effects on household composition and architecture need to be analyzed over a large geographic region. We need to understand the pre-deerskin economy and architectural variation before we can make conclusions about the effects of the post-deerskin economy. Joshua Piker and I have recently argued that the social history of individual Creek Indian towns was unique (Foster 2003b, 2004c; Piker 2003). Consequently, generalizations about the social history of all the people who were called Creek Indians have limited utility. This study and others (Foster 2004d) have demonstrated that archaeological data demonstrate significant but not unexpected variation between individual towns.

CONCLUSIONS

In this chapter I have analyzed the architectural variation of Lower Muskogee Creek Indians who lived along the Chattahoochee River watershed in central Alabama and Georgia during the Lawson Field phase (circa 1715–1836). All known structures (n=25) that have been investigated archaeologically were described in order to quantify the geographic variation and temporal variation of eighteenth- to early-nineteenth-century architecture. This analysis has shown that there were three types of structures used by the Lower Muskogee Creek Indians: rectangular vertical post wattle and daub residential structures, rectangular horizontal aboveground log-cabin structures, and round vertical post wattle and daub public structures. The log-cabin type was used only for a short period during the early nineteenth century and by a limited number of individuals. The other two types were used throughout the eighteenth and early nineteenth centuries. No subterranean rounded winter houses (Hally 2002) are known to have been used by the Lower Muskogee Creek Indians between 1715 and 1836.

While the deerskin market may have altered the society of the Southeastern Indians during the eighteenth century, the current archaeological evidence indicates that the Lower Creek Indians had already abandoned the rounded subterranean winter house style by the early eighteenth century. We need to characterize the geographical and temporal variations in architectural styles before we can accurately measure the effects of the deerskin trade on the household composition and culture of the Southeastern Indians.

6
Botanical Remains

Mary Theresa Bonhage-Freund

In this chapter I summarize and interpret the archaeobotanical remains that have been reported from Creek Indian archaeological sites. Since plant remains can also contribute to our understanding of the paleoenvironment, some of these results are discussed in Chapter 2. The paleoethnobotanical analysis is based exclusively on macroplant remains that are interpreted in conjunction with the historic record, and it consists of three parts. First, the historic data are reviewed for first-person insights into the character of early historic Creek subsistence. These data include both historic accounts, including government records, and significant scholarly interpretations of these texts. Second, there follows an assessment of archaeobotanical remains reported from excavated Lower Creek sites in Georgia and Alabama. Third, a paleoethnobotanical model of early historic Creek subsistence and ecology is advanced based on the joint consideration of historic and archaeobotanical data.

HISTORIC OVERVIEW

Several European-Americans recorded their firsthand impressions of early historic Creek ecology and economic activities, with varying degrees of scientific notation, accuracy, and ethnocentrism (Adair 1968; Foster 2003a; Harper 1998; Romans 1999, among others). I summarize historically documented details of the human-plant interaction at the lower Creek town of Cussetuh and the upper Creek towns known collectively as Okfuskee (Piker 2004). Creek towns and villages shared many culture traits, yet each possessed unique social and natural environments to which its people responded, possibly generating local variants of subsistence strategies. Thus, overgeneralization to other towns and villages must be approached with caution (Piker 2004).

Cussetuh Town (9CE1) is the probable locus of an eighteenth- to nineteenth-century Creek administrative and ceremonial center (Foster 2005a; O'Steen et al. 1997). The town experienced regular fluctuations in population as a function of the annual ceremonial cycle. Historic documents indicate that this complex system relied on field agriculture (Brannon 1925). In the 1830s, agricultural soils proximate to Cussetuh town were in decline, and the town itself showed signs of preparing for relocation (Foster 2003b, 2005b). However, the villages associated with Cussetuh town exhibited well-fenced fields that were cultivated by plows. They raised cattle, hogs, and horses. Some villages planted apples, peaches, and grapes (Foster 2003a).

In the early 1770s, Okfuskee (Oakfuske) was likely positioned at a ford on the Tallapoosa River where a major trade route traversed the river. The Okfuskee Creek took full advantage of this location, practicing a mixed subsistence strategy which almost certainly included agriculture, animal husbandry, hunting, trade, and bounty hunting of runaway slaves (Piker 2004:91, 111–112).

Josh Piker documented some details of these activities. Women collected firewood and wild plants, often accompanying men on hunting trips to perform these and other domestic tasks. In these temporary encampments, people fashioned lean-tos of bark and poles. In late March through early April, men and women together planted small fields with maize, with a second round occurring in May when larger fields were seeded with maize and other "provisions." By the 1750s, economic pressures obliged men to remain in hunting camps until the Busk in mid-July, leaving only briefly in April to plant the fields. Unfenced communally farmed fields were located some distance from the town, but by the 1760s and 1770s each household maintained a fenced kitchen garden (Piker 2004:113–115). Women alone planted and maintained the private gardens. The maize planted in these infields was a quick-growing variety which ripened in about two months, in contrast to the more slowly growing types planted in the communal outfields (Piker 2004:118).

Piker argues that an intercultural frontier exchange economy developed in Creek country during the second half of the 1750s, but the Upper Creek towns such as Okfuskee did not participate until this system was about to collapse in the 1760s. By then, Creek Indians and colonists in Georgia and South Carolina informally exchanged small amounts of food. Creeks traded venison for produce and other provisions. The Lower Creek Indians probably participated in this exchange economy. Chapter 7 describes animal remains found at archaeological sites.

In the early eighteenth century, Yuchi was the second largest of the Lower Creek towns (Boyd 1949). Benjamin Hawkins reported that the *E-ne-hau-ul-gee,* or those men second in command to the town's *Micco,* supervised the preparation of the communal agricultural fields (Foster 2003a). They also prepared the ceremonial tea known throughout the early historic Southeast as the "Black Drink" (Hudson 1976). This highly caffeinated tea was typically prepared from the toasted leaves of yaupon holly (*Ilex vomitoria*) and was central to Creek social and ceremonial life (Hudson 1979). Calabashes or gourds were sometimes used to serve it (Foster 2003a; Swan 1855).

Bartram described the structures of Yuchi Town as constructed on a wooden frame and neatly roofed with cypress bark or shingles (Harper 1998). He also visited the home of an elite man about two miles south of Yuchi Town (1RU109) and described part of the compound as featuring a cedar-roofed canopy, covered by "checquered mats woven of splints of canes dyed of different colours" (Harper 1998). The pavilion contained storage areas for sweet potatoes and other roots, underneath a "corn crib" (Waselkov and Braund 1995).

The Yuchi maintained garden patches on the town border, and each spring they burned these fields to prepare for planting. In addition, each household maintained a "dooryard garden" where they tended plants like tobacco. As suggested by the presence of corn cribs, maize, especially a flint race, was the primary staple crop (Speck 2004). Other cultivated plants included beans, sweet potatoes, melons, pumpkins, squashes, and gourd (Speck 2004). While Creek maintained an impressive agricultural complex, they did not rely on it to supply all plant foods. Wild plants, including hickory nuts and various berries, were incorporated into the diet (Newsom and Ruggieo 1998; Speck 2004).

In 1797, Benjamin Hawkins journeyed through Upatoi on the Hatcheeth-lucco, where he ate potatoes and coffee in the village of Tussekiah Mico. As the guest of Coosa Mico near Usachee Hatchee, Hawkins enjoyed potatoes, hickory milk, pumpkin, and beans, with hickory nut oil, ground peas, and chestnuts. Coosa Mico's people cultivated corn (maize) on the flatlands and potatoes on the hillsides. A month after his visit to Upatoi, Hawkins instructed his assistant and others in a plan to encourage "proper" agriculture among the Creek. This plan would include the cultivation of potatoes, peas, and wheat and the introduction of the plow (Foster 2003a).

DETAILS OF CREEK SUBSISTENCE

The Creek year was tied to phases of the moon and began with the most important of two principal annual feasts, the Busk, Boosketah, Poskita, or Green Corn ceremony. This pan-Southeastern renewal ceremony occurred when the maize ears were large enough for roasting, generally in July or August (Hewitt 1939; Swan 1855). Maize was the staple cultivated crop, as discussed in Chapter 1.

Hudson (1976) describes pan-Southeastern agriculture as "riverine." All of the large town and village sites discussed in this volume are proximate to large patches of loamy riverine soils. Frequently, canebrakes are noted near the communities, and, in fact, cane and maize thrive in similar environments (Hudson 1976:291–292). This suggests that the potential to farm maize was critical in selecting community locations. The availability of firewood was a second limiting factor (Hudson 1976).

Like other Southeastern Indians, the Creek used a complex system of multicropping and intercropping (see Hudson 1976:289–299 for a more comprehensive discussion of agricultural methods). Hudson asserts that the larger communal fields were planted with only a single crop of late-ripening maize that required time to dry on the stalk. Multicropping of smaller plots involved the scheduling of successive crops on the same field in one season. Some crops, like goosefoot and pigweed, would alone yield two distinct crops in one season: greens in the spring, seeds in the fall. Intercropping involves the planting together of complementary crops such as the well-known combination of maize, beans, and squash, as well as lesser-known maypops and purslane and probably others (Bonhage-Freund 1997; Gremillion 1989; Hudson 1976).

Creek women performed much of the "labor of the field" in the late eighteenth century. However, as observed at Okfuskee, both men and women planted the town fields and contributed to their cultivation (Romans 1999; Swanton 1979). Swan (1855) observed that Creek women "carry burdens, pound corn, and perform all the hard labor."

The Creek Indians raised "grain and pulse" for their household consumption but purchased "a good deal of rice." Their crops included several kinds of maize (*Zea mays*), beans (*Phaseolus vulgaris*), hyacinth beans (*Dolchios lablab*), "an abundance of melons, squashes and pumpkins" (*Cucurbita* spp.) (Romans 1999:93–94). Bartram (1909) specifically noted an absence of certain common European crops, including wheat, barley, spelt, rye, and buckwheat, turnips, parsnips, and salad (Table 6.1).

In addition to cultivated foods, the Creek people ate wild-collected plant foods. Romans (1999) believed that the Creek limited the extent of their agriculture because of the high productivity of the local environment. They made a "caustick salt" out of "a kind of moss that grows at the bottom of creeks and rivers." They dried peaches (*Prunus persica*) and persimmons (*Dysopyros virginianum*), chestnuts (*Castanea dentata*), and the fruit of the "blue palmetto" or "needle palm" (*Rapidophyllum hystrix*). Women prepared a cake of maypops (may apple pulp, *Passiflora incarnata*) (Romans 1999). Throughout the Southeast, Indians probably encouraged maypops to grow in cultivated fields (Gremillion 1989). Starchy wild plant foods included oak acorns (*Quercus* spp.), prepared as "acorn bread," two members of the morning glory family, described as potatoes or "sweet potatoes" (*Ipomoea batata, I. pandurata*), and several kinds of "panicum" (*Panicum* spp.; Romans 1999:93–94). The reported panicum may actually include sorghum (*Sorghum drummondii*), wild rice (*Zinzania aquatica?*), and cockspur grass (*Echinochloa crusgalli*) (Swanton 1979).

Firsthand accounts describe Creeks making oil from hickory, acorns, and

Table 6.1: Historically documented plant used by the Creek Indians

Taxon	Citation						Notes
	Bartram (1909); in-cludes work of B.S. Barton	Romans (1999)	Swan (1855)	Swanton (1979) - clarifying Bartram, Barton, Romans, Swan	Hariot et al. (1927)	Speck (2004)	
Native							
"... a vast variety of wild or native vegetables, both fruits and roots..."				x			
Bean, common; hyacinth [Dolchios] (*Phaseolus vulgaris*)	x	x		x		x	Speck (2004) lists this as a secondary food crop
Corn / Maize (*Zea mays*), several varieties	x	x		x		x	Speck (2004) identifies a flint race of maize and maize was primary food crop
Cane (*Arundinaria* sp.)							
Chestnut (*Castanea dentata*)		x	x				also chestnut oil
Cockspur Grass? (*Echinochloa crusgalli*)			?				

Food				Notes/Source
Grape (*Vitis rotundifolia*)	x			"lay up for winter and spring" - Barton (in Bartram 1909; 49-50)
Hickory Nut, Smoked Hickory Nut, Hickory Milk (*Carya* sp.)	x	x		"All kinds of Juglans" - Barton, probably includes hickory (in Bartram 1909:49-50); hickory were processed for storage by various means (Speck 1909:44)
Locust, Honey (pods) (*Gledetsia multiloba* [*meliloba* Walt.]; *G. triacanthos*)				
Locust, Water				
Moss				
Mulberry; mulberry, red (*Morus rubra*)	x			
Oak Acorn (*Quercus* spp.)	x	x		and acorn oil
Palmetto, blue (*Rhapidophyllum hystrix*)	x			
Panicum maximum and others	x			
Peas (*Pisum* spp.)				
Persimmon (*Diospyros virginiana*)	x			
Plum (*Prunus* sp.)				
Rice, wild (*Zinzania* sp.)			x	

Continued on the next page

Table 6.1: *Continued*

Taxon	Bartram (1909); includes work of B.S. Barton	Romans (1999)	Swan (1855)	Swanton (1979) - clarifying Bartram, Barton, Romans, Swan	Hariot et al. (1927)	Speck (2004)	Notes
	Citation						
Greenbriar (*Smilax pseudochina*) root	x						
Squash. Pumpkin (*Cucurbitae*)	x			x		x	Speck (2004) lists this as a secondary food crop
Sweetpotato, wild (*Ipoemoea batata; I. pandurata; Convulvulis batata*)	x	x		x		x	Speck (2004) lists this as a secondary food crop
Tobacco (*Nicotiana* sp.)						x	
Walnut (*Juglans* sp.; probably *J. nigra*)	x						
Introduced							
Apple (*Malus* sp.)	x						
Figs	x						
Maypops (*Passiflora incarnata*)		x					

Crop				Notes
Melons (unspecified genus)		x	x	Speck (2004) lists this as a secondary food crop
Muskmelon				
Oranges	x			Grown only by some Lower Creeks living in or near Florida
Peach (*Prunus persica*)	x	x		
Plums, Chickasaw (*Prunus*)	x			
Rice (*Oryza* sp.; *Zizania aquatica*?)	x	x		Farmed in hills on dry ground in gardens. Raised only for family's personal use
Sorghum (*Sorghum drummondii*?)		?		
Watermelon	x	x		
Noted as not grown				
cucemeres	x			
farinaceous grains: (wheat, barley, spelts, rye, buckwheat)	x			
turnips	x			
parsnips	x			
salads	x			

chestnuts (Swan 1855:692). In the Southeast, hickory nuts were sometimes smoked and dried on reed mats elevated over a fire (Hariot et al. 1927:29). Acorns usually required more extensive processing than other nuts because of their high tannin content. Some acorns were edible after merely being parched, but most required boiling in water to remover the bitter and poisonous tannic acid. The boiled acorns were pounded into a pulp that was dried into meal and used in much the same way as hominy. Acorns were sometimes boiled like potatoes (Swanton 1969; Watt and Merrill 1975). In addition to the above, Swanton (1979:293) inventoried the following "vegetable foods" used by the Creek: peas ("a variety of beans"), cane, grape, honeylocust, mulberry, panic grass (*Panicum maximum*), persimmon, plum, wild rice, greenbriar (*Smilax* spp.), and walnut.

While historic documents by Euro-Americans do not generally document fuel wood, it was specifically noted that oak (*Quercus* spp.) and cane (*Arundinaria* sp.) were used in the "spiral fire" at councils (Foster et al. 2004; Swanton 1946). Cane was also used in the weaving of mats, which were sometimes used in wall construction. Cypress bark and cedar were used for roofing shingles (see Chapter 5).

The historic record (summarized in Table 6.1) suggests that Lower Creek Indians followed similar subsistence strategies. Settlements were preferentially located on agricultural soils and abandoned in stages as their fertility declined (Foster 2003b). Successional growth on abandoned fields yielded many wild plants that contributed substantially to the diet. Very few exotic species were adopted, but peach was a major exception. Potatoes, too, are frequently documented. These patterns are similar to those observed among twentieth-century Yanomamo Indians of Venezuela. As soils wear out and they prepare to relocate the community, Yanomamo control succession and harvest wild "crops" from their abandoned fields. At the same time they plant other local fields and also prepare fields at a new location some distance away (Chagnon 1996).

PALEOBOTANICAL REMAINS FROM LOWER CREEK INDIAN SITES

There is much variation in sampling strategies for plant remains at archaeological sites over space and time. Phase I reconnaissance projects typically include no formal analysis of plant remains. In more comprehensive projects, archaeologists often collect flotation samples only from features containing visible charcoal, or they exclude postmolds because of the presumption that they contain only wood charcoal. This protocol skews the assemblage and severely compromises its robustness. A comprehensive collection of samples from each context is ideal, as taxa are usually unevenly distributed across any given site.

Certain uncommon, poorly preserved, small, or differentially distributed taxa are likely to appear primarily or exclusively in a single category of cultural features within a particular site (Bonhage-Freund 1997). Pearsall (1989:Chapter 2) reviews sampling strategies as well as procedures for the optimal operation of several different flotation systems.

Many of the early historic Creek archaeological projects discussed elsewhere in this volume lack a paleoethnobotanical component. A few of these report only macroplant remains that were incidentally recovered during field excavations. Four projects stand apart from the others in the broad scale of their floral recovery programs. Relatively extensive paleoethnobotanical analyses were an integral part of the research designs of the Cussetuh (9CE1), Buzzard Roost (9TR41, 9TR54), Yuchi Town (1RU63), and Ochillee Creek (9CE379) data recovery programs. In this section I first summarize macroplant remains excavated at sites where the recovery of archaeobotanical materials was of low priority, and then I consider those sites having substantial paleoethnobotanical components.

In this section I summarize the archaeobotanical data from sites reporting only limited amounts of charred plant remains. Many of these sites are part of phase I archaeological surveys, while others were excavated prior to the development of effective flotation systems. In the latter cases, archaeologists typically recovered only the largest and most visible plant and animal remains. Among those sites are Hitchiti (9Sw50) (Kelly et al. 1961) and Victory Drive (9ME50). Also represented are sites from archaeological investigations at 9Me42, 9ME395, 9ME372, 9ME479, and 9ME394 (Elliott et al. 1996, 1999).

The Walter F. George Basins Archaeological Salvage project, along the Chattahoochee River, reports minimal amounts of archaeobotanical materials from several sites (DeJarnette 1975). These include the Shorter village (1BR15), Jackson (1BR35), McLendon (1RU28), and Fort Apalachicola (1RU101). Methods for these surveys are discussed in detail in Chapter 3.

Wood charcoal is the most common macroplant remain at most sites, but it is often not reported and only rarely analyzed in the Creek Indian archaeological projects. Maize (*Zea mays*) cobs or kernels were reported in 8 of these 11 sites. Peach (*Prunus persica*) pits were found in four sites. Two sites reported hickory (*Carya* spp.) nutshell. Unidentified seeds were mentioned at two sites. The Jackson site (9BR35) is the only one to report wattle and daub, an indirect evidence of plant use.

The Victory Drive site (9ME50) is the only one of these sites that yielded acorn (n=1), squash (n=44 fragments), cultivated bean (n=3), and persimmon (n=1), all from a single large pit (Ledbetter 1997:252). The maize from this pit included nine measurable cob fragments with a mean cupule width of 9.9 mm, and most likely represents 10-row maize. (See the discussion of maize classification below.) A total of 104.2 grams of charred plant material from this pit were examined (Ledbetter 1997).

"Corn (maize [*Zea mays*]) cob pits" or "smudge pits" were specifically noted in four of these site reports, even if no other plant remains were mentioned. Maize and charcoal typically dominate the fill of these grapefruit- to dinner-plate-sized pits. Archaeologists who first encountered this feature type often interpreted it as serving a ceremonial function (eg., Kelly et al. 1961:31). We now know maize cob-filled features served many functions over space and time in the Southeast and Midwest, including smudging of pots, smoking of hides, meat, and plant foods, as insect repellent, and possibly in ceremonies (Binford 1967; Bonhage-Freund 2005; Mason 1973; Morse and Morse 1960; Schroedl 1986; Skinner 1913).

FULL PALEOETHNOBOTANICAL ASSESSMENTS

As discussed above, the Cussetuh (9CE1), Buzzard Roost (9TR41 and 9TR54), Ochillee Creek (9CE379), and Yuchi Town (1RU63) research programs each included full paleoethnobotanical assessments. There is significant overlap in the methodology, laboratory procedures, and analytical approaches employed in the first three of these projects. This section begins with a summary of these common approaches.

In the laboratory, each light fraction flotation sample was first weighed, then passed through nested geologic sieves for ease of sorting. Except in the case of extremely large samples from the Buzzard Roost sites, each size-graded light fraction was full-sorted under low magnification. Some very large samples from Buzzard Roost were subsampled (see Bonhage-Freund 1999 for details and discussion).

All charred seeds and plant tissue were collected from the 2.0 mm and larger sieves and quantified by material type and count. Nutshell, maize cob, and charred and uncharred wood were both counted and weighed. Fractions smaller than 2.0 mm were visually scanned, but only carbonized seeds were removed. Identifications of taxa were made by comparison to modern charred and uncharred reference collections, positively identified archaeological specimens, and standard reference volumes (Delroit 1970; Martin and Barkley 1973; Montgomery 1977). Wood charcoal was sampled and analyzed separately. All charred plant remains are considered to be of archaeological significance, but most noncharred seeds are presumed to be modern (Bonhage-Freund 2003, 2004).

Wood charcoal dominates the floral assemblage of nearly every sample. Identifications were attempted on a minimum of 20 and a maximum of all wood charcoal fragments from each provenience (Bonhage-Freund 1997; Minnis and Ford 1977:82; O'Steen and Raymer 1999). Wood charcoal specimens less than 2.0 mm in size were only evaluated in the absence of larger fragments; it is the minimum size likely to possess all the structural features needed for a reasonable identification. In fact, most fragments above 2.0 mm could only be identified to the genus, and some could only be classified as ring porous, diffuse porous, or hard or soft wood. Wood taxa were identified by comparison with charred and natural transverse, tangential, and radial thin sections of modern wood (Bonhage-Freund 1999, 2003; Ledbetter et al. 2002). Several analytical tools are routinely used to assess taxon significance by compensating for differential preservation. A discussion of those methods used in these studies follows.

In comparing taxa, it is not completely accurate to equate nutshell or maize cob fragments with seed count, because a single nutshell or maize cob produces multiple fragments. Both nutshell and maize cob are deliberately discarded by-products of food production, and both may be used as fuel, enhancing their potential for preservation. In the cases to be discussed, nutshell and maize cob are not included in the seed count calculations.

Ubiquity measures the percentage of proveniences in which each taxon occurs (Popper 1988). Each unique feature is regarded as one provenience, regardless of how many samples of its fill or how many levels were examined. In calculating ubiquity, taxa are scored on presence, regardless of their counts or weights. Ubiquity analysis is based on two premises. First, those taxa that were more prevalent at the site at the time of its occupation are expected to be present in a greater number of archaeological proveniences than are those that were less common. Second, each provenience is independent. Accordingly, if a taxon preserves poorly and yet was ubiquitous at the time of deposition, it is still possible that a single element of it will survive in each of multiple contexts, even though its gross count or weight will be insignificant (Johannessen 1984; Yarnell 1982).

Ubiquity does not provide absolute measures of taxon magnitude, but it is a reliable measure of relative significance. An important characteristic of this technique is that the score of one taxon does not affect the score of another, and thus the tallies of different taxa can be evaluated independently (Popper 1988). A disadvantage of ubiquity analysis is that it can be affected by disposal patterns. For example, if a taxon is more likely to appear in features than postmolds for any reason, and trash pits are larger but fewer in number in one time period versus another, the ubiquity score of this taxon will be lower in the period with fewer trash disposal areas. If the ubiquity score of one or more taxa departs from the trends revealed by other methods of inquiry, variations in disposal patterns should be considered. In the 2001 Cussetuh project, no postmolds were analyzed (Redwine et al. 2004; Smith 2004), so any remains that would be differentially deposited in such features will be absent or underrepresented.

Ubiquity aids in the reconstruction of catchment characteristics, recognition of activity areas, and discernment of disposal patterns. Ubiquity is useful only at sites where multiple features are studied, and its utility increases proportionally with the number of distinct proveniences under consideration. In other words, a ubiquity of 100 percent is meaningless if there is only one feature. I next address two strategies that can be used under any circumstances.

Density is a calculation of count per liter of sediment floated. By using the total amount of sediment in the sorted sample as the common denominator, macroflora from samples of varying sizes can be compared on an equal basis. Mean counts of seeds, nut shell, grass stem, cane stem, bark, tuber, and unidentifiable macroplant fragments are used as a measure of the abundance of each taxon. Unless soil sample sizes are based on geometric calculations of the soil *in situ*, rather than by physically measuring the sample in a device like a marked bucket, density is the least reliable of the assessment tools used in this study. Soil samples measured after excavation can vary according to the texture of the soil, the amount of compression used in filling the bucket, and the skill of the excavator. Although results can be affected by the technique used to measure the samples, intrasite measures should be reasonably uniform.

Ratios focus attention on two mutually exclusive variables and can be used either to assess the effects of different preservation contexts or to identify different use contexts (Miller 1988). Wood charcoal is often used in lieu of soil volume as the normalizing variable to quantify density for proveniences where it is reasonably certain that charcoal represents ordinary household fuel (Miller 1988). Wood charcoal is used to control for the likelihood of preservation in the Cussetuh and Buzzard's Roost projects. If seeds are preserved accidentally, "a greater concentration of burned seeds in a volume of charcoal should signify increased use" (Bohrer 1988). If fuel use has been fairly constant over time at any given site, macroplant remains should exist in proportion to the intensity of activities involving fire at that site. This presumes that both wood charcoal and other macroplant remains were subject to similar depositional and postdepositional forces (Asch and Asch 1985; Pearsall 1989). By comparing quantities of other taxa to wood charcoal, the use of the former may be tracked over time or compared across space in a relative sense. In order to avoid the mixing of building materials and fuel, only the contents of features other than postmolds are used in calculating these ratios in the Cussetuh site analysis. Absolute numbers are not important; rather, ratios are considered (Miller 1988).

Proportions or percentages are frequently employed to standardize sample contents and to facilitate the evaluation of relative importance among taxa. Within each taxonomic division, the proportion of each component is calculated as a means to explore the relative contributions of each taxon to the category.

Wood charcoal is examined in an effort to reconstruct paleoenvironment, as an independent measure of anthropogenic effects on the environment, and in an effort to discern patterns of selective resource exploitation. The first two of these goals is addressed in Chapter 2, this volume, and the final goal is considered here.

Unless otherwise specified, wood count, rather than weight, is used to evaluate the significance of taxa in these analyses. This is done in recognition of the varying properties of different wood types, which result in more or less thorough combustion and ultimately differential archaeological preservation (Bonhage-Freund 2005).

This concludes the discussion of methodology and analytical tools used in the Buzzard Roost, Cussetuh town, and Ochillee Creek paleoethnobotanical analyses. Discussions of the individual projects follow.

CUSSETUH (9CE1)

The Cussetuh Town site (9CE1) served as a ceremonial center. As a function of the annual ceremonial cycle, the town experienced regular fluctuations in population size. This paleoethnobotanical analysis extends our knowledge of that annual cycle.[1]

Archaeobotanical and zooarchaeological evidence was extracted from 77 flotation samples representing 26 unique features (Bonhage-Freund 2003, 2004). These samples represent all feature categories except postmolds. Preservation of macroplant remains was fair, but no controls, such as Gail Wagner's (1982) poppy seed test, were used to assess the recovery rate of the flotation system. Nevertheless, modern pigweed (*Amaranthus* sp.) and carpetweed (*Mollugo* sp.), among the smallest size classes of seeds anticipated in these samples, were noted in up to 49% of the samples. However, the assemblage contains no modern or archaeological examples of the very smallest seeds, such as rush (*Juncus* sp.) or tobacco (*Nicotiana* spp.). There is no way to determine if these smallest seeds were actually absent, or if they were lost in processing (Table 6.2).

Nut mast was an important food in Cussetuh Town. Nutshell/nutmeat have 54% ubiquity, 0.269 density, and a 1.25 ratio of count per g of wood charcoal. Hickory shell or nutmeat (*Carya* spp.) represents 66% of the nut remains and has 39% ubiquity. While beechnut (*Fagus grandifolia*) makes up 24% of the nutshell, it has only 12% ubiquity compared to acorn (*Quercus* spp.), which has

Table 6.2: Summary of macroplant remains from historic Creek Indian sites.

		9CE1 (Bonhage-Freund 2003)	
		Count	Percent
Domesticated Grains and Other Crops			
European cereals (unidentified)		19	43.18%
c.f. barley	*Hordeum vulgare*	1	2.27%
maize kernel	*Zea mays*	23	52.27%
sumpweed	*Iva annua var. macrocarpa*		
maygrass	*Phalaris sp.*	1	2.27%
Total		44	17.19%
Other Domesticated Crops			
cotton	*Gossypium hirsutum*		
bean	*Phaseolus vulgaris*		
squash seed, stem, rind	*Cucurbitae*		
bottle gourd	*Lagineria siceraria*		
Total		0	
Other Grasses			
c.f. manna grass	*Glyceria sp.*	3	60.00%
grass, Panicoid - seeds	*Panicum sp.*		
grass, unidentified - seeds	*Gramineae*	2	40.00%
Total		5	1.95%
Starchy and Oily Seeds			
ragweed	*Ambrosia artemisiaefolia and c.f. Ambrosia artemisiaefolia**	3	4.35%
pigweed	*Amaranthus sp.*	3	4.35%
goosefoot / chenopod - wild type	*Chenopodium sp.*	5	7.25%
goosefoot - wild type	*c.f. Chenopodium album*	1	1.45%
sumpweed	*Iva c.f. fructescens*	1	1.45%
smartweed	*Polygonum c.f. hydropeperoides*	6	8.70%
knotweed	*Polygonum sp.*	48	69.57%
knotweed family	*Polygonaceae*	2	2.90%
bean, wild	*Fabaceae*		
Total		69	26.95%

9TR41 (Bonhage-Freund 1999)		9TR54 (Bonhage-Freund 1999)		9CE379 (O'Steen & Raymer 1999)		1RU63 (Newsom and Ruggiero 1998)	
Count	Percent	Count	Percent	Count	Percent	Count	Percent
1		22					
2		37		5		228	
		1					
4		66					
7	22.58%	126	31.19%	5	12.50%	228	84.76%
		2					
		2				6	
		1				5	
						1	
0		5	1.24%			12	4.46%
						1	
3		3				2	
3	9.68%	3	0.74%			3	1.12%
1							
2		1				5	
		2					
						6	
6	19.35%	3	0.74%			11	4.09%

Continued on the next page

Table 6.2: *Continued*

	9CE1 (Bonhage-Freund 2003)	
	Count	Percent
Greens (Pot Herbs)		
dock *Rumex sp.*		
goosefoot /chenopod - wild type *Chenopodium sp.*	x	
goosefoot - wild type *c.f. Chenopodium album*		
mustard *Brassica sp.*	1	3.13%
pepperweed *Lepidium virginicum*	1	3.13%
pokeweed *Phytolacca americana*	20	62.50%
purslane *Portulaca oleraceae*	10	31.25%
Total	32	12.50%
Medicinal Plants		
copperleaf *Acalypha sp.*		
mouse-ear chickweed *c.f. Cerastium sp.*		
dogwood *Cornus sp.*		
doveweed *Croton sp.*		
spurge *Euphorbia maculata*	15	50.00%
spurge *Euphorbia sp.*	6	20.00%
bedstraw *Galium spp.*		
lettuce, wild *Lactua sp.*		
false mallow *Malvastrum sp.and c.f. Malvastrum sp.*	5	16.67%
clover *Melilotus sp.*		
beebalm *Monarda punctata*	1	3.33%
c.f. checkermallow *Sidalcea sp.*	1	3.33%
greenbriar *Smilax sp.*		
clover *Trifolium sp.*	1	3.33%
arrowwood *Viburnum sp.*		
cocklebur *Xanthium sp.*	1	3.33%
Total	30	11.72%
Fruits and Edible Pods		
honey locust pod *Gledetsia triancanthos*	2	2.94%
serviceberry *Amelanchier sp.*		
persimmon *Diospyros virginiana*		
huckleberry *Gayylussacia sp.*		
mulberry *Morus sp.*		

9TR41 (Bonhage-Freund 1999)		9TR54 (Bonhage-Freund 1999)		9CE379 (O'Steen & Raymer 1999)		1RU63 (Newsom and Ruggiero 1998)	
Count	Percent	Count	Percent	Count	Percent	Count	Percent
				19			
x		x				x	
1		113					
		1				8	
1	3.23%	114	28.22%	19	47.50%	8	2.97%
1		49					
						1	
1							
3		4					
		1				1	
		4					
5							
		1					
		3					
1							
11	35.48%	62	15.35%			2	0.74%
		2					
				1+		1	
				1		1	

Continued on the next page

Table 6.2: *Continued*

		9CE1 (Bonhage-Freund 2003)	
		Count	Percent
maypops	*Passiflora incarnata*	23	33.82%
peach	*Prunus persica*	1	1.47%
blackberry/raspberry	*Rubussp.*	40	58.82%
elderberry	*Sambuccus canadensis*	1	1.47%
grape/ grape family	*Vitaceae*		
c.f. fleshy fruit, small		1	1.47%
Total		68	26.56%
Other Economically Useful Taxa			
sedge	*Carex sp.*	5	
flatsedge	*Cyperus sp.*	2	
nutsedge	*Scleria sp.*	1	
Total		8	3.13%
Total Seeds Only		256	

		Count	wt (g)
Maize Cob, cupules	Zea mays	113	0.7

Nutshell		Count	Percent
hickory	*Carya sp.*	88	66.17%
hazel nut	*Corylus americana*	1	0.75%
beech	*Fagus grandifolia*	32	24.06%
walnut family	*Juglands sp.*	3	2.26%
oak acorn	*Quercus sp.*	9	6.77%
Total		133	100.00%

Miscellaneous Macroplant Remains			
maple seed	*Acer sp.*		
bark		2	
capsule			
composite family	Compositae		
grass stem fragments		5	
miscellaneous plant tissue (unidentifiable)		4	
pine cone			

9TR41 (Bonhage-Freund 1999)		9TR54 (Bonhage-Freund 1999)		9CE379 (O'Steen & Raymer 1999)		1RU63 (Newsom and Ruggiero 1998)	
Count	Percent	Count	Percent	Count	Percent	Count	Percent
		32				2	
1		47		14**+		x	
2		2					
		2				1	
		6					
3	9.68%	91	22.52%	16	40.00%	5	1.86%
		1					
0							0.00%
31		404		40		269	100.00%
wt (g)		wt (g)		ct	wt (g)	ct	wt (g)
29.07		319.14		219	2.76	50061	>874.4
Count	Percent	Count	Percent	ct	%		
37	88.10%	882	93.73%			229	95.42%
5	11.90%	14	1.49%				
		45	4.78%			11	4.58%
42	100.00%		100.00%	284		240	100.00%
		1					
		77		0.32			
		1					
		1					
2		29		12			
		2					
				3			

Continued on the next page

Table 6.2: *Continued*

	9CE1 (Bonhage-Freund 2003)	
	Count	Percent
plant fibers (not identified)	4	
testa or seed coat	26	
thorn or plant hair	5	
twine	2	
nutlet, not identifiable	2	
seed, unknown/unidentified	21	
stem	1	
rhizome		
root/tuber	2	
	74	
		wt (g)
Resin	318	4.36
wood charcoal		107.7
partly charred wood		2.59
uncharred wood		1.65

* "c.f." (compares favorably to) indicates a strong similarity to a taxon, but not a firm identification
**fragments of one stone
"*"=recovered in excavation

27% ubiquity but makes up only 7% of the nutshell. The balance of nut remains consists of walnut family husk (*Juglandaceae*) and hazelnut (*Corylus* sp.), which have 12% and 4% ubiquity, respectively.

Maize was the staple agricultural crop for the Cussetuh Town population (Foster 2003b). Overall, domesticated grains scored 48% ubiquity, 0.315 density, and have a 1.446 ratio of count per g of wood charcoal. Maize (*Zea mays*) kernels and cob, including cupules, made up about 86% of the cultivated grain assemblage. If only the kernels are considered, maize represents 52% of the cultivated cereals and scores 28% ubiquity. European cereal grains, together with possibly barley (*Hordeum vulgare*), comprises 45% of the cereal assemblage but scores only 12% ubiquity. A single maygrass grain (*Phalaris* sp.) is the only other evidence of possible crops.

Wild or naturally occurring grasses are poorly represented at Cussetuh. Overall wild grasses score 8% ubiquity, 0.01 density, and gave a 0.046 ratio of

9TR41 (Bonhage-Freund 1999)		9TR54 (Bonhage-Freund 1999)		9CE379 (O'Steen & Raymer 1999)		1RU63 (Newsom and Ruggiero 1998)	
Count	Percent	Count	Percent	Count	Percent	Count	Percent
		2					
						1	
		1					
2		3		1		3	
						1	
		1					
4		35					
8		153					
	wt (g)				wt (g)	wt (g)	
					4.69		
9TR41 and 9TR54 combined	660.13					>92.8	
					383.32		

count per gram of wood charcoal. These calculations are based on only five seeds of manna grass (*Glyceria* sp.) and grasses not identifiable to genus.

Wild or naturally occurring starchy seeds other than grasses yield scores of 27% ubiquity, 0.131 density, and a ratio of 0.605 per gram of wood charcoal. Smartweed (*Polygonum* c.f. *hydropeperoides*), knotweed (*Polygonum* sp.), and their relatives (Polygonaceae), together dominate the noncultivated starchy seed assemblage (82%). Ragweed (*Ambrosia artemisiaefolia* and c.f. *Ambrosia artemisiaefolia*), pigweed (*Amaranthus* sp.), goosefoot (*Chenopodium alba, Chenopodium* sp), and nondomesticated sumpweed (*Iva* c.f. *fructescens*) are all represented by small numbers of seeds. While the goosefoot and pigweed recovered from these samples do not meet the profile of the domesticated species, it is possible that they were encouraged taxa (Bonhage-Freund 1997; Lopinot and Woods 1993).

Greens or potherbs have fair representation, achieving an overall 27% ubiquity score, 0.066 density, and a ratio of 0.307 per g of wood charcoal. Pokeweed (*Phytolacca americana*) represents the greatest proportion of this category at 62%, and purslane (*Portulaca oleraceae*) is second at 31%. One seed each of wild mustard (*Brassica*), buttercup (*Ranunculus* sp.), and pepperweed (*Lepidium virginicum*) each represents 3% of the potherb assemblage. Purslane is not only edible but may have played a role in the agricultural system. Those modern Pueblo Indians who use traditional farming methods encourage purslane to grow among the maize. It helps to maintain moisture in the soil and is itself harvested as a crop (Martinez, personal communication, 1991; Bonhage-Freund 1997). Buttercup is an alien plant that has become naturalized (Fernald 1950; Moerman 1998).

Evidence of a limited number of fleshy fruits and edible pods is present, scoring 38% ubiquity, 0.135 density, and a ratio of 0.622 per g of wood charcoal. Blackberry/raspberry (*Rubus* sp.) seeds (58.8%) dominate this category. Complementing this discovery are six thorns recovered in two features. While these are not included in the fleshy fruit analysis, they do compare favorably to the thorns of raspberries and were recovered from the same features. Maypop (*Passiflora incarnata*) seeds are second most abundant in this category (33.8%). Two fragments of probable honey locust pod (*Gleditsia triacanthos*) (2.9%) were recovered, as was one elderberry seed (*Sambuccus* sp.) (1.5%). A single unidentifiable fleshy fruit (1.5 × 1.25 mm) was also retrieved but is not included in these calculations. All of these are wild taxa that flourish in edge zones and old fields. A single fragment of peach stone (*Prunus persica*) (1.5%) is the only domesticated fleshy fruit noted in these samples.

Overall, medicinal plants have a ubiquity of 19%, density of 0.052, and a ratio of 0.23 per g wood charcoal. One checkermallow (*Sidalcea* sp.), native to the Southwest and Mexico, is an unexpected find, and the identification should be regarded as tentative. In its natural range it is used to treat an internal injury (Moerman 1998). Spurge (*Euphorbia maculate, Euphorbia* sp.), beebalm, clover, and cocklebur all have medicinal uses (Moerman 1998) and are present in small amounts in assemblages.

Some plants have multiple common economic uses so it is difficult to classify them under another heading. Multiple-use plants have a ubiquity of 19%, density of 0.018, and a ratio of 0.05 per g of wood charcoal. Sedge seeds (*Carex* sp.) make up 56% of this category. This taxon was used as medicine and in basketry (Moerman 1998). Flatsedge, nutsedge/nut-rush (*Scleria* sp.), and bulrush (*Scirpus* sp.) seed were also noted. Southeastern tribes used various of these species as medicine and building materials and to weave matting (Moerman 1998). All of these seeds are few in number, with raw counts ranging from one to five.

Four plant fibers, five grass stem fragments, and two roots or twine may be related to weaving of mats or baskets or creation of smoke or fire or may be incidental inclusions. Bark may be part of the fuel, but it was sometimes used to deliberately create smoke, to line pits, and as building and roofing material. Some species of bark may have been collected for medicinal preparations (Moerman 1998).

Trace amounts of unidentifiable plant and two unidentified nutlets were found. Fifty-four unidentifiable seeds or seed coats (*testa*) or fragments of seeds or seed coats are included in the assemblage. These unidentified seed remains have no distinguishing characteristics that would aid in their identification. One stem fragment, measuring approximately 2 by 0.33 mm, is likely from a small fruit such as elderberry. Elderberry was not found in the same feature as this stem, but it was identified at the site. Nine small root or tuber fragments were recovered (19% ubiquity), while greens and medicinal plants have a moderate presence.

Wood remains are analyzed independently of other macroplant remains. One purpose of this separate treatment of wood is to provide an independent measure of anthropogenic effects on the environment, and a second is to discern patterns of selective resource exploitation. Wood data are summarized in Table 6.3.

Wood charcoal generally comprises the bulk of any light fraction flotation sample from open sites, and this was true in all of the Cussetuh samples. Every feature contained wood charcoal, although not every sample did. A total of 107.65 g was recovered. A minimum of 318 fragments of resin (ca 4.36 g) was recovered from 20 unique features, a ubiquity of 76.9%. Resin is often associated with burned pine (*Pinus* sp.) in southeastern sites. The ratio of resin to wood charcoal is 2.95 fragments per g of wood charcoal, or 0.041 g of resin per g of wood charcoal. It is not possible to determine if the resin is solely derived from pine, but it is likely that most is from that source.

An attempt was made to identify 1,739 wood charcoal fragments, and of these, 1,729 fragments were identifiable to some extent. The distribution of identified wood charcoal is 80.16% conifer or softwood, 16.89% dicot or hardwood, 2.95% monocot. In addition, there are unidentified bark, unidentified root, and identifiable wood charcoal. While softwoods dominate the assemblage by count, there is more variety among the hardwood.

As in most southeastern sites, pine at 82.57% of the identified wood charcoal clearly dominates the wood charcoal assemblage (Table 6.3). Oak, the dominant hardwood, at 9.59% is the only other taxon present in significant quantities. While the early wood is occluded by tyloses, as in white oak, the late wood resembles red oak. Therefore, all oak is considered as one category in the analysis. In addition to oak, there are 12 unique hardwood genera (Table 6.3). Most of the oak at this site has characteristics of both red and white oak groups.

Table 6.3: Wood charcoal identifications, Cussetuh, Buzzard Roost, Ochillee Creek, and `

	Cussetuh Town (9Ce1) (Bonhage-Freund 2003)	Cussetuh Town (9Ce1) (Bonhage-Freund 2003)	Proportion of specifically identified wood.	Buzzard Roost (9Tr41) (Bonhage-Freund 1999)	Buzzard Roost (9Tr41) (Bonhage-Freund 1999)
Monocot					
cane (*Arundinaria* sp.)	7		0.42%	9	
maize stem (c.f. *Zea mays*)	12		0.72%		
rattan (c.f. *Calamus* sp.)				1	
Unidentified monocot; c.f. monocot	32				
Proportion of all charcoal identified to general or specific category		2.95%			0.87%
Hardwood					
ash (*Fraxinus* sp.)	4		0.24%	3	
basswood (*Tillia americana*)	3		0.18%		
blackgum (*Nyssa sylvatica*)	5		0.30%		
buckeye (*Aesculus* sp.)	22		1.33%		
cherry / plum - wild (*Prunus* sp.)				3	
chestnut (*Castanea dentata*)					
elm / hackberry (*Ulmus* sp. / *Celtis* sp.)	11		0.66%	2	
hickory (*Carya* spp.)	14		0.84%	11	
holly (*Ilex* sp.)	5		0.30%		
honey locust (*Gledetsia triancanthos*)	1		0.06%		
maple (*Acer* sp.)	9		0.54%		
ALL oak combined (*Quercus* sp.)			9.59%		
oak (*Quercus* sp.)	1				
oak, red (*Quercus rubra*)	115			44	
oak, white (*Quercus alba*)	44			44	
oak bark (*Quercus* sp.)					
persimmon (*Diospyros virginiana*)					
poplar (*Populus* sp.)	4		0.24%		
sumac (*Rhus* sp.)					
sweetgum (*Liquidambar styraciflua*)					
sycamore (*Platanus occidentalis*)	9		0.54%	2	

Yuchi Town

Proportion of wood identified to at least the family.	Buzzard Roost (9Tr54) (Bonhage-Freund 1999)	Buzzard Roost (9Tr54) (Bonhage-Freund 1999)	Proportion of wood identified to at least the family.	Ochille Creek (9Ce379) (O'Steen and Raymer 1999)	Ochille Creek (9Ce379) (O'Steen and Raymer 1999)	Proportion of wood identified to at least the family.	Yuchi Town (1Ru63) (Newsom and Ruggiero 1998)
0.91%	11		1.02%				x
	16						
			2.15%			0.00%	
0.30%				1		0.30%	
				2		0.60%	
	1		0.09%				
0.30%							x
	5		0.46%				
0.20%	8		0.74%	1		0.30%	
1.12%	33		3.06%	13		3.88%	x
				2		0.60%	
8.94%			12.60%			8.66%	
	2			6			x
	81			4			63
	36			19			x
	17						
							x
	1		0.09%				
	2		0.19%				
0.20%			0.00%				

Continued on the next page

Table 6.3: *Continued*

	Cussetuh Town (9Ce1) (Bonhage-Freund 2003)	Cussetuh Town (9Ce1) (Bonhage-Freund 2003)	Proportion of specifically identified wood.	Buzzard Roost (9Tr41) (Bonhage-Freund 1999)	Buzzard Roost (9Tr41) (Bonhage-Freund 1999)
tulip tree (Liriodendron tulipfera)					
walnut, black (*Juglans nigra*)	1		0.06%	10	
walnut family (*Juglandaceae*)	16		0.97%		
unidentified diffuse porous	3			6	
unidentified ring porous	23			4	
unidentified hardwood	2			147	
Proportion of all charcoal identified to general or specific category		16.89%			24.13%
Softwood / Conifer					
baldcypress (*Taxodium distichum*)	2		0.12%		
eastern redcedar (*Juniperus virginianum*)	4		0.24%		
ALL pine combined (*Pinus* sp.			82.57%		
pine (*Pinus* sp.)	1254			731	
pine, eastern white (*Pinus strobus*)					
pine, southern yellow (*Pinus* sp.)				91	
pine bark (*Pinus* spp.)	115			34	
conifer, other unidentified	11			2	
Proportion of all charcoal identified to general or specific category		80.16%			75.00%
TOTAL of charcoal identified to a general or specific category	1729	100.00%		1144	100.00%
TOTAL of charcoal identified to at least the family	1658		99.94%	984	
Other					
unidentifiable wood charcoal					
unidentified charred bark	1				

Proportion of wood identified to at least the family.	Buzzard Roost (9Tr54) (Bonhage-Freund 1999)	Buzzard Roost (9Tr54) (Bonhage-Freund 1999)	Proportion of wood identified to at least the family.	Ochille Creek (9Ce379) (O'Steen and Raymer 1999)	Ochille Creek (9Ce379) (O'Steen and Raymer 1999)	Proportion of wood identified to at least the family.	Yuchi Town (1Ru63) (Newsom and Ruggiero 1998)
	1		0.09%				
1.02%	8		0.74%				
	5		0.46%				
	1						x
	10						
	148			12			x
		28.63%			17.29%		
	2		0.19%				
86.99%			80.26%				
	668			287		85.67%	>50
	138						
	60						
		69.22%			82.71%		
	1254	100.00%		347	100.00%		>113
100.00%	1079		100.00%	335		100.00%	
	38			16			
	103						

Continued on the next page

Table 6.3: *Continued*

	Cussetuh Town (9Ce1) (Bonhage-Freund 2003)	Cussetuh Town (9Ce1) (Bonhage-Freund 2003)	Proportion of specifically identified wood.	Buzzard Roost (9Tr41) (Bonhage-Freund 1999)	Buzzard Roost (9Tr41) (Bonhage-Freund 1999)
unidentified charred root	9				
resin	318/4.36g			72	
charred pine scales and needle attachment points				2	
PARTLY CHARRED WOOD					
pine (*Pinus* sp.)	12				
UNCHARRED WOOD					
bark	1				
unidentified	3				
pine (*Pinus* sp.)	109				

Uncharred macroplant remains are generally not considered to be of archaeological origin in prehistoric sites. However, in more recent sites, particularly in historic sites, uncharred plant remains often dominate the assemblage (Bonhage-Freund 2002; Pluckhahn 2003). Radiocarbon dating would be the only reliable way to ascertain the age of these wood fragments. All of the partially charred and uncharred wood is pine, except for one fragment of bark and four fragments of hardwood.

Discussion

Complementary results are observed for proportion, ubiquity, density, and wood charcoal ratio. All of these measures indicate that nutshell and domesticated cereal grains played a prime role in subsistence, but wild collected seeds, fruits, pods, and greens contributed to the diet. Nuts and cultivated grains are the most abundant macroplant remains in the Cussetuh Town assemblage.

Hickory (*Carya* sp.) shell or nutmeat accounts for two-thirds of the nutshell assemblage, with oak acorn, beechnut, walnut family, and hazelnut accounting

Proportion of wood identified to at least the family.	Buzzard Roost (9Tr54) (Bonhage-Freund 1999)	Buzzard Roost (9Tr54) (Bonhage-Freund 1999)	Proportion of wood identified to at least the family.	Ochille Creek (9Ce379) (O'Steen and Raymer 1999)	Ochille Creek (9Ce379) (O'Steen and Raymer 1999)	Proportion of wood identified to at least the family.	Yuchi Town (1Ru63) (Newsom and Ruggiero 1998)
139							
11							

for the remainder. This abundance of hickory is a common archaeological pattern. Hickory nutshell was sometimes used as fuel in the Southeast, affording it more opportunities for preservation.

In contrast, acorn and other thin-shelled nuts are usually underrepresented in the archaeological record because they do not preserve well. The small amount of acorn (n=9) relative to beechnut (n=32) is unusual, considering that acorns are repeatedly mentioned in period documents (Table 6.1). Acorn and beechnut have similar potential for preservation. It is likely that this greater showing of beechnut results from sampling error as oaks are abundant in the wood charcoal assemblage while beech is not.

Maize is clearly a staple food, but it is difficult to evaluate the role of European cereal grains at this site. While maize kernels and European cereal grains are present in similar amounts, maize dominates by ubiquity and was probably a larger component of crops. This discrepancy may result from differential preservation. Maize cob persists longer and is more easily identifiable than the stalks and chaff of other cereals. Like hickory nutshell, maize cob was sometimes deliberately burned as fuel or for smudging, increasing the likelihood of its preservation.

The relative abundance of maize cob helps to confirm its importance and to demonstrate that it was locally grown. If the maize had been transported to Cussetuh town, it may have been removed from the cob to save weight. It is not clear if the European cereal grains were regularly included in the human diet or if they were used to feed the newly adopted European farm animals (Chapter 7). Raising these introduced crops may have been in the experimental stage or may have served to diversify crop production as a backup crop. These findings support early historical records describing field agriculture in the floodplain.

In addition to these field crops, small amounts of maygrass, pigweed and goosefoot provide limited evidence that traditional Eastern crops were raised as a hedge against maize crop failure (see Bonhage-Freund 1997 for discussion). Maygrass is a component of the pre-maize "Eastern Tradition"[2] suite of plants cultivated in the Midwest and Southeast (Smith 1992). It is virtually impossible to distinguish the cultivated maygrass from that which occurs naturally, so its placement here is arbitrary. Manna grass is the only "wild" or naturally occurring grass represented at Cussetuh Town.

Knotweeds and their relatives dominate the naturally occurring starchy seeds. The other four taxa making up this group are ragweed, pigweed, goosefoot, and sumpweed. All of these are pioneering genera and related to varieties domesticated and cultivated by Eastern people since the Archaic Period. As discussed earlier, pigweed and goosefoot are considered as starchy seed producers, but they actually would have been harvested twice. In spring the young shoots would be pinched back and used as greens, resulting in increased branching and seed production (Bonhage-Freund 1997; Martinez 1991, personal communication).

Starchy seeds, wild greens, fruits, and edible pods together made up a sizable portion of the potential diet of Cussetuh Town, adding variety and nutrients. Blackberry and maypops, prolific seed producers, are most abundant and were probably included in the diet. Elderberry also yields abundant seeds but is only 1% of the assemblage and perhaps an incidental inclusion. In contrast, the single fragment of peach stone comes from a single-seeded fruit and so is more significant. Peach is the only domesticated fruit noted here, and there is no evidence of the arbors and vineyards described in early historic accounts of nearby villages. In fact, peaches often escape and are quite weedy in nature (Strausbaugh and Core 1977) and may have been one of the "managed" taxon rather than one requiring much human intervention.

Based on living traditions, it is likely that old fields were managed to produce a succession of economically useful species as part of an integrated agricultural system (Alcorn 1984; Chagnon 1996; Foster 2003b) (see also Chapters 1 and 2). Useful plants such as blackberry/raspberry, elderberry, and even peach, as well as browse for game, would be encouraged to grow (Bonhage-Freund 1997; Scarry and Reitz 1990). This practice could account for the lag between the movement of agricultural fields and the abandonment of Cussetuh Town village. The macroplant assemblage indicates that medicines, cordage, basketry, construction, and fuel needs could be met by the local plant communities. Based on these data, a picture emerges of a mixed economy, combining agriculture, resource management, and the collecting of wild plants (Hann 1986; Moerman 1998).

Several small fragments of unidentified roots or tubers may also represent food or medicine. In particular, aquatic roots and tubers from cattails, American lotus, arrowhead, and several members of the sedge family were widely exploited in eastern North America. Sweet flag rhizomes were an important medicine.

The small number of seeds from plants of documented medicinal use suggests an intimate knowledge of and relationship to the local plant communities. Some plants used for food or for material culture might have doubled as medicines as well (Hann 1986; Moerman 1998).

Finally, it is worth noting some anticipated taxa that were not recovered at Cussetuh. There are no examples of squash (*Cucurbita* sp.) or bean (*Phaseolus* sp.) seeds, rind, or pods. Beans and squash would never have been as abundant as grain at a site and, by this relatively smaller presence, would have fewer opportunities to be incorporated into the archaeological record. Squash rind and bean pods are composted more readily than maize cobs so even their waste products have a lower chance of survival than maize. Thus absence does not preclude the use of these genera.

On the Alabama side of the Chattahoochee River, a recent study evaluated witness tree data (Black et al. 2002; Foster et al. 2004). While a total of 65 species were noted, overall the region was dominated by pine, oak, and hickory. Pine is the most abundant genus in the poorer and drier landscapes of the Coastal Plain and Piedmont, but it is negatively associated with the richer bottomlands (Black et al. 2002). Eighteen identifiable genera were in the wood charcoal assemblage. Both historic and modern descriptions of the Cussetuh site environs note pine forests along with floodplain hardwood forests and canebrakes.

Pine produces a hot, messy fire. It is ideal for smudging and warding off insects but not for cooking. However, it was plentiful, burns readily, and was probably used not only to start fires but as a fuel as well. Different types of pine have different burning characteristics, but it is not possible to differentiate the species in these samples to detect any preferences. Hardwoods of all kinds, but particularly oak, provide a long-burning coal with even heat. These hardwoods frequently burn to ash, in contrast to pine that often leaves some residual charcoal (Bonhage-Freund 2005), thus contributing to the superabundance of pine charcoal relative to hardwood charcoal. It is presumed that the hardwood charcoal of the Cussetuh samples was primarily fuel wood. Pine was commonly used as a construction wood throughout the Southeast even into early historic times (Bonhage-Freund 2005), but in this study there were no samples associated with construction so this usage cannot explain the high percentage of pine.

Locally collected plants provided cordage, dyes, and raw materials for basketry, matting, and pipe stems and hold potential for many other purposes. While the European cereal grains and peach support European contact described in Chapter 2, the Creek still had the resources to maintain an independent life.

There is evidence from the paleobotanical remains of year-round occupation at Cussetuh Town, as might be expected for an agricultural community. Agricultural people would have needed to maintain at least a skeleton population near the fields from spring through harvest to protect the crops. Maize would be planted in spring, as soon as the floods subsided. Some native groups planted two succeeding crops of maize that would bring the site occupation through to early fall (Swanton 1969). While the majority of identified taxa ripen in late summer, maygrass, which matures in late spring to early summer (Fernald 1950), was recovered. Other identified taxa ripen at various times from summer to fall, including goosefoot, peach, blackberry/raspberry, pigweed, and knotweed (Bonhage-Freund 1999; Ledbetter et al. 2002).

The presence of maize cob and nutshell suggest that these foods were processed nearby, and, being both heavy and also being staples, they likely were stored for winter use. The presence of maize indicates that Cussetuh was populated in both spring and late summer, when the crops needed attention in the form of planting, protecting, and harvesting. The plant remains found at Cussetuh Town ripen over the course of every season but winter.

There is evidence that the people of Cussetuh town interacted with people outside their immediate community. The possible presence of checkermallow may indicate long-distance contact with Southwestern native people. It is unknown from this study if this taxon slowly drifted into the Southeast along with maize or if it indicates direct trade.

European cereal grains and peach reflect direct or indirect contact with Europeans. The amounts or contexts of these taxa indicate that they supplemented native cultigens but did not replace them. While the Historic Creek at Cussetuh Town had incorporated into their subsistence system those articles of European culture that they found useful, they were not yet dependent upon them for subsistence. Creek people of Cussetuh Town engaged in a highly mixed economy, in every sense of the term. They farmed, harvested nut mast, and supplemented their diet with wild fruits, seeds, and possibly tubers. Their agriculture was based on at least three different traditions: Eastern, Meso-American/ Southwestern, and European. Evidence presented elsewhere in this volume indicates that hunting, animal husbandry, and trade were meshed with plant food production and acquisition.

BUZZARD ROOST (9TR41 AND 9TR54)

Buzzard Roost (Salenojuh) was a daughter village of Cussetuh, occupied in the late eighteenth century.[3] This archaeobotanical analysis is based on flotation and dry-screened samples taken from 80 postmolds and features associated with multiple structures and activity areas in two related sites, 9TR41 and 9TR54. Samples represent the full range of recorded features consisting of postmolds, fireplaces or hearths, smudge pits, trash pits, rectangular "cellars," and a variety of miscellaneous features, including pits and basins. The field crew used a Sandy System (Archmat 1995) to process 211 liters of flotation samples from 9TR41 and another 462 liters from 9TR54.

The gross volume and condition of macroplant remains from the Historic Creek occupation of these sites were reported to be satisfactory. No controls, such as Wagner's (1982) poppy seed test, were used to assess the recovery rate of the flotation system. However, samples contained modern and archaeological seeds even in the 0.25 mm geological sieve, suggesting that the flotation was efficient.

The overall macroplant recovery by count was higher at 9TR54 than at 9TR41, partly because more than double the quantity of soil was floated at the former site than at the latter. Even with this in mind, the disparity between the two assemblages is noteworthy but unexplained. A total of just 31 seeds and other small macroplant remains appeared in the Historic Creek samples of 9TR41, while those of 9TR54 produced 404.

The samples from the two sites contained a total of 660.14 g of wood charcoal ± 2mm. Light fractions yielded 374.86 g (57%) while heavy produced 285.28 g (43%). It is expected that most macroplant remains, including wood charcoal, should be recovered in the light fraction; nevertheless, large or waterlogged charcoal fragments may sink into the heavy fraction. When it is considered that there were 29 fewer heavy fractions than light in this study, the amount of wood charcoal recovered in heavy fractions is magnified. This may be explained by the fact that most of the wood charcoal recovered from the heavy fractions came from hearth features where larger fragments of wood charcoal tend to be relatively abundant. A visual inspection of the samples found them to be free of soil, supporting this explanation.

All of the nutshell classified as "walnut family" is likely hickory, as it is the most abundant member of that family in the region. In most cases the fragments are too small to hold the diagnostic traits needed to place them in the hickory category. With this fact in mind, it is probable that 100% of the nutshell recovered from 9TR41 was hickory shell. At a minimum, 88% was hickory and the remaining 12% a close relative like black walnut or butternut. By count, hickory also dominates the nutshell assemblage of 9TR54 and, combined with walnut family shell, comprises 95% of the nutshell. In contrast to 9TR41, acorn shell makes up a full 5% of the nutshell fragments from 9TR54. Overall, nutshell has a ubiquity of 34% at 9TR41 but is almost double that at 9TR54 with a ubiquity of 76%.

Agricultural crops comprised 22.58% of all identifiable seeds at 9TR41 and 32.43% at 9TR54 and also have high ubiquity at both sites. At 9TR41, 26.67% of features including postmolds, small and large pits, and smudge pits contained agricultural seeds or maize cob. At 9TR54, the overall ubiquity of agricultural taxa was 79%, coming from postmolds, fireplaces, small pits, root cellars, trash pits, large pits, "smudge pits," and additional miscellaneous features.

The assemblage featured maize, a Meso-American domesticate, maygrass, traditionally cultivated in the Eastern tradition, and two exotic taxa, European cereal grain and peach. Several additional taxa were recovered at 9TR54, including the balance of the well-known Meso-American trio of maize, common bean, and squash (rind); the Eastern tradition marshelder; and exotic cotton. The cotton seeds were found in a single trash pit feature and were not charred but were deteriorated. While it is possible that this taxon was cultivated by the Creek, these two seeds more likely represent modern contamination.

While the composition of these assemblages is not unusual, the proportions and ubiquity of the potential staple grains is noteworthy. Although maize cob and cupules score a ubiquity of 75.8% at 9TR54, they score only 39% at 9TR41. At each site, maygrass was recovered in two proveniences that contained no maize. This might indicate that maygrass was exploited prior to the first maize harvest of the year. Maygrass dominated maize by seed count, representing 52.6% of the combined seeds of the two sites compared to maize at 29.3%. The ubiquity of maygrass (7.3%) is higher than maize (4.8%) at 9TR41 but noticeably lower than maize kernels (31%) at 9TR54, where maygrass scores 6.9%. European cereal grains make up 17.2% of the combined agricultural seeds from the two sites but have very low ubiquity of 2.4% at 9TR41. At 9TR54, the 17.2% ubiquity of European cereal grains dominates maygrass but maintains a distance from maize.

Old World crops were well integrated into the Historic Creek agricultural system at Buzzard Roost, according to ubiquity evidence. European cereal grains appeared in 40% of the structural posts of 9TR54 and 3% of those at 9TR41, as well as in 100% of the large pits and 33% of the root cellars at 9TR54. Peaches are represented in 50% of the large features at 9TR41, fireplace/hearth (50%), small pits (20%), trash pits (60%), and miscellaneous pit features (50%) at 9TR54. Again, cotton's inclusion here is tenuous.

In the eastern United States, archaeological maize is generally forced into the three-part typology—Eastern Eight-Row ("flint" type), Midwestern Twelve-Row ("flour" type), or Northern American Pop—that Cutler and Blake (1976) developed using data from the Northeast and Midwest. More recent studies indicate great variability in the morphology of archaeological maize in the Southeast and call into question a strict tripartite classification system. However, a viable alternative has not yet been developed. Ethnohistoric accounts clearly indicate that multiple types of corn were cultivated in the Southeast, and sufficient variation in collections of southeastern cobs has been identified to verify this fact. Cob row number is considered to be a useful diagnostic trait in determining if more than one cultivar is present at a site (Scarry 1994).

Southeastern cob populations with mean row numbers greater than 10 are usually considered to be dominated or at least influenced by the Midwestern Twelve-Row varieties of corn (Scarry 1994). Those with mean cob rows fewer than 10 are considered more closely related to the original corn introduced into the East, the Eastern Eight-Row, or Northern Flint. Eastern Eight-Row tends to have small cupules and kernels, while Midwestern Twelve-Row has larger cupules and kernels. While the population of measurable cobs and kernels is small in the assemblage under investigation, it conforms more closely with the Midwestern Eight-Row.

At these two sites, not every maize cob fragment was measurable for every characteristic, and some cobs were too degraded for any meaningful assessment. Thus the total cobs evaluated in Table 6.4 are not uniform. Maize cobs were evaluated for row number, cob shape, and condition at time of processing. Maize kernel shape was also assessed, where possible.

Nine percent of the maize cobs possessed 8 rows (n=5), 21% had 10 rows (n=12), 47% had 12 rows (27), 12% had 14 rows (n=7), and 11% had 16 rows (n=6). Four cob shapes were noted, including straight, tapered, and cigar (Table 6.4). There were only two classifiable 8-row cobs, one tapered and the other cigar-shaped.[4] All of the 16-row and the majority of the cobs having 10, 12, and 14 rows were straight (cylindrical) in form. Twelve-row cobs showed the most variety, containing examples of all three shapes. One cigar-shaped 14-row cob was also noted. Overall, straight cobs dominated the assemblage (77%), with tapered (14%), and cigar-shaped (9%) a distant second and third.

Table 6.4: Summary of maize cob shape data from Buzzard Roost (9TR41 and 9TR54) (Bonhage-Freund 1999)

Row #	8	10	12	14	16	Total/%
Cob Shape						
Straight (cylindrical)		6	18	4	5	33/77%
Tapered	1	3	2			6/14%
Cigar	1		2	1		4/9%
Total	2	9	22	5	5	43/100%

Three main kernel shapes were present: round (n=9), crescent (n=6), dent (n=4), and heart-shaped (n=2). Most of these were distorted to some extent, so this discussion is meant only to give an idea of the potential variation in the assemblage rather than to give a definitive evaluation.

It is likely that the majority of this maize is either Midwestern Eight-Row type or is strongly influenced by that cultivar. However, 30% of the assemblage had 10 or fewer rows, making it more similar to the Eastern Eight-Row type. The kernels with an indentation caused by soft starch (dent) is diagnostic of flour corn, but the rounded kernels—especially high, rounded "popcorn-like" kernels—are more characteristic of the flint corns. It is likely that the Midwestern Twelve-Row corn dominates this assemblage but that at least one variety of Eastern Eight-Row was cultivated. Farmers planted a variety of grains, probably in an effort to hedge against unanticipated events and to take advantage of double-cropping opportunities in their fields. It is likely that they grew several types of maize for similar reasons.

Mature maize leaves little or no residue in the cob when the kernels are removed: maize cobs look "clean." Cobs that are processed green have bits of the outer layers of the kernels clinging to them where the kernels were cut or bitten off of the cob. Ninety-one percent of the maize cobs at these sites appear to have been processed "green" (n=49) whereas 9 percent were dry (n=5). This does not mean that all, or even most, of the crop was eaten at the time of harvest. It means only that cobs from green corn were used for fuel in the features at this site. Since most of the cobs came from smudge features, it is likely that these cobs were used soon after the kernels were removed and not dried for later burning. Fresh maize cobs would produce dense smoke, which is the purpose of smudge pits.

Unidentified wild grasses made up 9.68% of the identified seed assemblage at 9TR41 and just 0.74% at 9TR54. The prominence of this taxon at 9TR41 is likely an artifact of the small sample size. The proportion of wild grasses at 9TR54 is similar to that of the Cussetuh site.

Uncultivated starchy seeds represent 19.35% and 0.74% of the 9TR41 and 9TR54 seed assemblages, respectively. Pigweed and goosefoot are the only two starchy wild seeds found at 9TR41, although these plus goosefoot and knotweed are found at 9TR54. While all four of these taxa are related to cultivated Eastern tradition plants, the species recovered at these two sites were definitely not domesticated.

Greens or potherbs account for 3.23% of the 9TR41 seeds and 28.22% of the 9TR54 seeds. Pokeweed accounts for all but one of the seeds classified as greens at these two sites. Similar to pigweed and goosefoot, only the new shoots are edible and are harvested in early spring. Seeds are not produced until late summer or fall, when they are used as dyes and medicines. The fact that only a single purslane seed was recovered may reflect incomplete seed recovery. Purslane is a prolific seed producer, but these are among the smallest seeds anticipated.

Fleshy fruits are well represented at both sites, making up 9.68% of the identified seeds at 9TR41 and 22.52% at 9TR54. Again, the small sample skews the significance of the single fragment of peach pit and two blackberry/raspberry seeds identified in the 9TR41 samples. The larger 9TR54 assemblage is probably more representative with maypops and peach, each associated with agriculture jointly approaching 81% of this category. Small amounts of serviceberry, blackberry/raspberry, elderberry, and grape, all associated with abandoned agricultural fields, constitute the balance.

Medicinal plants represent a significant 35.48% of the 9TR41 identified seeds and 15.35% of those at 9TR54. Nine distinct species make up this category. Nevertheless, many other identified taxa may have been used medicinally on occasion (Moerman 1998).

Miscellaneous macroplant remains are those archaeological seeds and plant tissues that did not fit neatly into another category or had no diagnostic characteristics. These are mainly comprised of unidentifiable seeds, tissues, and roots or tubers. Miscellaneous plant remains are found at both sites. Root/tuber and unknown or unidentifiable seeds were noted at both sites. Two grass stem fragments, two unidentified seeds, and fragments of roots or tubers were recovered from 9TR41. In addition, bark, maple, capsule, composite family seed, leaf/shoot, and rhizome were recovered at 9TR54.

Discussion of Macroplant Remains Exclusive of Wood

There is unambiguous evidence of farming at these sites. European introductions, including a cereal grain, peach, and perhaps cotton, can be explained by the practice of agriculture. The New World "Three Sisters" of agriculture—corn, beans, and squash/gourds—are noted. Members of the Eastern horticultural tradition are also observed, including maygrass and marshelder. These data suggest that maygrass played an important seasonal role in the diet, making up a large proportion of the seeds but found in a limited number of features.

An abundance of maize cob indicates that maize was probably produced locally and was an important staple. Several different varieties of maize are represented in the assemblage, suggesting the planting and harvesting were staggered. In addition, different types of maize possess unique properties, filling different needs. Flour "corn" is soft and can be easily ground into meal, processed into hominy, or roasted. The flint types of maize, including "pop corn," when dry, store better and have greater resistance to insect damage. Mature dent kernels are dented because of having a soft flour heart and hard flint sides. These can be ground and in modern times are also fed to animals and processed into beer. *Zea mays* served many ritual functions among Historic Creek and other Indians. It may also have been used medicinally (Native Seeds/SEARCH 2005).

In addition to cultivated foods, a large amount of acorn, hickory, and walnut family shell signals the regular harvesting and processing of nuts. Multiple species of both hickory and acorn would have been locally abundant. Black walnut and butternut are seen in minor amounts. Wood charcoal evidence (below) indicates that black walnut was locally available. This nut is difficult and time-consuming to process and probably would have been a luxury. The scarcity of this nut in the assemblage indicates that at least some degree of selectivity was practiced in resource exploitation.

Wild fruits, including blackberry/raspberry, elderberry, grape, and maypop, as well as the seeds of potherbs such as goosefoot, pigweed, and purslane, and seed-bearers like knotweed, all suggest that wild foods added variety to the diet. Human activity including agriculture creates ideal conditions for these pioneering species (see Chapter 2). In summary, the macroplant remains provide evidence of both local plant food production and the harvesting of wild resources. The subsistence system was a complex balance of agriculture and the collection of wild foods.

Wood Charcoal and By-Products

Once again it is noted that wood charcoal dominates the archaeobotanical assemblage. Identifications were attempted on 2,552 randomly chosen charcoal fragments dating to the Historic Period. Pine predominates, but several hardwood taxa are represented. The majority of identifiable hardwood species were

Table 6.5: Wood charcoal from Buzzard Roost (9TR41) (Bonhage-Freund 1999)

9TR41	Postmolds				Features			
	20th	a1	s1	s2	s	lg	sm	tr
HARDWOOD								
ash	1						1	
black walnut	3		2				5	
cherry/plum	3							
elm/hackberry				2				
hickory				4			7	
oak, red			13	23		1	7	
oak, white			11	27			6	
sycamore	1		1					
diffuse porous							6	
ring porous				2			1	
hardwood, unidentifiable	30	6	19	71		9	12	
TOTAL HARDWOOD	38	6	47	130	0	10	45	0
% OF WOOD IN GIVEN CATEGORY	22.75%	16.20%	40.90%	19.40%		11.20%	59.20%	
CONIFER								
bark, pine (including pine bark scales)	27						2	
conifer		2						
pine	63	29	60	468	21	70	19	1
pine, Southern Yellow	38		2	48		3		
TOTAL CONIFER	128	31	62	521	21	73	21	1
% OF WOOD IN GIVEN CATEGORY	76.60%	83.70%	53.90%	77.80%	96.50%	82.00%	27.60%	100%

Continued on the next page

Table 6.5: *Continued*

9TR41	Postmolds				s	Features		
	20th	a1	s1	s2		lg	sm	tr
MONOCOT								
Cane	1			6	1	1		
c.f. rattan				1				
TOTAL MONOCOT	1	0	0	7	1	1	0	0
% OF WOOD IN GIVEN CATEGORY	0.60%			1.00%	4.50%	1.10%	0	0
MISCELLANEOUS								
unidentifiable			6	12		1	10	
TOTAL MISCELLANEOUS	0	0	6	12		1	10	0
% OF WOOD IN GIVEN CATEGORY	0		5.20%	1.80%		1.1	13.20%	0
TOTAL WOOD	167	37	115	670	22	85	76	1

KEY:
Postmolds: 20th=20th century
s1=structure 1   s2=structure 2   a1=activity area 1   lg=large
Feature pits: s=small   tr=trash   sm=smudge

Table 6.6: Wood charcoal from Buzzard Roost (9TR54) (Bonhage-Freund 1999)

9TR54	Postmolds				Features						
	rc	sl	u	rk	fp/h	s	lg	sm	tr	rc/rec	misc
HARDWOOD											
blackgum											1
black walnut							5	3			
butternut											
chestnut		5									
elm									7		
elm/hackberry									1		
hickory							3	26	4		
oak								2			
oak, bark					17						
oak, red	6	1				1	18	30	5	9	11
oak, white	3	8		2	5		5	60	49	2	2
sumac									1		
sweetgum		2									
tulip tree										1	
walnut family								4		1	
diffuse porous			1								
ring porous		5									
hardwood- unidentifiable or unknown		21	1		8	9	16	35	1	9	4
TOTAL HARDWOOD	9	42	2	2	30	10	47	164	113	22	18
% OF WOOD IN GIVEN CATEGORY	18.00%	27.30%	10.50%	8.00%	65.20%	29.40%	34.60%	34.10%	29.90%	19,30%	25%

Continued on the next page

Table 6.6: *Continued*

9TR54	Postmolds				Features						
	rc	sl	u	rk	fp/h	s	lg	sm	tr	rc/rec	misc
CONIFER											
bark, pine (including pine bark scales)	5		1	7	5		4		27	11	5
Eastern redcedar								2			
pine	25	101	13	14	5	23	70	126	173	70	48
pine, Eastern White								2	13		
pine, Southern Yellow	10	1			9		6	87	25		
TOTAL CONIFER	40	102	14	21	14	23	80	217	238	81	52
% OF WOOD IN GIVEN CATEGORY	80%	66.20%	73.70%	84.00%	30.40%	67.60%	58.80%	45.10%	63.00%	71.10%	73.60%
MONOCOT											
cane		3							6	2	
monocot stem or stem node		2					4	2	7	1	
TOTAL MONOCOT	0	5	0	0	0	0	4	2	13	3	0
% OF WOOD IN GIVEN CATEGORY	0	3.20%	0	0	0	0	2.90%	0.40%	3.40%	2.60%	0
MISCELLANEOUS											
bark	1	5		2	2	1	4	85	8	8	1
unidentifiable	1		3	2	2		1	13	6	8	1

TOTAL MISCELLANEOUS	1	5	3	2	2	1	5	98	14	8	2
% OF WOOD IN GIVEN CATEGORY	2.00%	3.20%	15.80%	8.00%	4.30%	2.90%	3.70%	20.40%	3.70%	7.00%	2.80%
TOTAL WOOD	50	154	19	25	46	34	136	481	378	114	72

KEY:

Postmolds:
un=unassociated or unassigned
sl= structure 1
rc=root cellar

Feature pits:
rk=rock hearth (probably archaic)
fp/h=fireplace or hearth
s= small
tr= trash
sm= smudge
lg= large
rc/rec=root cellar or rectangular pit
misc.= miscellaneous pits including basin

from the hickory, black walnut, and oak genera (Tables 6.5 and 6.6) reflecting the local forest composition.

In this analysis, wood counts, rather than weights, are used to evaluate the significance of taxa. This is done in recognition of varying properties of different wood types, resulting in more or less thorough combustion, and ultimately differential archaeological preservation (Bonhage-Freund 2005). In addition, much of the wood came from structural contexts, rather than fuel, which, as discussed, make it inappropriate for use as a normalizing variable.

Several fire-related features are among those sampled across the two sites. The typical fuels in smudge pits were pine, supplemented by oak (especially white oak group), cane, and bark. The two hearths at 9TR54 contain a mean of 65.5% hardwood. Pine and oak are "self-pruning" species. These data suggest that locally collected "dead and down" wood was the primary fuel.

Despite the diversity of specifically identified hardwood taxa, conifers dominate the archaeological assemblage by count, and pine accounts for 77% of all wood charcoal in postmolds. At 9TR41, 24.1% of the identifiable wood charcoal was hardwood, compared to 75.0% conifer and less than 1.0% monocot (Table 6.5). There is a similar situation at 9TR54 where 28.6% of the sample was assigned to the hardwood category and 69.2% to the conifer category (Table 6.6). Buzzard Roost postmolds hold tenuous clues to which woods were preferred for construction. At the two Buzzard Roost sites, pine made up between 54% and 80% of postmold wood charcoal.

The data from these Buzzard Roost sites suggest that the early Historic Creek population of the Flint River valley practiced a highly mixed economy. They farmed, harvested mast and wood from local forests, and supplemented their diet with wild fruits, seeds, and possibly tubers. Their farming was based in at least three different agricultural traditions—Eastern (maygrass, marshelder), Meso-American/Southwestern (corn, squash), and European (Eurocereal, peach, domesticated livestock). Maygrass might have served as a staple in spring, before the first maize harvest. Nuts were as much a staple as grains. Wild fruits and potherbs rounded out the diet, and wild plants were their medicines. In addition, local fauna were harvested and domesticated livestock were also kept (see Chapter 7). The European cereal grains, along with evidence presented elsewhere in this volume, hint that trade with non-Indians was an integral component of subsistence.

As is common throughout the Eastern Woodlands, people focused on local raw materials to satisfy economic needs. They harvested wild resources such as fire and construction wood, grass, sedge, and bark for use in basketry/matting, food smoking, as medicines, and for building materials. Most of the identified taxa are available in late summer or fall, probably for no other reason than this is a season of abundant harvest. Maygrass, which matures in late spring to early summer (Fernald 1950), and several other taxa mature at various times throughout the summer into fall. Further evidence of spring occupation is the fact that two features containing maygrass had no maize remains. Frequently, stored nut reserves were depleted by early spring, and there would be no remnants to be mixed with the new crop of maygrass. There is no winter crop, but corn and nuts are highly storable and would be bulky to transport over great distances. These factors lead to the conclusion that the site was permanently occupied. Local woods were used as fuel and for building material (Bonhage-Freund 1999). These two sites were almost certainly occupied throughout the year.

OCHILLEE CREEK SITE (9CE379)

The Ochillee Creek site (9CE379) is part of the Fort Benning research program.[5] The Phase II and limited Phase III research included paleoethnobotanical analysis of a single feature cluster from a late-eighteenth- to early-nineteenth-century Creek Indian context (Cowie 2001). This small farmstead offers insight into what was probably the basic unit of production in the Creek subsistence system, the family.

Seventeen 2–9-liter flotation samples, totaling 94 liters, were collected from the west sector of the site. These features included two fire-related features, four deep refuse-filled pits, and one shallow rectangular pit, among others. Prior to archaeobotanical analysis, each flotation sample was processed through a Shell Mound Archaeological Project–type flotation device (SMAP machine) similar to that described by Watson (1976). The heavy fraction trap was lined with 0.80 mm mesh. Also considered are macroplant remains recovered during the excavation of several features. The quantity of wood charcoal found in the greater than 2.0 mm portions of the light and heavy fractions indicates that flotation separation of samples from this site was excellent. Whereas 382.57 grams of wood charcoal was tabulated in the greater than 2.0 mm light fractions, the greater than 2.0 mm heavy fractions were found to contain only 0.75 grams of wood (Cowie 2001; O'Steen and Raymer 1999).

Despite the low seed count and lack of controls, recovery of carbonized macroplant remains was reported to be excellent. This assessment is based primarily on a high weight density of 4.08 grams of wood charcoal per liter of floated soil. Maize remains, in contrast, had a density of 0.31 grams or 2.34 fragments per liter of floated soil.

Maize cob, cupules, and kernel fragments are virtually the only evidence of agriculture at this site. A single peach pit (14 fragments) is the only other domesticate (Cowie 2001; O'Steen and Raymer 1999). Maize cupules and cob fragments exhibited 41% ubiquity across the sampled proveniences, while kernels were found in just 12% of the samples. All maize kernels, cob, and cupules considered jointly had a ratio of 2.383 units per liter of flotation, a ratio of 0.31 grams per liter of flotation, and 1 gram per 130 grams of wood charcoal.

No charred nutshell was recovered in either flotation or excavation. Dock and mulberry were the only nondomesticated species recovered (Table 6.2). These taxa provide tenuous evidence that collected wild plants contributed to subsistence. These species are among those favoring anthropogenic habitats including edge zones and old fields.

Nut mast is conspicuously absent from this assemblage. This fact, combined with a mostly spring through early summer seed assemblage, strongly suggests that this feature cluster was used on a seasonal basis. Mulberry and peach ripen in late spring through early summer (Strausbaugh and Core 1977). In order for dock to produce seeds from summer through fall, it would logically have been available for consumption as tender greens in the spring. In early summer it would already be producing the seeds that were not likely to have been eaten. In addition, Raymer (Cowie 2001; O'Steen and Raymer 1999) notes that the maize presence is low compared to contemporary Creek sites and that this finding also supports a seasonal use of this feature cluster.

It is possible that the western sector of the farmstead was used only as a kitchen in spring through early summer. This does not negate the possibility that different parts of the site were used in other seasons (Cowie 2001; O'Steen and Raymer 1999). Nevertheless, it seems likely that if that were the case, at least a few nutshell fragments would have made their way into the features during routine site maintenance (see discussion of ubiquity above).

The zooarchaeological assemblage at this site needs to be considered here, as it was much richer than and complementary to the archaeobotanical collection. The faunal assemblage represents approximately half wild and half domesticated species, but overall the wild species dominate slightly. There is evidence that while cattle and pigs were raised for trade, they were seldom eaten by the Creek (Piker 2004) (see also Chapter 7). The fact that just under half of the projected biomass base represented domesticated animals, about 30% of them cattle, implies that people were driven to slaughter their productive stock. These data complement the scarce floral remains to suggest a spring occupation because spring is often considered to be a "starving time" among Eastern Native Americans. Winter stores are depleted, and the shoots and fruits of spring provide few calories and protein.

Leslie Raymer (Cowie 2001; O'Steen and Raymer 1999) established that the wood charcoal consists of remnant fuel and, as such, may not be representative of the full spectrum of tree species growing in the area during the site's Creek occupation. Pine was recovered from every sample and accounts for 85.6% of the specifically identified wood charcoal, and it also was the most ubiquitous.

A mixture of oaks is the second most abundant at 8.6% of the identified wood species, followed by hickory at 3.8%. The remaining four taxa—ash, basswood, elm/hackberry, and maple—represent less than 1% each of the identified wood charcoal (Table 6.3).

Pine, oak, and hickory provided the bulk of fuel at this site. While pine was the most abundant taxon by all scores, oak scored 41% ubiquity and hickory scored 35% ubiquity. As discussed in Chapter 2, oak and hickory are often associated with fire-related features and, by modern standards, are excellent fuel woods. While quantities of these two taxa are relatively low, their ubiquity is quite a bit higher. It is likely that a scarcity of oak and hickory in the assemblage reflects in part the fact that these hardwoods tend to have more complete combustion than pine (Bonhage-Freund 2005). In addition, there may have been a preference for harvesting wood close to its consumption point. The prevalence of pine, in combination with the low species diversity, is indicative of a pine-dominated forest (Cowie 2001; O'Steen and Raymer 1999).

Discussion

As at Cussetuh Town and Buzzard Creek, occupants of the Ochillee Creek site probably incorporated both domesticated and wild gathered plants into their subsistence system. The maize-to-wood ratios and maize ubiquity are extremely low compared to those of contemporary Creek and Cherokee sites, and the only other domesticated species is peach (O'Steen and Raymer 1999; Raymer et al. 1997). However, Ochillee Creek represents a family farmstead. No other Creek farmsteads have been extensively analyzed from a paleoethnobotanical perspective.

In farmsteads in the Oconee drainage of Georgia in the Protohistoric Late Bell phase (circa 1580–1680), the ubiquity of maize is similar to that of Ochillee Creek (Kowalewski and Hatch 1991; Kowalewski and Williams 1989). For the Bell phase of the Sugar Creek site (9MG4), all agricultural taxa combined, primarily maize, had 46.1% ubiquity, while at the Lindsey site (9MG231) the ubiquity was 28.3%, compared to 41% at the Ochillee Creek site. In addition, the Ochillee Creek assemblage exhibits a density ratio of maize (0.536 count per liter of flotation) similar to the agricultural seeds (not including cob) of the Sugar Creek site (0.780 count per liter of flotation). The Lindsey site agricultural seed density ratio was 2.475 per liter of flotation, but that site displayed unusually good seed preservation (Bonhage-Freund 1997). The Ochillee Creek ratio of 0.31 grams of maize per liter of soil surpasses the Sugar Creek Bell phase ratio of 0.114 grams of maize cob per liter of soil and also that of the Lindsey site, 0.055 grams cob per liter of soil. Ochillee Creek's 1 gram of maize (primarily cob) per gram of wood charcoal surpasses the cob:wood ratio of both the Sugar Creek (0.010) and Lindsey (0.33) sites. If only seeds are considered, as they were in the Bell phase sites being discussed, maize kernels and peach stone fragments make up 47.5% of the recovered seeds at Ochillee Creek, compared to all cultigens at Sugar Creek (46.9%) and Lindsey (65.8%). But if the 14 peach pit fragments at Ochillee Creek are counted as one stone, this proportion drops to 15% (Bonhage-Freund 1997; O'Steen and Raymer 1999). The Ochillee Creek site lacks any evidence of either Eastern Tradition or European-introduced agricultural taxa other than peach.

At the Sugar Creek and Lindsey sites, evidence of successional management and both archaeobotanical assemblages include species that ripen in every season except winter. The presence of dock and mulberry at the Ochillee Creek site tenuously indicates that a similar system of field management was in place among Creek farmsteaders. In addition to semiwild crops for human consumption, old fields and edge zones provide forage for domesticated animals and for deer, both of which are represented in the faunal assemblage (O'Steen and Raymer 1999).

The one obvious difference between the subsistence evidence at this site and most other Southeastern sites of the same time period is a total absence of nutshell. This is strong evidence against a fall occupation of this site. At the very least, the western portion of the site was utilized primarily in spring through early summer and abandoned before fall.

From the paleoethnobotanical perspective, the subsistence system at the Ochillee Creek site was likely a complex mixture of agriculture, wild plant gathering, hunting, animal husbandry, and probable trade with Euro-Americans. While this supposition is based on limited evidence from one section of the site, in some important ways it compares favorably to early historic farmsteads elsewhere in Georgia. While this site's macroplant remains lack the variety of agricultural taxa found at contemporary Creek sites and at the two protohistoric farmsteads considered here, ubiquity, density, and two comparative ratios indicate that maize agriculture may well have been practiced at the site. At the very least, maize was the staple cereal food of the site's inhabitants, and the large amount of maize cob recovered relative to maize kernel points to its production in the not-too-distant vicinity. Unlike Creek town and village sites considered elsewhere in this chapter, the Ochillee Creek site produced no evidence of either traditional starchy and oily-seeded crops or European-introduced cereals. As is typical of Creek sites of this period, there is evidence of animal husbandry.

While agricultural crops are less evident at Ochillee Creek than at other contemporary Creek sites, this could be related to the fact that the population was also smaller there. The site's occupants, likely an extended family, may have produced only enough to feed themselves. Maize could have been stored in another part of the site. They would have shared the produce of the old fields with game and domestic animals. These animals, in turn, could serve as a critical food resource in the spring. Alternatively, agriculture might have been minimal or absent at the Ochillee Creek site. In the latter case, Ochillee Creek might represent a special-use site where domesticated animals were grazed in old fields in the spring.

In any case, the Ochillee Creek macroplant assemblage, lacking both nutshells and most postspring fruiting species, suggests that this western feature cluster was used seasonally, in spring and early summer (O'Steen and Raymer 1999). No archaeobotanical research was reported from test units from other areas of the site (Cowie 2001), so it cannot be certain whether activity shifted to other parts of the site in other seasons.

YUCHI TOWN (1RU63)

The Yuchi Town site (1RU63) represents one of the largest and most important Creek towns in the early eighteenth century (Boyd 1949). During excavations conducted in 1958, David W. Chase recovered charred maize cobs, unidentified nut hulls, and peach pits, along with a host of other artifacts and ecofacts (Foster 2004a; Weisman 2000). Michael R. Hargrave supervised the excavation of 77 cultural features in 1998, among them "several corn cob filled smudge pits" (Foster 2004a; Weisman 2000). Data from Yuchi town excavations are largely unreported. Between the 1958 and 1998 excavations, looters destroyed much of the site. Thus, the macroplant remains are from a skewed sample and must be viewed with caution.

As part of the 1998 project, Newsom and Ruggiero (1998) analyzed 48 archaeobotanical samples including 35 flotation samples and 13 direct excavated or *in situ* samples. The latter consisted of fill from several of the maize cob–filled smudge pits. Flotation samples were processed using a SMAP machine (Watson 1976; Pearsall 1989).

Four agricultural taxa are represented in this sample: maize, common bean, and two members of the gourd/squash family, *Cucurbita* spp. (pumpkin, squash) and gourd (*Lagineria siceraria*). Maize is the most ubiquitous of all taxa, having 84% ubiquity with more than 50,000 individual examples of maize identified. The remaining garden species have less than 4% ubiquity each.

Analysis of sample maize kernels and cob established the presence of at least two varieties. Twenty-seven whole or nearly complete maize kernels from three features were selected for analysis from among the 228 specimens recovered from seven features In addition, 56 cob midsections from four features, but primarily from Feature 12, were evaluated (Newsom and Ruggiero 1998 for more details and data). Maize remains were analyzed and classified following Bird (1994) and King (1987).

Maize kernels were either wedge- or crescent-shaped, but the crescent form predominated (n=24; 89%). The size and shape of the crescent-shaped kernels associate them with the Eastern Eight-Row ("Eastern Complex"). This type of maize has kernels with floury or flinty endosperm. Lee Newsom (Newsom and Ruggiero 1998) observed that this might be the maize mentioned in Frank Speck's (2004:18, 45) account of the Yuchi Indians.

The wedge-shaped kernels were restricted to a single feature. They represent 11.11% of all the classifiable kernels. While small in number, this morph type is significant because it compares favorably to the cultivar Hickory King that is seen in the Southeast beginning around A.D. 1700 (Wagner 1994:337). The Yuchi Town wedge-shaped kernels lack the shallow denting of the Hickory King but otherwise resemble that cultivar; thus an affiliation with this group is highly likely (Newsom and Ruggiero 1998).

Maize cob row number is predominantly eight- and ten-row, with nearly even proportions of each (43% eight-row, 55% ten-row), and a mean row number of 10.8. A single twelve-row cob came from a feature that is not associated with wedge-shaped kernels. In general, row pairing was moderate to strong. Median external cupule width for the entire assemblage is 7.87 mm (Newsom and Ruggiero 1998:202–204 for complete data). Jointly considering characteristics of kernels and cobs, Newsom (Newsom and Ruggiero 1998) believes that the majority of Yuchi Town maize is most consistent with a modified form of Eastern Eight-Row maize (Blake 1986).

Nutshell was nearly ubiquitous. Hickory shell scored 64% ubiquity, acorn 13%. Hickory is second only to maize in ubiquity. Small amounts of goosefoot and wild bean represent starchy seeds. The goosefoot at this site is definitely the nondomesticated type. Wild bean, while classified here as noncultivated, may actually have been another species that was encouraged to grow in or near agricultural fields (see Bonhage-Freund 1997 for discussion.)

Purslane, a taxon commensal with agriculture and perhaps encouraged, is the third most common seed type by ubiquity (29%). Chenopod (goosefoot) scored 13% ubiquity. Both were used as potherbs, and goosefoot seeds may have been harvested as well.

Fleshy fruits identified include persimmon, huckleberry, maypops, and elderberry (Newsom and Ruggiero 1998). Each was recovered from only one sample except maypop, which appeared in two. Finally, unidentified thick seed coat and stem fragments may be belong to a member of the palm family, such as saw palmetto or cabbage palm (Newsom and Ruggiero 1998).

Wood charcoal identification includes at least five genera of tree species in the Yuchi Town samples: wild cherry, hickory, oak (red and white groups), persimmon, and pine (hard or yellow, aka "Southern Yellow") (Table 6.3). Most of the samples contained fewer than ten fragments that could be identified to genus, so preferential wood uses are far from definite.

In considering the combined assemblage, pine is the most common, appearing in 82% of the samples and over the full range of contexts including postholes, cob pits, other pits, possible house structural remains, and the basin fill from Structure 1. Red oak was found in 18% of the samples and is the predominant wood charcoal associated with the roof/wall samples from Structure 1. White oak group, wild cherry, hickory, persimmon-like wood, and diffuse-porous (c.f. maple) were identified in one provenience each. Cane stem fragments were recognized in just two proveniences, a posthole and a basin within Structure 1 (Newsom and Ruggiero 1998).

The diversity of species associated with the individual cultural contexts sampled is generally low, typically with one to three wood types documented from any particular provenience. A single wood, usually pine, is identified from each of the cob pits, though hardwoods (oak and hickory) were also present in three of these features. While postholes and possible postholes typically featured pine, a few contained oak or probable oak, and one also contained persimmon wood. A wall trench contained some oak, as did a hearth feature. General pit features occasionally held a few fragments of hardwoods, in addition to the dominant pine (Newsom and Ruggiero 1998). Overall, wood charcoal reflects the local forest composition, but red oak does seem to be differentially associated with Feature 1 construction. There is no evidence of the cypress shingles observed by Hawkins (Foster 2003a).

Seeds produced in different seasons attest to seasonal use of some of the features considered in this study. All maize cob–filled features contained at least some examples of late summer–fall ripening taxa such as elderberry, huckleberry, panicoid grass, chickweed and spurge, and other maize cob–filled features species (Tables 6.2 and 6.5). Lee Newsom (Newsom and Ruggiero 1998) proposes that the deposition of seeds in late summer through fall may reflect either their seasonal abundance or seasonal use of these features. With an abundance of cobs, fruits, nuts, meats, and hides, late summer–fall would hold potential as a season for smoking hides or drying foods for winter, and these procedures have been observed historically (Speck 2004). However, the fact that these late-ripening foods were routinely preserved also means that they could be deposited in features in virtually any season (Newsom and Ruggiero 1998).

Discussion

Maize, wood, and nutshell (hickory and acorn) were found in nearly every Yuchi Town provenience. Beans and two members of the gourd/squash family

(*Cucurbita* sp.) were also present, as were wild foods—persimmon, huckleberry, maypops, elderberry, purslane, and small grain seeds (chenopod, panicoid grass) (Weisman 2000). "Calabashes or gourds" are among those fruits used in ceremonies (Foster 2003b; Swan 1855), but they probably also served many storage and serving functions in domestic settings. Newsom (Newsom and Ruggiero 1998) surmises that a member of the palm family may be represented by unidentified thick seeds and stems. This is consistent with historic references to similar taxa (Bartram 1909; Romans 1999).

While this pattern is consistent with those discerned at other sites discussed in this chapter, it could alternatively be related to skewed sampling and disturbed contexts. While the samples were assessed to be from the Historic Creek occupation, they were collected from the northwest end of the site where early Lawson Field Phase and Blackmon Phase materials predominate. These samples may predate the widespread adoption of calabashes and gourds (Newsom and Ruggiero 1998; Weisman 2000).

While Bartram described storage facilities for sweet potatoes "and other roots" at Yuchi Town, these are conspicuously absent from the assemblage (Harper 1998). Equally lacking were examples of introduced cultigens such as musk melons, watermelon (*Citrullus lunatus*), peaches, cowpeas (*Vigna unguiculata*), and cotton (*Gossypium hisrutum*), all of which are known from historic sources to have been utilized by the Yuchi during the eighteenth century. Newsom and Ruggiero (1998) consider the preponderance of indigenous cultivars and wild plant foods as an indication of the traditional or conservative practices by the Yuchi Town inhabitants. On several occasions Hawkins reflected on the reluctance of the Yuchi to adopt new technologies, preferring to "adhere to the old times" (Swanton 1922). Finally, there is no evidence of yaupon holly or, with the exception of cane, of the plant-based construction and matting materials described by Hawkins (1982). For this information we must for now rely on history.

Conclusions

Like Ochillee Creek, the Yuchi Town report is skewed. Samples come only from the northwest portion of the site, and there is a high probability that at least some of the samples are from disturbed contexts. Nevertheless, the macroplant remains provide insights into the site's subsistence, and the results are consistent with those of the other sites discussed. Maize was the staple crop and the only cultivated grain recovered. Maize, beans, and squash remains indicate that a fully developed field agricultural system was in place, but neither the Eastern Tradition crops nor any European introductions were evident. Chenopods and panicoid grasses are related to Eastern Tradition crops and may have been harvested from the wild. Purslane may have been encouraged to grow among the corn, as described above.

Wild foods were a significant part of the diet. Hickory and oak acorns provided a wild staple food. A variety of edible pods and fruits attest to the existence of old fields or edge zones and suggest that these foods were incorporated into the diet. It is likely that they were integrated into a complex agricultural system as described above. While specific medicinal plants and other nondietary plants of economic use were not identified, it is likely that they were collected locally.

The historic record leads to the conclusion that this archaeobotanical record is incomplete. The large amount of disturbance at the site makes it unlikely that additional studies could improve the recovery. However, the historic and archaeological records are complementary. Euro-American chroniclers did not generally recognize the complex nature of the Creek subsistence system, nor could they be expected to note any wild species that were not processed or used in their presence. Some introduced species, like potatoes, are rare and hard to recognize in the archaeological record but are well described historically. Although a few pieces are still missing from the puzzle, based on the historic and archaeological data it appears that the Yuchi Town subsistence system was similar to that of Cussetuh Town (9CE1).

DEVELOPING A MODEL OF
EARLY HISTORIC CREEK PLANT USE

In developing a model of the Creek plant use, it is important to recognize the limitations of the data. Plant remains have not been systematically collected at all archaeological projects. Where they have been conscientiously collected, for a variety of reasons preservation or recovery may be poor. Some plant remains are more likely to be preserved than others, owing to differential discard patterns, durability, or preservation, especially by charring.

Plant foods that are cooked before consumption have an increased chance of preservation because of accidental charring as results from cooking mishaps. Similarly, those parts of the plant that were considered to be waste have a much higher chance of being preserved than those that were not. Even under the best conditions, macroplant analysis cannot recover all taxa used at a site, nor can there be an expectation that the proportions of taxa will reflect their initial abundance. There is no guarantee that all recovered macroplant remains were actually used at the site, and undoubtedly many more taxa were exploited than find their way into the archaeological record. The use of the analytical devices described helps to compensate for these disparities. With careful analysis, much can be learned about the past relations between plants and people. By considering historic records, we are able to fill in the gaps of the archaeo-botanical record and also to clarify or correct misconceptions of eighteenth-century Eurocentric observers.

DIET AND SUBSISTENCE SYSTEM

Historic Creek people practiced a highly mixed and integrated economy, in every sense of the term. They farmed, harvested mast, and supplemented their diet with wild fruits, seeds, and possibly tubers. Agriculture, the base of Creek sub-sistence, drew from at least three different traditions, Eastern, Meso-American/Southwestern, and European, although this is not evident at every site. As Piker (2004) cautions and the combined results of this book are showing, some variation in subsistence is to be expected between individual communities.

Maize is the dominant domesticated grain in all assemblages, while may-grass and sumpweed appear in the Cussetuh Town and Buzzard Roost assem-blages. This pattern is a legacy of the Mississippian Period when maize largely replaced the traditional cultivation of the weedy and starchy taxa. The Eastern Tradition crops, with their weedy origins, were more reliable but less produc-tive than the Meso-American complex. At the Buzzard Roost sites, it is likely that maygrass was a seasonally important crop.

European cereal grains are noted by B. S. Barton as conspicuously absent in early Historic Creek communities (Bartram 1909), but the archaeological re-cords from Cussetuh Town and Buzzard Roost contradict this observation. The Historic Creek might have raised these grains as food for the European animals they were raising rather than for their own consumption. These crops may have not yet been proven reliable, or perhaps the knowledge of how to cultivate them lagged behind the availability of the seeds. Furthermore, by planting a variety of crops, rather than monocropping, people avoided total crop loss in case of drought, pestilence, or other natural disaster. The historic record docu-ments that Native Americans planted crops on a schedule to ripen at various times through the season and may have double-cropped some fields (Swanton 1979).

Cultivation is not a clearly definable set of activities but rather may be re-garded as a technological continuum, much of which is invisible in the ar-chaeological record (Ford 1985). Economically useful wild plant taxa might have been selectively weeded, tolerated, encouraged, or transplanted (Ford 1985). Recent ancestors of the Creek had already incorporated peaches into their agricultural system, and naturalized maypops were encouraged or culti-vated as well (Bonhage-Freund 1997; Gremillion 1989). During the seventeenth and eighteenth centuries, the Creeks participated in trade with the European-

Americans and gradually experimented with exotic agricultural crops such as rice, wheat, sweet potatoes, white potatoes, cotton, and others. The current archaeobotanical evidence implies that these played a very small role in the agricultural systems and diets of the Creeks.

While the archaeological record provides abundant evidence for agriculture, it is historic documents that describe community fields, private gardens, and some details of their cultivation. With peaches ubiquitous and grape appearing once, the macrobotanical remains recovered from all of these sites are consistent with historic accounts of agricultural fields and orchards as described by Hawkins (Foster 2003a).

Early descriptions indicate that the historic Creek maintained a system of "infields" and "outfields," at least in the larger towns and villages. Men and women together planted the communal fields, which might be some distance from the residences. Women alone planted and tended the smaller infields or household kitchen gardens. When communal fields declined, new fields were established. There is archaeological evidence that these old fields took on a new role in the subsistence system.

There is evidence that the historic Creek managed succession on the old fields to provide "wild crops" for themselves and browse for game and livestock. Some economically useful plants recovered archaeologically include blackberry/raspberry, elderberry, honeylocust, huckleberry, mulberry, persimmon, serviceberry, and even peach. Plant collection was primarily the work of women. The old-field habitat would also attract game and could serve as forage for the Creeks' domesticated animals (Bonhage-Freund 1997; O'Steen and Raymer 1999). Recently acquired livestock may have been turned into harvested fields, but this practice was not evident in the archaeobotanical studies.

Nuts constituted a dietary staple food of historic and prehistoric people throughout the Eastern Woodlands (Gremillion 1989). Ochillee Creek is the only major project considered in this chapter that lacks evidence of this fact. Historic observers agree that hickory and acorn were regularly exploited and describe multiple methods of preservation and preparation. Nut oils or "milk" are mentioned in particular, and even modern Cherokee consider *Ku-Nu-Che*, a hickory nut soup, to be an important traditional dish (Bartram 1909; Fritz et al. 2001; Romans 1999; Swan 1855). Other nuts were occasionally used.

Hickory provides a greater energetic return than all other readily available mast resources, the most important wild seeds, and most traditionally cultivated species. Even when maize comes to dominate agriculture in the late Prehistoric Period, hickory continues to play an important role in Eastern subsistence (Gremillion 1998). Use of hickory as a staple is energetically efficient. Based on native harvesting and processing methods, it is estimated to return 2,565 kcal per hour, compared to 1,107 kcal per hour for acorn (Gremillion

1998). Nuts and grains, particularly hickory and maize, are nutritionally complementary. Hickory is superior to both maize and acorns as a source of nine of the ten essential amino acids (Gardner 1992).

In summary, it is the nature of human activity, in the process of carving spaces for their dwellings, to create areas of ecotone, teaming with diverse and economically important species. Thus people and plants co-evolve in a dance of survival, so seamless that it is not always recognized. Projecting backward in time, we see that the Historic Creek subsistence system is clearly based upon a traditional local subsistence system (Bonhage-Freund 2002).

SUBSISTENCE VARIATION BETWEEN TOWNS

As discussed in Chapter 1, Creek Indian towns often split into daughter populations. Since the paleobotanical remains discussed above are from mother and daughter populations, it is informative to discuss variation in subsistence that can be determined between these related towns and villages. Yuchi Town was one of the most important eighteenth-century Creek towns, but the residents were linguistically and culturally different from the other Muskogee towns discussed here. Cussetuh Town was a primary-tier political center, and Buzzard Roost was one of its daughter villages. Ochillee Creek was probably a family farmstead of Muskogee-speaking people, possibly from Cussetuh. Within the limits of the available data, there seems to be no significant difference in the subsistence system of the first three of these sites. Maize-based agriculture, local mast, and wild plants harvested from old fields and edge zones were three pillars of the subsistence system. The seasonally used feature cluster of the Ochillee Creek site lacks nut remains but does suggest a maize-based diet and possible the harvesting of old field taxa. Data cited elsewhere in this chapter and in Chapter 7 indicate that hunting was universally practiced and that domesticated animals were integrated into the existing agricultural, primarily as living trade goods. These data seem to indicate that each settlement, regardless of its size, was essentially an independent economic unit, participating in trade networks but locally producing the bulk of their diet and other subsistence needs.

CONCLUSIONS

Until recently, little has been known of Historic Creek lifeways. We now know that the Historic Creek built their settlements in areas of ecotone and relied on local fields and forests for food, medicines, raw materials, and fuel. They drew on the traditions of their ancestors and cautiously incorporated foreign taxa and trade goods into their resource base. In studying the complex mixture of the material remains of Historic Creek livelihood, one undeniable fact emerges: Their culture was neither stagnant nor in decline. It was flexible, adaptive, and yet still unique. The end result is an amalgam of North American, Meso-American, and European traditions, steeped in the heritage of the Prehistoric Southeast. The Historic Creek did not abandon the ways of their ancestors. They built on them.

NOTES

1. Unless otherwise stated, the source of all data related to 9CE1 macroplant remains is Bonhage-Freund (2003).

2. Formerly known as the "Eastern Agricultural Complex."

3. Unless otherwise stated, the source of all data related to 9TR41 and 9TR54 is Bonhage-Freund (1999).

4. It should be noted that these evaluations are subjective and that none of the cobs was complete. Thus it is possible that, given a more complete cob, the shape assignment could be different. For example, a "straight" cob segment might actually be the central portion of a "cigar-shaped" cob.

5. Unless otherwise stated, the source of all data related to 9CE379 is O'Steen and Raymer (1999).

7
Animal Remains

Lisa O'Steen

Prior to contact with Europeans during the sixteenth and seventeenth centuries, Native Americans in Georgia subsisted primarily on deer, turtles, and turkeys. Other native wild mammals and birds, fish, and shellfish supplemented the diet. There is no archaeological evidence of diet among the Lower Creek in the seventeenth or early eighteenth century, although historical accounts of the Upper Creek indicate that they had been introduced to, and were acquiring, some domesticated animals and birds from their Spanish and English neighbors by the early eighteenth century (Piker 2004). Historical accounts indicate that while the Lower Creek raised domestic livestock and drove them to coastal markets, they did not believe in eating these animals except in famine situations (Ethridge 1996, 2003; Piker 2004). The changes brought about by owning domestic livestock would play an integral role in all aspects of Lower Creek life over the next several decades.

Europeans noted that there was little difference in Creek clothing or houses based on individual status, although "possessions" included jewelry, agricultural and hunting tools, cooking vessels and utensils, and animal hides. Of these, deer hides were the only items of value to the colonists. Hides were the only commodity the Maskókî had to trade for desirable European goods, including metal tools, cooking pots, guns, powder, shot, rum, glass beads and bottles, and European ceramics. Many of these items, particularly metal tools and guns, were valued because they reduced the amount of energy expended on agricultural, domestic, and hunting activities of Creek men and women (Braund 1993; Hahn 2004; Saunt 1999). Prior to the 1760s, the deerskin trade had not had much influence on the relationships between Maskókî and their concept of property, most of which was communally "owned," worked, and hunted (Braund 1993). Exchange of "gifts" was informal and was based on matrilineal kinship ties. Much to the chagrin and confusion of colonial Spanish and English leaders, the Maskókî had little interest in accumulating or possessing property. Ranching of domestic animals by the Maskókî and the interaction with colonists required to support this activity would eventually have profound effects on Creek social, political, and economic systems.

Maskókî established kin relationships with British traders via marriage, which made the exchange of goods reciprocal and obligatory rather than solely commercial. By the middle of the eighteenth century, intermarriage had produced a generation of ethnically mixed children (Saunt 1999). This change corresponded with the increasing population of white Georgians and black slaves, which together quadrupled between 1745 and 1760 and reached 36,000 by 1775. At this time, Creek population was estimated at 14,000 (Swanton 1922). At the same time, the number of cattle owned by white settlers increased and encroached more and more on Lower Creek lands (Ethridge 2003).

A 1756 letter to Governor Reynolds from the Lower Creek stated that white people "spoils our hunting Ground and frightens away the Deer." Another letter, in 1759, reported that whites who "have Guns that will kill Deer as far Distant as they can see them" were "wandering all over the Woods destroying our Game, which is now so scarce that we cannot kill sufficiently to supply our Necessities." The Maskókî believed that incursion by whites and their cattle was responsible for the depletion of deer, bear, and "buffalo" on their hunting lands. Cattle and pigs also destroyed the natural habitats that attracted the native animals. By the 1750s South Carolina was overstocked with cattle, and white ranchers continued expanding into the neighboring colony of Georgia and Lower Creek lands (Saunt 1999:46, 48, 50).

Prior to the Revolutionary War there are records of Maskókî owning domestic livestock. They had adopted pigs and chicken, both of which were common in their towns before the middle of the eighteenth century. Piker (2003:199–202) found 1735, 1737, and 1749 accounts of cattle ownership among the Maskókî, although such accounts became much more common later in the century. In many cases, these were probably free-ranging animals that were appropriated after they wandered into Creek towns and crop fields.

Despite some ownership of livestock among the Maskókî, the invasion of colonists' and traders' cattle was a major Creek grievance in treaties between the Maskókalkî and Britain in 1717, 1763, and 1765. When land was ceded to Georgia in these treaties, one condition was to "keep your slaves [who herded the cattle] & Cattle" within those boundaries. However, cattle and settlers continued to encroach on Creek lands. In a 1771 letter, Upper Creek headmen remarked that "it was promised that no more Cattle should be drove thro' our Nation but that the Path should be always kept Green" (Saunt 1999:48–49). Most of the complaints were directed toward stock that was owned by white traders and brought into Creek country. During this period, raids on colonists by Maskókî reportedly involved the stealing of horses, which were considered useful pack animals, and the killing of cattle and pigs (Ethridge 1996, 2003; Piker 1998, 2004; Saunt 1999). However, by the middle of the eighteenth century, some Maskókî, especially those of mixed British heritage, began accumulating large cattle herds (and slaves) themselves. The Lower Creek and Seminoles may have been less resistant than the Upper Maskókî to acquiring livestock, and even during the 1760s some accounts mentioned that some Maskókî had only a few cattle (Piker 1998, 2004).

In 1777, British surveyor Bernard Romans described animals and foods that he observed among the Lower Creek:

> Their way of life is in general very abundant; they have much more of venison, bear, turkies; and small game in their country than their neighbors have, and they raise abundance of small cattle, hogs, turkeys, ducks and dunghill fowls (all of which are very good in their kind) and of these they spare not. . . . They have more variety in their diet than other savages: They make pancakes; they dry the tongues of their venison; they make a caustick salt out of a kind of moss found at the bottom of creeks and rivers, which although a vegetable salt, does not deliquiate on exposing to the air; this they dissolve in water and pound their dried venison till it look like oakum and then eat it dipped in the above sauce; they eat much roasted and boiled venison, a great deal of milk and eggs. (Saunt 1999:50; Swanton 1946:285)

A 1773 account noted that although Maskókî fenced their towns and household gardens, communal crop fields were not fenced. Horses were tied up, and pigs were penned from early spring through the harvest (Piker 1998:205).

By the middle of the eighteenth century, the deer population was declining, owing in large part to overhunting for the hide trade. Habitat destruction caused by cattle and pigs and white settlements, and the territoriality and long gestation period of deer, also contributed to population decline. The number of deer hides exported to Europe had peaked and begun to decline by the 1770s. During and after the Revolutionary War, politics also played a role in the declining importance of deer hide trading to the Maskókî (Braund 1993:72, 165–170). Based on historical accounts of the Upper Creek town of Okfuskee, Piker (1998, 2004) observed that as the deer population decreased, the length of the hunting season gradually increased, and hunters had to travel farther to find deer. Creek hunters may have been forced to harvest younger and younger deer (Braund 1993:153). Instead of the traditional short-term summer and winter hunts, by the late eighteenth century there is historical evidence that the hunting season began earlier in the year, often in September, and continued into early summer of the following year. Despite a longer hunting season, the number of hides produced and traded to stores in Augusta and Savannah, Georgia, continued to fall, and the deer population became even more depleted. It was also during this time that cattle ranching became more important (Piker 2004).

The growth of cattle ranching during the late eighteenth century was likely related to the increasing need to replace deer hides with cowhides. In 1776, the Georgia Council of Safety recommended the payment of Indians in cattle, citing that it would result in a "tendency not only of attaching them to our interest from gratitude, be a means of civilizing them, and by fixing the idea of property would keep them honest and peaceable with us" (Saunt 1999:50). In 1783, William Bartram noted that one of the cattle ranches that he visited was producing cowhides for trade (Saunt 1999: 159).

During the late eighteenth century, there were a number of conflicts between the Maskókî and their American neighbors related to the stealing of cattle, pigs, and horses from white settlers and the damage these animals caused to unfenced Creek crop fields. A 1793 inventory of debts owed by Maskókî at the town of Salenojuh or Buzzard's Roost listed payments owed to Georgia settlers for several stolen cattle and horses (Ledbetter et al. 2002). In many cases, these activities involved the capture of semiferal cattle, horses, and pigs that had encroached on Creek lands or cases when they were found plundering unfenced Creek crops.

Benjamin Hawkins was appointed by George Washington in 1796 and served until 1816 as the U.S. Government's agent to the Southern Indian nations. Since the official U.S. policy at that time was to "civilize" the eastern tribes, Hawkins's mission was to introduce the Maskókî to American ideals of civilization, primarily animal husbandry, cotton cultivation, cloth spinning, and Christianity. The plan for animal husbandry focused on fencing crops from ranging livestock and spreading communities out so that livestock and crops were separated geographically.

Ranching may have had an effect on the social structure and settlement patterning of Lower Creek towns during the late eighteenth century. Hawkins noted in 1799 that "The raising of stock is more relished by the Maskókî [typically men] than any other part of the plan devised for their civilization" (Saunt 1999:159). Traditionally, Creek kinship was matrilineal, and Creek women managed and produced the most important subsistence resources, the corn crop and the growing and harvesting of other domestic and wild plant foods. As the stock herds grew, ranchers established patriarchal settlements away from the town households controlled by women. These isolated, fenced farms were surrounded by thousands of acres of grazing land. During the 1770s, William Bartram noted few farms that were not visible from the towns, but this pattern of settlement may have changed to some degree by the 1780s and 1790s to one of outlying farms or plantations rather than nuclear towns with households headed by women (Saunt 1999:159).

In *A Sketch of the Creek Country In the Years 1798 to 1799*, Hawkins (Foster

2003a:45s), referring to the Upper Creek town of Ocfuskee, stated that the "Indians have recently moved out and settled in villages, and the town will soon be an old field." He noted that this dispersal had been repeatedly urged by the agent for Indian affairs and that there were already seven satellite villages belonging to Ocfuskee. Many of the dispersed ranches in Lower Creek country similarly developed into satellite communities of the larger nuclear towns. They served the valuable function of protecting vital unfenced farm crops (maintained by the women) from pillaging livestock (maintained primarily by the men).

Livestock ranching affected other aspects of Lower Creek social life, including those of communal ownership and sharing of resources. Poor harvests and starvation were documented during the middle and late eighteenth century, but the Maskókî endured together and shared food resources until they were exhausted. In 1756, several Maskókî died from starvation, but only after all "Stock and every Thing" was eaten (Saunt 1999:213). A September 1777 letter stated that the Maskókî were starving and that the British Indian agent had resorted to eating dogs and horses.

By the turn of the nineteenth century, the spirit of sharing food with others for the good of the community may have changed in some cases. During the winter and spring of 1803–1804, women were still farming with hoes in the old towns, the soil was exhausted, and hunting did not provide enough meat. Some people starved; others, particularly those with ranch herds, ate well. Ranchers were also able to clothe themselves during the winter, while others could not. Although the U.S. government provided funds to help, the money was hoarded by wealthy Maskókî and not equally distributed. A string of droughts, hurricanes, failed crops and hunts, and disease among nutritionally weakened people led to further breakdown and corruption. Instead of banding together against a common cause—the U.S. government and intruding white settlers—as neighboring Native American groups had, the Maskókî blamed corrupt leaders within their own ranks.

During this period a number of treaties were signed that ceded more Creek lands in return for cash payments. Some of the money was embezzled, and some was provided to towns that supported the government plan for "civilizing" the Maskókî. These towns received hoes, axes, and salt to sustain livestock and preserve "domestic meats" (Saunt 1999:220). Towns that resisted the plan did not receive such supplies.

During a devastating famine in 1807, the Creek national council purchased blankets, hoes, bullets, flints, iron, and steel, but no food. The controversial treaties of Washington and Fort Wilkerson, the breakdown of the traditional Creek socioeconomic and political system, internal dissension, the accumulation of unshared wealth by Creek planters and ranchers, the collection of debts by white traders, natural disasters, years of crop failure, depletion of wild game, and disease led to mistrust and, in many cases, rejection of the U.S. Government plan for the civilization of the Creek Indians. This famine, in turn, led to several years of war, massacres, socioeconomic and political instability and breakdown, and land cessions that ended with removal of the Maskókî from Georgia during the 1830s (Saunt 1999:214–290).

In this study I will examine the archaeological evidence for the use of animals and for diet among the Lower Creek within the framework of ethnohistorical accounts. Although a number of Lower Creek sites have been systematically excavated, zooarchaeological analysis of nonhuman bone remains has been conducted on only six of them. Taphonomic factors like poor preservation because of high soil acidity, destructive food preparation and disposal techniques, other cultural modifications, and scavenging animals have often resulted in unidentifiable bone fragments or very small samples of identifiable material.

Over many decades, at least 30 Lower Creek sites in Alabama and Georgia have been excavated using systematic and nonsystematic methodologies. A comprehensive list of sites and associated reports is given in Chapter 3. Systematic zooarchaeological analysis of nonhuman bone remains has been conducted on only six of these sites, predominantly because of the taphonomic factors noted above. In other cases, the bone preservation was good, but remains were not systematically collected.

One goal of this study is to present all of the systematically excavated and analyzed zooarchaeological data from the known Lower Creek sites and synthesize the results. One systematically analyzed late-eighteenth to early-nineteenth-century site, 9ME348, produced only six identifiable faunal remains from one postmold, so these data are not included in the overall database (Pavao-Zuckerman in Keith 2003). Detailed analyses and reporting of these zooarchaeological assemblages are available in site reports produced by Southeastern Archeological Services, Southern Research, and Panamerican Consultants (Boyko 2004; Ledbetter et al. 2002; O'Steen in Ledbetter 1997; O'Steen and Raymer in Cowie 2001; Pavao-Zuckerman in Keith 2003).

ANALYTICAL TECHNIQUES

Zooarchaeological remains from features at five Lower Creek sites in Georgia were identified using standard zooarchaeological analysis techniques and comparative skeletal collections, including those at the University of Georgia Zooarchaeology Laboratory. Faunal assemblages included in this study were systematically collected from 0.64 cm (¼ in) and 0.32 cm (⅛ in) screened and feature flotation samples. Zooarchaeological remains from the other four sites in this study—Ochillee Creek Farmstead (9CE379) (Cowie 2001), Salenojuh or Buzzard's Roost Town (9TR41 and 9TR54) (Ledbetter et al. 2002), and the Cowetuh Settlements (9ME50)—were analyzed and reported by the author (Ledbetter et al. 1996). Wayne C. J. Boyko (Boyko 2004) conducted the analysis and reporting of vertebrate remains from Cussetuh Town (9CE1). Analysis techniques were very similar and systematically applied. The zooarchaeological assemblages are presented from earliest date of occupation to latest.

Each bone fragment submitted for analysis was examined and included in these analyses. Faunal remains were identified to the most specific taxonomic classification possible. Size categories for classes of unidentified taxa were subjective but were believed to be informative as to general sizes of unidentified classes of animals. The criteria used in making these distinctions were the overall size and thickness of bone fragments for birds and mammals. Unidentified small bird bone fragments represent perching or quail-sized birds; unidentified medium bird bone represents duck- or chicken-sized individuals; unidentified large bird bone fragments represent turkey- or heron-sized birds. Most of the unidentified large mammal fragments represent deer and the two domestic mammals, pigs and cows. Unidentified medium mammal bone represents animals the size of raccoons, opossums, or Native American dogs. Unidentified small mammals represent animals in the size range of small rodents up to squirrel- or rabbit-sized animals. Boyko (2004) used the diameter of fish vertebrae to assess size classes for unidentifiable fish. Because of their fragmentary condition, these remains could not be identified more specifically than to the class level. Differential preservation due to acidic soils, food preparation techniques and other cultural modifications, and attrition caused by scavenging animals reduced the degree of recovery and identification of taxa in these assemblages.

Zooarchaeological analysis spreadsheets were used to record all remains by provenience, most specific taxonomic identification, number of individual specimens (NISP), body part, proximal and distal element fusion, element side, burning or calcining, cut marks, animal gnaw marks, and weight. Elements that cross-mended were counted as one specimen. A comments column was used to record cross mends, bone pathologies, age and sex data, and any other relevant data not provided for in other categories of the spreadsheet.

Two types of cuts, hacked marks and superficial cuts, were identified. Hacked cuts, made with an ax or cleaver, cut through the bone or broke or cracked the bone. Spiral fractures were probably produced when breaking or chopping bones across an anvil. In most cases, spiral fractures were made by ax or cleaver-like tools, but the cuts could not be seen because of exfoliation of the bone surface. Superficial knife cuts were characterized by shallow, smooth incisions when viewed under low-power magnification.

The minimum number of individuals (MNI) was calculated for each species, genus, family, or other appropriate taxonomic classification (where appropriate) from analyzed features or other analytical groupings. Unless noted, MNI was calculated separately for each feature or other discrete depositional context. It was calculated using paired left and right elements. Where possible, comparative age, sex, and size of animals were determined and utilized in calculation of MNI.

Biomass was calculated separately for the taxa identified in 0.64 cm (¼ in) screened and flotation samples. Biomass calculations are based on the biological premise that the weight of bone is related to the amount of flesh it supports. These calculations provide an estimate of the amount of meat that would have adhered to a particular weight of shell or bone (Reitz and Cordier 1983; Reitz and Wing 1999). These calculations provide a balance to the NISP and MNI methods of quantification and account for the presence or absence of partial and complete skeletons.

There are acknowledged problems with this formula and with many other techniques that have been used to estimate the importance of animals in faunal assemblages, especially in small assemblages (Reitz and Wing 1999). The combined faunal assemblage from all of the sites should be large enough to provide significant results using this calculation. Even if this formula is used only as a statistical indicator of the relative contribution of different species in the represented diet, it provides useful and comparable data.

The species list(s), including NISP, MNI, Weight (gm), Biomass, and Percent Biomass from each site in this study, are presented and discussed separately by site. These data were then compiled into a summary table presenting the identified taxa recovered from all of the sites.

Element distribution tables group identified elements of mammal species in the collections by site. These categories group elements by head (skull elements), loose teeth, axial (ribs and vertebrae), forequarter (scapula, humerus, radius, ulna), hindquarter (pelvis, femur, tibia, fibula), and ankle and foot bones (tarsals, carpals, metapodials, phalanges). These categories provide a representation of the body parts of mammals that are present in the collections. Teeth and ankle and foot bones are relatively dense parts of the skeleton; they are often better preserved than less dense elements and may have been broken up less often than other body parts for marrow extraction or during other food preparation techniques. These biases must be considered in evaluating these data. These tables were compiled for each site assemblage, and then they were combined to provide a summary table for all of the analyzed data.

The percentages of MNI and biomass for wild and domestic taxa were tabulated for each site. These data were then compiled to produce a summary table for all of the analyzed assemblages. These tables compare the number of wild and domestic individuals and the amount of wild and domestic biomass represented in the assemblages.

VERTEBRATE ZOOARCHAEOLOGICAL REMAINS FROM CUSSETUH

The portion of Cussetuh Town that was examined in this study was the second manifestation of this Lower Creek town during the eighteenth century. Data recovery excavations were undertaken to mitigate impacts associated with the Lawson Army Airfield on Fort Benning, Georgia. Based on artifacts—including Creek and European ceramics, glass, beads, metal tools, and other artifacts— recovered from archaeological investigations, the area of Cussetuh represented in this study was occupied between 1750 and 1775. Zooarchaeological analysis and reporting of vertebrate remains from the site were conducted by Boyko (2004).

A total of 19,171 vertebrate remains were recovered from Cussetuh, 15,986 from 88 different feature and postmold contexts (Table 7.1). Although some of the vertebrate assemblage was recovered from flotation samples, the vast majority was recovered from 0.64 cm screened (¼ in) and laboratory excavated contexts. Vertebrate remains represent a minimum of 89 individuals and 89.13 kg (197 lbs) of biomass. Shellfish from the site were not analyzed and are not included in this analysis. Four percent (N=639) of vertebrate remains were identifiable to family, genus, or species.

Three large trash-filled pits, Features 501, 502, and 516, produced the greatest variety of identified taxa from the excavations at Cussetuh. These features produced most of the fish, all of the turtles and amphibians, and all of the identifiable bird remains. Identified wild and domestic mammal remains were found in these and many other features, and mammal remains were much more ubiquitous across the site than were fish, reptile, amphibian, and bird remains.

Differential preservation owing to acidic soils, scavenging animals, and cultural factors relating to food preparation and refuse disposal probably resulted in a lower rate of recovery for very small delicate bones, especially those from fish and birds. Boyko (2004) noted that even preservation of much of the mammal bone was poor, with much surface exfoliation. Despite the relatively poor overall preservation, some very small delicate bones such as fish and amphibians were identified.

Fish

A total of 551 fish remains were recovered. Identifiable fish remains were recovered from 8 out of 88 feature contexts (Table 7.2). Most of these remains were

Table 7.1: Faunal material recovered from feature contexts at Cussetuh Town
(after Boyko 2004: table 20)

Taxon	NISP	MNI	Weight (gm)	Biomass (kg)	Biomass %
Amia calva (Bowfin)	2	2	0.2	0.01	<0.1
Micropterus spp. (Bass)	2	2	0.3	0.01	<0.1
Ictalurus punctatus (Channel Catfish)	7	2	0.4	0.01	<0.1
Ictalurus spp. (Catfish)	58	9	3.0	0.06	0.1
Selachimorpha (Shark Superorder)	4	3	3.4	0.36	0.4
Salmonidae (Bass Family)	4	1	0.7	0.02	<0.1
Unidentified Fish	348	—	12.3	0.23	0.3
Unidentified Large Fish	17	—	2.3	0.06	0.1
Unidentified Medium Fish	44	—	1.8	0.05	0.1
Unidentified Small Fish	65	—	1.4	0.04	<0.1
TOTAL FISH	551	19	25.8	0.85	1.0
Bufo sp. (Toad)	4	2	0.3	0.03	<0.1
Unidentified Amphibian	16	—	0.3	0.03	<0.1
TOTAL AMPHIBIAN	20	2	0.6	0.06	0.1
Apalone sp. (Softshell Turtle)	7	1	1.3	0.04	<0.1
Terrapene carolina (Box Turtle)	29	2	8.1	0.13	0.1
Unidentified Turtle	174	—	18.7	0.23	0.3
Unidentified Reptile	46	—	3.5	0.07	0.1
TOTAL REPTILE	256	3	31.6	0.47	0.5
Sturnus vulgaris (Starling)	1	1	0.1	<0.01	<0.1
Bonasa umbellus (Ruffed Grouse)	1	1	0.7	0.02	<0.1
Anas spp. (Duck)	2	1	0.8	0.02	<0.1
Meleagris gallopavo (Turkey)	4	2	4.6	0.08	0.1
Unidentified Bird	48	—	1.9	0.04	<0.1
Unidentified Large Bird	92	—	17.8	0.28	0.3
Unidentified Medium Bird	34	—	1.6	0.03	<0.1
Unidentified Small Bird	5	—	0.1	<0.01	<0.1
TOTAL BIRD	187	5	27.6	0.47	0.5
Castor canadensis (Beaver)	1	1	6.1	0.13	0.1
Tamias striatus (Chipmunk)	3	1	0.1	<0.01	<0.1
Ursus americanus (Black Bear)	10	2	59.4	1.04	1.2

Table 7.1: *Continued*

Taxon	NISP	MNI	Weight (gm)	Biomass (kg)	Biomass %
Bos spp. (Domestic Cow)	83	17	2786.2	33.15	37.2
Odocoileus virginianus (White-tailed Deer)	339	39	1178.2	15.28	17.1
Artiodactyla (Even-toed Ungulate Order)	326	—	57.3	1.01	1.1
Large *Artiodactyla* (Even-toed Ungulate Order)	74	—	47.0	0.84	0.9
Unidentified Mammal	4900	—	213.0	3.28	3.7
Unidentified Large Mammal	2047	—	2703.7	32.27	36.2
Unidentified Medium Mammal	70	—	11.7	0.24	0.3
Unidentified Small Mammal	19	—	1.4	0.04	<0.1
TOTAL MAMMAL	7872	60	7064.1	87.28	97.9
Unidentified Bone	7113	NA	102.7	NA	NA
TOTAL FAUNAL REMAINS	15999	89	7252.4	89.13	100.0

*Not Applicable

found in Features 209, 501, and 502. A minimum of 2 bowfin (*Amia calva*), 11 catfish (*Ictalurus* ssp.), and 2 bass (*Micropterus* ssp.) were identified. Three sharks were represented by four teeth from three features. No actual sharks may have been brought to Cussetuh. Rather, shark teeth may have been picked up nearer the Gulf Coast or acquired through trade with coastal residents. Unidentifiable fish bone was recovered from the same array of features as the identifiable fish remains (Boyko 2004).

Evidence of food preparation techniques may be seen in the type and number of fish bones that were burned or calcined (Table 7.3). Twenty-seven percent of fish remains (n=150) from Cussetuh were burned. These included 45 freshwater catfish pectoral spines, 2 catfish dorsal spines, 75 unidentified fish vertebrae, and 28 unidentified fish elements. Catfish were at least occasionally roasted over an open fire, where spines were burned. However, these and the burned vertebrae and other elements may have been disposed of in hearths.

Amphibians

Amphibian faunal remains (n=20) were recovered from only 2 out of 88 features at Cussetuh. Toad remains (*Bufo* ssp.; MNI=2) were identified from both

Table 7.2: Faunal material recovered by specific feature context at Cussetuh Town (from Boyko 2004: table 21)

Taxon	Features
Amia calva (Bowfin)	501, 502
Micropterus spp. (Bass)	66, 502
Ictalurus punctatus (Channel Catfish)	502
Ictalurus spp. (Catfish)	66, 476, 501, 502, 516
Selachimorpha (Shark Superorder)	96, 209, 637
Salmonidae (Bass Family)	501
Unidentified Fish	66, 476, 501, 502, 516
Unidentified Large Fish	501, 502
Unidentified Medium Fish	501, 502
Unidentified Small Fish	501, 502, 516
Bufo spp. (Toad)	501, 502
Unidentified Amphibian	501
Apalone sp. (Soft-shell Turtle)	501
Terrapene carolina (Box Turtle)	501
Unidentified Turtle	501, 502, 516
Unidentified Reptile	501, 502
Sturnus vulgaris (Starling)	501
Bonasa umbellus (RuffedGrouse)	501
Anas spp. (Duck)	501
Meleagris gallopavo (Turkey)	501, 502
Unidentified Bird	96, 501, 502
Unidentified Large Bird	96, 185, 323, 476, 501, 502
Unidentified Medium-sized Bird	501, 502
Unidentified Small Bird	501
Castor canadensis (Beaver)	502
Tamias striatus (Chipmunk)	502
Ursus americanus (Black Bear)	66, 502
Bos spp. (Domestic Cow)	106, 165, 209, 317, 323, 345, 375, 377, 386, 493, 501, 502, 516, 528, 622
Odocoileus virginianus (White-tailed Deer)	66, 165, 209, 323, 375, 429, 434, 445, 468, 476, 478, 480, 493, 501, 502, 503, 516, 539, 540, 599, 634, 635
Artiodactyla (Even-toed Ungulate Order)	67, 96, 165, 209, 382, 383, 386, 431, 445, 488, 489, 494, 502, 516, 520, 528, 540, 573, 613

Table 7.2: *Continued*

Taxon	Features
Large *Artiodactyla* (Even-toed Ungulate Order)	40, 67, 209, 382, 488
Unidentified Mammal	28, 36, 37, 38, 41, 66, 96, 106, 165, 173, 185, 209, 323, 330, 331, 332, 375, 376, 382, 390, 399, 429, 432, 434, 461, 468, 476, 478, 479, 490, 492, 493, 494, 501, 502, 503, 516, 520, 539, 541, 546, 573, 576, 577, 616, 633, 637
Unidentified Large Mammal	28, 37, 38, 41, 66, 96, 165, 185, 209, 298, 314, 317, 323, 375, 376, 378, 381, 382, 384, 388, 390, 399, 429, 432, 444, 445, 468, 476, 478, 479, 490, 492, 493, 494, 501, 502, 503, 516, 520, 523, 524, 528, 539, 540, 541, 546, 559, 573, 599, 616, 635, 637, 661
Unidentified Medium-sized Mammal	185, 323, 502
Unidentified Small Mammal	479, 501, 502, 573

these features, and unidentified amphibian remains were also recovered from one of them (Table 7.2). These individuals were not skeletally complete, and two burned unidentified amphibian fragments were recovered from one of the features. Boyko (2004) believed that the toad and other amphibian remains recovered from Cussetuh were commensal species that had burrowed into features and died. This belief was based on their limited spatial distribution on the site and the low incidence of cultural modification of the amphibian assemblage.

Reptiles

Reptile remains (n=256) were recovered from 4 out of 88 features. Most of the reptile remains, and the identifiable box (*Terrapene carolina*) and softshell (*Apalone* ssp.) turtle remains, were recovered from Feature 501, a large trash-filled pit. The majority of the unidentified turtle remains probably represent members of the Emydidae family, pond and box turtles. None of the fragments could be conclusively identified (Boyko 2004). Twenty-nine percent (n=74) of reptile remains, most of which were turtle shell fragments, were burned. Two burned box turtle shell fragments and five burned softshell turtle shell fragments were recovered from Feature 501. Fifty-five burned unidentified turtle

Table 7.3: Faunal assemblage modifications (from Boyko 2004: table 22)

Taxon	Burned/ Calcined	Carnivore Gnawed	Cut Marks
Ictalurus punctatus (Channel Catfish)	2		
Ictalurus sp. (Catfish)	45		
Unidentified Fish	22		
Unidentified Large Fish	6		
Unidentified Medium Fish	30		
Unidentified Small Fish	45		
Unidentified Amphibian	2		
Apalone sp. (Soft-shell Turtle)	5		
Terrapene carolina (Box Turtle)	2		
Unidentified Turtle	55		
Unidentified Reptile	12		
Unidentified Bird	4		
Unidentified Large Bird	45	1	1
Unidentified Medium-sized Bird	19		
Unidentified Small Bird	1		
Ursus americanus (Black Bear)		3	
Bos spp. (cow)		7	1
Odocoileus virginianus (White-tailed Deer)	22	16	
Artiodactyal (Even-toed Ungulate Order)	3		
Unidentified Mammal	971		
Unidentified Large Mammal	453	46	
Unidentified Medium-sized Mammal	43	3	
Unidentified Small Mammal	13		
Unidentified Bone	1077		
Total Modified Remains	2877	76	2

shell fragments and 12 burned unidentified reptile remains were also recovered (Boyko 2004).

Birds

Bird remains (n=187) were recovered from 6 out of 88 features at Cussetuh (Table 7.2). Features 501 and 502 produced the majority of the identified avian material—a minimum of one duck (*Anas* ssp.), a grouse (*Bonasa umbellus*), two turkeys (*Meleagris gallopavo*), and a starling (*Sturnus vulgaris*) (Boyko 2004). The one starling faunal element was considered by Boyko to be intrusive, since the starling is a European bird not native to North America. Starlings were released in New York City in the 1890s and were first recorded in Georgia in 1917 (Burleigh 1958:476).

Most (n=55; 73%) of the burned bird bone was found in Features 501 and 502, the remainder in Features 476 and 323. One cut was identified on a large bird bone fragment, and one turkey humerus was spiral fractured (Feature 501). One carnivore-gnawed large bird bone fragment was found in Feature 502 (Boyko 2004).

Mammals

Mammal remains were recovered from numerous feature contexts (Table 7.2). Deer (*Odocoileus virginianus*) and cattle (*Bos* ssp.) were the most ubiquitous identified mammals. Cattle were identified in 15 features and deer in 22 features out of the 88 analyzed (Table 7.2). A beaver (*Castor canadensis*), a chipmunk (*Tamias striatus*), and a bear (*Ursus americanus*) were identified from Feature 502. Another bear was identified in Feature 66. It was unclear whether the chipmunk bones in the Cussetuh faunal assemblage represented intrusive modern taxa. The bones were not culturally modified in any way, and all the recovered elements occurred in a small area. However, the absence of a complete skeleton suggested that the few remains recovered may have been from a consumed animal (Boyko 2004).

Most of the deer and cattle remains represented cranial elements, teeth, or lower leg bones (Table 7.4). Deer and cattle skull elements were represented primarily by teeth (n=168) but included a cranial fragment and three mandibles. Lower leg bones were represented by the astragalus, calcaneus, metacarpus, metapodial shafts, metatarsus, cubonavicular, phalanges, sesamoids, tibia, and ulna. The upper leg was represented by the femur and humerus. The axial skeleton was represented by ribs, vertebrae, and an innominate (pelvis) fragment (Boyko 2004).

All bear elements were lower leg, ankle, and foot bones. One spiral fractured and four carnivore-gnawed bear lower hind leg elements were recovered from Feature 502. Most modifications of cattle bone were found on four lower leg and foot elements. All but one modified element were found in Feature 502. Spiral fractures were found on a metapodial (ankle), a femur (upper hind leg; Feature 377), and a tibia (lower hind leg). Transverse hacked marks were found on a cow ulna (lower foreleg). Carnivore gnaw marks were found on seven cow elements, including some of those with spiral fractures and cut marks. Cuts and spiral fractures on these elements probably represent the removal of the

Table 7.4: Skeletal representation of cow and deer elements
(after Boyko 2004)

Portion	Deer	Cow
Skull and Teeth	172	59
Lower Leg	157	21
Upper Leg	5	3
Axial	5	0
Total	339	83

lower legs, ankles, and feet from the meatier, upper leg portions (Table 7.4; Boyko 2004).

Several elements of deer exhibited modifications (Table 7.3). Many elements exhibited multiple modifications. Almost all modifications (burning/calcining [n=21], spiral fractures [n=28], and carnivore gnaw marks [n=15]) were found on lower leg, ankle, and foot elements. Exceptions were two spiral fractured tibias (one burned), two spiral fractured humerii (one carnivore gnawed), two burned teeth, and a calcined skull fragment (Boyko 2004). The presence of these elements indicates that lower legs and feet of deer were frequently brought back to site, either attached to hides or as part of hind- or forequarters or sides, and were not (always) left at hunting or butchering camps. Burning found on deer lower legs and feet probably indicates preparation of larger quarters over a hearth, where the less meaty extremities were burned. It may also indicate disposal of removed ankles and feet in fires. Carnivore gnaw marks also indicate that these parts were sometimes fed to dogs or were not immediately buried or burned, making them accessible to scavenging animals.

The fact that only one cow element (an ulna) exhibited evidence of hacked or "chop" marks was not surprising to Boyko, given the overall preservation of the faunal material. In many cases the bone surfaces had either disintegrated or exfoliated, so that distinguishing cut marks on much of the assemblage was all but impossible (Boyko 2004).

Unidentifiable mammal remains were recovered from several features (Table 7.2). The unidentifiable large mammal material was likely deer or cow but could not be identified with any greater degree of certainty. The unidentified mammal bone category likewise contained much material that, if preservation conditions were more favorable, could have been identified. The unidentified large artiodactyl and unidentified artiodactyl categories were based on teeth and fragmentary teeth. The unidentified artiodactyl remains were likely either deer or cow but could not be distinguished (Boyko 2004). The large number (n=400) of fragmented artiodactyl teeth reflects processing of deer and cattle mandibles and maxillae.

Types of modifications recorded for unidentified mammal categories are tabulated in Table 7.3. Less than 1 percent (n=49) of unidentified mammal elements were carnivore-gnawed. Twenty-one percent (n=1480) of the unidentified mammal bone assemblage from Cussetuh was burned or calcined fragments. In some cases, burning may indicate more intensive processing of the animal protein attached to mammal bone, as well as of the bones themselves. Larger bone fragments were broken into smaller ones that became leached and bleached, and these smaller fragments were eventually deposited in trash features at Cussetuh. Long bones were often broken up to access the marrow cavity, as well as to break up larger bones for preparing stew and other dishes and bone grease. Sometimes marrow was eaten directly from the bone. Much of the unidentified mammal bone was spiral-fractured (Boyko 2004).

Summary of Lower Creek Diet at Cussetuh

The vertebrate assemblage from Cussetuh indicates that by 1750 to 1775, cattle supplied over one-third of the dietary biomass, while deer, bear, beaver, fish, turkeys, grouse, turtles, and amphibians provided 20 percent. The remaining biomass was provided by unidentified specimens of birds and medium-to-large mammals. A total of 64 wild mammals and 17 cattle provided 98 percent of the biomass and 67 percent of the MNI. As a group, 19 fish provided the next largest amount of MNI and biomass (1%), followed by 5 birds and 3 turtles (0.5% each).

The amount of spiral fracturing and the locations of these fractures indicate that carcasses were similarly divided, particularly the deer and cattle. Although few cut marks were identified, there was a pattern of carcass division represented by cuts likely made with axes or cleavers. The weathered and exfoliated surfaces of most mammal bone made cut marks very difficult to identify. A few superficial cuts indicated deboning of large mammal elements and disarticulation of leg and ankle joints. The spiral-fractured portions represented large roast-sized portions or the removal of jowls or tongues, heads, and lower legs and feet. Most of the elements represented head, loose teeth, and ankle and foot elements. The large number of artiodactyl tooth fragments indicates that jaws distal to the articulation with the rest of the head were often crushed, either during butchering or some later processing of jaws.

Data available for aging wild and domestic mammals indicate that most animals exploited by the residents of Cussetuh were adults. Most cattle ranged between two and less than four years at time of death. One cow older than three to four years was identified (Reitz and Wing 1999:76). At least one deer less than two years of age and one aged more than four years were identified.

Most deer ranged in age from two years to four or five years at time of death (Gilbert 1980:102; Reitz and Wing 1999:76). The two bears were represented by fused hind ankle and foot elements. Marks and Erickson (1966) noted that the upper foreleg bones of bears don't fuse until after four to six years but provided no data on foot elements. Since ankle, foot, and pelvis elements fuse earlier than upper leg bones in most species, the bears from Cussetuh are probably adults but could have been more or less than four to six years at time of death. No sexual characteristics were identified on elements in the assemblage.

Carnivore gnawing indicates that very little of the Cussetuh bone debris was exposed to dogs and other scavengers. Some bones were undoubtedly completely consumed by Creek dogs or other scavengers and disappeared from the faunal record. Less than 1 percent (n=76) of the entire bone assemblage exhibited carnivore gnaw marks. No evidence of rodent gnawing was noted, although this may be partly because of the poor preservation of many remains. The limited evidence of carnivore gnawing and the lack of evidence of rodent gnawing may also result from a combination of thorough processing and disposal of bone refuse. This processing may have resulted in the consumption of most nutritional substances in bone by humans and rapid burial, which resulted in fewer bones being available to scavengers (Boyko 2004).

The large number of burned or calcined mammal fragments may have resulted from the preparation of bone grease (Boyko 2004). Burning, breakage, and other modifications indicate that animal carcasses and skeletal remains at Cussetuh were usually utilized completely prior to disposal. Burned and calcined bone indicates that many meats, fish, birds, and turtles were roasted in or over cooking fires.

ZOOARCHAEOLOGICAL REMAINS FROM BUZZARD ROOST

Sites 9TR41 and 9TR54 were part of the middle-to-late eighteenth-century Lower Creek town of Salenojuh (Salanotkhee, Suala-nocha, Sulenojuh; English names Buzzard's Roost, Buzzard Roost, the Roost), located on a bluff overlooking the Flint River (Ledbetter et al. 2002). These sites were excavated under the direction of Jerald Ledbetter of Southeastern Archeological Services, Inc. for the Georgia Department of Transportation. The areas investigated were determined by direct project impacts within a highway widening right-of-way (see Figures 5.6 and 5.7, this volume).

As described in Chapter 5 on architecture, the remains of at least three Lower Creek structures and associated yard areas produced Lawson Field Phase ceramics, as well as Euro-American wrought nails and metal tools, flintlock gun parts, musket balls, gun flints, kaolin pipe fragments, olive and clear bottle glass, glass beads, a salt-glazed stoneware bottle, and a slipware mug. Artifacts and historic descriptions suggest that the main occupation of the town was during the middle to late eighteenth century (ca. 1770–1790) (Ledbetter et al. 2002:197–210). The following sections summarize the zooarchaeological analysis of vertebrate and invertebrate faunal remains recovered from Creek farmsteads excavated at Salenojuh or Buzzard's Roost during this time frame. More detailed zooarchaeological data and analysis of these sites are provided in Ledbetter et al. (2002:241–249, Appendix C).

A total of 208 faunal remains were recovered from nine features at site 9TR41. Feature 3, a large midden-filled pit located west of Structure 2, contained 57 faunal remains. These remains were collected from 0.64 cm (¼ in) screens. The majority (n=54; 95%) was unidentified medium-to-large mammal fragments. Three deer elements, all lower hind leg bones, were identified. One fused deer metatarsal (ankle) indicated an individual more than 2–2.5 years of age (Reitz and Wing 1999:76).

The remaining features, postmolds associated with Structure 2, produced an additional 151 faunal remains. These remains were recovered from the heavy fractions of flotation samples of feature fill. None of these remains was identifiable beyond the class level. Half of these very tiny fragments (n=76) were classified as unidentified bone, and all weighed less than 0.1 gram each. Unidentified bird long bone (<0.1 gm) was found in Feature 112, and unidentified turtle shell (0.1 gm) was found in feature 113, while the remainder was unidentified mammal fragments. Most of these remains (n=124; 82%) were burned or calcined. No sex or age characteristics were found. The total bone weight from all of the posts was 1.9 grams, suggesting that many of these fragments represent floor sweepings or tiny fragments that accumulated around the interior wall of the structure.

A total of 1,949 vertebrate and invertebrate remains were recovered from 19 features at site 9TR54. The fill of nine of these features was processed as flotation samples. These features represent trash pits and postmolds associated with Creek structures and associated yard and activity areas. Table 7.5 presents the faunal remains recovered from 0.64-cm screened feature fill, most of which were recovered from large trash pit Features 29, 30, 33, 69 (Southern Structure 1 Cluster), 36, 39, 68 (Northern Structure Area), 88 (Structure 1 area), 90 (Structure 1 area), and 133, a small pit in the interior yard area (Figure 5.7). A minimum of 12 deer (*Odocoileus virginianus*), 5 domestic cattle (*Bos* cf. *taurus*), 2 domestic pigs (*Sus scrofa*), 2 unidentified birds, a river cooter (*Pseudemys* cf. *concinna*), 2 unidentified turtles, and a freshwater mussel (Unionidae family) were identified.

A total of 21.71 kilograms (48 lbs) of dietary biomass was represented in the screened feature fill. Ninety-nine percent of biomass was contributed by mammals—32 percent by deer, 29 percent by cattle, and less than 0.5 percent by pigs; turtles provided 1 percent, mussels and birds less than 0.5 percent.

Table 7.5: Species list: Salenojuh or Buzzard's Roost Town (9TR54) Features, 0.64 cm (1/4 in) screen (from Ledbetter et al. 2002)

Taxon	NISP	Weight (gm)	MNI	Biomass (kg)	% Biomass
Unionidae (Freshwater Mussel Family)	7	2.0	1	<0.01	<0.1
Pseudemys c.f. *concinna* (Prob. River Cooter)	10	12.4	1	0.17	0.8
Unidentified Turtle	2	1.0	2	0.03	0.1
TOTAL TURTLE	12	13.4	3	0.20	0.9
Unidentified Bird	12	1.8	2	0.04	0.2
Odocoileus virginianus (White-tailed Deer)	180	496.8	12	7.02	32.4
Bos c.f. *taurus* (Domestic Cow)	18	436.4	5	6.25	28.8
Sus scrofa (Domestic Pig)	2	2.5	2	0.06	0.3
Unidentified Medium-Large Mammal	1285	558.4	NA	7.80	36.0
Unidentified Mammal	167	15.0	NA	0.30	1.4
TOTAL MAMMAL	1652	1509.1	19	21.43	98.9
Unidentified Bone	12	0.4	NA	NA	NA
TOTAL FAUNAL REMAINS	1695	1526.7	25	21.67	100.0

NA=Not applicable

Table 7.6 presents remains from the flotation of smaller pit and post feature fill at 9TR54. Most of these smaller features (Features 31, 32, 34, 37, 40, 41, 75) contained domestic refuse associated with the exterior activity area, a relatively open ground between Structure 1 and the Northern Structure. Features 44 and 45 were small pits located south of the large trash pit Features 29, 30, and 33 and Structure 1 (Ledbetter et al. 2002; see Figure 5.7, this volume).

A minimum of one mussel, one unidentified fish, two small unidentified turtles, two deer, and one cow were recovered from flotation samples (Table 7.6). Approximately three pounds of biomass (1.11 kg) was represented, most of which was contributed by mammals. Cow contributed 44 percent of the biomass (based on one element), followed by deer (5%) and turtles (3%).

Invertebrates

Ten very small fragments of freshwater mussel (Unionidae family) were recovered from Features 31 and 33, located in the Exterior Activity Area. These remains comprise a negligible portion of the dietary biomass (<0.1%) but do indicate that mussels were occasionally exploited. Three shell fragments were burned.

Table 7.6: Species list: Salenojuh or Buzzard's Roost Town (9TR54), Feature Flotation Samples

Taxon	NISP	Weight (gm)	MNI	Biomass (kg)	% Biomass
Unionidae (Freshwater Mussel Family)	3	<0.1	1	<0.01	<0.1
Unidentified Fish	1	<0.1	1	<0.01	<0.1
Unidentified Small Turtle	6	1.1	2	0.03	2.7
Unidentified Bird	1	<0.1	1	<0.01	<0.1
Odocoileus virginianus (White-tailed Deer)	4	2.0	2	0.05	4.5
Bos c.f. *taurus* (Domestic Cow)	1	25.7	1	0.49	44.1
Unidentified Medium-Large Mammal	143	23.9	NA	0.46	41.4
Unidentified Mammal	91	3.5	NA	0.08	7.2
TOTAL MAMMAL	239	55.1	3	1.08	97.2
Unidentified Bone	4	<0.1	NA	NA	NA
TOTAL FAUNAL REMAINS	254	56.2	8	1.11	100.0

NA=Not applicable

One fish spine was recovered from Feature 31. It could not be identified beyond class. This element indicates that fish were consumed, at least occasionally, but suggests that they did not constitute a major component of the diet on this part of the site (<0.1% of biomass).

Ten burned fragments of the shell of a river cooter (*Pseudemys* cf. *concinna*) were found in Feature 133, a small pit in the Interior Yard Area. These remains probably represent a single individual. Unidentified turtle shell (n=8) was found in four features (29, 31, 33, and 45) in the Structure 1 yard area. Based on size and morphology, these probably represent four individuals of the Emydidae (box and pond turtle) and/or Kinosternidae (mud and musk turtle) families. None of the fragments could be conclusively identified. Five (63%) were burned. Turtles often provided the second or third largest amount of dietary biomass in many Southeastern prehistoric aboriginal assemblages. They supplied only 0.9 percent of the biomass at 9TR54.

No bird species were identified, although 13 fragments of unidentified bird bone were recovered from Feature 30, a large trash pit near Structure 1, and Feature 31, a thermal pit in the Exterior Activity Area. Most of the bird remains represent a medium-sized individual(s), in the size range of a chicken or duck. Three long bone fragments were burned. Birds provided 0.2 percent of the dietary biomass, an unusually low percentage of bird biomass compared with most Southeastern aboriginal assemblages.

A total of 1,891 mammal bones were recovered (Tables 7.5 and 7.6). The remains of at least 14 deer (*Odocoileus virginianus*), 6 cows (*Bos* cf. *taurus*), and 2 pigs (*Sus scrofa*) were identified from the features at 9TR54. Among the identified species, deer bone comprised the largest percentage of remains, bone weight, and biomass, followed by cows. Pigs provide a much lower percentage of the remains and biomass in the assemblage (fourth-ranked after turtles). Mammals overall provided 98 percent of the total dietary biomass in the assemblage, a much higher percentage of mammal to bird and turtle biomass than is usually observed in Southeastern prehistoric assemblages. Most of the mammal remains (n=1,450; 74%) were found in the three large trash-filled pits, Features 29, 30, and 33, located in the Structure 1 yard area. All of the pig and cattle bone was found in features near Structure 1. Interestingly, no bone remains were recovered from a large pit, Feature 69, also located in this cluster of features.

Deer were the most ubiquitous species identified, occurring in 8 out of 19 features in both the Northern Structure and Southern Structure 1 areas. Twenty-six percent (n=46) of the deer remains represent hocks, ankle, and foot elements (Table 7.7). Sixty-five percent (n=116) represent deer cranial elements or teeth. However, most of these remains (n=100) represent one skull (*in situ*) from Feature 33. Fifteen loose deer teeth and a jaw fragment were recovered from Features 29 and 33, in a yard area near Structure 1. The remaining 9 percent represent other deer body parts, upper leg bones and vertebrae.

Twenty-two fragments of deer bone were burned (14 skull, 3 teeth, 1 carpal/tarsal, 1 astragalus, and 3 long bone fragments). Deer humeri from Features 29 and 68 exhibited possible hacked marks. Seven deer were aged more than 2–3 years, and one was aged less than 2–3 years at time of death (Reitz and Wing 1999:76). One buck was represented by an antler fragment.

Cattle were identified in 5 (Features 29, 30, 33, 88, and 90 near Structure 1) out of 19 features at 9TR54. Most body parts were represented (Table 7.7). However, 56 percent (n=9) of the elements were skull, tooth, ankle, or feet fragments. A cow femur (upper hind leg) from Feature 29 was burned and had superficial cuts along the shaft. An *in situ* cow scapula was found in Feature 88, a pit associated with Structure 1. Hacked marks were identified on a metatarsal (hind ankle) and humerus from Feature 30 and on a cow long bone fragment from Feature 33. Fused vertebrae represented a cow more than 7–9 years old at time of death (Reitz and Wing 1999:76).

Pig remains consisted of two tooth fragments that were identified in Features 29 and 30, located near Structure 1. The contributed proportion of pig biomass was approximately equal to that of birds in the screened assemblage.

Table 7.7: Element distribution: Salenojuh or Buzzard's Roost Town
(9TR41, 9TR54) (from Ledbetter et al. 2002)

Portion	Deer		Cow		Pig	
	NISP	%	NISP	%	NISP	%
Head	101	56.7	4	25.0	0	0
Loose Teeth	15	8.4	1	6.3	2	100.0
Forequarter	12	6.7	3	18.8	0	0
Axial	2	1.2	3	18.8	0	0
Hindquarter	2	1.2	1	6.3	0	0
Ankles and Feet	46	25.8	4	25.0	0	0
TOTAL	178*	100.0	16**	100.0	2	100.0

* 6 deer elements were unidentified long bone fragments—not included on table
** 3 cow elements were unidentified long bone fragments—not included on table

It is possible that additional remains of pigs were present but were reduced to unidentifiable fragments through processing or disposal activities.

The majority of mammal bone (n=1,686; 89%) was not identifiable beyond class. The large number of unidentified medium-to-large mammal bone fragments indicates that additional processing of long bones and other elements of deer and cattle beyond that required by butchering took place.

Summary of the Lower Creek Diet at Salenojuh

When compared with other Southeastern prehistoric faunal assemblages, the Historic Salenojuh assemblage is skewed toward mammal biomass. The mammal bone assemblage is heavily weighted toward skull and lower leg portions that are traditionally considered butchering refuse, or parts that result from the processing of by-products, such as hides, gelatin, or glue. Other meatier body parts are present in lower numbers and exhibit cut marks, indicating both butchery and portioning of carcasses of cattle and deer, probably the breaking of upper leg bones to extract marrow or to prepare bone grease, and the slicing of meat from a cow femur (upper hind leg).

Burning or calcining were found on 22 percent (n=479) of the bone in the 9TR41 and 9TR54 assemblages, indicating food preparation techniques that resulted in burning of ankle and foot bones, skull and teeth, and a few long bones of deer (n=24). The only burned cow bone, a femur, was also the element with superficial cut marks. Hacked cuts were found on two deer and three cattle elements (2 deer humeri [upper foreleg], 1 cow humerus, 1 cow metatarsal [hind ankle], and 1 cow long bone fragment). No rodent or carnivore gnaw marks were identified in the assemblage, indicating that bones were either completely consumed by scavenging animals or were usually buried and not left exposed to such animals.

The bone assemblage, particularly from the large trash pits at 9TR54, is heavily weighted toward skull and lower leg portions that are traditionally considered butchering refuse. Given the uneven representation of cow, pig, and deer body parts, these remains from the large trash pits may reflect specialized activities, such as processing of deer and cow hides, as well. Deer heads and feet were, at least occasionally, brought to the site still attached to hides and may be discard resulting from hide processing. Over half of the deer exploited were more than two years old. One cow was more than seven years of age when butchered.

Burning was observed on three long bones of birds, three mussel shells, the shell of a river cooter, and an unidentified small turtle shell. Ninety-one percent (n=438) of burned remains were unidentified mammal and bone fragments. Turtles may have been baked in the shell, while larger mammal portions may have been cooked over an open hearth, where less meaty exposed bones burned. Other food preparation techniques, such as stewing, baking, or deboning and drying meat, would not have resulted in burned elements. Preparation of bone grease may explain the large number of burned or calcined mammal bone fragments. This process involved smashing the bones, then cooking them repeatedly in a vessel to extract grease.

Few conclusions can be made about the remains from 9TR41. One deer more than two years at time of death was identified. Most remains were recovered from postmolds of a structure. These very small remains may be floor sweepings from the structure interior. The poor representation of birds, turtles, and fish in this riverine setting is unusual, although differential preservation of bone remains owing to soil acidity, and cultural factors such as trampling, animal scavenging, and food processing and disposal techniques must be considered. The zooarchaeological analysis suggests that bone remains from the large trash pits (Features 29, 30, 33, and 68) at the 9TR54 farmstead may not represent a strictly domestic diet but rather a mixture of domestic diet and animal hide-processing refuse.

Occupations at Salenojuh represent a transitional period just before and following the Revolutionary War (1770–1790), when the deerskin trade was waning and perhaps was being supplemented with trade in cowhides. The presence of deer and cow elements representing meatier portions indicate that Creek households at Salenojuh consumed these animals. The evidence for consumption of domestic animals may reflect famine conditions at Salenojuh by the 1780s, since historical accounts indicate that the Maskókî raised, but usually did not consume, domestic cattle and pigs (Braund 1993; Ethridge 1996, 2003; Foster 2003b; Piker 1998, 2004). The residents may have simply decided to add domestic meats to their traditional diet. If they were killing cattle for hides, they probably were consuming the meat. This may be especially true if it was a more cost-effective alternative to venison, which was becoming scarce.

ZOOARCHAEOLOGICAL ANALYSIS OF THE COWETUH SETTLEMENTS

Site 9ME50 represents a small portion of the Cowetuh settlements (Ledbetter et al. 1996). The settlements were located on a broad, flat alluvial terrace on the east side of the Chattahoochee River, at the confluence of Bull Creek, and across from Cowetuh Town proper (see Figure 3.6, this volume). Part of the site was excavated under the direction of Jerald Ledbetter of Southeastern Archeological Services, Inc. for the Georgia Department of Transportation. The project was conducted to mitigate the impacts of the Columbus Riverwalk project in Columbus, Georgia (Ledbetter et al. 1996). Ledbetter also reported on previous excavations undertaken in the project area.

Artifacts recovered from these Cowetuh out-settlements included late Creek Lawson Field Phase ceramics. Late-eighteenth-century European ceramics, glass, and metal artifacts were also found in association with the Lower Creek component. Zooarchaeological analysis focused on two large Creek pits, Features 1 and 2. Feature 1 was a previously excavated and unscreened sample (Schnell 1970); Feature 2 was systematically excavated and screened (Ledbetter et al. 1996).

Over 3,900 vertebrate and invertebrate remains were recovered from two large trash-filled pit features, Features 1 and 2, at site 9ME50. These remains represent a sample of the Lower Creek animal diet at households in the Cowetuh settlements circa 1800. Feature 1 was a large trash-filled pit excavated in 1969 (Schnell 1970). Bone remains were not systematically excavated or collected, so a systematic analysis was not attempted. Instead, faunal remains from Feature 1 were scanned for identifiable species. Those represented in this unscreened sample included domestic cow (*Bos* cf. *taurus*), deer (*Odocoileus virginianus*), bear (*Ursus americanus*), domestic pig (*Sus scrofa*), turkey (*Meleagris gallopavo*), domestic chicken (*Gallus gallus*), freshwater mussel (Unionidae family), box turtle (*Terrapene carolina*), and cooter/slider turtle (*Pseudemys/ Trachemys* ssp.). Most of the bone represented cow and deer, and most of the bone was unburned.

In Feature 1, hacked marks, made with an ax or cleaver, were found on deer, bear, and cow bone (Figures 7.1 and 7.2). Superficial cuts were noted on astragali of both deer and cow. These cuts probably represent the removal of lower legs and feet at the hock joint or some additional processing of this body part. Most of the elements represent adult animals. One unfused cow ulna indicated an animal less than 3.5 years of age. A cow maxillary fragment with an erupted second molar and erupting third molar indicated an animal less than 2–2.5 years of age. Other cow elements indicated that most cattle were at least 1.5 years of age, e.g., fused calcanei and phalanges (Reitz and Wing 1999:76; Schmid 1972:77).

Most of the remains from Feature 1 represent what is usually considered butchering refuse, including head, lower leg, and foot elements. Few bones representing the meatiest portions of these animals were observed. Many of these remains may represent refuse primarily associated with processing of deer, and possibly cow, hides. The hide trade was an important activity to the Lower Creek during the eighteenth century in Georgia, although its importance waned following the Revolutionary War. Food remains were also included in the pit. The pit probably represents a mixture of domestic and trade-oriented activities that occurred on Lower Creek households circa 1820.

Faunal remains from Feature 2 were systematically collected from 0.64 cm (¼ in) screened, 0.32 cm (⅛ in) screened, and feature flotation samples. Thirty-nine percent (n=1,539) of remains from this feature were identified to family, genus, or species. Vertebrate and invertebrate bone remains from this feature represent a diet composed of primarily mammal biomass, most of which was contributed by deer and a domestic cow (Table 7.8). These included 4 deer (*Odocoileus virginianus*), 1 domestic cow (*Bos* cf. *taurus*), and 3 domestic pigs (*Sus scrofa*). Four birds, 3 turtles, 6 fish, 4 frog/toads, and 7 freshwater mussels comprised smaller portions of the diet. Birds, turtles, and fish, respectively, provided the second, third, and fourth highest proportion of the represented biomass. A total of 28.61 kilograms (63 lbs) of dietary biomass was calculated for this pit.

Among all of the identified mammal species, four deer provided one-third of the dietary biomass in the assemblage. A domestic cow and three pigs provided the second and third highest mammal biomass in Feature 2. The two mice (cf. *Peromyscus* ssp.) from Feature 2 were considered commensal, since they are scavengers attracted to human garbage.

Table 7.9 presents the distribution of mammal elements. Almost all body parts of all three species were identified, indicating that they were being butchered and used for food for the household. Axial elements, ribs and vertebrae, can be difficult to identify to species and may be underrepresented in this table. Ankle and foot bones may be overrepresented because they are very dense and have small marrow cavities. They may have preserved better and may have been broken up less often for marrow or bone grease.

Head, loose teeth, and ankle and feet bones comprised 88 percent of the deer remains. The large proportion of deer ankle and foot bones may indicate processing of raw hides that were brought to the site with the lower legs and feet

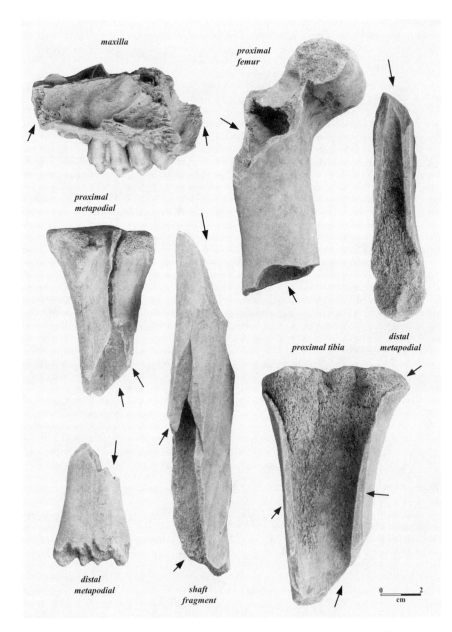

Figure 7.1. Butchered cattle elements from Feature 1, Cowetuh Settlements (9ME50).

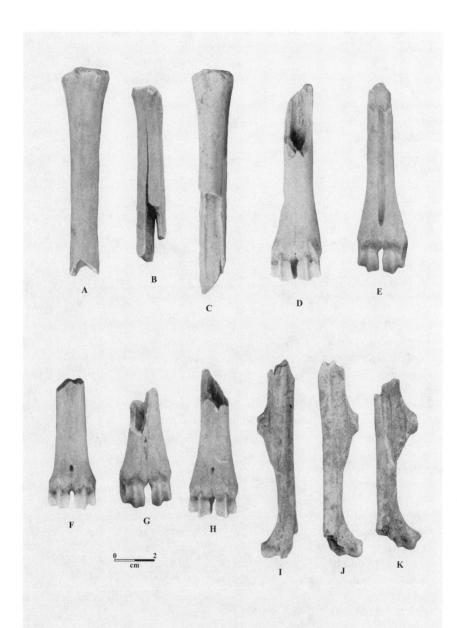

Figure 7.2. A–H, butchered deer metapodials from Feature 1; I–K, breakage pattern and cut spurs on turkey metatarsals, Feature 2, Cowetuh Settlements (9ME50).

Table 7.8: Species list: Cowetuh Settlements (9ME50), Feature 2, 0.64 cm (1/4 in) screened (from O'Steen in Ledbetter 1997)

Taxon	NISP	Weight (gm)	MNI	Biomass (kg)	% Biomass
Unionidae (Freshwater Mussel Family)	73	77.6	7	0.02	0.1
Ictalurus cf. *punctatus*. (Prob. Channel Catfish)	29	2.9	3	0.06	0.2
Micropterus cf. *salmoides*. (Prob. Largemouth Bass)	37	7.3	3	0.15	0.5
Micropterus ssp. (Bass)	12	0.5	NA	0.02	0.1
Unidentified Fish	1034	48.8	NA	0.69	2.4
TOTAL FISH	1112	59.5	6	0.92	3.2
Rana c.f. *catesbiana* (Prob. Bullfrog)	39	1.0	4	0.08	0.3
Terrapene carolina (Box Turtle)	2	11.6	1	0.16	0.6
Pseudemys sp. (Cooter/Slider)	27	31.3	1	0.32	1.1
Dierochyles reticularia (Chicken Turtle)	114	268.0	1	1.34	4.7
TOTAL TURTLE	143	310.9	3	1.82	6.4
Meleagris gallopavo (Wild Turkey)	100	92.1	2	1.25	4.4
Gallus gallus (Domestic Chicken)	936	25.7	1	0.39	1.4
Passeriformes (Perching Bird Order)	1	<0.1	1	<0.01	<0.1
Unidentified Medium-Large Bird	188	35.6	NA	0.53	1.9
TOTAL BIRD	1225	153.4	4	2.17	7.7
Sciurus carolenensis (Grey Squirrel)	2	0.2	1	0.01	<0.1
C.f. *Peromyscus* ssp. (Prob. Mouse)	8	0.1	2	<0.01	<0.1
Odocoileus virginianus (White-Tailed Deer)	117	695.4	4	9.51	33.2
Sus scrofa (Domestic Pig)	28	44.1	3	0.80	2.8
Bos taurus (Domestic Cow)	15	349.8	1	5.12	17.9
Unidentified Small Mammal	13	1.9	NA	0.05	0.2
Unidentified Medium-Large Mammal	1200	583.4	NA	8.12	28.4
TOTAL MAMMAL	1383	1674.9	11	23.61	82.5
TOTAL FAUNAL REMAINS	3975	2277.3	35	28.62	100.0

NA=Not Applicable

Table 7.9: Element distribution: Cowetuh Settlements (9ME50), Feature 2

Portion	Deer		Cow		Pig	
	NISP	%	NISP	%	NISP	%
Head	1	0.9	3	12.0	6	21.4
Loose Teeth	6	5.2	2	8.0	9	32.1
Forequarter	3	2.6	1	4.0	1	3.6
Axial	7	6.1	11	44.0	0	0
Hindquarter	4	3.5	3	12.0	1	3.6
Ankles and Feet	94	81.7	5	20.0	11	39.3
TOTAL	115	100.0	25	100.0	28	100.0

attached, in addition to butchering debris from deer carcasses or quarters of venison that were brought to the site for consumption.

The largest percentage of cattle elements represented vertebrae and ribs. The presence of these elements, and the representation of all body parts, supports the butchering and consumption of these animals. All parts of pigs, except vertebrae and ribs, were identified. Ninety-three percent of pig bones were head, loose teeth, and ankle and foot bones. The representation of almost all cattle and pig body parts supports butchering, preparation, and consumption of these animals at this household.

All ageable deer were more than 1–1.5 years; one was less than 2–2.5 years, and one was more than 2.5 years at time of death (Gilbert 1980:102; Reitz and Wing 1999:76). A male, a female, and a juvenile pig were identified. The male pig and female pig were over one year of age (Schmid 1972:77).

Deer elements with superficial cuts and a possible hacked cut identified on a metacarpal (lower foreleg) are depicted in Figure 7.3. The hacked mark suggests removal of a foreshank portion or disarticulation of the lower from the upper foreleg. The remaining identified cuts on deer bones were superficial and appear to represent either slicing or carving meat off of large portions and the disarticulation of the knee joint and hock joints. No cuts were definitely identified on any other mammal bone, including cow and pig remains.

Thirty-one percent (n=422) of mammal elements were burned or calcined. Most of these were unidentifiable beyond class. Burning on deer elements suggests that portions were occasionally prepared over an open hearth, where less meaty portions such as ankles and feet were burned. Two deer ribs and five ankle and foot elements were burned. No cow bone was burned. Six pig metapodials (ankle bones) were burned. Two hind leg elements of a juvenile squirrel were burned.

9 ME50 Feature 2

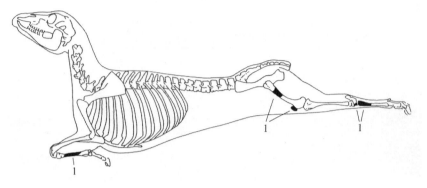

Figure 7.3. Diagram of hacked cuts on deer elements, Feature 2, Cowetuh Settlements (9ME50).

As a group, birds provided the second largest amount of dietary biomass, following mammals. Among identified bird species, two male turkeys (*Meleagris gallopavo*) provided the largest proportion of the represented diet. Approximately 97 percent (n=909) of the domestic chicken (*Gallus gallus*) bone was eggshell fragments. One small perching bird (Passeriformes order) was identified by a tibia (lower leg bone). No cut marks were found on bird bone, but a breakage pattern was noted on the distal condyles of male turkey metatarsals. This breakage pattern probably represents the removal of lower legs and feet from the upper torso of these birds (see Figure 7.2). Interestingly, the male spurs on these metatarsals had been cut off. These spurs are used to strike predators, and they are often cut off of captive male turkeys. Spurs are removed to prevent injuries to turkey hens, among fighting males, and to their human keepers. The size and morphology of turkey remains in the assemblage fall within the ranges for wild turkeys, and they were identified as such. However, the cut spurs could indicate a group of wild turkeys that was kept penned or otherwise contained until needed. Five percent (n=65) of the bird bone was burned, including three turkey leg bones, a chicken wing tip, and three chicken leg or wing elements. The remaining burned bone was unidentifiable.

As a group, turtles provided the third highest proportion of biomass in Feature 2. Three species, a box turtle (*Terrapene carolina*), a cooter/slider (*Pseudemys/Trachemys* ssp.), and a chicken turtle (*Dierochyles reticularia*) were identified. The chicken turtle remains represent one large individual from the north half of Feature 2. All but one turtle element represented shell and carapace fragments. A total of 17 turtle shell fragments (9.3 percent of turtle remains) were burned. No cut marks or other modifications were noted.

Three freshwater catfish (*Ictalurus* cf. *punctatus.*) and three largemouth bass (*Micropterus* cf. *salmoides*) were identified in Feature 2. Fish provided the fourth highest percentage (3 percent) of the dietary biomass from the feature. Most of these remains represent very small fish that could have been easily caught in nets or with small hooks. Some may represent food consumed by larger fish. Approximately 92 percent (n=950) of fish remains were scales, spines, ribs and vertebrae that were difficult to identify to even the family level. Approximately 7 percent (n=76) of the fish bones was burned, including catfish vertebrae, bass skull fragments, and unidentified fish spines, ribs, and skull fragments. No cuts or other modifications were noted.

The four probable bullfrogs (*Rana* cf. *catesbiana*) may have been commensal species, since they often burrow into the soil. However, most remains were leg and pelvis fragments (n=27; 78%). One skull fragment and vertebrae were also identified. The lack of skeletal completeness and burning on two elements suggests that they may have been a very minor dietary element (0.3% of biomass). It may also be the result of differential preservation of these small remains. Seven freshwater mussels (Unionidae family) provided even less of the biomass than frogs, only 0.1 percent of the total. None of the shellfish remains were burned. No other modifications were noted on frog and shellfish elements.

Summary of Lower Creek Diet at the Cowetuh Settlements

Approximately 4,000 vertebrate and invertebrate faunal remains were recovered from the circa 1800 Creek Features 1 and 2 at site 9ME50. Bone remains from Feature 1 were scanned for identifiable species. Those represented in this unscreened sample include domestic cow, deer, bear, domestic pig, turkey, domestic chicken, freshwater mussel, box turtle, and cooter/slider turtle. Most of the bone represents cow and deer, and most of it is unburned. Hacked marks were found on deer, bear, and cow bone. Superficial cuts noted on the hock joints of both deer and cow probably represent the removal of lower legs and feet at this joint. No sawed cuts were observed. Most of the elements represent adult animals aged 1–3.5 years at time of death. Most of the remains from Feature 1 represent what is usually considered butchering refuse, including head, lower leg, and foot elements. Few bones representing the meatiest portions of these animals were observed.

Bone remains from Feature 2 at site 9ME50 represent a diet composed of primarily mammal biomass, including 4 deer (33%) and 1 domestic cow (18%). A minimum of 3 pigs, 1 squirrel, 4 birds, 3 turtles, 6 fish, 4 bullfrogs, and 7 freshwater mussels comprised smaller but consistent portions of the diet. Following deer and cows, birds (8%), turtles (6%), fish (3%), and domestic pigs (3%) provided, respectively, the second, third, fourth, and fifth largest proportion of the biomass.

One possible hacked mark probably represented the disarticulation of a deer foreleg. The remaining identified cuts were superficial and appear to represent either carving meat off of large portions or the disarticulation of the knee joint and hock joints. No cuts were identified on any other mammal bone, including cow and pig remains. Burning was observed on deer, squirrel, and pig leg and foot elements and on bird legs and wings. Burning suggests that these animals were occasionally roasted over an open fire, where less meaty, exposed portions such as ankles, feet, and wings were burned. This also suggests that these animals were often roasted prior to removal and discard of these body parts, so these burned bones probably do not represent butchering refuse.

These results provide further support to the idea that by circa 1800, the Lower Creek at the outlying Cowetuh household had incorporated Euro-American domestic animals and chickens into their diet. This pattern may indicate hardship conditions, wherein the Maskókî were forced to consume animals that were documented historically to be raised only for sale. These changes were probably hastened by the documented depletion and habitat destruction of wild animals, including deer, bears, and turkeys, during the eighteenth century.

Hunting, fishing, and collecting supplied most of the meat protein in the Lower Creek diet at the turn of the nineteenth century. Wild species, including deer, turtles, turkeys, fish, and river mussels provided most of the meat protein and probably most of the hides. By this time, however, domestic cattle, pigs, and chickens comprised about one-fifth of the Lower Creek diet at the Cowetuh Settlements.

ZOOARCHAEOLOGICAL ANALYSIS OF
THE OCHILLEE CREEK FARMSTEAD

The Ochillee Creek site was named for the Chattahoochee River tributary on which it is located. Although this outlying farmstead has not been definitely associated with a known Lower Creek town, artifacts, architecture, and proximity suggest that this was probably a farmstead associated with the people of Cussetuh (see Chapter 5 on architecture). Artifacts recovered at the site indicate occupation of the farmstead from circa 1800 to 1820 (Cowie 2001). Excavations at Ochillee Creek were conducted under the direction of Dean Wood and Sarah Cowie of Southern Research. The work was conducted to mitigate the impacts of installing utility poles associated with a rail loading facility. Only a limited part of the site was excavated (see Figure 5.8, this volume). The site report by Southern Research (Cowie 2001) provides a complete recordation and reporting of all analyzed zooarchaeological data from 0.64 cm (¼ in) screened feature proveniences and feature flotation samples. In the original site report, the zooarchaeological data were tabulated and discussed separately for the appropriate analytical units (fill episodes) in Feature 8 and individually for the other features. These results are lumped below for Feature 8 and summarized for the other Lower Creek features.

A total of 1,281 faunal remains were analyzed in this study. Vertebrate and invertebrate remains (n=754; 59%) were recovered from 0.64 cm (¼ in) screened deposits from seven features. An additional 327 faunal remains (26%) were recovered from feature flotation samples. Most remains were recovered from Feature 8 (n=881; 69%).

The majority (n=663; 89%) of 0.64 cm (¼ inch) screened faunal remains were recovered from Feature 8, hypothesized to be a clay extraction pit that was eventually filled with site refuse. This pit, 1.2 by 1.3 meters, contained four major fill episodes, including primary and secondary deposits of Creek and European ceramics, brass and bone buttons, clay pipe stems, olive green bottle glass, metal tools and nails, burned clay, and animal bone. An additional 218 faunal remains (66.7%) were recovered from 24 liters of flotation samples from this feature. The following presents a summary of the zooarchaeological analysis of Feature 8.

Screened remains from Feature 8 represented 17.56 kg (39 lbs) of dietary biomass (Table 7.10). A minimum of one freshwater mussel (Unionidae family), a channel catfish (*Ictalurus* cf. *punctatus*), one unidentified fish, four turtles (Kinosternidae family), two domestic chickens (*Gallus gallus*), one rabbit (*Sylvilagus* ssp.), one raccoon (*Procyon lotor*), three domestic cows (*Bos* cf. *taurus*), five domestic pigs (*Sus scrofa*), six deer (*Odocoileus virginianus*), one black bear (*Ursus americanus*), and one juvenile even-toed ungulate (Order Artiodactlya) were identified. Twenty percent (n=130) of faunal remains from Feature 8 were identified to family, genus, or species.

Deer provided 35 percent of biomass, followed by cattle (23%), pigs (11%), turtles (1%), and the bear and chickens (<1% each). Fish, small mammals, and a freshwater mussel provided less than 0.2 percent each of biomass from the feature. The bear was represented by two canines that represent an adult female. If these teeth represent an entire bear carcass, which is approximately 200–300 lbs. (Golly 1962), bear would have been a more significant part of the diet than is indicated by the biomass calculation. The remainder of this carcass may be in unexcavated features, or it could have been disposed of elsewhere on or off the site.

Hacked marks were found on 169 identified and unidentified bones from Feature 8 (discussed below). Two fragments of unidentified medium-to-large mammal bone appeared to have abraded or utilized edges. One deer radius was abraded, either by a tool or by unusual carnivore gnawing activity. This element is also rodent-gnawed, indicating that it was exposed for some time to scavenging animals.

Thirty-six percent (n=239) of remains were burned or calcined. Eight car-

Table 7.10: Species list: Ochillee Creek Farmstead, Feature 8, all strata combined, 0.64 cm (1/4 in) screen (from O'Steen and Raymer in Cowie 2001)

Taxon	NISP	Weight (gm)	MNI	Biomass (kg)	% Biomass
Unionidae (Freshwater Mussel Family)	1	<0.1	1	<0.01	<0.1
Ictalurus cf. *punctatus* (Prob. Channel Catfish)	1	0.1	1	<0.01	<0.1
Unidentified Fish	2	0.1	1	0.01	<0.1
TOTAL FISH	3	0.2	2	0.01	<0.1
Kinosternidae (Mud and Musk Turtle Family)	2	0.4	1	0.02	0.1
Unidentified Turtle	30	8.3	3	0.19	1.1
TOTAL TURTLE	32	8.7	4	0.21	1.2
Gallus gallus (Domestic Chicken)	19	5.6	2	0.10	0.6
Unidentified Medium Bird	8	1.3	NA	0.03	0.2
TOTAL BIRD	27	6.9	2	0.13	0.8
Procyon lotor (Raccoon)	1	0.9	1	0.02	0.1
Sylvilagus floridanus (Cottontail Rabbit)	1	0.1	1	<0.01	<0.1
Ursus americanus (Black Bear)	2	5.6	1	0.12	0.7
Odocoileus virginianus (White-tailed Deer)	57	383.8	6	6.15	35.0
Order *Artiodactyla* (Even-toed Ungulate juvenile)	3	0.6	1	0.02	0.1
Bos cf. *taurus* (Domestic Cow)	16	244.7	3	4.02	22.9
Sus scrofa (Domestic Pig)	30	102.8	5	1.89	10.8
Unidentified Medium-Large Mammal	483	280.1	NA	4.98	28.4
Unidentified Small Mammal	1	0.4	NA	0.01	<0.1
TOTAL MAMMAL	594	1019.0	18	17.21	98.0
Unidentified Bone	6	1.9	NA	NA	NA
TOTAL FAUNAL REMAINS	663	1036.7	27	17.56	100.0

nivore-gnawed and two rodent-gnawed elements were recovered. One cow tibia exhibited both rodent and carnivore gnaw marks. Carnivore gnaw marks were found on a cow long bone, a deer calcaneus (ankle bone), a pig humerus (foreleg), and four unidentified medium-to-large mammal fragments. Rodent gnaw marks were found on a mammal rib fragment.

Two cattle more than 1.5–2 years at time of death were identified. One pig aged greater than 1–2 years and one aged less than 1.5 years at time of death were represented (Reitz and Wing 1999:76; Schmid 1972:75). A laying hen was identified by the presence of spongy medullary deposits inside two chicken long bones.

An antler fragment identified a male deer. Two deer were aged more than 1–2 years, and one was more than three years of age at time of death. Two bear canines represent an adult female at least 12 months of age (Gilbert 1980:102, 108; Reitz and Wing 1999:76). A small, porous pig scapula fragment may indicate a juvenile individual; however, this is not conclusive since the adult pigs in this assemblage were about half the size of modern adult skeletons. Three elements of an unidentified artiodactyl were determined to be from a juvenile, based on the porous texture of the remains.

Remains from Feature 8 flotation samples (n=218) represent at least two more unidentified fish, *Kinosternid* (mud and musk) and *Emydid* (pond and box) turtles, a small perching bird (*Passeriformes* order), and another unidentified small bird. Chicken eggshell was also recovered. A cow long bone fragment, a pig phalange (toe bone), and a deer metapodial (ankle bone) were also identified in these samples. Seventy-two percent (n=156) of flotation remains were burned (O'Steen and Raymer in Cowie 2001:Appendix B).

Feature 8 Meat Cuts and Processing

All but two cuts in the Ochillee Creek assemblage (from Features 5 and 57) were identified from Feature 8. Figure 7.4 illustrates the portions of elements of deer, cow, and pig that had hacked cut marks. Thirty-four cuts of venison, eight cuts of pork, and seven cuts of beef were recorded. All of these were hacked cuts, probably made with an ax or cleaver. Two unidentified medium-to-large mammal long bone fragments had superficial cut marks. Superficial cuts were found on the proximal end of a deer phalange (toe) and three cow phalanges. No sawed cuts were identified.

Most cuts or cut marks on all species represent portioning of head, lower legs, and fore- and hindquarters (Figure 7.4). Two deer antlers had hacked cuts where they were removed from the skull. Many of the cuts on lower leg and foot elements represent multiples of the same body part. The numbers on Figure 7.4 represent the number of duplicate cut locations. Some cuts probably represent further division or processing of larger portions for marrow, bone

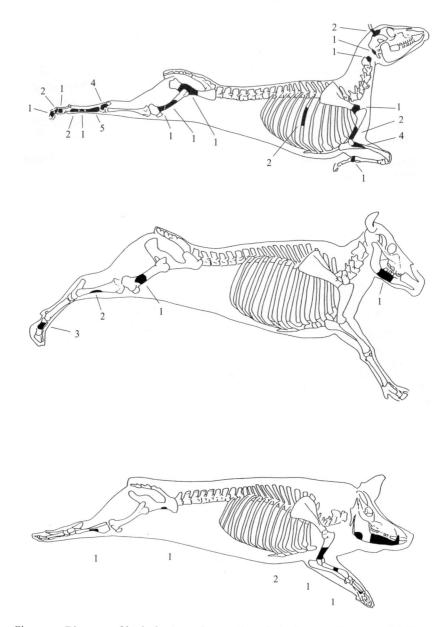

Figure 7.4. Diagrams of hacked cuts on deer, cattle, and pig elements, Feature 8, Ochillee Creek Farmstead (9CE379).

grease, stew, gelatin, or glue making. Many of the unidentified mammal long bone fragments suggest this type of additional processing and may represent the larger, marrow-rich elements, such as the humerus and femur.

For deer, 18 (53%) cuts represented cutting or removal of lower legs and feet, 3 (9%) represented forequarter roasts, 4 (11%) represented foreshank removal or stew bones, 3 (9%) represented roast-sized hind leg cuts, 4 (11%) represented removal of the head and antlers, and 2 (6%) represent rib segments (Figure 7.4). For pork, one cut (13%) represented removal of a forefoot, two (25%) represented head or jowl processing following removal of the sinuses, one (13%) represented a foreshank or stew bone, two (25%) represented forequarter or shoulder roasts, and two (25%) represented roast-sized ham and ham shank cuts. For cattle, one cut represents head or jowl processing, three represented roast-sized hindquarter portions, and three probably represent removal of hind feet. On the three cow toes, cuts were made diagonally across the proximal end of the first phalange. One cut mark was identified on a chicken tibiotarsus (lower hind leg). This cut was probably used to sever the lower leg and foot from the upper leg.

A fairly even distribution of deer and pig elements was found in the assemblage (Table 7.11). All body parts of deer and most pig body parts were identified. No forequarter elements, vertebrae, or ribs were identified for cattle. In all three animals, head, teeth, and foot and ankle elements dominated the assemblage (deer 75%; pig 72%; cow 67%). Because of difficulties in identifying ribs and vertebrae to the genus level, axial parts of skeletons may be underrepresented. Ribs, skull, and teeth fragments and long bone fragments that were recorded as unidentified medium-to-large mammal could represent deer, pigs, or cattle, but mammal vertebrae were almost absent from the assemblage. One deer cervical vertebra and two rib fragments were the only identifiable axial elements in the assemblage.

While at least three cows supplied the second highest amount of biomass in Feature 8, the uneven distribution of elements and beef cuts may indicate that only head and hindquarter portions of cow carcasses were brought to, or consumed at, the Ochillee Creek farmstead. It is possible that when a cow was butchered, portions were distributed among several families or related households. This may have been a more efficient way to use a fresh beef carcass, especially during warm weather. This practice, sometimes referred to as a "meat ring," was a cooperative system documented among nineteenth-century rural Euro-American households (Hilliard 1969:5). Several families usually contributed to the care of a cow, then the carcass was divided up and distributed among those families when the cow was butchered. In other cases, neighbors borrowed fresh meat and repaid later as their own animals were slaughtered. Since beef does not preserve as well as pork, this may have provided fresh beef

Table 7.11: Distribution of elements of deer, pig, and cattle at the Ochillee Creek Farmstead, Feature 8 (from O'Steen and Raymer in Cowie 2001)

Portion	Deer	Pig	Cow
Head	13 (23.6%)	3 (12.0%)	1 (11.1%)
Teeth	2 (3.6%)	10 (40.0%)	2 (22.2%)
Forequarter	8 (14.5%)	4 (16.0%)	0
Axial	3 (5.5%)	0	0
Hindquarter	3 (5.5%)	3 (12.0%)	3 (33.3%)
Feet	26 (47.3%)	5 (20.0%)	3 (33.3%)
TOTAL	55	25	9

for several households at a time. It is also possible that the head and foot elements represent the detritus of cowhide processing, an activity that had begun to replace the deer hide trade. Since the entire site was not excavated, it is possible that the missing portions of cow carcasses were located in unexcavated features, or they were discarded elsewhere on the site.

Additional Creek Features at 9CE379

A total of 91 remains (7%) were identified from the screened fill of Features 4, 5, 57, 61, 66, and 70 (O'Steen and Raymer in Cowie 2001:Appendix B). These features included three steep-sided, oval-to-circular pits (Features 5, 57, and 66), two smudge pits (Features 4 and 61), and a circular basin-shaped pit (Feature 70). A total of 200 remains were recovered from 0.64-cm (¼ in) screened feature fill (n=91) and flotation samples (n=109). Poor preservation was evidenced by the surface exfoliation of many of the bones.

A minimum of two pigs, three deer, two cows, a cooter or slider turtle (*Pseudemys/Trachemys* ssp.), and a small bird were represented by 17 remains (8.5% of assemblage). Deer contributed 57 and 67 percent of the biomass in two features, the turtle contributed 4 percent in one feature, cattle contributed 32 and 52 percent in two features, and pigs provided 18 and 33 percent in two features. The remainder was unidentified bone or unidentified mammal remains. Twenty-seven percent (n=25) of screened remains and 39 percent (n=42) of flotation remains were burned or calcined.

A deer ulna and a humerus (foreleg) fragment from Features 5 and 57 were hacked. Carnivore gnaw marks were found on a deer toe in Feature 5. This deer toe and a fused distal humerus from Feature 57 identified two deer more than 1–2 years of age at time of death. A fused cow toe from Feature 57 indicated an individual greater than 1.5–2 years at time of death (Gilbert 1980:102; Reitz and Wing 1999:76).

Summary of Lower Creek Diet at the Ochillee Creek Farmstead

While preservation in Feature 8 was exceptionally good, preservation in the other features was very poor. Feature 8 was associated with a circa 1800–1820 kitchen and summer house of the household compound. The diet represented by remains from these features indicates that domestic mammals (five cattle and seven pigs) and two chickens contributed 48 percent of the dietary biomass, while wild mammals (nine deer, a bear, a raccoon, and a rabbit), five turtles, and four fish contributed 52 percent of the biomass. Overall, mammals contributed the vast majority of dietary biomass, followed by turtles, chickens and unidentified small-to-medium-sized birds, fish, and shellfish.

With the exceptions of pig and cow vertebrae and ribs and cow forequarter elements, all body parts of deer, cattle, and pigs were represented. Evidence of butchering, food preparation, and refuse disposal at Ochillee Creek suggest that residents were indeed consuming all three of these species, along with bear, smaller wild mammals, chickens, turtles, fish, and shellfish. With the exception of one juvenile artiodactyl, which was probably a deer, and one juvenile pig, the animals that could be aged were at least one year of age. At least one male deer and an adult female bear were identified. Laying hens and eggs were also consumed.

Thirty-two cuts of venison, eight cuts of pork, and seven cuts of beef were recorded. All of these were hacked cuts, probably made with an ax or cleaver. Superficial cuts were found on the proximal ends of deer and cow phalanges (toes). Two unidentified medium-to-large mammal long bone fragments had superficial cut marks. Most cuts on all species represent removal and further processing of head, lower legs and feet, and fore- and hindquarters. However, portions of the meatier quarters of deer, cattle, and pigs indicate that roast-sized portions were prepared, presumably for consumption by the household. Many cut and fractured unidentified mammal bones probably represent further division or processing of larger, marrow-rich elements for marrow, bone grease, stew, gelatin, or glue. Superficial cuts likely represent the slicing of meat from larger portions and the disarticulation of feet of large mammals.

SUMMARY OF ZOOARCHAEOLOGICAL REMAINS FROM LOWER CREEK SITES

The data summarized in Tables 7.12–7.15 were derived from the zooarchaeological analysis of the five previously discussed sites, Salenojuh Town (9TR41, 9TR54), the Cowetuh Settlements (9ME50), Cussetuh Town (9CE1), and the Ochillee Creek farmstead (9CE379). These assemblages represent the most comprehensive summary of the faunal remains from Lower Creek households between circa 1750 and 1820 that has been published to date. The comprehensiveness of these data allows us to begin to make systematic and empirically derived conclusions about the faunal adaptations of the late Historic Period Maskókalkî.

Several biases must be considered in evaluating these assemblages. The size of some site faunal assemblages is small. In two instances, the Cowetuh Settlements and the Ochillee Creek farmstead, the majority of zooarchaeological remains were recovered from one large trash-filled feature at each household. This bias may be offset by the fact that at Cussetuh, where 88 features of all types were analyzed, 53 percent (n=8,478) of all remains, and the majority of identifiable remains, were recovered from four large trash-filled pits. Faunal remains from postmolds and other feature types were generally small and unidentifiable. Remains from postmolds appeared to represent floor sweepings from structure interiors. If this is true, the large trash-filled pits are probably representative of diet at the associated households. At Salenojuh and Ochillee Creek, excavations of only part of three household compounds were conducted. In all cases, the area of the sites excavated was limited to the area to be impacted by development so only parts of the known site areas could be examined.

Taphonomic processes that introduced biases included high soil acidity, which resulted in preservation that varied between features on the same site or resulted in poor overall preservation. Burning for refuse disposal, food-processing techniques that involved breaking bones for marrow or cooking bones down to small fragments, trampling by site residents, and scavenging of bone by wild and domestic animals also affected the preservation of remains in these assemblages. Excavation sampling and analytical biases also exist. These biases, many of which were noted in the individual site discussions, must be considered in evaluating these assemblages. The importance of disseminating the data of assemblages that have been systematically analyzed using comparative skeletal collections counteracts many of these problems. The original analyses from the Lower Creek sites in this study are found primarily in archaeological site reports that were printed and distributed in very small numbers.

Table 7.12 presents a list of taxa identified from Lower Creek sites. Over 22,000 faunal remains from these sites were analyzed, and this table presents the 13 percent of remains that could be identified to order or more specific classification. A minimum of 187 individuals was identified. Deer (37%) contributed the largest percentage of MNI, followed by cattle (16%), fish (14%), pigs (7%), birds (6%), shellfish (6%), turtles (6%), and amphibians (3%). Mammals contributed 95 percent of the dietary biomass, and 89 percent of the mammal biomass was contributed by cattle (51%) and deer (38%). Pigs contributed only 3 percent of the represented diet. Following mammals, turtles, birds, and fish, respectively, provided the next highest amounts of biomass. No bison (*Bos bi-*

Table 7.12: Taxa identified on Lower Creek sites, eighteenth to early nineteenth centuries: Salenojuh or Buzzard's Roost Town, Cowetuh Settlements, Cussetuh Town, and Ochillee Creek Farmstead, screened and flotation contexts

Taxon	NISP	MNI	% MNI	Weight (gm)	Biomass (kg)	% Biomass
Unionidae (Freshwater Mussel Family)	84	11	5.9	79.6	0.02	<0.1
Amia calva (Bowfin)	2	2	1.1	0.2	0.01	<0.1
Micropterus ssp. (Bass)	18	3	1.6	1.5	0.04	<0.1
Micropterus cf. *salmoides* (Prob. Largemouth Bass)	37	3	1.6	7.3	0.15	0.2
Ictalurus punctatus (Channel Catfish)	37	6	3.2	3.4	0.06	0.1
Ictalurus ssp. (Freshwater Catfish)	58	9	4.8	3.1	0.06	0.1
Selachimorpha (Shark Superorder)	4	3	1.6	3.4	0.36	0.4
TOTAL FISH	156	26	13.9	18.9	0.68	0.8
Dierochyles reticularia (Chicken Turtle)	114	1	0.5	268.0	1.34	1.5
Pseudemys c.f. *concinna* (Prob. River Cooter)	37	3	1.6	44.1	0.51	0.6
Terrapene carolina (Box Turtle)	32	4	2.1	20.0	0.29	0.3
Kinosternidae (Mud and Musk Turtle Family)	3	2	1.1	1.0	0.02	<0.1
Apalone ssp. (Softshell Turtle)	7	1	0.5	1.3	0.04	<0.1
TOTAL TURTLE	193	11	5.8	334.4	2.20	2.5
Rana/Bufo ssp. (Frog/Toad)	43	6	3.2	1.3	0.11	0.1
TOTAL AMPHIBIAN	43	6	3.2	1.3	0.11	0.1
Gallus gallus (Domestic Chicken)	955	3	1.6	31.3	0.47	0.5
Meleagris gallopavo (Wild Turkey)	104	4	2.1	96.7	1.31	1.5
Anatinae (Duck Subfamily)	2	1	0.5	0.8	0.02	<0.1
Bonasa umbellus (Ruffed Grouse)	1	1	0.5	0.7	0.02	<0.1

Passeriformes (Perching Bird Order)	2	2	1.1	0.1	0.01	<0.1
TOTAL BIRD	1064	11	5.8	129.6	1.83	2.1
Castor canadensis (Beaver)	1	1	0.5	6.1	0.13	0.2
Sylvilagus floridanus (Cottontail Rabbit)	1	1	0.5	0.1	<0.01	<0.1
Tamias striatus (Chipmunk)	3	1	0.5	0.1	<0.01	<0.1
Sciurus carolenensis (Grey Squirrel)	2	1	0.5	0.2	0.01	<0.1
Procyon lotor (Raccoon)	1	1	0.5	0.9	0.02	<0.1
C.f. *Peromyscus* ssp. (Prob. Mouse)	8	2	1.1	0.1	<0.01	<0.1
Ursus americanus (Black Bear)	12	3	1.6	65.0	1.13	1.3
Odocoileus virginianus (White-tailed Deer)	697	69	36.9	2822.5	33.54	37.8
Bos c.f. *taurus* (Domestic Cow)	133	30	16.0	3897.3	44.84	50.5
Sus scrofa (Domestic Pig)	60	13	7.0	157.4	2.50	2.8
Artiodactyla (Even-toed Ungulate Order)	403	NA	NA	104.9	1.73	2.0
TOTAL MAMMAL	1321	122	65.1	7054.6	83.90	94.6
TOTAL FAUNAL REMAINS	2861	187	99.7	7618.4	88.74	100.0

NA=Not Applicable

Table 7.13: Comparison of MNI and biomass percentages for identified taxa from Lower Creek Sites, eighteenth to early nineteenth centuries, screened and flotation contexts

	Salenojuh/ Buzzard's Roost Town (circa 1770–1788) % MNI	Salenojuh/ Buzzard's Roost Town (circa 1770–1788) % Biomass	Cowetuh Settlements (circa 1800) % MNI	Cowetuh Settlements (circa 1800) % Biomass
Domestic Mammals	21.1	48.8	11.4	29.7
Wild Mammals	47.4	49.3	14.3	47.8
Domestic Birds	0*	0*	2.9	2.0
Wild Birds	0*	0*	8.6	6.3
Turtles	15.8	1.8	8.6	9.1
Amphibians	0	0	11.4	0.4
Fish	7.9	0.1	17.1	4.6
Shellfish	7.9	<0.1	20.0	0.1
Commensals	0	0	5.7	<0.1
TOTAL #MNI/ BIOMASS (KG)	38**	14.84**	35**	19.91**

	Ochillee Creek Farmstead (circa 1800–820) % MNI	Ochillee Creek Farmstead (circa 1800–1820) % Biomass	Cussetuh Town (circa 1750–1775) % MNI	Cussetuh Town (circa 1750–1775) % Biomass
Domestic Mammals	32.6	46.3	19.3	64.9
Wild Mammals	30.2	51.2	48.8	32.2
Domestic Birds	4.7	0.7	0*	0*
Wild Birds	2.3	<0.1	4.6	0.2
Turtles	18.6	1.7	3.4	0.9
Amphibians	0	0	2.3	0.1
Fish	9.3	0.1	21.6	1.7
Shellfish	2.3	<0.1	0	0
Commensals	0	0	0	0
TOTAL #MNI/ BIOMASS (KG)	43**	14.08**	88**	51.10**

*Unidentified bird bone was recovered
**Includes MNI and Biomass from unidentified fish and turtle categories

son) were identified in these assemblages, although many cattle elements (aside from lower legs and feet) were highly fragmented. Braund (1993:72) reported that "buffalos" were extinct in Creek country by the early eighteenth century. However, because of the potential for identifying bison, the large artiodactyl remains were examined carefully. Small mammals, including a beaver, a rabbit, a chipmunk, a squirrel, and a raccoon, were relatively uncommon and comprised a very minor amount of biomass (1.5%). Preservation factors may have affected the recovery of small mammal remains.

The most commonly exploited fish were catfish and bass. The shark teeth from Cussetuh probably represent trade items acquired from coastal groups. Fish contributed less than 1 percent of the biomass. Turkeys and chickens were the most common birds consumed. Chicken turtles, box turtles, mud and musk turtles, and softshell turtles were eaten. Birds and reptiles provided approximately equal amounts of biomass (2–2.5%). Bullfrogs may have been minor, perhaps incidental, dietary elements. Hudson (1976:309) noted that snakes, frogs, lizards, snails, insects, and insect larvae were eaten by Southeastern Indians during times of famine. It is possible that some of the amphibian and reptile remains in the Lower Creek assemblages reflect periods of famine. They may also represent incidental species that were captured in fishing nets and may or may not have been consumed.

Overall, among all Lower Creek sites in this study, domestic mammals and chickens contributed 53 percent of the diet, and wild resources represented the remaining 47 percent. Most of the diet was contributed by deer and cattle, but pork, aquatic and terrestrial turtles, wild and domestic birds, bears, fish, small wild mammals, freshwater mussels, and bullfrogs served to vary the meat protein in the diet at Lower Creek households.

Tables 7.13 and 7.14 present comparisons of MNI and biomass for the five sites separately for wild and domestic groups of animals and for all sites combined. Remains from the 1750–1790 households at the towns of Salenojuh and Cussetuh indicate that domestic mammals were raised and consumed by the residents and contributed 49–65 percent of the dietary biomass. The bulk of this biomass was beef. Two pigs from Salenojuh represented less than 1 percent of the biomass. No domestic birds were identified at either site. Wild resources, primarily deer, contributed 35–51 percent of the biomass during this period. Deer bone from Salenojuh may represent both domestic diet and the disposal of lower legs and feet that were brought to the households still attached to raw deer hides. At one structure at Salenojuh, the butchering of cattle was likely represented by the skull and lower leg and foot elements. Cowhide processing may have also taken place in this area. The unexpectedly high amount of domestic cow biomass at these towns may reflect the presence of major trading paths and resident traders. Traders kept their own herds and would have driven

Table 7.14: MNI and biomass percentages combined for Lower Creek sites in Georgia, 1750–1820

	MNI	% MNI	Biomass (kg)	% Biomass
Domestic Mammals	43	21.1	52.68	52.7
Wild Mammals	79	38.7	40.48	40.5
Domestic Birds	3	1.0	0.49	0.5
Wild Birds	8	3.9	1.37	1.4
Turtles	20	9.8	2.80	2.8
Amphibians	6	2.9	0.18	0.2
Fish	32	15.7	1.91	1.9
Shellfish	11	5.4	0.02	<0.1
Commensals	2	1.0	NA	NA
TOTAL	204**	100.0	99.93**	100.0

**Includes MNI and biomass from unidentified fish and turtle categories

cattle through these towns on a regular basis. As cowhides began to replace deer hides as important trade items during the late eighteenth century, the Maskókî in these towns may have been more amenable to ranching than those in outlying villages. Butchery of cattle for hides would have resulted in more beef for consumption.

At the two households at the Cowetuh Settlements and the Ochillee Creek farmstead, circa 1800 to 1820, the domestic diet included chickens, pigs, and cattle. Domesticated resources comprised 32–47 percent of the diet at these sites. The larger percentage of wild meat in the diet may reflect easier access to game because more locations were isolated, away from the larger towns. Given that by the 1750s deer and bear were reportedly extinct from large areas of Creek country (Braund 1993), it is interesting that deer provided one-third of the meat at these households. At Cowetuh, spurs cut off the legs of male turkeys indicate that these birds were probably kept penned. Turkeys provided most of the bird biomass at that household.

Table 7.15 illustrates element distributions for deer, cattle, pigs, and bears from Lower Creek sites. The majority of identified elements of deer (94%), cattle (74%), pigs (85%), and bears (100%) were skull, loose teeth, and ankle and foot elements. The high proportion of head and lower leg elements represents butchering debris, the removal of feet from hides or hind- and forequarters, and the processing of skulls. Jaws and teeth of mammals were highly fragmented, indicating additional processing of heads and jowls and tongue removal.

The lack of larger, marrow-filled upper leg portions probably represents the

Table 7.15: Element distribution: Lower Creek sites, eighteenth to early nineteenth centuries (Salenojuh or Buzzard's Roost Town, Cowetuh Settlements, Cussetuh Town, and Ochillee Creek Farmstead)

Portion	Deer		Cow		Pig		Bear	
	NISP	%	NISP	%	NISP	%	NISP	%
Head	401	41.4	17	12.2	9	16.4	0	0
Loose Teeth	192	19.8	61	43.9	21	38.2	2	16.7
Forequarter	26	2.7	8	5.8	5	9.1	0	0
Axial	15	1.6	16	11.5	0	0	0	0
Hindquarter	15	1.6	12	8.6	4	7.3	0	0
Ankles and Feet	318	32.9	25	18.0	16	29.1	10	83.3
TOTAL	967	100.0	139	100.0	55	100.0	12	100.0

additional processing of these elements for marrow and bone grease. The large numbers of unidentified mammal fragments likely indicate this type of processing. Ribs and vertebrae are also unequally represented, but many of these elements were also highly fragmented and could not be identified to genus or species. According to many historical accounts, deer were butchered, meat was deboned and dried, meat and marrow were consumed, and hides were processed at hunting camps. These activities would result in only portions of carcasses being returned to towns and villages. However, at least some deer were returned to Lower Creek towns either as whole carcasses or as quarters with feet still attached. Raw skins may have been returned with feet and heads attached.

Burned and calcined bones represent both food preparation and disposal techniques. There is evidence that mammals, birds, turtles, fish, and possibly bullfrogs were roasted over fires. Burning was evident on the lower legs and feet of mammals, birds, and frogs, on bird wings, turtle shells, and on fish spines, head elements, and vertebrae. Turtles were at least occasionally roasted in the shell, probably buried in ashes or over active fires. The large number of burned, fragmented, medium-to-large mammal bones may represent the residue of bone grease processing, wherein the bone was cooked until there was little left. Some of these burned bone fragments were probably the result of disposal in fires prior to deposition of ash in trash pits. Some bone may have also been burned *in situ* in trash pits. Other food preparation techniques found in historical accounts, such as stewing, baking, or deboning and drying meat, would not have resulted in burned elements.

The Lower Creek faunal assemblages were assessed for evidence of a prolonged hunting season during the late eighteenth century, as documented by Piker (1998, 2004). Unfortunately, there are little seasonality, sex, or age data for deer that could address the historical evidence. Deer breed year-round in Georgia, so even the presence of fawns in a collection does not constitute clear seasonality data. Certainly, today, more fawns are born in the spring, but they are also born throughout the year. If the Maskókî were hunting from September through early summer of the next year, some indicators might be evidence of shed antlers, probably a higher population of juveniles, or perhaps fetal bones (from pregnant does). If the goal was the largest skins, it seems that adults would have been selected. However, if they were indiscriminately killing every deer they encountered, it seems that there would be a large range of ages, sizes, and sexes. The data from the Lower Creek sites indicate that all but two deer were adults, at least one year or older. Most deer were 2–3 years, and a few were older than three years. Bucks were identified at the Ochillee Creek farmstead and Cussetuh, but these had antlers that were still attached to the skull. Given larger assemblages, where zooarchaeological analysis records age, sex, and size attributes, these questions may be better addressed.

During his travels among the Maskókî between 1796 and 1816, Indian agent Benjamin Hawkins wrote numerous letters and journals documenting the wild and domestic animals, birds, and fish that he encountered, as well as the foods that he was served in Creek households. His journals give us the most thorough account of the interaction of the Maskókalkî with the animals during the late eighteenth century. The following sections review some of Hawkins's accounts of interactions of the Maskókî with settlers and traders that involved wild and domestic animals, the types of foods that were eaten, how animals and fish were captured or raised, and evidence of seasonal abundance and exploitation of various species (Foster 2003a).

Hawkins observed that the country was "extensive and wild . . . so much in a state of nature" that he expected to see "game in abundance." He said, however, that it "is difficult for a good hunter . . . to obtain enough for his support" (Foster 2003b:24s). This observation, made during the late 1790s, probably reflects the depletion of game because of overhunting for the deer hide trade. He makes few references to deer, although he was served it in Creek households. Since one of his goals was to introduce American animal husbandry techniques, his accounts were focused on livestock.

There is historical evidence that by the early eighteenth century, Maskókî were already maintaining herds of cattle. However, they were slow to adopt American concepts of agriculture, and it appears that they were likewise slow to adopt the government plan for animal husbandry. Hawkins expressed doubts about succeeding there in establishing a program of animal husbandry because of "old habits of indolence, and sitting daily in the squares. . . . The Cussetuhs have some cattle, horses, and hogs, but they prefer roving idly through the woods . . . to attending to farming or stock raising" (Foster 2003a:53s, 61s). He was told that, when needed, free-ranging cattle were hunted like deer. Livestock and deer would have been fairly easy to capture or hunt in the summer. Hawkins reported that cattle, horses, and deer gathered at shoals with salt moss in the summer (Foster 2003a:28s): "They have in the range a place called a stamp, where the horses have salt every spring, and here they gather of themselves at that season. The cattle come to the creek for the moss, the bottom being covered with it. And at this season all the stockholders make a gathering" (Foster 2003a:31).

Hawkins's plan for animal husbandry urged ranchers to fence their crops or to spread out their settlements to separate pillaging livestock and unfenced crops. He cited an instance where the Upper Creek residents of Hoithle Waule were "inconvenienced" because the town was located across the Tallapoosa River from their crop fields and livestock. Apparently the mix of free-roaming animals and unfenced crops was causing them problems. He reported that the town divided "against itself; the idlers and ill-disposed remained in the town, and the others moved across the river and fenced their fields" (Foster 2003a:32s). In his writings, Hawkins regularly noted whether towns had fenced or unfenced fields, so fencing of fields was obviously a very important component of the animal husbandry plan.

Adoption of cattle and pigs varied from town to town. In 1796, Hawkins noted that a trader named Bailey had moved away from the Upper Creek town of Auttosse because the Indians were "in the habit of destroying hogs or cattle whenever they trespass on the fields under cultivation. By this removal they were three years without a trader, and the Indians sent several messages to them to return" (Foster 2003a:49). The trader refused to return until he had some guarantee that his stock would be secure. In a letter of January 1798 from Cussetuh, Hawkins wrote that the Indians were averse to a white man having cattle, but "they never seem dissatisfied when asked to partake of beef, hogs, or the produce of the garden" (Foster 2003a:477). This statement indicates that, certainly by this time, the Maskókî did eat beef and pork and that they were not raised for marketing only.

Hawkins mentioned cattle and hogs being kept for, or taken to, market a few times. In one account in November 1796, he encountered two Indian women on horseback, "driving ten very fat cattle to the station for a market" (Foster 2003a:16). Ten horses were loaded with deerskins. In December of that year, he noted that a Creek leader, The Tarrapin, claimed that he had raised some cattle of 1,200 pounds; the inference is that they were marketed (Foster 2003a:24). In 1798, he mentioned a chief in Nauchee who had 90 hogs "fit for market" (Foster 2003a:42s). The few accounts of marketing of cattle and hogs are unusual, since

one of Hawkins's goals was encouraging and improving animal husbandry among the Maskókî. He regularly reported the size of herds and who owned them. Perhaps the marketing of animals was not mentioned more because it was so common that it was not notable and was the obvious result of raising livestock herds. Hawkins noted that by 1799, a satellite village of Cussetuh, Auputtaue, had a "regular market, and weights and measures are introduced." Prices were established for pork, bacon, beef, fowls, eggs, butter, cheese, hickory nut oil, corn, potatoes, pumpkins, and ground and field peas. Pork could be purchased by gross or net weight at $3.00 per cwt. or $4.00 per 100 pounds net weight. Bacon was $10.00 and beef $3.00 per 100 pounds net. Capons (castrated male chickens) were available at $0.25 per pair, and fowls at $0.25 for four. Eggs were 12½ cents a dozen (Foster 2003:61s).

In 1796, Hawkins noted at least two towns, Soocheah and Soguspogase, whose names were derived from the Musckogean word for hog (sooccau) were called "hog range" by traders. These appear to have been satellite towns where hog raising was a major activity (Foster 2003a:48s).

Sheep were mentioned twice and goats once in Hawkins's writings. In January 1801, sheep were presented to Mr. Cornels, an Upper Creek chief and interpeter, by the local Indian agent. Timothy Barnard, a trader and interpreter who lived near Salenojuh in the late 1790s, had "forty sheep, some goats, and stock of every description" (Foster 2003a:31s, 67s). In 1796, Hawkins was served venison, beef, pork "stakes," stewed fowls, and ducks in Creek households during his travels through Creek country (Foster 2003a:49–50). None of the accounts mentioned the consumption of bears, small wild mammals, sheep, goats, fish, shellfish, or turtles. Hawkins reported that he was provisioned with a pair of "fat hens," for which Creek women requested a pint of salt. The women told him "where they were able to supply themselves plentifully with meat, they were unable to preserve it for want of salt. They raised hogs, some cattle, and a great many poultry" (Foster 2003a:21). Creek women were obviously familiar with salt curing of meats.

Hawkins only mentioned wild mammals a few times. He noted that every Creek town had an area called the "beloved bear-ground" that was preserved as a bear habitat (Foster 2003a:33s). He noted a 40-acre beaver pond at Cussetuh. His opinion was that it could be drained successfully, so apparently beavers were not considered a useful resource (Foster 2003a:53s).

In January 1797, Hawkins reported that ponds on flats of Chattahoochee River tributaries and river islands and shoals near Cussetuh and Cowetuh were abounding with ducks and geese, which were feeding on acorns (Foster 2003a:28s). In October 1797, Hawkins noted that that the wild geese had arrived (Foster 2003a:24j). In the winter of 1798, he noted a large aggregation of swans, ducks, and geese at a large shoal on the Tallapoosa River (Foster 2003a:61).

Wild aquatic birds were seasonally most abundant, and hunting of these birds would have been most cost-effective during these winter aggregations. Although he never mentioned eating fish, Hawkins provided several accounts of communal fishing. He reported that during the summer the Indians pounded buckeye root with clay in a mortar, then put it in a creek. He was told that it poisoned the fish for eight miles, and 60 to 80 persons picked up as many as they could carry home (Foster 2003a:23). He described two large fisheries (basically two long narrow channels) at the base of the large falls near Cowetuh Town, one belonging to the Cussetuhs and one to the Cowetuhs. The fish there were caught with scoop nets, and "As soon as the fish make their appearance, the chiefs send out the women, and make them fish for the *square*" (Foster 2003a:53s, 60). In August 1798, he noted that "All the men, women, and children of Tuckabatchee turned out a-fishing; their seine was made of cane platted, 160 feet long, 30 feet at each end, tapering, and the middle about 4 feet broad. Men & women, boys and girls swimming and supporting the seine, & about 30 strong men at each end, hauling it with grape vine; they caught a few" (Foster 2003a:490).

Hawkins reported, "They get fish plentifully in the spring season . . . rock, trout, buffaloe, red horse and perch" (Foster 2003a:41s). During spring and summer, hickory shad, rockfish, trout, perch, catfish, red horse, suckers, and sturgeon were taken with scoop nets, and perch and rockfish were also caught with hooks. He described the large numbers of rockfish "at its month during the summer season" in a tributary of the Flint River below Salenojuh (Foster 2003a:73). The fish gathered in great numbers and were caught using a hook with a long line fixed to float down the river. The repetition of the species Hawkins mentions in his accounts indicates that these fish were most abundant or easier to capture or that they were preferred species. These accounts indicate that fishing was a communal spring and summer activity. Although Hawkins does not mention them, aquatic turtles like the softshell, mud turtles, and cooters/sliders could also have been captured using scoop nets or hooks and were probably also caught incidentally in fishnets.

Hawkins mentions "fish ponds" several times. One community name was derived from "thlotlo," the Muskogean word for fish (Foster 2003a:33). These ponds, usually located on tributaries, were probably seasonally filled pools or flats where fish accumulated or were stranded. These were obviously important locations that were significant enough to merit place-names.

Capture Techniques

Hawkins described capture techniques specific to the Maskókî with whom he interacted with during the late eighteenth and early nineteenth centuries. The following sections summarize ethnohistorical accounts of methods used by

Native Americans to capture the types of fish, turtles, birds, and mammals identified in the Lower Creek assemblages. Most of the species in these assemblages could have been found in the rivers and creeks that were near the sites or in old fields and areas of secondary forest succession that surrounded many of the Creek settlements. The size of the catchment area would have depended upon factors such as human population pressure and habitat destruction by humans and domestic animals.

Harvesting fish populations was accomplished in a variety of ways but with two procurement aims. The first was mass fishing, where all individuals of all species were targeted. The second was individual fishing, where individuals or a few individuals were targeted. Both methods were used by the Lower Creek. Small hand nets, fish weirs and traps, and fish poison were mass fishing techniques used, given the wide range of fish sizes present in the assemblages. Fishing for larger individuals was accomplished with spears, fishhooks, and bows and arrows (Hudson 1976).

Adair (1968 [1775] #101), Swanton (1946), and Harrington (1913) all noted that in the Southeast, fish were poisoned by ground roots and other plants scattered and dissolved in creeks or ponds. These plants included green walnuts, horse chestnuts, and buckeyes. Fish floated to the top and were gathered in baskets. Cumbaa (1972:51) noted that weaker poisons only marginally affect some species of fish. He added that sunfishes are highly susceptible to poisons, but that bowfin, catfish, and gar are very tolerant of environmental pollutants, including poisons. Swanton's informant, Jackson Lewis, told him that the Maskókî usually used fish poisons in July and August when the water was low (Swanton 1946:342–343).

Lewis also described another mass capture technique to Swanton that was used by the Maskókî. They constructed a drag, something like a fence, the width of the pool. They placed it at the lower end of the pool, then walked upstream, keeping the drag face vertical. Once they reached the shallow end, there were hundreds, sometimes thousands of trapped fish that could be harvested. The drag was a single-use tool and was discarded after use (Swanton 1946:344).

Fishing techniques such as spearing or hook and line would have been practical for species such as bowfin and gar, as well as larger individuals of other species. Use of sharpened spears and fine-mesh nets would have been most effective and efficient during winter months when fish were concentrated in deeper pools (Cumbaa 1972).

Cleland (1966:177) suggested that the use of seine nets or fish traps—both nonselective methods—should be detectable in the archaeological record from the diversity in the sample of fish bones present. Limp and Reidhead (1972:75) challenged this assumption, noting that preservation conditions select against small species as does the consumption of entire small fish. Screen size also affects the recovery of small fish bones. Fish elements from Lower Creek sites represented all sizes of fish and probably reflect both selective and nonselective fishing techniques.

Several species of turtles could have been harvested while harvesters waded through shallow areas at shoals, particularly bottom-dwelling ones like the softshell and mud and musk turtles (Carr 1952). The technique of poisoning water for fish capture would have also stunned softshell and other aquatic turtles. Aquatic turtles could also be caught easily by hook and line (Carr 1952:29). Baited hoop nets, box traps, and basking traps would have also been effective for catching aquatic turtles. They could be captured by hand as they lay on the bottom in shallow water, partly concealed under sand or mud. The cost of capturing small amphibians and reptiles was probably very low. Aquatic turtles and amphibians were probably caught in fishing nets or on hooks. The small territorial range of terrestrial turtles, such as the box turtle, would have made them fairly easy to find.

Archaeological and historic reports indicate that waterfowl and other avian species were harvested fairly regularly by aboriginal groups in eastern North America. Bow and arrow hunting (Speck 2004:19–22; Trigger 1968:31), nets (Rogers 1973:57–60), and snares or slingstones (Reidhead 1976:183) were used to capture birds. Of all these techniques, netting seems to have been most productive. The winter months would have been the most efficient season to hunt aquatic birds and wild turkeys. Flocks are larger at this time: higher population densities occur between November and March (Smith 1975:80). Most ethnohistorical accounts, at least indirectly, indicate fall to winter hunts of turkeys (Schorger 1972:377–408).

Lower Creek hunted deer east and north into the Ogeechee and Oconee valleys and south and west into the Florida peninsula. Deer fur was thicker and deer were fattest in the late fall, and the bucks went into rut in the early winter, becoming less wary during their search for mates. During the rut, the bucks chased the does, and all ages and sexes of deer became easier prey. Deer hunting was accomplished using bows and arrows until guns became available. Fire drives, wearing decoy deerskins, and creating artificial clearings around oak and chestnut trees were techniques used by the Maskókî to capture deer. Family groups participated in hunts, and by the late eighteenth century Creek towns were almost deserted during the hunting season. The aged, infirm, unmarried women, and widows and children were the only residents left behind. Creek hunters skinned the deer they killed, but their wives butchered the carcasses, smoked the meat, and processed the deerskins for home consumption and trade. Upon their return to villages and towns, smoked and dried venison was distributed to the elderly and those unable to hunt for themselves. Young hunters reportedly stripped the deer of their hides and left the meat to rot. Some hunters claimed to kill 300 to 400 deer per year (Braund 1993:61–76).

Few black bear remains were identified in the Lower Creek assemblages. The harvest of bears could have occurred at any time of the year, although bears are at their optimum nutritionally in the late fall. The average weight of black bears harvested in Georgia during modern times is 90.7 to 136.1 kg (200–300 lbs) (Golley 1962). Ethnohistoric accounts from the Southeast indicate that bears were hunted in the late fall or winter while they were hibernating (Trippensee 1947). Each Creek town maintained a bear habitat composed of canebreaks and hardwood forests where settlements and hunting were restricted. Bear could be hunted only at certain times of the year in these areas (Braund 1993:65). According to Swanton (1946:371), bears were valued for the fat rather than for the meat. The small number of bears in the Lower Creek assemblages may reflect depopulation of bears resulting from habitat destruction. Braund (1993:178) noted that by the 1790s, former bear preserves had been turned into range for cattle and pigs.

Lower Creek hunters could have hunted beavers in three different ways: capturing them out of water, submerging traps, or capturing them in lodges or burrows. The fall would have been the best period for capturing beaver out of the water by trapping or by stalking, especially at beaver landing sites. If the quality of the beaver pelt was important to the hunter, beaver were probably hunted later in the year. Beaver pelts do not get prime until December (Smith 1975:84–86). Other small mammals, such as the squirrel, raccoon, and rabbit, were probably captured through the use of fire hunting, bow and arrow, and snares or traps (Lawson in Swanton 1946).

Creek women prepared a diverse array of vegetable and animal foods. They preserved meat by drying or salting it, and bear fat was considered a prized seasoning for foods. Meat and fish was boiled, broiled, fired, roasted, and smoked. Meat and vegetable stews were common fare, and meat was used to season vegetable dishes (Braund 1993; Hudson 1976). Fish were gutted but often not scaled or beheaded. Some Florida aboriginals (Swanton 1946:371) used fish grease as "butter." Fish were preserved for future use by smoking and drying, either by the sun or over a fire. Dried fish were then stored in baskets (Le Moyne in Swanton 1946:376–378). Skinner (Swanton 1946:369) described the roasting of turtles in hearths, which the Lower Creek may have practiced, as indicated by burned or calcined shell fragments. Besides the use of turtles for food, shells were also fashioned into rattles as well as bowls and ladles or spoons (Swanton 1946:252). Swanton's (1946:374–375) Creek informant, Jackson Lewis, described the processing and preservation of deer meat:

They first made an incision down the middle of the deer's belly and then stripped the body meat off of the bones from front to back. The resulting piece was large and flat. It was dried in the sun, and as others were dried they were made into a pile, which was carried back to the village on the back of a pony. The thighs were treated in this way. First the long bones were removed, and then the meat was cut up into chunks somewhat larger than baseballs. Withes or sticks were passed through these and they were placed over a fire until nearly cooked, by which time the meat had shrunk to about the size of a baseball. It had also shrunk away from the stick leaving a large hole, and by means of these holes a great many such chunks of meat were strung together for transportation. The meat of 10 deer was all that could be gotten upon 1 horse.

Another informant to Swanton (1946:375) provided additional information on deer processing:

Charlie Thompson, afterward made chief of the Alabama Indians in Texas, gave a slightly different account. According to him one piece was made of the ribs and the flesh adhering to them, a thin, flat piece was stripped off of the ribs and breast, and two separate pieces were made of the loins and thighs. Sticks were run through these and they were placed on a low scaffold about 3 feet high and 3–4 feet each way, where they were roasted. Sometimes a much higher scaffold was used, depending probably upon the weather and the size of the fire. Pieces intended for immediate consumption might be impaled on a single stick over the fire, the other end of the stick being planted in the ground. The dried meat was strung together and carried home from camp packed on either side of the hunter's horse along with the deer hides, the hunter himself walking and driving the animal. Finally, the meat was stored in the corncrib, where it would usually keep for an entire year. If it had not been dried sufficiently, screw-worms would breed in it. (From what I was told by some old white settlers, however, it would appear that the Indians did not have insuperable objections to wormy meat.) When dried venison was to be eaten, it was washed, pounded in a mortar, mixed with bear's grease, and partaken of with bread.

If deer were very plentiful, they sometimes threw away the ribs, shoulders, and other less desirable cuts, and occasionally are said to have hunted the deer for their hides alone, but on other occasions they might eat even the marrow and liver. When an unusually large number of deer had been killed, or there was to be a special feast at the ballground, they would sometimes string the tongues and hearts by themselves on cords of bass fiber.

This description of deer processing provides at least a partial explanation for the skeletal incompleteness of the deer skeletons on the Lower Creek sites. When processed at some distance from settlements, much of the meat was removed from the heavy bones before transport back to the towns and villages. In conjunction with the harvesting of deer for the hide trade, the expected pattern would be like that of deer bone from the Lower Creek sites in this study. If free-ranging cattle were hunted like deer, similar processing of beef carcasses for transport home may have occurred. These accounts may explain the low number of ribs, vertebrae, shoulder, and other portions of deer and cattle found in these assemblages.

Pigs and cattle were probably butchered when the weather began to cool in the fall, when they would have been at maximum weight and when preservation or storage of meat was easier in the cooler weather. The cattle, and perhaps pig, carcasses from these households were likely shared, exchanged, or traded with other families or relatives, since they were incomplete, and not all body parts were found at any household. Since beef does not preserve as well as pork, this practice would have provided several people or families with fresh beef and prevented spoilage and waste.

Bears have thick layers of fat. This fat was separated from the lean meat, which was cooked or dried like other meats. The fat was cooked in earthen pots and the oil extracted from it. This fat was used as cooking oil, condiment, and cosmetic (Hudson 1976:300).

One ethnohistorically documented method of processing animal protein was boiling meat and bone in a stew-type dish (Hudson 1976; Swanton 1946). This method would not necessarily require smashing the bone into small fragments. A second method was the making of bone grease or "butter" (Leechman 1951; Vehik 1975). In this type of processing, bones were pulverized to increase surface area and then placed in boiling water. Grease was periodically skimmed from the surface of the water and stored. This process was repeated until the bones were leached of nutrients and became bleached in appearance. The resulting bone mass was then discarded. Based on the fragmented and burned condition of much of the mammal bone from Lower Creek sites, it is likely that both methods were used.

Meats were also roasted, baked, broiled, dried, and salt cured (Foster 2003a; Hudson 1976). According to historical accounts, livestock was sold to visitors or travelers on the hoof and in preserved form (Ethridge 2003). The high value of salt, which was sometimes traded for provisions of livestock and poultry, indicates that salt curing of meat took place at Creek households. In one of Hawkins's accounts, he traded a pint of salt for two chickens. The Creek women told him that they had plenty of meat but not enough salt to preserve it. Hawkins also described being served stewed chicken, ducks, venison, beef, and pork steaks in Creek households during his travels in the 1790s (Foster 2003a). Small mammals like raccoons, rabbits, and squirrels were minimally dressed before cooking. Most were skinned and cooked whole. Whole small mammals, whole fish, and larger pieces of meat were cooked impaled on a sharpened stick, with the stick inclined toward the fire. The stick was turned periodically for even roasting (Hudson 1976:301).

DISCUSSION OF LOWER CREEK DIET

Based on historic accounts from the eighteenth and early nineteenth centuries, it is apparent that domestic animals and chickens were often acquired informally from Euro-American settlers and traders and probably also from relatives. Chickens were reputedly common on Creek farmsteads, and eggs and poultry were "regular food and trade items" (Ethridge 1996:256). Frontier settlers and Native Americans preferred chickens to other yard fowls because chickens roost off the ground and, therefore, were not as vulnerable to predators as geese and ducks were (Hilliard 1969). Chickens foraged for food scraps, which were probably plentiful since most Creek cooking and food preparation took place out of doors. The small number of chickens identified on Lower Creek sites is surprising but may be related to preservation factors. Most of the bird bones were unidentifiable fragments. There is some evidence that wild turkeys were kept penned at the Cowetuh settlements, and turkeys provided more of the diet than chickens at that household.

No sheep or goats were identified on Lower Creek sites. Sheep and goats were never popular because they required constant herding, were sensitive to heat and humidity, and were vulnerable to predators. Southern wool was not of good quality, and goatskins and milk were not profitable (Ethridge 1996:256). Although initially wary and resentful of cattle and pigs, the Maskókî eventually realized they could be profitable and could provide an economic alternative to the declining deerskin trade. According to Ethridge (1996:257), cattle and pigs were not usually consumed because the Maskókî believed that consuming the flesh of these unwieldy, slow animals would impart these qualities to the consumer. More important, cattle and hogs competed with humans, deer, bears, wild turkeys, and other game animals for wild plants, other forage, and nut mast. Since allowed to roam freely, cattle and pigs also destroyed unfenced crops.

Compared to northern herds, southern livestock were of poor quality. A southern cow rarely weighed over 700 pounds, and the average meat yield of a southern hog was 130–150 pounds per hog. These differences in quality were attributed in part to free ranging, which produced smaller hogs and cattle than pasture-fed stock, and to a lack of selective breeding. Under free-range conditions, a cow could gain up to 200 pounds during the spring and summer, then lose it during the winter months when forage was not as plentiful (Ethridge 1996:259). Livestock bred with feral animals, producing leaner, smaller offspring. Although the conclusion is subjective, owing to the small number of measurable bones, both cattle and pigs from Lower Creek sites were roughly one-third to one-half smaller than modern comparative specimens.

Throughout the eighteenth century, domestic livestock owned by white traders and settlers were a bone of contention among the Maskókî and their Euro-American neighbors. They figured into disputes over political boundaries and in treaty negotiations, especially concerning poaching or stealing of free-ranging animals by Maskókî and intrusions of animals into unfenced Indian gardens and crops. Maskókî had their own livestock herds during this period, some of which were probably captured or stolen free-ranging animals, so most of these complaints were really concerns about the encroachment of white settlers into Indian lands.

According to Ethridge (1996, 2003), cattle and pigs were raised by the Maskókî primarily as trade or market commodities that brought profits to both men and women. Livestock were often butchered for or sold on the hoof to Euro-American travelers. Cattle and pigs were rounded up and driven to markets in Savannah, Darien, Ocmulgee, and Pensacola in late summer or early fall, when the stock was fattest from spring and summer foraging (Ethridge 1996:268). Beef steers were sold by age at $2.50 per year. Market prices for hogs were not recorded, but bacon sold for 30 cents a pound (Ethridge 1996:151). By the 1790s markets were being opened in Lower Creek towns. Hawkins cited prices in 1796 of $3.00 to $4.00 per 100 pounds weight for pigs at a market in a Cussetuh town. Beef was sold for $3.00 per 100 pounds net weight (Foster 2003b:61s). Venison was not listed for sale at the Cussetuh market.

By the middle of the eighteenth century, cowhides may have begun to replace deer hides for trade. Increasing consumption of beef probably reflected the rise of the cowhide trade. Instead of being driven to market, cattle were skinned at Creek households, and only the skins were sent to market. Killing of cattle at Creek households may have resulted in more beef available for eating. Since deer hunters had to travel great distances and spend large amounts of time away from home to procure fewer and fewer deer hides, the use of cattle would have been more energy efficient. According to historical accounts, cattle and pigs did not become numerous among the Maskókî until after the American Revolution. By the late eighteenth century, Indian agent Benjamin Hawkins found that almost every Creek town had chickens and herds of cattle and hogs, some ranging from 30 to 150 head (Foster 2003a). The results of zoo-

archaeological analysis coupled with historical and ethnographic documentation provide support to the idea that by the middle to late eighteenth century,
the Lower Creek had adapted in part, whether by choice or necessity, to frontier
Euro-American subsistence patterns just as the Euro-Americans had adopted
items from the Indian diet.

Domestic cattle and pigs that had been butchered and consumed were present in Creek assemblages circa 1750 to 1790 from two nuclear towns, Salenojuh
and Cussetuh. Beef made up at least half of the diet at these towns (see Tables
7.13 and 7.14). Cattle, primarily, had become significant economic and dietary
elements in the Lower Creek diet prior to the Revolutionary War. The addition
of beef to the traditional Indian diet probably reflects the presence of resident
traders with livestock herds, the presence of major trading paths, and the increasing need for cowhides. Because of these factors, and the availability of a
steady supply of cattle carcasses, Lower Creek assimilated beef into their diet.

By the early nineteenth century, domestic animals and birds supplied at least
a third of the diet on Lower Creek Cowetuh Settlement and Ochillee Creek
farmsteads (see Tables 7.13 and 7.14). The Cowetuh settlements may have resulted from an attempt to separate crops and domestic animal herds from each
other. The circa-1800 household that was examined archaeologically was located across the river from Cowetuh Town itself. Ochillee Creek farmstead
(circa 1800–1820) also represents a satellite household probably associated with
the Cussetuh people. It is the latest dated assemblage analyzed in this study,
and, like the Cowetuh settlements, probably represented a household on an
outlying ranch or farm that had resulted from the introduction of domestic
animal herds into the Lower Creek economy, and the need to separate pillaging
herds from unfenced crops.

Most of the diet on these outlying satellite ranches or farms was still supplied by deer, bear, small wild mammals, wild birds, turtles, shellfish and fish,
the traditional elements of native diet prior to contact with Europeans. Hunting, fishing, and the collection of shellfish, fish, turtle, and wild birds were
likely seasonal activities that were still practiced by Lower Creek households.
Deer, turkey, and bear populations had been severely depleted as a result of the
hide trade, the environmental effects of domestic animal herds, and increased
and encroaching human populations. By 1800, travelers through Georgia reported traveling long distances without seeing any deer, although they were
often served deer meat by their Native American hosts (Foster 2003a:24s). Perhaps these more isolated households had easier access to wild animals than
those in the larger, more populated Lower Creek towns. The sharing of fresh
carcasses with other households or relatives may have also resulted in fewer
domestic remains and less complete carcasses.

To date, no bison (*Bison* ssp.) remains have been identified on Lower or Upper Creek sites in Georgia or Alabama. Although there are abundant historical references to buffalo and wild cattle throughout the eastern United States beginning in the 1500s, very few buffalo remains have been recorded from archaeological sites in Georgia. Plotting the eastern range of buffalo is problematic due to the small amount of archaeological evidence for these animals. Rostlund (1960:402) and Belue (1996:9) report that, in 1873, Charles C. Jones found a well-preserved buffalo skull, with horns still attached, that had been plowed up in a field in Brooks County, Georgia. Bones identified as *Bison bison* were reported in 1941 from a site dated A.D. 1600 at Irene Mound in Chatham County, Georgia.

Spanish explorers sighted buffalo throughout the Southeast by the 1670s. In 1716, explorer Diego Pena crossed the Ochlocknee River and entered Georgia in a buffalo hide boat. During September of that year, he reported killing both domestic cattle and buffalo in south Georgia and slept on buffalo skins at an Indian village near the confluence of the Flint and Chattahoochee Rivers (Belue 1996:30–31). In 1733, former general and member of Parliament James Oglethorpe noted that the wild animals in Georgia included deer, elk, bears, wolves, and buffalo. Buffalo hunts were reported near Darien, Georgia, in 1735. Several herds numbering 60 or more animals were hunted west of the Oconee River in Laurens County, Georgia, in July 1739. That same year, Oglethorpe's men also hunted buffalo in Screven County, Georgia, on the Ogeechee River, and described them as plentiful. Belue's (1996) research into historical accounts of buffalo suggests that herds were much smaller than the vast herds of the West. The hides never became as important in the hide trade as those of deerskins, furs, or other peltry. Eastern buffalo herds usually numbered 100 head or less; many numbered around 20 animals.

Buffalo were probably utilized by the Lower Creeks by the 1720s or earlier. The meat was considered delectable, and robes, shoes, ornamental clothing, and spoons were made from the by-products. In August 1739, at a Creek town on the Chattahoochee River (Russell County, Alabama), Oglethorpe's men observed Creek men hunting turkeys, deer, geese, and buffalo. At another Creek town in Alabama, the white hunters observed that the Indians "spend much time in hunting deer, turkeys, and bison" (Belue 1996:63). During the 1740s, accounts of fairly large buffalo herds continued in Georgia. By the 1750s and 1760s, trader James Adair and others reported that buffalo had become scarce in the Carolinas. The last known "wild buffalo" in Georgia was killed in 1800 on the Turtle River near Brunswick. The two last reported wild buffalo east of the Mississippi River were killed in Wisconsin in 1832 (Belue 1996:62–65).

Historical accounts that overlap with the occupation dates of the sites in this study indicate that buffalo were present in small herds and hunted by both whites and Indians. Mention is made of clothing and bedding made from buffalo skins, but there are no accounts of buffalo hides being traded. Buffalo were probably becoming scarce by the 1770s in Florida, South Carolina, Georgia, and Alabama. They may have already become extinct in some parts of Lower Creek country. Some historic accounts state that buffalo bred, or were deliberately bred, with domestic or feral cattle and produced offspring that could reproduce. Crossbreeding might mask the identification of these animal remains, especially in small bone assemblages. It is likely that buffalo herds were present in small scattered groups and that they were extinguished within 150 years of historical documentation east of the Mississippi. However, it remains an intriguing question why such distinctive bone remains have not been identified on late-seventeenth and middle-eighteenth-century Creek sites in Alabama and Georgia.

Domestic mammals and chickens may have provided more readily available meat with less energy expenditure than wild ones. Pigs, cows, and chickens foraged on fallow crops, garbage, nut mast, grasses, and other wild plant and animal foods and could be rounded up when needed. Chickens and eggs could have been consumed fresh on an as-needed basis, and laying hens were at least occasionally eaten at the Ochillee Creek farmstead.

Aside from Creek food taboos and historical accounts of killing and eating livestock only during famines, the concept that domestic animals were not part of the Creek diet is based on zooarchaeological analyses of two Upper Creek towns in Alabama. At the town of Tukabatchee, no postcranial elements of cattle were identified in the Historic Creek component, leading Knight (1985) to conclude that cattle were butchered only for sale, with the heads left and the entire remaining carcass removed from the town. At Fusihatchee, domestic birds and mammals were minor components of the bone assemblage by 1700 and comprised only 2 percent of the biomass. Similarly to the results of this study, domestic birds contributed a low percentage of biomass at Fusihatchee throughout the eighteenth and early nineteenth centuries. By 1780, domestic mammals still constituted only 9 percent, but by 1814 they made up 61 percent of the biomass at Fusihatchee (Pavao-Zuckerman 2000:139). These results indicate that the Upper Maskókalkî in the central Alabama towns did not fully incorporate domestic animals into their diet until the early nineteenth century.

Like the Maskókî, the Cherokee Indians were involved in the deerskin trade and had access to domestic animals by the middle of the eighteenth century (Gilbert 1943:360). At the Cherokee town of Toqua (1600–1819) in Tennessee, domestic mammal and bird bone was present but in very small quantities (Bogan 1982; Polhemus 1987a, b). At a small Cherokee settlement in north Georgia, domestic animals were absent from Early Qualla households (seventeenth to early eighteenth century), but domestic pigs, cattle, and chickens were present at a Late Qualla structure (late eighteenth to early nineteenth century) (O'Steen 2000). Aside from the addition of domestic species, the traditional array of wild species was very similar between the Early and Late Qualla households. These findings suggest that the Indian groups farther to the north and west of the Lower Creek were more resistant to subsistence change, perhaps owing to distance and less direct participation in the colonial economic system. These zooarchaeological assemblages reflect less change in diet over time than is indicated by changes in the material culture of the Upper Maskókî and Cherokees.

The results of this study indicate that major changes in Lower Creek diet had occurred by the middle of the eighteenth century. The Maskókî continued to exploit the native species that were part of the prehistoric and protohistoric diet but added a significant amount of domestic meats and fowl during the eighteenth century. Domestic cattle played a significant role in Lower Creek economy and subsistence by the 1760s. Domestic mammals were both marketed and consumed by the Lower Creek, although pork was consumed much less often than beef. The use of domestic species was still secondary to that of wild species in the late eighteenth to early nineteenth century at the outlying farmsteads or ranches, but they consistently provided half of the meat consumed in large towns between 1750 and 1790. This pattern of domestic animal use was probably hastened by the depletion of wild animals such as deer, bears, and turkeys and by the decline of the deer hide trade during the eighteenth century. Cattle and pigs (and reportedly dogs and horses) were consumed during periods of famine, and there are a number of such accounts in Hawkins's and other records during this time period (Foster 2003a; Manuelshagen and Davis 1967; Saunt 1999).

No zooarchaeological data are currently available for Lower Creek components from the seventeenth or early eighteenth centuries, so the exact time when these changes began among the Lower Creek cannot be established. Additional zooarchaeological studies should be able to address when the Lower Creek incorporated domestic mammals and birds into their diet and if these changes did indeed take place among all Lower Creek earlier than among the neighboring Upper Maskókî and Cherokees. Changes observed in this study may be related to the sites being associated with two large Lower Creek towns, Cussetuh and Cowetuh, which were located on major trading paths. Smaller, more isolated Lower Creek settlements may have been less influenced by Euro-American contact, and this may be reflected in the diet. Zooarchaeological data from late-seventeenth and early-eighteenth-century Lower Creek sites can be used to address the question of when dietary changes occurred. The examination of additional zooarchaeological assemblages from contemporary Upper and Lower Creek and Cherokee sites will provide more insights into the stability of subsistence and socioeconomic systems among the Lower Creek and their neighbors.

8
Conclusion

Owing to the amount of research on Creek Indian sites over the last few decades, archaeologists are beginning to discern patterns and can measure and characterize variation among the archaeological sites. Now that we have a relatively comprehensive data set, we should reevaluate our archaeological models, our metrics of material culture, by comparing archaeological and historical data. We have accurate and consistent information about migration and population stability throughout the eighteenth century in the form of accurate maps, descriptions, and large-scale archaeological surveys. Chapter 3 synthesized what is known about the location and population movements of each individual town. Consequently, we can begin to compare mother and daughter towns in order to understand migration and fission of Southeastern Indian towns that may contribute to chiefdom cycling (Anderson 1994; Blitz 1999).

A goal of this book was to set a baseline of knowledge about the archaeological remains of the Lower Creek Indians. I used a direct historic and regional approach to define empirically the archaeological assemblage composition of individual Creek talwas. I used the current archaeological knowledge to define comprehensively the regional and temporal variation in the "population" of Lower Creek Indian archaeological remains so that smaller assemblages could be evaluated in terms of samples from the larger population in a sort of middle-range theory. Archaeologists and other researchers need to study the Maskókalkî at the level of the talwa or tribal population rather than larger regional units.

We have spent a significant amount of time explaining the archaeological context of the data that have been collected. Since archeological data are samples of some population, archaeologists have to understand what kind of sample that was collected relative to the population. We have to understand the validity of the archaeological data so that we can adequately assess samples of them. We have attempted to clarify the biased nature of the samples and the archaeological perspective put forth here by explicitly describing the context from which it came. This is not to say that archaeological data are not useful. As with any sample of data, if you understand the biases, you can control for them. Furthermore, the data give us a unique perspective on the past that cannot be obtained by oral histories, documents, or modern descendants. We feel that our comprehensive approach has been useful at delineating and clarifying the diversity of the Maskókalkî of the Lower Chattahoochee and Flint River watersheds of the eighteenth century.

This book has also been a study of archaeological metrics and units of analysis. By isolating the limits of the analysis to a single archaeological phase, we have been able to characterize and quantify the variation within the phase. That monolithic unit has impeded the analyis of talwas at the proper level of analyis. By lumping all Lawson Field sites together, we were unable to distinguish between the unique cultural units. I hope that this study has shown that the Lawson Field phase and the Lower Creek Indians that it represents were composed of a diverse people. There is no reason to believe that this finding is limited to the Historic Period. Archaeologists need to reassess their understanding of the dynamics within prehistoric archaeological phases in order to use them properly. My approach has been to describe fully the archaeological variation in an attempt to create a sort of "population" from which subsets and further samples can be compared. If we know the geographic and temporal variation in the population, then we will be better able to assess samples of that population (Orton 2000:44–57; Orton and Tyers 1990, 1992). For example, by fully describing the population of ceramic vessels and surface types, we can better assess variation between archaeological assemblages as representing change through time versus change over space versus a sampling bias. Certainly, not all of the data sets described here are comprehensive enough to accomplish that, but it is a start. Only by doing this can we begin to measure culture change among these Southeastern Indians. Following, I will summarize the major themes covered.

The Lower Maskókî (Creek) Indians were a loose collection of culturally similar but independent talwas or towns. The Maskókalkî settled on the Lower Chattahoochee and Flint River watersheds in various waves of migration throughout the seventeenth and eighteenth centuries. These Indians were the direct descendants, both biologically and culturally, of Mississippian period Indians of central and northern Alabama and Georgia intermixed with other Indian populations. They were of course not an isolated population and were, instead, fluid. Individual towns were constantly experiencing emigrations and immigrations that contributed to the dynamic nature of the society and material culture over time.

There is more continuity than discontinuity between the Historic Creek Indians and their ancestors. Most important, the discontinuity is, at least partly,

measurable. Assuming that the Historic Creek Indians are too culturally distinct from the Mississippian populations to make historical connections, an
analogy is an uncritical overgeneralization (Muller 1997:55). The monolithic
view of the Southeastern Indians as drastically different than their ancestors
has dominated the study of the Maskókalkî for decades (Jackson 2003:17, 290).
We know too much and can measure too well the changes that occurred, and
the degree of those changes, to disregard the relationship of the Historic Period
to the Prehistoric Period. The division between those two periods is an artificially created research boundary. I argue that archaeological data are uniquely
able to characterize the transition and adaptation of the people of the southeastern United States during the Protohistoric and Historic Periods.

Assuming that the Indians were unique biological populations that did not
undergo dramatic changes before the Europeans arrived is naive. I would argue
that we can actually quantify and characterize those changes. We have a lot to
learn about prehistory by looking at the historic institutions and social organization of the historic peoples (Muller 1997:402). Recent ethnographic and ethnohistoric research has documented significant continuities between the prehistoric people and their modern descendants (Bell 1999; Jackson 2003; Urban
1994; Wickman 1999).

The Hitchiti-speaking populations were settled on the Chattahoochee at
least by the beginning of the seventeenth century and likely well before that.
Apalachicola and Hitchiti towns were home to the original inhabitants of the
Lower Creek region during the Historic Period. The Muskogee speakers, who
came to be the dominant population of the Creek Indians, migrated from the
west some time during the middle of the seventeenth century. The Muskogee
towns such as Cussetuh and Cowetuh have migration myths that describe their
travels to the Chattahoochee Valley. They fought "flat"-headed Indians and
then settled among the Palachicola (Hitchiti-speaking Apalachicola people)
who were already settled near the Chattahoochee River (Swanton 1928b:37, 39,
50). In the late seventeenth century, practically all of the Lower Creek Indians
abandoned the Chattahoochee River watershed and moved to the Ocmulgee
River watershed to be closer to the European colonies and to get away from the
Spanish in Florida. After the Yamassee War, many of the towns migrated back
to the Chattahoochee. These chapters have synthesized the ethnohistoric and
archaeological remains of those Indians after that last migration back to the
Chattahoochee, which occurred around 1715. One of the most abundant and
useful artifact types encountered in these archaeological sites is pottery.

Pottery styles remained relatively unchanged for over 100 years and even
after the Creek Indians were removed to the Indian territories (Gettys 1995;
Quimby and Spoehr 1950). The pottery analysis in this book has characterized
the population of ceramic wares that were in use by the Lower Creek Indians.

I used a direct historic and regional approach, including a vessel analysis, in order to counteract the problems of biases in ceramic assemblages found at archaeological sites. One of my goals was to describe comprehensively, with as little bias as possible, the population of pottery wares in use in the Lower Creek Indian towns of the eighteenth to early nineteenth century.

Because of the statistical bias of broken pottery in assemblages, we have characterized the population of vessels from which any given assemblage was drawn to make comparisons between assemblages (Orton and Tyers 1990, 1992). Consequently, I analyzed the quantitative variation of the Lower Creek Indian pottery assemblages over space and time and by ethnolinguistic association and in a minimum vessel analysis. These results indicate, unsurprisingly, that pottery styles varied over time and space. What is surprising is the type of variation.

Pottery characteristics such as surface treatment and pottery temper correlated with time, space, and linguistic affiliation. It is traditionally thought that the vast majority of Creek Indian pottery was manufactured for the cooking and preparation of corn hominy, or sofke. These pots were large vessels that were decorated on the exterior with a type of roughening and are classified as Chattahoochee Roughened. This type of pottery is spatially variable. It increases in frequency from south to north, which is also correlated with a change from Hitchiti-speaking people to Muskogee-speaking people. The red painted wares, Mission Red Filmed, were relatively constant over space. This finding partially contrasts the traditional view of this type as originating to the far south. Mission Red Filmed wares were in fact the most frequent type of decoration in the minimum vessel analysis (22.65%), although Chattahoochee Roughened was very similar in frequency (21.18%). Since relative frequencies from the minimum vessel analysis are less biased than counts of pottery sherds, we can conclude that Mission Red Filmed and Chattahoochee Roughened were approximately equally occurring decorative features on pottery in use by the Lower Creek Indians during the eighteenth to early nineteenth centuries. Vessels with red painting were not as rare as traditionally thought. They may have had a more public or common function than originally assumed.

These results indicate that archaeologists need to reevaluate their definition of the Lawson Field archaeological phase. This phase has been used to identify Lower Creek Indian sites for decades. It is primarily defined by the presence of Chattahoochee Roughened pottery types. These results indicated that Mission Red Filmed pottery types should have equal weight in the definition of that phase. In addition, shell tempering may not be a temporal characteristic of the phase.

The Lawson Field phase has been defined as a reduction in the relative frequency of shell tempering compared to the previous Blackmon phase (1650–

1715) (Knight 1994b; Knight and Mistovich 1984; Schnell 1998). As demonstrated here, shell tempering may be an ethnolinguistic trait. If this is true, then we need to reconsider our assessment and delineation of seventeenth-century, pre–Yamassee War archaeological sites from eighteenth-century, post–Yamassee War sites. This change in pottery styles over time is one of the reasons that I limited this book's temporal scope to a well-defined migratory boundary that occurred after the Yamassee War (circa 1715). It is also why such detailed and comprehensive analyses of the constituents of archaeological phases need to be made from a regional perspective, particularly when most of the sites, or the type-sites, are single component. Archaeologists need to characterize spatial and temporal variation in ceramic assemblages. As I stated above, we have to understand the validity of the Lawson Field archaeological phase before we can adequately use it as an archaeological metric.

Social organization and labor roles of the Lower Creek Indians may have changed during the eighteenth century. Traditionally and among their modern descendants (Bell 1999; Jackson 2003), the majority of the Lower Creek Indians were matrilineal. Men and women had very specific roles that reflected that descent system. Adult women contributed the majority of the subsistence foods and owned the household property. Her children received their names from her. Men contributed hunted meat and animal products to the household economy. Women made pottery vessels, worked in the agricultural fields, and processed animal skins.

During the eighteenth century, many of the Creek Indians began hunting deer in greater numbers than in their recent past. This increase occurred because the Indians wanted to trade the deerskins with colonists in Georgia and South Carolina. The increase in deer hunting intensified and eventually may have altered the male-female roles of at least some portion of Creek Indian society. Some males probably hunted for longer periods of time and were therefore separated from the village society for longer periods. Claudio Saunt (1999) has argued that women may have lost some "economic status" in the later part of the eighteenth century because of the trade in unprocessed deer hides. We see evidence of the trade in unprocessed deer hides in the archaeological data. These hides still had the hooves attached, and researchers have demonstrated an unusually high ratio of hooves to other deer bone parts in the archaeological remains from that time period. So the archaeological remains are consistent with the historic documents by indicating that the deerskin trade became a part of the economy of some Creek Indians. No one has analyzed how widespread that trade practice was, so we don't know if the effect on women or the economy actually manifested or the degree of that effect. Saunt further argued that the character of towns was altered to a degree that implied changes from female-centered social organization to male-centered (1999:159–161). With little or no justification for his conclusions, he says that Benjamin Hawkins "meant to refer to men" (1999:159, 161) when Hawkins observed that some of the "Creeks" were ranching. Saunt uses this interpretation of Hawkins to argue that the traditional female horticulture was being replaced by "male dominated" cattle ranching.

Archaeological remains are consistent with the historic documents in the degree to which cattle and hogs became important to the Indians. Lisa O'Steen's analysis and synthesis of the zooarchaeological remains from all known Lower Creek Indian towns indicate that at least by the latter half of the eighteenth century, domesticated animals were a major contribution to the material culture of the Muskogee people. Her analyses indicate that the relative contribution of domesticated animals to the estimated biomass of meat at individual towns increased to over half of the total at those towns. However, the relative contribution of biomass of domesticated animal meat varies among towns and villages. While biomass is frequently used as a proxy for consumable meat, we are not empirically positive that beef significantly contributed to the diet of the Indians. This type of evidence could be obtained from chemical studies of the osteological remains from burials of eighteenth-century Indians, but modern Muskogee descendants do not want such analyses (Foster 2005a).

Historians have concluded that the Creek Indians adopted cattle husbandry (Ethridge 2003), but the faunal remains from archaeological sites indicate that the Maskókî adoption of domesticated animals was variable (Pavao-Zuckerman 2005). Faunal analyses in this book indicate that the Lower Creek Indians probably adopted domesticated animals at a greater rate than their Upper Creek relatives. Faunal remains at the Upper Creek town of Tukabatchee are consistent with the interpretation that domesticated animals were only used for sale and were not consumed (Knight 1985:152, 181). This conclusion was based on the fact that no postcranial cow or pig bones were identified from the late-eighteenth-century assemblage at Tukabatchee. The ethnohistoric review in Chapter 7 indicates that postcranial bones, particularly long bones, are unlikely to have been brought back to the villages because they were processed and preserved during hunting away from the village. The pattern of no postcranial elements at village sites, thus, is consistent with a skin trade and a meat-processing interpretation.

The archaeozoological data indicate that the Creek Indians maintained a relatively traditional diet while *some* individuals began trading and raising domesticated animals toward the late eighteenth to early nineteenth centuries. The animal diet probably consisted of venison, beef, turkey, chickens, small game such as squirrel and rabbit, wild birds, fish, turtle, bear, and other animal products such as fat and eggs. These animal products were processed by roasting, smoking, boiling, baking, and salting. There was variation in the zooarchaeological remains between the smaller villages and the larger towns. For instance, the larger towns, such as Cussetuh, showed a higher frequency of domesticated animals whereas the village settlements showed a higher frequency of wild zooarchaeological remains. This zooarchaeological pattern, interestingly, contradicts the explanation for the documented dispersal from the central towns to out-settlements and the transition from a diet based on wild animals to one based on domesticated animals (Ethridge 2003:159–174; Saunt 1999:159–162).

What is clear from the historic documents and archaeological data is that domesticated animals were present and used by some people. Hawkins says that practically all towns had herds of cattle and hogs, and the archaeological data support that observation. However, we do not have the data to characterize how widespread was the use of domesticated animals within a town. Based on the sample described in this book, we can characterize the differential adoption between towns and village populations and between Upper and Lower Creek towns. Zooarchaeological remains from daughter village out-settlements and Upper Creek towns are less likely to demonstrate evidence for the adoption of domesticates in their diet. The archaeological and historical data are equally consistent with the interpretation that only traders who lived in the towns raised domesticated animals. This interpretation is consistent with domesticated animals having been more frequent in larger towns than in outlying settlements.

Domestication of animals was of interest to the Europeans, especially Benjamin Hawkins (Foster 2003a), so the few instances of Indians raising domesticated animals were emphasized in the historic documents and correspondence. Historic sources such as the journals of Benjamin Hawkins and legal documents support the interpretation that the Creek Indians domesticated animals and changed their diet. Historians have adopted the view that the Creek Indians began using domesticated animals in large numbers, but archaeological investigations show that these Southeastern Indians were more resilient to change (Waselkov 1998) and more variable in their adoption of domesticated animals into their diet than the historic documents suggest. Pavao-Zuckerman (2005) argues that domestic animals were present but not abundant in Upper Creek Indian towns until the last few years before removal. The results from the Lower Creek Indian sites indicate that some populations in larger towns such as Cussetuh were adopting domesticated animals relatively early. Cussetuh and Buzzard Roost were on major trade routes and both had resident traders. Smaller, more dispersed settlements that were formed relatively late, such as Ochillee Creek, were more resistant to change and did not begin using domesticated animals at the rate observed at the larger towns. This observation contradicts the common thesis (Braund 1993; Ethridge 2003; Saunt

1999) derived from historic sources such as Hawkins that the Creek Indians were dispersing from larger villages into smaller villages toward the end of the eighteenth century in order to have rangeland for cattle and pigs.

The Upper Creek towns cited by Waselkov (1998) and Pavao-Zuckerman (2005) were on major trade routes similar to the locations of Cussetuh and Buzzard Roost; nevertheless, the data from the Upper Creek sites indicate that domesticated animals were not adopted until very late. The Lower Creek sites along trade routes and those having resident traders adopted domesticated animals earlier. There is variation in how individual towns adapted to the changing frontier environment. Simply being a mother town or being on the trade routes does not explain the variation in the acceptance of domesticated animals as an economic alternative. I suspect the answer lies at the level of individual decisions at individual households.

In contrast to Pavao-Zuckerman's analyses of Upper Creek sites, the zooarchaeological remains from the Lower Creek sites show a higher ratio of domesticated animals relative to wild animals. Before we can make conclusions about dietary change, archaeologists need to quantify the ratio of meat from domesticated animals that was preserved and traded relative to the meat that was consumed by the Indians. In addition, it should be noted that none of the zooarchaeological samples analyzed in detail in this book (Chapter 7) were from Hitchiti people, which may bias our conclusions.

Botanical remains indicate a pattern of subsistence that had persevered for hundreds of years. Traditionally, the Creek Indians grew corn and a variety of other crops such as squash. During the eighteenth century, some Indians began to experiment with new crops like rice, sweet potatoes, and white potatoes, but these additional crops did not make a significant contribution to their diet. Certainly, the contribution of foreign crops varied and was probably greater among the Lower Creek Indians than the Upper Creek towns because the former were closer to Benjamin Hawkins, who was trying to persuade the Indians to grow new crops. Archaeological results support the interpretation that a relatively "traditional" plant diet was consumed at many of the Lower Creek Indian towns.

The Maskókalkî exploited a wide variety of habitats for plant foods. Wild foods collected included nuts, blackberry/raspberry, elderberry, grape, honeylocust, huckleberry, mulberry, persimmon, and serviceberry. The archaeological evidence supports the historic descriptions of wild plants gathered. The collection of these plant foods was primarily the work of women.

If the plant portion of the subsistence economy was managed and performed by women in the eighteenth-century Maskókî households, then the sexual division of labor and gender role changes postulated by Saunt (1999) and others may be evident in the archaeological record. The paleobotanical remains at the sites analyzed and synthesized in Chapter 6 indicate that the Lower Creek Indians were resilient in the utilization of foreign plant foods in their subsistence economy. Archaeological evidence of plant foods from Cussetuh, Buzzard Roost, Yuchi, and Ochillee Creek indicates the presence of nonnative plants but shows that the traditional Eastern and Meso-American food traditions were still dominant up until the time of forced removal by Euro-Americans (circa 1825–1836). As opposed to the paleobotanical remains, the faunal remains indicate a greater adoption of Euro-American domesticated animals. If having domesticated animals was predominately a male activity and raising plant foods was predominately a female activity, then the archaeological record supports the thesis of gender division during the eighteenth century.

The Creek Indians were not passive recipients of their natural environment. Quantitative historic ecology research has shown that the Creek Indians altered the composition of the forests through hunting, collecting nuts, and farming. I have shown through the analysis of historic maps, ecological spatial analysis, and the study of ancient pollen that the Creek Indians were active participants in the shaping of their landscape and biophysical environment (Foster and Cohen 2005; Foster et al. 2004). The frequency of hickory trees was abnormally high within the first few thousand meters of Creek Indian towns because of harvesting and central place foraging of nuts. Burning of agricultural fields decreased the number of tree species that were fire-adverse and increased the number of early succession species within and around their agricultural fields. Burning of the forests was also increased because of deer hunting, particularly as a result of the deerskin trade in the eighteenth century (Foster and Cohen 2005; Foster et al. 2004).

Research into horticultural management decisions indicates that the Creek Indians were risk minimizers. Instead of farming for maximum crop harvests, their farming techniques were designed to maximize their chance of obtaining a certain minimum harvest each year (Foster 2003b, 2005b). This means that their horticultural management decisions—when to move gardens, which crops to grow, and when to harvest—were oriented toward obtaining a certain minimum harvest amount instead of maximizing their yield in any given year. This finding has profound consequences for the study of prehistoric Indian populations in the Southeast, particularly because some researchers argue that agricultural productivity and population dispersal contributed to social organization and Mississippian development (Muller 1997). I believe that institutions within the Maskókalkî social organization that minimized risk are probably ancient and probably contributed to Mississippian Period social organization. Patricia Wickman argues that prehistoric and modern Maskókî culture is defined by reciprocity (1999:91). These institutions of reciprocity such as collective farming may show continuity with the Mississippian Period. Examples of risk minimization strategies can be reciprocity, increased trade, coalescence of people in a single location, sharing, and redistribution (Real and Caraco 1986; Winterhalder et al. 1999). I suspect that the public granary that was managed by the Mico was one of those risk-minimizing strategies and that the institution of the public granary and its management was in existence during the Prehistoric Period as part of an overall horticultural strategy. James Adair, and recently Josh Piker, described the Maskókalkî "religious economy" that linked subsistence with social organization and religion (Piker 2004:148). This connection of horticultural management through risk linked the collective behaviors of individuals within a talwa and created an institution of status that may have contributed to the formation of stratification among prehistoric chiefdoms of the Southeast.

Each Lower Creek town had a town council for public decisions. It made collective decisions that affected the members of a town and was presided over by the Mico. The Mico held a centralized position but did not have the power that has been attributed to centralized leaders of the Mississippian Period. There is ethnohistoric evidence that, over time, some of these Micos were attributed more status and power because of their relationship with European representatives. The bureaucratic European governments wanted to deal with single individuals for more efficient legal transactions.

There may be evidence of increased status in the form of material culture and property ownership changes in the archaeological record. Cameron Wesson (2000) has argued, though problematically (see Chapters 1 and 5), that households and burial treatment demonstrate a decrease in centralized power from the protohistoric to the Historic Period among the Maskókalkî. Some Creek Indians began to possess exotic trade items in greater frequency, as is evident in the archaeological record, but we don't know that those individuals had higher status or more power as a result. Wesson's argument is that items that were considered to be "prestige goods" during the early eighteenth century were still "prestigious" in the late eighteenth century. He used this conclusion to argue that, since these European trade goods were more frequent in the late eighteenth century, power had been decentralized from chiefly elites. This static view of the function and meaning of artifacts distorts our ability to understand the Maskókalkî as a dynamic people (Jackson 2003; Wickman 1999). In addition, just because Europeans gave status to some individuals does not mean that Europeans altered the social status institutions that were in place for hundreds of years. Many of these religious and political roles still exist today among modern descendants (Moore 1994:126–141; Swanton 1928b; Urban 1994; Wickman 1999). The documented status given by the European politicians and traders probably existed parallel to the traditional social organization. For example, the historically venerated Emperor Brims was attributed power and given power by European colonists, but that does not necessarily negate the existing religious and political roles that existed among the Maskókalkî of the early eighteenth century nor does it mean that the effect was equal among all of the towns' populations. Each town was affected differently.

I would argue that generalizing about the Creek Indians based on a few sites or ethnohistoric descriptions is not very useful. There was so much variation in the towns and the response to European trade and the frontier economy that generalization is not accurate in any one case. It is known that some of the Upper Creek Indians felt that European trade goods were a sign of negative changes and growing demands on their land. Josh Piker has argued that cattle represented unwanted change to some of the Creek Indians, not opportunities to acquire European trade goods (2004:99–100). So high status may be measured differently in different towns and should be assessed according to the talwa. Markers of status among the Lower Creek were not the same as they were among the Upper Creek.

We have no reason to believe that status was not variable by town prehistorically also. Each town was an independent political unit with its own people acting on their own. While they were participating and interacting collectively as the common Maskókalkî, they were also reacting at their own pace and in response to different environmental constraints. We can learn about the reaction to power change and institutional reorganization of the Mississippian societies by studying the reactions and political adaptation of the eighteenth-century people.

By examining the variation of the archaeological record, we have shown that the Maskókalkî were a persistent and adaptable group of people. This book has set a beginning point for the study of the historic Maskókalkî and their ancestors. We have learned that each talwa was a politically and socially independent unit. The view of the Southastern Indians as a monolithic unit is not useful for the study of the historic or prehistoric people. Subsistence and material culture variation existed between talwas as well as within them. Consequently, further study of the Maskókalkî should be at least at the level of talwas, both historically and prehistorically. Ideally it would be at the individual or household level. Hopefully, we can take this knowledge to identify how each culture developed and adapted to new social and economic environments in the past. By clearly identifying the economic variation at each town and between towns, we should be able to understand change over time. The Historic Maskókalkî have a lot to teach us about the prehistoric Southeastern Indians.

Bibliography

Abrams, Marc D.

1992   Fire and the Development of Oak Forests. *Bioscience* 42(5):346–353.

Adair, James

1968   *The History of the American Indians, Particularly those Nations adjoining to the Mississippi, East and West Florida, Georgia, South and North Carolina, and Virginia.* Series in American Studies. Johnson Reprint Corp., New York.

Alcorn, Janis B.

1984   *Huastec Mayan Ethnobotany.* University of Texas Press, Austin.

Anderson, David G.

1994   *The Savannah River Chiefdoms: Political Change in the Late Prehistoric Southeast.* University of Alabama Press, Tuscaloosa.

Archmat

1995   *Supplies for Archaeology.* Archmat, Merrimack, New Hampshire.

Asch, Nancy B., and David L. Asch

1985   Prehistoric Plant Cultivation in West-Central Illinois. In *Prehistoric Food Production in North America,* edited by R. I. Ford. Anthropological Paper No. 75. Museum of Anthropology, University of Michigan, Ann Arbor.

Ashley, Margaret E., and Frank T. Schnell

1928   Mound and Village Sites in Harris, Muscogee and Chattahoochee Counties, Georgia. Report on File at the Columbus Museum of Arts and Sciences in Columbus, Georgia.

Baden, William M.

1987   A Dynamic Model of Stability and Change in Mississippian Agricultural Systems. Ph.D. dissertation, University of Tennessee, Knoxville.

Barker, W.

1795   Georgia from the Latest Authorities. Pages engraved for Carey's American Edition of *Guthrie's Geography.* Rucker Agee Map Collection, Birmingham Public Library.

Bartram, William

1909   *Observations on the Creek and Cherokee Indians.* Facsimile reprint of 1853 ed. Transactions of the American Ethnological Society, vol. 3. New York.

Battle, Henry B.

1921   Sawokli Town. *Arrow Points* 3(5):81–82.

Beasley, Virgil

2003   Investigations at the Quartermaster Site, 9CE42, Fort Benning, Georgia, Report Submitted to Fort Benning, Georgia. Panamerican Consultants, Inc., Tuscaloosa.

Bell, Amelia R.

1999   Separate People: Speaking of Creek Men and Women. *American Anthropologist* 92:332–345.

Belue, T. F.

1996   *The Long Hunt: Death of the Buffalo East of the Mississippi.* Stackpole Books, Mechanicsburg, Pennsylvania.

Benton, Jeffrey C. (editor)

1998   *The Very Worst Road: Travellers' Accounts of Crossing Alabama's Old Creek Indian Territory, 1820–1847.* The Historic Chattahoochee Commission, Eufaula, Alabama.

Binford, Lewis R

1967   Smudge Pits and Hide Smoking: The Use of Analogy in Archaeological Reasoning. *American Antiquity* 32(1):1–11.

Bird, Robert M.

1994   Manual for the Measurement of Maize Cobs. In *Corn and Culture in the Prehistoric New World,* edited by S. Johannessen and C. A. Hastorf, 5–22. Westview Press, Boulder, Colorado.

Black, Brian, H. Thomas Foster II, and Marc Abrams

2002   Combining Environmentally Dependent and Independent Analyses of Witness Tree Data in East-Central Alabama. *Canadian Journal of Forest Research* 32:2060–2075.

Blake, Leonard W.

1986   Corn and Other Plants from Prehistory into History in Eastern United States. In *The Protohistoric Period in the Mid-South, 1500–1700: Proceedings of the 1983 Mid-South Archaeological Conference,* edited by David H. Dye and Ronald C. Brister, 3–13. Archaeological Report No. 18. Mississippi Department of Archives and History, Jackson.

Blanton, Richard E., Gary M. Feinman, Stephen A. Kowalewski, and Peter N. Peregrine

1996   A Dual Processual Theory for the Evolution of Mesoamerican Civilization. *Current Anthropology* 37(1):1–14.

Blitz, John H.

1999   Mississippian Chiefdoms and the Fission-Fusion Process. *American Antiquity* 64(4):577–592.

Bogan, Arthur E.

1982   Archeological Evidence of Subsistence Patterns in the Little Tennessee River Valley. *Tennessee Anthropologist* 7(1):38–50.

Bohrer, Vorsila

1988   Ethnobotanical Aspects of Snaketown, a Hohokam Village in Southern Arizona. *American Antiquity* 50:102–116.

Bonhage-Freund, Mary Theresa

1997   Paleoethnobotany of the Georgia Piedmont: Four Lamar Period Farmsteads in the Middle Oconee Upland. Ph.D. dissertation, Pennsylvania State University.

1999   Flint River Data Recovery: A Paleoethnobotanical Analysis of Sites 9TR41 and 9TR54. Report Submitted to Southeastern Archaeological Services, Inc. Alma College, Alma, Michigan.

2002   Final Paleoethnobotanical Analysis of Flotation Samples from the Kolomoki 2001 Project (9ER1). Report submitted to the Department of Anthropology, University of Georgia, Athens. Alma College, Alma, Michigan.

2003   Final Paleoethnobotanical Analysis of Flotation Samples from the Kasita III Project (9CE1). Submitted to Panamerican Consultants, Inc. Alma College, Alma, Michigan.

2004   Paleoethnobotanical Analysis of Flotation Samples. In Following in the Footsteps of Gordon Willey: Excavation at the Town of Kasita (9CE1). Draft Report Submitted to Fort Benning, Georgia. Panamerican Consultants, Inc., Tuscaloosa, Alabama. Report Submitted to Fort Benning, Georgia.

2005   An Experimental Approach to the Analysis of Two Maize Cob-Filled Features from Etowah (9BR1). *Early Georgia* 34(2).

Booker, Karen M., Charles M. Hudson, and Robert L. Rankin

1992   Place Name Identification and Multilingualism in the Sixteenth-Century Southeast. *Ethnohistory* 39(4):399–451.

Boyd, Mark F.

1949   Diego Pena's Expedition to Apalachee and Apalachicolo in 1716: A Journal Translated and with an Introduction. *Florida Historical Quarterly* 28:1–27.

Boyko, Wayne

2004   Faunal Analysis. In Following in the Footsteps of Gordon Willey: Excavation at the Town of Kasita (9CE1). Draft Report Submitted to Fort Benning, Georgia. Panamerican Consultants, Inc., Tuscaloosa.

Braley, Chad O.

1991   Archaeological Data Recovery at Yuchi Town, 1RU63, Fort Benning, Alabama. Southeastern Archeological Services, Inc., Athens, Georgia.

1995   Historic Indian Period Archaeology of the Georgia Coastal Plain. Laboratory of Archaeology Series, Report 34, Submitted to Department of Anthropology, University of Georgia.

1998   Yuchi Town (1RU63) Revisited: Analysis of the 1958–1962 Excavations. Southeastern Archaeological Services, Inc., Athens, Georgia.

Brannon, Peter A.

1909   Aboriginal Remains in the Middle Chattahoochee Valley of Alabama and Georgia. *American Anthropologist,* n.s. 2:186–198.

1920   Aboriginal Towns in Alabama. In *Handbook of the Alabama Anthropological Society,* edited by P. A. Brannon, 42–54. Brown Printing Company, Montgomery.

1922a   Aboriginal Towns in Alabama, Showing Locations by Present County Boundary Lines. *Arrow Points* 4(2):26–28.

1922b   Kasihta. *Arrow Points* 5(1):10.

1925   Casihta of the Lower Creeks. *Arrow Points* 10(3):44.

1926   Okchayudshi Town. *Arrow Points* 12(4–5):43–44.

1930   Coweta of the Lower Creeks. *Arrow Points* 17(4):37–47.

Braun, E. Lucy

1950   *Deciduous Forests of Eastern North America.* Free Press, New York.

Braund, Kathryn E. Holland

1986   Mutual Convenience—Mutual Dependence: The Creeks, Augusta, and the Deer-skin Trade, 1733–1783. Ph.D. dissertation, Florida State University.

1993   *Deerskins & Duffels: Creek Indian Trade with Anglo-America, 1685–1815.* Indians of the Southeast. University of Nebraska Press, Lincoln.

Brose, David S., and Nancy Marie White

1999   *The Northwest Florida Expeditions of Clarence Bloomfield Moore.* Classics in South-eastern Archaeology. University of Alabama Press, Tuscaloosa.

Brown, Ian W.

1993   William Bartram and the Direct Historic Approach. In *Archaeology of Eastern North America: Papers in Honor of Stephen Williams,* edited by J. Stoltman. Mississippi Department of Archives and History, Jackson.

Buchner, C. Andrew

1996   Archaeological and Historical Evidence for Broken Arrow, a Lower Creek Town, on Ft. Benning, Georgia. Paper presented at the 53rd Southeastern Archaeological Conference, Birmingham, Alabama.

Burleigh, Thomas Dearborn

1958   *Georgia Birds.* 1st ed. University of Oklahoma Press, Norman.

Caldwell, Joseph R.

1948   Palachacolas Town, Hampton County, South Carolina. *Journal of the Washington Academy of Sciences* 38(10):321–324.

Carr, A.

1952   *Handbook of Turtles.* Comstock, Ithaca, New York.

Chagnon, Napoleon

1996   *The Yanomamo.* 5th ed. Case Studies in Cultural Anthropology Series. Harcourt Brace and Company, Orlando.

Clayton, Lawrence A., Vernon J. Knight, and Edward C. Moore

1993   *The De Soto Chronicles: The Expedition of Hernando de Soto to North America in 1539–1543.* University of Alabama Press, Tuscaloosa.

Cleland, Charles Edward

1966   *The Prehistoric Animal Ecology and Ethnozoology of the Upper Great Lakes Region.* Anthropological Papers 29. Museum of Anthropology, University of Michigan, Ann Arbor.

Cottier, John W.

1977   Lawson Field: A Cultural Resource Survey and Evaluation of a Selected Portion of Fort Benning Military Reservation. Department of Sociology and Anthropology, Auburn University, Alabama. Submitted to Fort Benning, Georgia.

Cowie, Sarah

2001   Early Nineteenth Century Evidence of the Creek Square Ground Plain: Phase II Archaeological Testing and Limited Phase III Data Recovery of the Ochillee Creek

Site (9CE379), Fort Benning, Chattahoochee County, Georgia. Southern Research, Ellerslie, Georgia.

Crane, Verner W.
1918   The Origin of the Name of the Creek Indians. *Mississippi Valley Historical Review* 5:339–342.
2004   *The Southern Frontier, 1670–1732*. Originally published 1929. University of Alabama Press, Tuscaloosa.

Cumbaa, S. L.
1972   An Intensive Harvest Economy in North Central Florida. Master's thesis, University of Florida.

Cumming, William P., and Louis De Vorsey, Jr. (editors)
1998   *The Southeast in Early Maps*. 3rd ed. University of North Carolina Press, Chapel Hill.

Cutler, Hugh C., and Leonard W. Blake
1976   *Plants from Archaeological Sites East of the Rockies*. American Archaeological Report no. 1 (Microfiche). American Archaeology Division, University of Missouri, Columbia.

Dale, Virginia H., Lisa Mai Olsen, and H. Thomas Foster II
in press Landscape Patterns as Indicators of Ecological Change at Fort Benning, Georgia. *Landscape and Urban Planning*.

DeJarnette, David L.
1975   *Archaeological Salvage in the Walter F. George Basin of the Chattahoochee River in Alabama*. University of Alabama Press, Tuscaloosa.

Delroit, R. J.
1970   *Illustrated Taxonomy of Weed Seeds*. Agronomy Publications, River Falls, Wisconsin.

Dickenson, Martin F., and Lucy B. Wayne
1985   Chattahoochee River Valley Cultural Resource Study and Evaluation, Fort Benning Military Reservation, Russell County, Alabama and Chattahoochee County, Georgia. Water and Air Research, Inc., Gainesville, Florida.

Douthat, James L. (editor)
1995   *1832 Creek Census: Parsons-Abbott*. Institute of Historic Research, Signal Mountain, Tennessee.

Durrenberger, E. Paul, and Nicola Tannenbaum
1992   Household Economy, Political Economy, and Ideology: Peasants and the State in Southeast Asia. *American Anthropologist* 94:74–89.

Edwards, Thomas
1921   Map of East Central Alabama Showing Aboriginal Mounds, Townsites, & Villages of Upper and Lower Creeks and Alibamos Prior to 1832. *Arrow Points*.

Elliott, Daniel T.
1992   Cultural Resources Survey of Selected (FY-90) Timber Harvesting Areas, Fort Benning, Alabama and Georgia, Vols. 1 and 2. Gulf Engineers & Consultants, Inc., and Brockington and Associates, Atlanta.

Elliott, Daniel T., Rita Elliott, Dean Wood, Russell Weisman, and Debra Wells
1999   Archaeological Testing of Nine Sites in Compartment K-06 Fort Benning Military

Reservation in Muscogee County, Georgia. Southern Research, Historic Preservation Consultants, Inc. Submitted to Directorate of Public Works, Fort Benning, Georgia.

Elliott, Daniel T., Grace F. Keith, Russell M. Weisman, Debra J. Wells, and David S. Leigh

2001   A Cultural Resources Survey of Compartment Z-01, Fort Benning Reservation, Russell County, Alabama. November 2001. Southern Research, Historic Preservation Consultants, Inc. Submitted to Directorate of Public Works, Fort Benning, Georgia.

Elliott, Daniel T., Karen G. Wood, Rita Folse Elliott and W. Dean Wood

1996   Up on the Upatoi: Cultural Resources Survey and Testing of Compartments K-6 and K-7, Fort Benning Military Reservation, Georgia. Southern Research, Historic Preservation Consultants, Inc. Submitted to Directorate of Public Works, Fort Benning, Georgia.

Elliott, Daniel T., Grace F. Keith, George D. Price, Rita F. Elliott, Tracy M. Dean, Debra J. Wells, Robbie F. Ethridge, and David S. Leigh

2001   A Cultural Resources Survey of the Main Post, Fort Benning Military Reservation Chattahoochee and Muscogee Counties, Georgia. Southern Research, Historic Preservation Consultants, Inc. Submitted to Directorate of Public Works, Fort Benning, Georgia.

Epenshade, Christopher T., and Marian D. Roberts

1992   Archaeological Assessment of 1RU135, a Nineteenth Century Creek Site, Uchee Creek Recreation Area, Fort Benning, Alabama. Brockington and Associates, Inc., Atlanta, Georgia.

ESRI

2003   ArcView. 8.3 ed. Environmental Systems Research Institute, Redlands, California.

Ethridge, Robbie Franklyn

1996   A Contest for Land: The Creek Indians on the Southern Frontier, 1796–1816. Ph.D. dissertation, University of Georgia.

2003   *The Creek Country: The Creek Indians and Their World, 1796–1816.* University of North Carolina Press, Chapel Hill.

Fairbanks, Charles H.

1952   Creek and Pre-Creek. In *Archeology of the Eastern United States,* edited by James B. Griffin, 285–309. University of Chicago Press, Chicago.

1955   The Abercrombie Mound, Russell County, Alabama. *Early Georgia* 2(1):13–19.

2003   *Archaeology of the Funeral Mound, Ocmulgee National Monument, Georgia.* University of Alabama Press, Tuscaloosa.

Feest, Christian F.

1974   Creek Towns in 1725. *Ethno Logische Zeitschrift Zuerich* 1:161–175.

Fenenga, Franklin, and Barbara Wagner Fenenga

1945   An Archaeological Survey of the Vicinity of Columbus, Georgia. Manuscript on file at the Columbus Museum of Arts and Sciences, Columbus.

Fernald, M. L.

1950   *Gray's Manual of Botany—Illustrated.* American Book Company, New York.

Ford, Richard I.

1979 Paleoethnobotany in American Archaeology. In *Advances in Archaeological Method and Theory,* edited by M. B. Schiffer, 2:285–336. Academic Press, New York.

1985 The Process of Plant Food Production in Prehistoric North America. In *Prehistoric Food Production in North America,* edited by R. I. Ford, 1–18. Anthropological Papers no. 75, University of Michigan, Ann Arbor.

Foster, H. Thomas II

1993 An Analysis of Burial Depth at the King Site (9Fl-5). Paper presented at the 50th Annual Southeastern Archaeological Conference, Raleigh, North Carolina.

2000a Evolutionary Ecology of Creek Indian Residential Mobility. Paper presented at the Southeastern Archaeological Conference, Macon, Georgia.

2000b Temporal Trends in Creek Indian Paleodemography. Paper presented at the Southeastern Archaeological Conference, Macon, Georgia.

2001 Long-term Average Rate Maximization of Creek Indian Residential Mobility: A Test of the Marginal Value Theorem. Ph.D. dissertation, Pennsylvania State University.

2003a *The Collected Works of Benjamin Hawkins, 1796–1810.* University of Alabama Press, Tuscaloosa.

2003b Dynamic Optimization of Horticulture among the Muscogee Creek Indians of the Southeastern United States. *Journal of Anthropological Archaeology* 22:411–424.

2004a Archaeological and Ethnohistoric Evidence for the Yuchi Indians within the Chattahoochee and Flint River Watersheds in the Southeastern United States (1715–1830). Paper presented at the American Society of Ethnohistory, Chicago, Illinois.

2004b Benjamin Hawkins and the Creek Indians. Paper presented at the Alabama Frontier: Cultural Crossroads, Montgomery.

2004c Book Review, *Historic Indian Towns in Alabama, 1540–1838,* by Amos J. Wright, Jr. *American Antiquity* 69(4):791–792.

2004d Evidence of Historic Creek Indian Migration from a Regional and Direct Historic Analysis of Ceramic Types. *Southeastern Archaeology* 23(1):65–84.

2004e Structural Analysis at Cussetuh. In Following in the Footsteps of Gordon Willey: Excavation at the Town of Kasita (9CE1). Draft Report Submitted to Fort Benning, Georgia. Panamerican Consultants, Inc., Tuscaloosa.

2005a Excavation at the Muskogee Town of Cussetuh (9CE1). A Report Submitted to the U.S. Army Corp of Engineers and the University of Arkansas. Northern Kentucky University, Highland Heights, Kentucky.

2006 A Model of Long-Term Optimal Land Use and risk management among Shifting Horticulturalists of the Southeastern United States (1715–1825). *American Antiquity,* in review.

Foster, H. Thomas II, and Arthur Cohen

2006 Palynological Evidence of the Effects of the Deerskin Trade on Eighteenth-Century Forests of Southeastern North America. *American Antiquity,* in press.

Foster, H. Thomas II, Brian Black, and Marc D. Abrams

2004 A Witness Tree Analysis of the Effects of Native American Indians on the Pre-European Settlement Forests in East-Central Alabama. *Human Ecology* 32(1):27–47.

Fretwell, Mark E.

1954   Benjamin Hawkins in the Chattahoochee Valley: 1798. *Valley Historical Association Bulletin* 1 (Bulletin 1):1–30.

1962   Lower Creek Towns on the Chattahoochee. In Mark Fretwell Collection, Collection 119, Folder 108, Manuscript on file at Cobb Memorial Archives, Valley, Alabama.

1980   *This So Remote Frontier: The Chattahoochee Country of Alabama and Georgia.* Rose Printing Co., Tallahassee, Florida.

Fritz, Gail J., V. D. Whitekiller, and J. W. McIntosh

2001   Ethnobotany of Ku-Nu-Che: Cherokee Hickory Nut Soup. *Journal of Ethnobiology* 21(2):1–27.

Galloway, Patricia

1995   *Choctaw Genesis, 1500–1700.* Indians of the Southeast. University of Nebraska Press, Lincoln.

1997a   *The Hernando de Soto Expedition: History, Historiography, and "Discovery" in the Southeast.* Univerity of Nebraska Press, Lincoln.

1997b   The Incestuous Soto Narratives. In *The Hernando de Soto Expedition: History, Historiography, and "Discovery" in the Southeast,* edited by P. Galloway, 11–44. University of Nebraska Press, Lincoln.

Gardner, Paul

1992   The Cultural and Ecological Implications of Mast Exploitation Strategies. Paper presented at the Fryxell Symposium of the 57th Annual Meeting of the Society for American Archaeology, Pittsburgh.

Gatschet, Albert S.

1884   A Migration Legend of the Creek Indians: With a Linguistic, Historic, and Ethnographic Introduction. Library of Aboriginal American Literature, no 4. 2 vols. D. G. Brinton, Philadelphia.

Gettys, Marshall

1995   Historical Archaeology in Oklahoma. *Oklahoma Anthropological Bulletin* 44.

Gilbert, B. M.

1980   *Mammalian Osteology.* Modern Printing Company, Laramie, Wyoming.

Gilbert, W. H.

1943   *The Eastern Cherokees.* Anthropological Papers No. 23, Bureau of American Ethnology, Bulletin 133. Smithsonian Institution, Washington, D.C.

Golly, F. B.

1962   *Mammals of Georgia.* University of Georgia Press, Athens.

Grantham, Bill

2002   *Creation Myths and Legends of the Creek Indians.* University Press of Florida, Gainesville.

Green, Michael D.

1990   *The Creeks.* Indians of North America. Chelsea House, New York.

Gremillion, Kristen J.

1989   The Development of a Mutualistic Relationship Between Humans and Maypops (*Passiflora incarnata*) in the Southeastern United States. *Journal of Ethnobiology* 9:135–155.

1998   Changing Roles of Wild and Cultivated Plant Resources among Early Farmers of Eastern Kentucky. *Southeastern Archaeology* 17(2):140–157.

Hahn, Steven

2000   The Invention of the Creek Nation: A Political History of the Creek Indians in the South's Imperial Era, 1540–1763. Ph.D. dissertation, Emory University.

2004   *The Invention of the Creek Nation, 1670–1763.* University of Nebraska Press, Lincoln.

Hall, Basil

1829   *Forty Etchings, from sketches made with the Camera Lucida, in North America, in 1827 and 1828.* Cadell & Co., Edinburgh.

Hally, David J.

1971   The Archaeology of Euro-Indian Contact in the Southeast. In *Symposium on Indians in the Old South: Red, White, and Black.* Southern Anthropological Society Proceedings, no. 5. Southern Anthropological Society, Athens.

1986   The Identification of Vessel Function: A Case Study from Northwest Georgia. *American Antiquity* 51(2):267–295.

2002   "As caves below the ground": Making Sense of Aboriginal House Form in the Protohistoric and Historic Southeast. In *Between Contacts and Colonies: Archaeological Perspectives on the Prehistoric Southeast,* edited by C. B. Wesson and M. A. Rees, 90–109. University of Alabama Press, Tuscaloosa.

Hann, John H.

1986   The Use and Processing of Plants by Indians of Spanish Florida. *Southeastern Archaeology* 5(2):91–102.

1988   *Apalachee: The Land between the Rivers.* Ripley P. Bullen Monographs in Anthropology and History. University Presses of Florida, Gainesville.

1996   Late Seventeenth-Century Forebears of the Lower Creeks and Seminoles. *Southeastern Archaeological Conference* 15(1):66–80.

Hann, John H., and Bonnie G. McEwan

1998   *The Apalachee Indians and Mission San Luis.* University Press of Florida, Gainesville.

Hargrave, Michael L., Charles R. McGimsey, Mark J. Wagner, Lee A. Newsom, Laura Ruggiero, Emanuel Breitburg, and Lynette Norr

1998   The Yuchi Town Site (1RU63), Russell County, Alabama: An Assessment of the Impacts of Looting. Cultural Resources Research Center, U.S. Army Construction Engineering Research Laboratory, Champaign, Illinois.

Hariot, Thomas, René Goulaine de Laudonnière, Jacques Le Moyne de Morgues, and L. Ningler

1927   *Voyages en Virginie et en Floride.* Duchartre et Van Buggenhoudt, Paris.

Harper, Francis (editor)

1998   *The Travels of William Bartram.* Naturalist's Edition. University of Georgia Press, Athens.

Harrington, M. A.

1913   A Preliminary Sketch of the Lenape. *American Anthropologist* 15:208–235.

Hawkins, Benjamin

1807   A Concise Description of the Creek Country, with some Remarkable Customs

Practised among the Native Inhabitants. *The Medical Repository, and Review of American Publications on Medicine, Surgery, and the Branches of Science* 4:36–43.

Hewitt, J. N. B.

1939 Notes on the Creek Indians. In *Bureau of American Ethnology Bulletin,* 121–159. Anthroplogical Papers, No. 10. Smithsonian Institution, Washington, D.C.

Hilliard, S.

1969 Hog Meat and Cornpone: Food Habits in the Ante-Bellum South. *Proceedings of the American Philosophical Society* 113:1–13.

Holland, C. G.

1974 A Mid-Eighteenth Century Indian Village on the Chattahoochee River. *The Florida Anthropologist* 27(1):31–46.

Hudson, Charles M.

1976 *The Southeastern Indians.* University of Tennessee Press, Knoxville.

1994 The Hernando de Soto Expedition, 1539–1543. In *The Forgotten Centuries: Indians and Europeans in the American South, 1521–1704,* edited by C. Hudson and C. C. Tesser, 74–103. University of Georgia Press, Athens.

Hudson, Charles (editor)

1979 *Black Drink: A Native American Tea.* University of Georgia Press, Athens.

Hudson, Charles, and Carmen Chaves Tesser (editors)

1994 *The Forgotten Centuries: Indians and Europeans in the American South, 1521–1704.* University of Georgia Press, Athens.

Hudson, Charles M., Marvin Smith, David Hally, Richard Polhemus, and Chester DePratter

1985 Coosa: A Chiefdom in the Sixteenth-Century Southeastern United States. *American Antiquity* 50(4):723–737.

Hurt, Douglas A.

2000 The Shaping of a Creek (Muscogee) Homeland in Indian Territory, 1828–1907. Ph.D. dissertation, University of Oklahoma.

Hurt, Wesley R.

1947 An Archaeological Survey, Chattahoochee Valley, Alabama, 1947. Manuscript, University of Alabama, Office of Archaeological Services.

1975 The Preliminary Archaeological Survey of the Chattahoochee Valley Area in Alabama. In *Archaeological Salvage in the Walter F. George Basin of the Chattahoochee River in Alabama,* edited by D. L. DeJarnette. University of Alabama Press, Tuscaloosa.

Huscher, Harold A.

1959 Appraisal of the Archaeological Resources of the Walter F. George Reservoir Area, Chattahoochee River, Alabama and Georgia. Report to the Smithsonian Institution, Washington, D.C.

Huscher, Harold A., et al.

1972 Archaeological Investigations in the West Point Dam Area: A Preliminary Report. Department of Sociology and Anthropology, University of Georgia, Athens.

Jackson, Jason Baird

2003 *Yuchi Ceremonial Life: Performance, Meaning, and Tradition in a Contemporary American Indian Community.* Studies in the Anthropology of North American Indians. University of Nebraska Press, Lincoln.

Jackson, Paul D., Ryan A. Crutchfield, and Meghan LaGraff Ambrosino

1998   Archaeological Site Testing and Evaluation of Ten Selected Sites (1RU38, 1RU39, 1RU40, 1RU43, 1RU55, 1RU58, 1RU87, 1RU88, 1RU92, 1RU136) within the Fort Benning Military Reservation, Alabama. Panamerican Consultants, Inc. Submitted to National Park Service and the Directorate of Public Works, Fort Benning, Georgia.

Jackson, Paul D., Ryan A. Crutchfield, Meghan LaGraff Ambrosino, James N. Ambrosino, and Russell M. Weisman

1998   Archaeological Site Testing and Evaluation of Ten Selected Sites (1RU45, 1RU54, 1RU72, 1RU78, 1RU128, 1RU129, 1RU227, 1RU358, 1RU360, and 1RU361) within the Fort Benning Military Reservation, Alabama. Panamerican Consultants, Inc., Tuscaloosa.

Johannessen, Sissel

1984   Paleoethnobotany. In *American Bottom Archaeology: A Summary of the FAI-270 Archaeological Project*, edited by C. J. Bareis and J. W. Porter. University of Illinois Press, Urbana.

Johnson, Nathanial

1708   Letter to the Lords Proprietors, September 17, 1708. Records Pertaining to South Carolina, vol. 5, 203–210. British Public Records Office, Columbia.

Keith, Scot J.

2003   Archaeological Data Recovered at 9ME348, Muscogee Technology Park, Columbus, Georgia. Southern Research Historic Preservation Consultants, Inc., Ellerslie, Georgia.

Kelly, A. R.

1938   A Preliminary Report on Archeological Explorations at Macon, Ga. *Bulletin of the Bureau of American Ethnology* 119.

Kelly, Arthur R., Clemens de Bailiou, Frank T. Schnell, Margaret V. Clayton, Jr., Francis J. Clune, and Ann L. Schlosser

1961   *Excavations in Stewart County, Georgia: Summer and Fall, 1961.* Southeast Archaeological Center, National Park Service, Tallahassee, Florida.

King, Adam

2002   Creek Chiefdoms at the Temporal Edge of the Mississippian World. *Southeastern Archaeology* 21(2):221–226.

King, Frances B.

1987   Prehistoric Maize in Eastern North America: An Evolutionary Evaluation. Ph.D. dissertation, University of Illinois, Urbana-Champaign.

Knight, Vernon James, Jr.

1985   Tukabatchee: Archaeological Investigations at an Historic Creek Town, Elmore County, Alabama, 1984. Report no. 45. Office of Archaeological Research, Alabama State Museum of Natural History, University of Alabama, Tuscaloosa.

1994a   The Formation of the Creeks. In *The Forgotten Centuries: Indians and Europeans in the American South, 1521–1704*, edited by C. Hudson and C. C. Tesser, 373–392. University of Georgia, Athens.

1994b   Ocmulgee Fields Culture and the Historical Development of Creek Ceramics. In *Ocmulgee Archaeology: 1936–1986*, edited by D. J. Hally, 237. University of Georgia Press, Athens.

Knight, Vernon James, Jr. and Tim S. Mistovich
1984   Walter F. George Lake: Archaeological Survey of Fee Owned Lands, Alabama and Georgia. Office of Archaeological Research, University of Alabama, Tuscaloosa.

Kowalewski, Stephen A., and James W. Hatch
1991   The Sixteenth-Century Expansion of Settlement in the Upper Oconee Watershed, Georgia. *Southeastern Archaeology* 10(1):1–17.

Kowalewski, Stephen A., and Mark Williams
1989   The Carroll Site: Analysis of the 1936 Excavations at a Mississippian Farmstead in Georgia. *Southeastern Archaeology* 8(1):46–67.

Kurjack, Edward B.
1975   Archaeological Investigations in the Walter F. George Basin. In *Archaeological Salvage in the Walter F. George Basin of the Chattahoochee River in Alabama,* edited by D. L. DeJarnette, 86–195. University of Alabama Press, Tuscaloosa.

Lafitau, Joseph-François
1974   *Customs of the American Indians Compared with the Customs of Primitive Times.* Originally published 1724. The Publications of the Champlain Society, 48–49. Champlain Society, Toronto.

Ledbetter, R. Jerald
1996   The Bull Creek Site, 9ME1 Muscogee County, Georgia. Southeastern Archaeological Services, Inc., Athens, Georgia.
1997   The Victory Drive Site, 9ME50, Muscogee County, Georgia. Occasional Papers in Cultural Resource Management 8. Georgia Department of Transportation, Office of Environment, Atlanta.

Ledbetter, R. Jerald, Lisa D. O'Steen, Andrea B. Shea and John S. Lupold
1996   The Victory Drive Site, 9ME50 Muscogee County, Georgia. Southeastern Archeological Services, Inc., Athens, Georgia.

Ledbetter, Jerald, Robbie Ethridge, Mary Theresa Bonhage-Freund, William G. Moffat, Lisa D. O'Steen, and John Worth
2002   Archaeological Investigations at Buzzard Roost 9TR41, 9TR54, and 9TR106 Taylor County, Georgia. Southeastern Archaeological Services, Inc., Athens, Georgia.

Leechman, D.
1951   Bone Grease. *American Antiquity* 16:355–356.

Lescarbot, M.
1968   *The History of New France.* Originally published 1609. Translated by W. L. Grant III. The Champlain Society, Toronto.

Lewis, C. Thomas
2004   Aboriginal Pottery from the Lower Creek Indian Town of Kasita. In Following in the Footsteps of Gordon Willey: Excavations at the Town of Kasita (9CE1). Draft Report. Panamerican Consultants, Inc., Tuscaloosa, Alabama.

Limp, W. Fredrick, and V. A. Reidhead
1972   An Economic Evaluation of the Potential of Fish Utilization in Riverine Environments. *American Antiquity* 44(1):70–78.

Lolly, Terry L.
1996   Ethnohistory and Archaeology: A Map Method for Locating Historic Upper Creek Indian Towns and Villages. *Journal of Alabama Archaeology* 42(1).

Lopinot, Neal H., and William I. Woods

1993   Wood Overexploitation and the Collapse of Cahokia. In *Foraging and Farming in the Eastern Woodlands,* edited by C. Margaret Scarry, 206–231. Ripley P. Bullen Series. University Press of Florida, Gainesville.

Manuelshagen, C., and G. H. Davis

1967   The Moravians' Plan for a Mission Among the Creek Indians, 1803–1804. *Collections of the Georgia Historical Society* 5:358–364.

Marks, S. A., and A. W. Erickson

1966   Age Determination in the Black Bear. *Journal of Wildlife Management* 30(2).

Martin, Alexander C., and William D. Barkley

1973   *Seed Identification Manual.* University of California Press, Berkeley.

Martin, Jack B., and Margaret McKane Mauldin

2000   *A Dictionary of Creek Muscogee: With Notes on the Florida and Oklahoma Seminole Dialects of Creek.* Studies in the Anthropology of North American Indians. University of Nebraska Press, Lincoln.

Mason, Carol Irwin

1963   The Archaeology of Ocmulgee Old Fields, Macon, Georgia. Ph.D. dissertation, University of Michigan.

Mason, Otis Tufton

1973   Aboriginal Skin Dressing, a Study Based on Material in the U.S. National Museum. Annual Report of the Board of Regents of the Smithsonian Institutions (facsimile reproduction). In *Book Collection on Microfilm Relating to the North American Indian,* reel 1. Microfilming Corporation of America, Glen Rock, Michigan.

McCoy, Jill, and Kevin Johnston

2002   Using ArcGIS Spatial Analyst. ESRI Press, Redlands, California.

McMichael, Edward V., and James H. Kellar

1960   Archaeological Salvage in the Oliver Basin. University of Georgia, Laboratory of Archaeology.

McPike, James W.

1992   Site Analysis Through Extended Surface Collection and Research: 1Ru70— Hitchiti (McLendon)—Russell Co., Alabama. Report on file, Columbus Museum, Columbus, Georgia.

Mereness, Newton D. (editor)

1961   *Travels in the American Colonies.* Antiquarian Press, Ltd., New York.

Mihesuah, Devon Abbott (editor)

1998   *Natives and Academics: Researching and Writing about American Indians.* University of Nebraska Press, Lincoln.

Milfort, Louis LeClerc

1959   *Memoirs or, a Quick Glance at my various Travels and my Sojourn in the Creek Nation.* Translated by B.C. McCary. The Beehive Press, Savannah, Georgia.

Miller, Naomi Frances

1988   Ratios in Paleoethnobotanical Analysis. In *Current Paleoethnobotany,* edited by C. A. Hastorf and V. S. Popper. University of Chicago Press, Chicago.

Minnis, Paul E., and Richard I. Ford

1977   Analysis of Plant Remains from Chimney Rock Mesa. In *Archaeological Investiga-*

tions at Chimney Rock Mesa: 1970–1972, Memoir 1, edited by F. W. Eddy. Colorado Archaeological Society, Denver.

Mistovich, Tim S., and Vernon J. Knight, Jr.

1986 Excavations at Four Sites on Walter F. George Lake, Alabama and Georgia. Office of Archaeological Research, University of Alabama. Report no. 49.

Moerman, Daniel E.

1998 *Native American Ethnobotany.* Timber Press, Portland, Oregon.

Montgomery, F. H.

1977 *Seeds and Fruits of Plants of Eastern Canada and the Northeastern United States.* University of Toronto Press, Toronto.

Moore, Alexander (editor)

1988 *Nairne's Muskhogean Journals: The 1708 Expedition to the Mississippi River.* University Press of Mississippi, Oxford.

Moore, John H.

1994 Ethnoarchaeology of the Lamar Peoples. In *Perspectives on the Southeast: Linguistics, Archaeology, and Ethnohistory,* edited by P. B. Kwachka. Southern Anthropological Society Proceedings, vol. 27. M. W. Helms, general editor. University of Georgia, Athens.

Morse, Dan F., and Phyllis A. Morse

1960 9Go507: The Williams Site, Gordon County, Georgia. *Early Georgia* 13(4):81–91.

Muller, Jon

1997 *Mississippian Political Economy.* Plenum, New York.

Mulvihill, Frank J.

1925 Some Indications of Indian Occupancy along Bull Creek, near Columbus, Georgia. *Arrow Points* 10(3):36–43.

Myer, William Edward

1928 Indian Trails of the Southeast. In *Forty-Second Annual Report of the Bureau of American Ethnology to the Secretary of the Smithsonian Institution,* edited by J. W. Fewkes, 727–857. U.S. Government Printing Office, Washington.

Native Seeds/SEARCH

2005 www.nativeseeds.org.

Newsom, Lee A., and Laura Ruggiero

1998 Archaeobotany. In *The Yuchi Town Site (1Ru63), Russell County, Alabama. An Assessment of the Impacts of Looting.* Prepared for Environmental Management Division, Department of the Army, Headquarters U.S. Army Infantry Center, Fort Benning, Georgia, DoD Project No. 940683, edited by M. L. Hargrave. U.S. Corp of Engineers, Environmental and Development Research Center, Champaign, Illinois.

Olsen, Lisa, Virginia H. Dale, and Howard Thomas Foster II

2001 Landscape Patterns as Indicators of Ecological Change at Fort Benning, Ga. Paper presented at the ESRI Users Conference, San Diego, California.

Opler, Morris Edward

1952 The Creek "Town" and the Problem of Creek Indian Political Reorganization. In *Human Problems in Technological Change,* edited by E. Spicer, 165–180. Sage, New York.

Orton, Clive R.

1982   Computer Simulation Experiments to Assess the Performance of Measures of Quantity of Pottery. *World Archaeology* 14(1):1–18.

1985   Two Useful Parameters for Pottery Research. Paper presented at the Computer Applications in Archaeology 1985, London.

2000   *Sampling in Archaeology.* Cambridge Manuals in Archaeology. Cambridge University Press, Cambridge, U.K.

Orton, Clive R., and P. A. Tyers

1990   Statistical Analysis of Ceramic Assemblages. *Archeologia e Calcolatori* 1:81–110.

1992   Counting Broken Objects: The Statistics of Ceramic Assemblages. *Proceedings of the British Academy* 77:163–184.

Orton, Clive, Paul Tyers, and Alan Vince

1993   *Pottery in Archaeology.* Cambridge Manuals in Archaeology. Cambridge University Press, Cambridge, U.K.

O'Steen, Lisa D.

2000   Zooarchaeological Analysis of a Cherokee Settlement in North Georgia. *Early Georgia* 28(2):55–73.

O'Steen, Lisa, and Leslie Raymer

1999   Late Eighteenth to Early Nineteenth Century Creek Foodways at the Ochillee Creek Farmstead, Fort Benning, Georgia. New South Associates Technical Report #637. New South Associates, Atlanta.

O'Steen, Lisa D., John S. Cable, Mary Beth Reed, and J. W. Joseph

1997   Cultural Resources Survey Lawson Army Airfield, Ft. Benning, Georgia, and Alabama: Survey Results for 4,690 Acres Within Compartments V1-V4 and W1-W3 and Lawson Field. New South Associates, Inc., Atlanta.

Owen, T.

1950   Indian Tribes and Towns in Alabama. *Alabama Historical Quarterly* 12(1–4):118–241.

Paredes, J. Anthony, and Kenneth J. Plante

1983   A Reexamination of Creek Indian Population Trends: 1738–1832. *American Indian Culture and Research Journal* 6(4):3–28.

Pavao-Zuckerman, Barnet

2000   Vertebrate Subsistence in the Mississippian-Historic Transition. *Southeastern Archaeology* 19(2):135–144.

2005   Deerskins and Domesticates: Creek Subsistence and Economic Strategies in the Historic Period. In press.

Pearsall, Deborah M.

1989   *Paleoethnobotany: A Handbook of Procedures.* Academic Press, Inc., San Diego.

Peebles, Christopher S., and Susan M. Kus

1977   Some Archaeological Correlates of Ranked Societies. *American Antiquity* 42(3): 421–448.

Piker, Joshua A.

1998   "Peculiarly Connected": The Creek Town of Oakfuskee and the Study of Colonial American Communities, 1708–1785. Ph.D. dissertation, Cornell University.

2003   "White & Clean" & Contested: Creek Towns and Trading Paths in the Aftermath of the Seven Years' War. *Ethnohistory* 50(2):315–347.

2004   *Okfuskee: A Creek Indian Town in Colonial America.* Harvard University Press, Cambridge.

Pluckhahn, Thomas J.

1997   Archeological Investigation of the Tarver (9Jo6) and Little Tarver (9Jo198) Sites, Jones County, Georgia. Southeastern Archeological Services, Inc., Athens, Georgia.

2003   *Kolomoki: Settlement, Ceremony, and Status in the Deep South, A.D. 350 to 750.* University of Alabama Press, Tuscaloosa.

Polhemus, Richard R.

1987a   *The Toqua Site—40MR6: A Late Mississippian, Dallas Phase town.* Vol. 1. Tennessee Valley Authority. Submitted to University of Tennessee Department of Anthropology Report of Investigations No. 41, and Tennessee Valley Authority Publications in Anthropology No. 44.

1987b   *The Toqua Site—40MR6: A Late Mississippian, Dallas Phase town.* Vol. 2. Tennessee Valley Authority. Submitted to University of Tennessee Department of Anthropology Report of Investigations No. 41, and Tennessee Valley Authority Publications in Anthropology No. 44.

Popper, Virginia S.

1988   Selecting Quantitative Measurements in Paleoethnobotany. In *Current Paleoethnobotany,* edited by C. A. Hastorf and V. S. Popper. University of Chicago Press, Chicago.

Quimby, George I., and Alexander Spoehr

1950   Historic Creek Pottery from Oklahoma. *American Antiquity* 3:249–251.

Raymer, Leslie, Lisa O'Steen, and Mary Theresa Bonhage-Freund

1997   Subsistence Studies. In A Picture Unsurpassed: Prehistoric and Historic Indian Settlement and Landscape, Brasstown Valley, Towns County, Georgia. Report prepared for the Georgia Department of Natural Resources. New South Associates Technical Report 457, edited by J. Cable. New South Associates, Atlanta, Georgia.

Real, Leslie, and Thomas Caraco

1986   Risk and foraging in stochastic environments. *Annual Review of Ecology and Systematics* 17:371–390.

Redwine, Charles III, C. Thomas Lewis, and Robert J. Scott

2004   Laboratory Methods. In Following in the Footsteps of Gordon Willey: Excavations at the Town of Kasita (9CE1), edited by M. T. Bonhage-Freund and others. Panamerican Consultants, Inc., Tuscaloosa.

Reidhead, V. A.

1976   Optimization and Food Procurement at the Prehistoric Leonard Haag Site, Southeast Indiana: A Linear Programming Analysis. Ph.D. dissertation, Indiana University.

Reitz, E. J., and D. Cordier.

1983   Use of Allometry in Zooarchaeological Analysis. In *Animals and Archaeology,* no. 2, edited by C. Grigson and J. Clutton-Brock, 237–252. BAR International Series 183, London.

Reitz, Elizabeth Jean, and Elizabeth S. Wing

1999   *Zooarchaeology.* Cambridge University Press, Cambridge, U.K.

Rice, Prudence M.

1984   *Pots and Potters: Current Approaches in Ceramic Archaeology.* Monograph 24. Institute of Archaeology, University of California, Los Angeles.

Richardson, Rick R., and Eric A. Duff

1998   Phase I: Archaeological Investigation of Site 1RU11, Russell County, Alabama. Report submitted to Alabama Historical Commission, Montgomery.

Rogers, E. S.

1973   *The Quest for Food and Furs: The Mistassini Cree, 1953–1954.* Publications in Ethnology 5. National Museum of Canada, Ottawa.

Rogers, J. Daniel, and Bruce D. Smith

1995   *Mississippian Communities and Households.* University of Alabama Press, Tuscaloosa.

Romans, Bernard

1999   *A Concise Natural History of East and West Florida.* University of Alabama Press, Tuscaloosa.

Rostlund, E.

1960   The Geographic Range of the Historic Bison in the Southeast. *Annals of the Association of American Geographers* 4:395–407.

Rubertone, Patricia E.

2000   The Historical Archaeology of Native Americans. *Annual Review of Anthropology.* 29:425–426.

Russell, Margaret Clayton

1976   Lamar and the Creeks: An Old Controversy Revisited. *Early Georgia* 3(1):53–67.

Saunt, Claudio

1999   *A New Order of Things: Property, Power, and the Transformation of the Creek Indians, 1733–1816.* Cambridge Studies in North American History. Cambridge University Press, Cambridge, U.K.

Scarry, C. Margaret

1994   Variability in Late Prehistoric Corn from the Lower Southeast. In *Corn and Culture in the Prehistoric New World,* edited by S. Johannessen and C. A. Hastorf, 347–367. Westview Press, Boulder.

Scarry, C. Margaret, and Elizabeth Jean Reitz

1990   Herbs, Fish, Scum, and Vermin: Subsistence Strategies in Sixteenth Century Spanish Florida. In *Columbian Consequences,* vol. 2: *Archaeological and Historical Perspectives on the Spanish Borderlands East,* edited by D. H. Thomas, 343–354. Smithsonian Institution Press, Washington, D.C.

Schmid, E.

1972   *Atlas of Animal Bones.* Elsevier Publishing Company, Amsterdam.

Schmitt, Karl

1950   Two Creek Pottery Vessels from Oklahoma. *The Florida Anthropologist* 3(1–2):3–8.

Schnell, Frank T., Jr.

1970   A Comparative Study of Some Lower Creek Sites. *Southeastern Archaeological Conference, Bulletin* 13:133–136.

1982   A Cultural Resources Investigation of Sites 1RU63 and 9CE66, Fort Benning, Alabama and Georgia. Columbus Museum of Arts and Sciences, Columbus, Georgia.

1984   Late 17th and Early 18th Century Sites on the Lower Chattahoochee. *LAMAR Briefs* 3:8–9.

1990   Middle Chattahoochee River Phase Characteristics. In *Lamar Archaeology: Mississippian Chiefdoms in the Deep South,* edited by J. Mark Williams and Gary Shapiro, 67–69. University of Alabama Press, Tuscaloosa.

1998   Ceramics in the Southern Half of the Chattahoochee Valley. *Journal of Alabama Archaeology* 44(1–2):99–130.

Schorger, E.

1972   *The Wild Turkey.* University of Oklahoma Press, Norman.

Schroedl, Gerald F.

1986   Overhill Cherokee Archaeology at Chota-Tanasee. Department of Anthropology, University of Tennessee, Knoxville.

2000   Cherokee Ethnohistory and Archaeology from 1540 to 1838. In *Indians of the Greater Southeast: Historical Archaeology and Ethnohistory,* edited by B. G. McEwan, 204–241. University Press of Florida, Gainesville.

Scott, Robert

2004   ARPA Damage Assessment of 1RU132, Russell County, Alabama. Panamerican Consultants, Inc. Submitted to Directorate of Public Works, Fort Benning, Georgia.

Sheldon, Craig T., Jr.

1997   Historic Creek "Summer" Houses of Central Alabama. Paper presented at the Annual Meeting, Society for American Archaeology, Nashville, Tennessee.

Silver, Timothy

1990   *A New Face on the Countryside: Indians, Colonists, and Slaves in South Atlantic Forests, 1500–1800.* Cambridge University Press, Cambridge, U.K.

Sinopoli, Carla M.

1991   *Approaches to Archaeological Ceramics.* Plenum Press, New York.

Skinner, Alanson

1913   Notes on the Florida Seminole. *American Anthropologist,* n.s. 15:63–77.

Smith, Bruce D.

1975   *Middle Mississippi Exploitation of Animal Populations.* Anthropological Papers, no. 57. University of Michigan, Ann Arbor.

Smith, Marvin T.

1987   *Archaeology of Aboriginal Culture Change in the Interior Southeast: Depopulation during the Early Historic Period.* Ripley P. Bullen Monographs in Anthropology and History, no. 6. University of Florida Press/Florida State Museum, Gainesville.

1992   Historic Period Indian Archaeology of Northern Georgia. Laboratory of Archaeology series, Report no. 30. Laboratory of Archaeology, University of Georgia, Athens.

2000   *Coosa: The Rise and Fall of a Southeastern Mississippian Chiefdom.* University Press of Florida, Gainesville.

Smith, Marvin, and David J. Hally

1992   Chiefly Behavior: Evidence from Sixteenth Century Spanish Accounts. In *Lords of* the Southeast: Social Inequality and the Native Elites of Southeastern North America, edited by A. W. Barker and T. R. Pauketat, 99–110. Archaeological Papers of the American Anthropological Association, no. 3. American Anthropological Association, Washington, D.C.

Smith, Patrick
2004   Cultural Features Overview. In Following in the Footsteps of Gordon Willey: Excavation at the Town of Kasita (9CE1), draft report, 421–438. Panamerican Consultants, Inc., Tuscaloosa.

Southerland, Henry DeLeon, Jr. and Jerry Elijah Brown
1989   The Federal Road through Georgia, the Creek Nation, and Alabama, 1806–1836. University of Alabama Press, Tuscaloosa.

Speck, Frank G.
2004   Ethnology of the Yuchi Indians. University of Nebraska Press, Lincoln.

Stahle, David W., and Malcolm K. Cleaveland
1992   Reconstruction and Analysis of Spring Rainfall over the Southeastern U.S. for the Past 1000 Years. Bulletin of the American Meteorological Society 73(12):1947–1961.

Steward, Julian
1942   The Direct Historical Approach to Archaeology. American Antiquity 7(4):337–343.

Stiggins, George
2003   Creek Indian History: A Historical Narrative of the Genealogy, Traditions and Downfall of the Ispocoga or Creek Indian Tribe of Indians by One of the Tribe, George Stiggins. Edited by William Stokes Wyman and Virginia Pounds Brown. University of Alabama Press, Tuscaloosa.

Strausbaugh, Perry Daniel, and Earl Lemley Core
1977   Flora of West Virginia. Seneca Books, Grantsville, West Virginia.

Swan, Caleb
1855   Position and State of Manners and Arts in the Creek, or Muscogee Nation in 1791. In Historical and statistical information respecting the history, condition, and prospects of the Indian tribes of the United States, edited by H. R. Schoolcraft. Lippincott, Grambo, & Co., Philadelphia.

Swanton, John Reed
1912   The Creek Indians as Mound Builders. American Anthropologist, n.s. 14(2):320–324.
1922   Early History of the Creek Indians & Their Neighbors. Southeastern Classics in Archaeology, Anthropology, and History. University Press of Florida, Gainesville, 1998.
1928a   Religious Beliefs and Medical Practices of the Creek Indians. In Forty-Second Annual Report of the Bureau of American Ethnology to the Secretary of the Smithsonian Institution, 1924–1925, edited by J. W. Fewkes, 473–672. U.S. Government Printing Office, Washington.
1928b   Social Organization and Social Usages of the Indians of the Creek Confederacy. In Forty-Second Annual Report of the Bureau of American Ethnology to the Secretary of the Smithsonian Institution, 1924–1925, edited by J. W. Fewkes, 23–472. U.S. Government Printing Office, Washington.
1946   The Indians of the Southeastern United States. U.S. Bureau of American Ethnology

Bulletin 137. U.S. Government Printing Office, Washington. 137. Reprint, Greenwood Press, New York, 1969.

1979   *The Indians of the Southeastern United States.* Classics in Smithsonian Anthropology 2. Smithsonian Institution Press, Washington.

Terrill, Helen Eliza, and Sara Robertson Dixon

1958   *History Stewart County, Georgia.* Columbus Office Supply Co., Columbus, Georgia.

Trigger, Bruce G.

1968   *The Huron: Farmers of the North.* Holt, New York.

1969   Criteria for Identifying the Locations of Historic Indian Sites: A Case Study from Montreal. *Ethnohistory* 16(4):303–316.

Trippensee, E.

1947   *Wildlife Management.* Vol. 1. McGraw-Hill, New York.

Urban, Greg

1994   The Social Organization of the Southeast. In *North American Indian Anthropology: Essays on Society and Culture,* edited by R. J. DeMallie and A. Ortiz. University of Oklahoma Press, Norman.

Utley, Francis Lee, and Marion R. Hemperly (editors)

1975   *Placenames of Georgia: Essays of John H. Goff.* University of Georgia, Athens.

Vehik, S. C.

1975   Bone Fragments and Bone Grease Manufacturing: A Review of Their Archaeological Use and Potential. *Plains Anthropologist* 22(77):169–182.

Wagner, Gail E.

1982   Testing Flotation Recovery Rates. *American Antiquity* 47:127–132.

1994   Corn in Eastern Woodlands Late Prehistory. In *Corn and Culture in the Prehistoric New World,* edited by Sissel Johannessen and Christine A. Hastorf, 335–346. Westview Press, Boulder, Colorado.

2003   Eastern Woodlands Anthropogenic Ecology. In *People and Plants in Eastern North America,* edited by P. E. Minnis, 126–171. Smithsonian Institution Press, Washington, D.C.

Waselkov, Gregory A.

1989   Seventeenth-Century Trade in the Colonial Southeast. *Southeastern Archaeology* 8(2):117–133.

1997   Changing Strategies of Indian Field Location in the Early Historic Southeast. In *People, Plants, and Landscapes: Studies in Paleoethnobotany,* edited by K. J. Gremillion, 179–194. University of Alabama Press, Tuscaloosa.

1998   The Eighteenth-Century Anglo-Indian Trade in Southeastern North America. In *New Faces of the Fur Trade: Selected Papers of the Seventh North American Fur Trade Conference, Halifax, Nova Scotia, 1995,* edited by J. Fiske, S. Sleeper-Smith, and W. Wicken, 193–222. Michigan State University Press, East Lansing.

Waselkov, Gregory A., and Kathryn E. Holland Braund (editors)

1995   *William Bartram on the Southeastern Indians.* University of Nebraska Press, Lincoln.

Waselkov, Gregory A., and Marvin T. Smith

2000   Upper Creek Archaeology. In *The Indians of the Greater Southeast: Historical Archaeology and Ethnohistory,* edited by B. G. McEwan. University Press of Florida, Gainesville.

Waselkov, Gregory A., and Brian M. Wood

1986   The Creek War of 1813–1814: Effects on Creek Society and Settlement Patterns. *Journal of Alabama Archaeology* 32(1):1–24.

Waselkov, Greg, John Cottier, and Craig T. Sheldon, Jr.

1990   Archaeological Excavations at the Early Historic Creek Indian Town of Fusihatchee (Phase 1, 1988–1989), Report submitted to the National Science Foundation, Grant No. BNS-8718934. University of South Alabama, Mobile.

Watkins, Joe

2000   *Indigenous Archaeology: American Indian Values and Scientific Practice.* Altamira Press, Walnut Creek, California.

Watson, Patty Jo

1976   In Pursuit of Prehistoric Subsistence: A Comparative Account of Some Contemporary Flotation Techniques. *MidContinental Journal of Archaeology* 1(1):77–100.

Watt, Bernice K., and Annabel L. Merrill

1975   *Composition of Foods.* U.S.D.A. Agricultural Handbook No. 8. U.S. Government Printing Office, Washington.

Wauchope, Robert

1966   *Archaeological Survey of Northern Georgia with a Test of Some Cultural Hypotheses.* Memoirs of the Society for American Archaeology, no. 21. Society for American Archaeology, Salt Lake City.

Weisman, Russell

2000   An Archaeological Study of the Yuchi Town Site (1Ru63), Fort Benning Military Reservation, Russell County, Alabama. Southern Research, Ellerslie, Georgia.

Weisman, Russell M., and Meghan LaGraff Ambrosino

1997   Phase I Archaeological Survey within Fort Benning, Compartments Z-2 and Z-3, Russell County, Alabama. Vols. 1 and 2. Panamerican Consultants, Inc. Submitted to Directorate of Public Works, Fort Benning, Georgia.

Wenner, David J., Jr.

1948   Preliminary Appraisal of the Archaeological Resources of the Eufaula Reservoir (Onapa and Canadian Reservoir Areas). Department of Anthropology, University of Oklahoma, Norman.

Wesson, Cameron B.

1997   Households and Hegemony: An Analysis of Historic Creek Culture Change. Ph.D. dissertation, University of Illinois, Champaign-Urbana.

1999   Chiefly Power and Food Storage in Southeastern North America. *World Archaeology* 31 (1, Food Technology in Its Social Context: Production, Processing, and Storage):145–164.

2002   Prestige Goods, Symbolic Capital, and Social Power in the Protohistoric Southeast. In *Between Contacts and Colonies: Archaeological Perspectives on the Protohistoric Period Southeast,* edited by C. B. Wesson and M. A. Rees, 110–125. University of Alabama Press, Tuscaloosa.

Wickman, Patricia Riles

1999   *The Tree that Bends: Discourse, Power, and the Survival of the Maskoki People.* University of Alabama Press, Tuscaloosa.

Will, George F., and George E. Hyde

1964   *Corn among the Indians of the Upper Missouri.* University of Nebraska Press, Lincoln.

Willey, Gordon R.

1938   Excavations at Lawson Field Site, Ft. Benning Reservation, Columbus, Ga. In Kasihta Town Report Records. Folder 10. National Park Service, Tallahassee, Florida.

n.d.   Stratigraphic Survey of Kasihta Chattahoochee No. 1. In Kasihta Town Report Records. Folder 12. National Park Service, Tallahassee, Florida.

n.d.   Excavation at the Lawson Field Site, Ft. Benning Reservation, Columbus, Georgia. In Kasihta Town Report Records. Folder 9. National Park Service, Tallahassee, Florida.

Willey, Gordon R., and William H. Sears

1952   The Kasita Site. *Southern Indian Studies* 4:3–18.

Williams, J. Mark, and Gary Shapiro

1990   *Lamar Archaeology: Mississippian Chiefdoms in the Deep South.* University of Alabama Press, Tuscaloosa.

Williams, Samuel Cole (editor)

1930   *Adair's History of the American Indians.* Promontory Press, New York.

Willoughby, Lynn

1999   *Flowing Through Time: A History of the Lower Chattahoochee River.* University of Alabama Press, Tuscaloosa.

Winterhalder, Bruce, Flora Lu, and Bram Tucker

1999   Risk-Sensitive Adaptive Tactics: Models and Evidence from Subsistence Studies in Biology and Anthropology. *Journal of Archaeological Research* 7(4):301–348.

Worth, John E.

1994   Late Spanish Military Expeditions in the Interior Southeast, 1597–1628. In *Forgotten Centuries: Indians and Europeans in the American South, 1521–1704,* edited by C. Hudson and C. C. Tesser, 104–122. University of Georgia, Athens.

1997   The Eastern Creek Frontier: History and Archaeology of the Flint River Towns, ca. 1750–1826. Paper presented at the Society for American Archaeology, Nashville, Tennessee.

2000   The Lower Creeks: Origins and Early History. In *Indians of the Greater Southeast: Historical Archaeology and Ethnohistory,* edited by B. G. McEwan, 265–298. University Press of Florida, Gainesville.

Wright, Amos J.

1999   Creek Indian Census. *Journal of Alabama Archaeology* 45(1):37–48.

2003   *Historic Indian Towns in Alabama, 1540–1838.* University of Alabama Press, Tuscaloosa.

Wright, J. Leitch

1986   *Creeks & Seminoles: The Destruction and Regeneration of the Muscogulge People.* Indians of the Southeast. University of Nebraska Press, Lincoln.

Yarnell, Richard Asa

1982   Problems of Interpretation of Archaeological Plant Remains of the Eastern Woodlands. *Southeastern Archaeology* 1(1):1–7.

Index